Introduction
to
Schenkerian
Analysis

Introduction
to
Schenkerian
Analysis

ALLEN FORTE

YALE UNIVERSITY

STEVEN E. GILBERT

CALIFORNIA STATE UNIVERSITY, FRESNO

W · W · NORTON AND COMPANY

NEW YORK · LONDON

Music typography by Mel Wildberger
Page makeup by Ben Gamit

Library of Congress Cataloging in Publication Data
Forte, Allen.
 Introduction to Schenkerian analysis.

 Includes index.
 1. Music—Theory. 2. Schenker, Heinrich,
1868–1935. I. Gilbert, Steven E., joint author. II. Title.
MT6.F642I6   781   81-22502
                          AACR2

W. W. Norton & Company, Inc.
500 Fifth Avenue, New York, N.Y. 10110
W. W. Norton & Company Ltd.
37 Great Russell Street, London WC1B 3NU

1 2 3 4 5 6 7 8 9 0

ISBN 0-393-95192-8

Contents

INTRODUCTION   1

PART ONE
Survey of Basic Concepts

CHAPTER 1   Melodic Diminutions   7
             The Neighbor Note as Motive   17
             The Passing Note as Motive   24
             The Arpeggiation as Motive   32
             Exercises   37
CHAPTER 2   Voice Leading: Counterpoint and Figured Bass   41
             The Species Counterpoint Model   41
             Figured Bass Notation   49
             Exercises   64
CHAPTER 3   Compound Melody   67
             Exercises   80
CHAPTER 4   Linear Intervallic Patterns   83
             Exercises   100
CHAPTER 5   Harmonic Relations   103
             Harmonic Relations   103
             Harmonic Functions of Diatonic Triads   105
             Harmonic Progressions   106
             Harmony and Voice Leading   106
             Harmony and Diminutions   108
             Conclusion   109
             Exercises   109

CHAPTER 6   Some Common Secondary Structural Features   110
             Voice Exchanges   110
             Implied Notes   119
             Register Transfer   123
             Exercises   126

PART TWO
Reductions of Small to Moderate Dimension

CHAPTER 7   Basic Axioms   131
             Structural Levels   131
             Models of Fundamental Structure   131
             Fundamental Structure in Thematic
                 Statements   133
             Rhythmic versus Analytic Notation   134
             Exercises   139
CHAPTER 8   The Concept of Prolongation   142
             Exercises   145
CHAPTER 9   Prolongation of the Primary Tone: Initial Ascent 149
             Exercises   151
CHAPTER 10   Prolongation of the Primary Tone: Arpeggiation 153
             Exercises   156
CHAPTER 11   Introduction to Musical Form;
                 Unfolding of Intervals   159
             Exercises   163
CHAPTER 12   Fundamental Structure in Complete Units   166
             Coupling of Registers   167
             Exercises   169
CHAPTER 13   The Harmonized Chorale   175
             Formal Aspects   175
             Techniques for Reduction   178
             The Chorale and the Octave Progression   180
             Exercises   184
CHAPTER 14   Elaborated Chorales: Instrumental Preludes
                 and Studies   188
             Exercises   194
CHAPTER 15   Musical Form and Fundamental Structure:
                 "One-Part" Forms   201
             Exercises   204
CHAPTER 16   Musical Form and Fundamental Structure:
                 "Two-Part" Forms   208
             Exercises   212

CHAPTER 17 Musical Form and Fundamental Structure:
                "Three-Part" Forms   214
            Exercises   217
CHAPTER 18 Register Transfer and Displacement   220
            Exercises   228

                      PART THREE
            Reductions of Larger Dimension

CHAPTER 19 Review and Refinement: Structural Levels
                and Linear Progressions   235
            Linear Progressions in the Upper Voices   237
            Linear Progressions in the Bass   238
            Dissonant and False Linear Progressions   240
            Exercises   246
CHAPTER 20 Review and Refinement: Unfolding, Register
                Transfer, Overlapping, Motivic Structures   250
            Register Designations   250
            Unfoldings of Small Scale   251
            Unfoldings of Larger Scale   257
            Register Transfers (Couplings)   260
            Overlappings   265
            Motivic Structures   267
            Exercises   271
CHAPTER 21 Sonata Form and Structural Levels   276
            The Design of the Sonata Form   276
            An Exemplar of Sonata Form   280
            Additional Examples of Sonata Form   293
            Sonatina Form   313
            Exercises   319
CHAPTER 22 Variation Form and Structural Levels   320
            Exercises   349
CHAPTER 23 Structural Levels in Compound and
                Rondo Forms   350
            Compound Ternary Forms   350
            Rondo Forms   367
            Exercises   387

INDEX OF MUSICAL EXAMPLES AND EXERCISES   389

GENERAL INDEX   398

Introduction
to
Schenkerian
Analysis

Introduction

Purpose

This book is intended to serve as a basic textbook on Schenkerian analysis, the analytical approach developed over a period of many years by the Austrian music theorist Heinrich Schenker (1868–1935). Schenker himself never undertook the preparation of a pedagogical work that would help students learn to apply his concepts of musical structure to the study of tonal compositions. His analytical ideas, of course, are amply illustrated in his voluminous publications.[1]

The book is addressed to college students of music who have had a year of instruction in tonal harmony and counterpoint. The courses for which it is appropriate are variously titled: for example, Analysis of Tonal Music or Form and Analysis.

Scope and Organization

The book begins with a thorough coverage of a number of elementary matters. This may be regarded either as a review or as a reorientation in preparation for the systematic presentation that follows. For example, the fundamentals of voice leading are examined with reference to the two models customarily used in teaching that subject: species counterpoint (Fux) and the figured bass.

Beginning in Part Two ideas that are more specifically Schenkerian are developed and applied to the analysis of short compositions. Since the book is

---

1. See David Beach, "A Schenker Bibliography," in Maury Yeston, ed., *Readings in Schenker Analysis and Other Approaches* (New Haven: Yale University Press, 1977). Another very useful reference is Larry Laskowski, *Heinrich Schenker; An Annotated Index to his Analyses of Musical Works* (New York: Pendragon Press, 1978).

1

also intended to cover all of basic standard form it has seemed logical to use this feature in organizing the material. Thus, Part Two ends with longer forms and Part Three covers the main large forms (sonata, rondo, and so on). The various types of Schenkerian prolongations are introduced gradually and discussed and illustrated thoroughly in the text. Each chapter ends with a set of exercises keyed to the topics that have been presented, and the student is given precise instructions for completing the exercises as well as occasional hints about pitfalls and special problems that they contain.

The instructor may find the *Instructor's Manual*, which is available from the publisher, to be of value, especially in working through the text for the first time.

Studying Schenkerian Analysis

Now that Schenker's ideas have been quite broadly disseminated, especially in the United States, and his concepts have gained wide acceptance, it is not necessary to offer an apologia for them. Suffice it to say that many musicians have discovered that Schenkerian principles, correctly applied, yield musical insights not obtainable from other methods of analysis. Far from being a dry and sterile process, musical analysis from the Schenkerian point of view is both musical and analytical in the best sense. The gaining of fluency in the use of the techniques, however, requires patient study, the development of a good ear, and musical intelligence. It is hoped that this textbook will encourage the student by providing the information he needs to carry out his own beginning analytical studies and enable him, in time, to express his own ideas about the structure of a work in a coherent and convincing manner.

Analysis lies at the very core of all musical studies, no matter how "intuitive" or how "intellectual" it may be. For the person with good musical intuitions the study of Schenkerian analysis will provide new insights and, if properly carried out, offers no counter-intuitive obstacles.

A Note on the Exercises

In the earlier chapters the authors have supplied the complete notation required for the exercises. In the later chapters this becomes impractical for reasons of space. Accordingly, we have often assumed that the reader will be able to obtain a copy of the required score, since all are standard works in the tonal repertory. A number of these will be found in published anthologies.

References to Schenker's Writings

Since we often have occasion in the text to refer to two of Schenker's major publications, we have abbreviated their titles as follows:

FGMA   *Five Graphic Musical Analyses*, edited by Felix Salzer (New York: Dover Publications, 1969)

FC   *Free Composition*, translated and edited by Ernst Oster (New York: Longman, in cooperation with the American Musicological Society, 1979)

Part One

Survey of Basic Concepts

1
Melodic Diminutions

This chapter introduces the student to a number of concepts essential to the work presented later in the book. In particular, it sets out those concepts within a Schenkerian orientation, emphasizing the differences between that orientation and the more conventional one in which basic components of musical structures are often accorded a perfunctory and mechanical treatment.

The present discussion is not intended to serve as a substitute for a thorough grounding in harmony and counterpoint. Rather it should be regarded as a combination of review and reorientation, in which certain fundamental ideas, terms, and analytical notational devices are presented, providing a firm basis for the far more comprehensive work to follow, and preparing the student to make the structural distinctions that underlie a good Schenkerian analysis.

Many of the ideas introduced in this chapter are brought in again in later sections of the book where they will be understood more directly in the context of the Schenker approach.

The topic of this chapter has a long history in the pedagogy of music, as will be illustrated below. First, however, a brief explanation. The term *diminution* refers to the process by which an interval formed by notes of longer value is expressed in notes of smaller value. The various kinds of musical events involved in this "diminishing" process are known collectively as *diminutions*, and they comprise the *passing note* (P), the *neighboring note* (N), the *consonant skip* (CS) and the *arpeggiation* (Arp), as well as subspecies of these.

The term diminution derives from the Italian word *diminuimento*. We can see precisely what it means by looking at a historical example, an illustration from an early Italian treatise on diminution which was used to train singers to improvise embellishments of vocal lines (*passagi*).[1]

Example 1 is taken from the first part of Bovicelli's book, in which he gives a systematic treatment of the diatonic intervals, illustrating in great detail how each interval formed by long notes may be expressed in notes of smaller value. Here we see four of the ways in which the ascending fifth D–A can be embellished.[2] (In all, Bovicelli offers twenty-four different diminutions of this fifth.)

EXAMPLE 1. Giovanni Battista Bovicelli, *Regole Passagi di musica* (1594)

In the first diminution of the ascending fifth, the top note, A, is approached by a motion that spans the third F–G–A, partially filling out the large interval. In the second diminution, the voice skips away from D to F, then returns before proceeding upward to complete the fifth. Then, in the third diminution, we see a complete stepwise motion between the first and last notes of the interval; and the remaining diminutions of the fifth are variants on this stepwise completion.

The English-language equivalent of the term diminutions is *divisions*. From an English treatise dating from 1659, we see that the tradition of systematic and explicit teaching of diminution technique is indeed a long and honorable one.[3] The process with which Simpson's treatise is concerned is "breaking the ground," which he describes as follows: "Breaking the ground (a melodic bass figure) is the dividing its notes into more diminute Notes. As for instance, a Semibreve may be broken into two Minims, foure Crotchets, eight Quavers, sixteen Semiquavers, etc."[4]

Example 2 is one of a large number in Simpson's book illustrating model divisions of a ground. For better legibility the notation has been transcribed in accordance with modern practice and the notes of the ground are aligned to coincide with those of the divisions (diminutions).[5]

The diminutions on the lower staff of Example 2 follow the five-note pattern repeated in the ground (a melodic sequence). Thus, in the diminu-

1. Giovanni Battista Bovicelli, *Regole Passagi di musica* (Rules of Musical Embellishment), Venice, 1594. Published in facsimile by Bärenreiter-Verlag, Kassel and Basel, 1955.
2. Ibid., p. 20. The example has been transcribed into modern notation.
3. Christopher Simpson, *The Division-Viol or, The Art of Playing Extempore upon a Ground*, 2nd ed., London, 1665. Published in facsimile by J. Curwen & Sons, London, 1955.
4. Ibid., p. 28.
5. Ibid., p. 56.

EXAMPLE 2. Christopher Simpson, *The Division-Viol* (1665)

tions the first of the three repeated notes of the ground has attached to it an ascending third, filled in by stepwise motion, while the second repeated note of the ground occurs as the skip downward to the fourth quarter note. The third repeated note, however, is represented in the diminutions by the ascending third which effects a stepwise connection to the fourth note of the ground. Thus, we see that the note receiving the diminutions need not actually be present in the diminutions; that is, the diminutions *represent* the note being embellished. This basic and important idea of melodic structure will become more apparent as we proceed. Another instance can be seen in the second measure (and corresponding measures) of the diminutions in Example 2. There the second F is represented in the diminutions by A before the literal statement of that note in the diminutions.

From the preceding historical material, it is quite evident that the theme-and-variations genre would provide an instructive corpus of music for the study of diminution procedures in tonal music, since it offers a prototypical musical structure (the theme) and a variety of diminutions (the variations) directly related to that structure. Three themes and variations will now be examined. In the process we introduce an elementary analytic notation which will eventually develop into the full-fledged graphics that are so essential to Schenkerian analysis.

Example 3 shows the well-known Air from Handel's *Leçon in B♭*, *a*, aligned with the third variation on the Air, *b*. The basis of the diminution for the variation is as follows: To each note of the theme is attached the *consonant skip* of a third, and this interval is filled in by a stepwise connective note called a *passing note*,[6] a basic type of diminution. It is remarkable that the first form of this diminution reflects the longer ascending third of the theme itself: B♭–C–D (Example 3e).

EXAMPLE 3. Handel, *Leçon in B♭*, Air

a. Air

b. Variation 3

---

6. Passing note and passing tone are interchangeable terms.

c. Rhythmic reduction

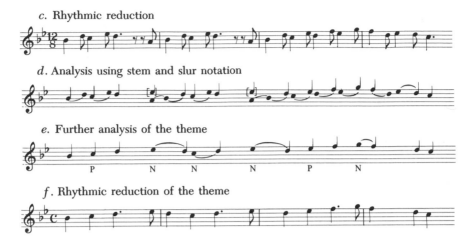

d. Analysis using stem and slur notation

e. Further analysis of the theme

f. Rhythmic reduction of the theme

Beginning with m. 2 of Example 3*b*, the diminution which originally served as a *suffix* to the main note of the theme is also to be construed as a *prefix*. Thus, the quarter note D of the theme *a* in m. 2 is represented by the diminution B♭–C–D. And in m. 3 the prefix-type diminution applies to the first three notes of the theme, as indicated by the diagonal lines of the illustration.

Example 3*c* omits the eighth-note passing tone to produce a *rhythmic reduction* of the first phrase of the theme. Here in m. 1 the reduction omits the passing eighth notes (P) shown at *b* and enlarges the first eighth note to a quarter and the fourth eighth note to a quarter to reveal the simpler underlying pattern. This procedure continues systematically for the remainder of the excerpt. Rhythmic reduction will be used frequently and to good advantage in subsequent portions of this book (e.g., in Chapter 7).

In Example 3*d* we abandon meter and barlines and introduce elementary analytic notation consisting of the stem and the slur. These symbols have special significance in Schenkerian analysis, since they provide a lucid way to represent relations among the pitches of a tonal configuration, in this case a melodic line. This process of differentiation is unequivocal in the case we are now considering, for we can refer to the basic structure of the theme in making analytic decisions. Thus, the stemmed notes are the notes of the theme as first revealed in the rhythmic reduction. (Compare 3*d* with 3*c*.) Slurs indicate *dependency*. The D attached to the initial B♭ is dependent upon that note, just as the subsequent E♭ is dependent upon C. With only stem and slur notation, it is possible to achieve a correct and convincing basic analysis from which a more refined reading may be obtained, using the full repertory of Schenkerian symbols which will be introduced gradually in the presentations that follow.

Since the variation can be subjected to analysis to reveal its relation to the theme, it seems reasonable to assume that the theme itself can undergo the same process. This is shown in Example 3e. To understand the analysis given there, it is necessary to introduce another basic type of diminution, the *neighbor note*.[7] The neighbor note, in its *complete* form, departs from the main note, the note upon which it is dependent, and returns to it. A good example of this is the lower neighbor note C in m. 2, which stands between two statements of D, the main note in this context. The reader can easily verify for himself that all the neighbor notes in the theme are of the complete type. For example, the upper neighbor note Eb at the end of m. 1 stands between two statements of D.[8]

Example 3f displays a rhythmic reduction of the theme, omitting or, rather, absorbing the diminutions which are operative within the theme itself. This final part of the rather large example is crucial, for it embodies one of the basic concepts of Schenkerian analysis: The elementary types of diminutions, such as the passing and neighbor notes introduced thus far, may and do occur in durationally expanded form; they are not restricted to the durations of short notes. Here (Example 3f) it is apparent that the passing note C in m. 1 has the duration of a quarter note. It is still a passing note, however, since it connects the two notes that form the tonal interval of a major third from scale degree $\hat{1}$ to scale degree $\hat{3}$, an interval which has structural priority here since it is a member of the tonic triad.[9] Similarly, C in m. 2 is a lower neighbor note to D, although it has full *metrical value*, the duration of a quarter note.

Example 4 gives the notation for the first variation by Brahms on Handel's *Air in Bb*. Here the lower neighbor note of the complete type is the characteristic diminution in the upper voice, while consonant skips involving sixteenth notes characterize the diminutions in the lower voices. (The deeper significance of repeated skips of this type will be taken up in the section on compound melody in Chapter 2.) Here, where the complete context is given—not just the upper voice, as in Example 3—a fundamental principle of Schenkerian analysis is illustrated in the most lucid manner: *The function of a note is determined by its harmonic and contrapuntal setting.* Thus, in the first beat of the first measure the upper-voice A must be read as a lower neighbor

---

7. The terms neighbor note and neighboring tone are interchangeable. The neighbor note is also known as the auxiliary note (tone).

8. A neighbor note is characterized by its placement with respect to the note upon which it depends as either upper or lower. A passing note is described by its direction in the configuration as either ascending or descending.

9. Scale degrees here and elsewhere are given as numbers with carets. We assume that the reader is familiar with the primal position of the tonic triad within the tonal system. See the section Harmonic Relations in Chapter 5.

note between two occurrences of B♭ because the harmony governing that quarter-note duration is the B♭ triad (I), and A can only be dependent upon B♭, since it is unsupported.[10] Within the second quarter note of the first measure, however, B♭ is the dependent lower neighbor note between two occurrences of C, because here C is the main note, as defined by the F triad (V) that governs that duration. One more fact requires emphasis here: C itself, on the second quarter, is a passing tone between B♭ and D in the theme, for it is a durational expansion of the passing-note type (recall Example 3 *f*). This function too is supported by the harmonic and contrapuntal context, for the F triad (V) on the second quarter note of the first measure is structurally dependent upon the two B♭ triads (I) which surround it. Corresponding to this structure, in the upper voice, the structural interval is the third from B♭ to D. Consider how disorienting it would be if one were somehow to understand B♭ on the first quarter as lower neighbor note to C on the second quarter and the following D on the third quarter as the upper neighbor to C. This would effectively destroy the coherent tonal relations presented at the beginning of the theme, even placing in jeopardy the integrity of the tonality (B♭) itself.

EXAMPLE 4. Brahms, Variation 1 on Handel's *Air in B♭*

As the second example of theme and variation, Example 5 presents, at *a*, the first two measures of J. S. Bach's *Aria variata alla maniera italiana* (BWV 989), together with his third variation on that portion of the aria, *b*, a rhythmic reduction in eighth and quarter notes, *c*, and analysis using slur and stem notation, *d*.

Let us first consider the diminutions and expanded diminutions in the variation theme (*Aria*) itself. The upper voice begins on the tonic note, A, which is then supplied with the lower neighbor note G♯, followed by A, to form a complete neighbor-note figure. On the fourth eighth note, B, the upper neighbor of A, enters. Since there is no return to A, this neighbor note is described as an *incomplete* upper neighbor note. To make the description complete, one would also want to observe that the neighbor note follows the

---

10. The expressions "harmonic tone" and "nonharmonic tone" are best avoided, here and elsewhere. They are misleading since they do not acknowledge the existence of structural levels in the Schenkerian sense. However, the reader does not have to concern himself with levels at present, since that concept will develop in a natural way as we proceed.

Example 5. Bach, *Aria variata* (BWV 989)

a. Aria

b. Variation 3

c. Rhythmic reduction

d. Analysis using stem and slur notation

main note here. That is, it is of the suffix, not the prefix type.[11]

In the second measure an expanded passing note B connects A to C with traditional embellishments indicated by symbols and small notation. These fixed embellishments are, of course, themselves diminutions which belong to the outermost surface of the music. For example the small note F♯ near the end of the first measure is a *descending* passing note. Notice that the bracketed skips in the first measure are only incidentally consonant skips. The direct motion from A to G♯ in the soprano is interrupted by the upper neighbor B. Compare *b* and *c* at this location in the music: the progression A–G♯ occurs there without interruption.

Variation 3 (Example 5*b*) introduces complicated diminutions, the components of which are labeled. The upper voice of the variation does not begin on A, but on C, which lies a consonant third above it. The reason for this will be suggested below. On the first two beats of the upper voice in the second

---

11. Incomplete upper neighbor suffixes are not uncommon. Incomplete lower neighbor suffixes, however, are quite rare. See the section The Neighbor Note as Motive, below.

measure is a figure composed of incomplete upper neighbor and incomplete lower neighbor, of suffix and prefix types respectively. The figure is complete, since the main note delimits it on both ends. The rhythmic reduction *c* removes the neighbor-note diminutions and restores the full quarter note value to the main notes A and B. A similar complete neighbor-note figure is the traditional turn—for example, B–A–G♯–A.[12]

The rhythmic reduction shown in Example 5*c* reveals an underlying design that is not immediately apparent in Variation 3: the succession of three thirds, bracketed in the example. The first of these comprises the motion from C to E through the passing note D; the second is the motion from G♯ to B through the passing note A; the third and final motion is from A to C through the expanded passing note B. The latter, of course, is part of the original melodic theme. Thus, it seems likely that the composer prepared the final third by the two faster preceding thirds, hence began the variation melody on C rather than on A. In the analysis presented in Example 5*d*, a further differentiation is effected; with the omission of the passing eighth notes in the upper voice of *c* the opening C has attached to it the consonant skip to E, and the next important structural note in the line, B, is introduced by the consonant skip from G♯. The bass, subjected to analysis, begins with an arpeggiation (Arp) of the A-minor triad.

Beginning in Chapter 7, the reader will be given more detailed and cogent reasons for analytical decisions such as those made in Example 5*d*. For the present we are concerned to demonstrate the role of diminutions in elaborating and otherwise transforming more basic structures. By reversing the diminutions process a convincing analysis revealing an even more basic structure is produced, as in Example 5*d*.

To conclude the discussion of Example 5, it is important to make a general observation, namely, that diminutions often displace the notes upon which they are dependent, sometimes causing musical elements which belong together to occur in different temporal locations. There is an example of this in the first four notes of the bass line in Variation 3 (Example 5*b*). The rhythmic reduction at *c* shows that the bass note B, a passing note, belongs together with the D of the upper voice, also a passing note. However, the diminution of A by the complete neighbor-note figure A–G♯–A in sixteenth notes causes the bass note B to be displaced by one sixteenth note, that is, by the second A, which completes the neighbor-note pattern.

The third and final illustration of diminution technique as practiced in the traditional theme-and-variation genre is given in Example 6. This shows a portion of the theme of the third movement of Beethoven's *Ninth Symphony*, *a*, the corresponding segment of the first variation, *b*, a rhythmic reduction to

---

12. A caveat is in order here, however; namely, the second note of the turn sometimes must be read as a passing note. See Example 11.

EXAMPLE 6. Beethoven, *Ninth Symphony*, III

a. Theme

b. Variation 1

c. Rhythmic reduction

d. Analysis using stem and slur notation

eighth-note and quarter-note values, *c*, and an analysis using stem and slur notation, as in Example 5*d*.

A rhythmic reduction of the outer voices of Variation 1 to eighth and quarter notes is shown at *c* in Example 6, and this can profitably be compared with the Theme at *a*, whose melodic contours it follows with completeness and exactitude. The first diminution consists of a consonant skip from D to B♭. This B♭ is then suspended above the bass E♭, where it becomes a neighbor note to A. Because of the preparation of B♭ as a consonance and its resolution to A, it is easily understood as a suspension, and that aspect of the rhythmic reduction is shown by the tie enclosed in parentheses here and in three analogous positions that follow. Up to the end of the second measure, the diminutions consist of the pattern consonant skip-neighbor note. There the passing note E♭ from the Theme is brought in and suspended over the bar line to resolve to D. Then begins an ascending motion which incorporates two neighbor-note prefixes (G–F and C–B♭). (Prefixes of this type are often called appoggiaturas.)[13] The goal of that ascending motion is D on the downbeat of m. 4, which then descends to resolution on C over the dominant harmony.

---

13. *Appoggiatura* and *échappée* are names used in the literature to refer to forms of neighbor notes.

Before it resolves, however, it is expanded by the consonant skip to F. This F is followed by E♭, the upper neighbor of D, as shown by the dotted line in Example 6c. Such *indirect* neighbor-note configurations—that is, situations in which the neighbor note is not directly adjacent to the note upon which it is dependent—are not uncommon in elaborate diminutions. Another instance is shown in Example 9.

The abbreviations above the top voice of Variation 1 (Example 6b), point out diminutions not shown in the rhythmic reduction at c. Thus, the consonant skip from D to B♭ in m. 1 is filled in by a passing note, as is the skip from C to A at the end of that measure. The characteristic diminution of the second half of the phrase is the turn, comprising upper and lower neighbor notes (that is, a form of the complete neighbor-note figure). This figure begins on the third beat of m. 2, where F is introduced by its upper and followed by its lower neighbor note. The figure on the next beat is somewhat more complicated. Here E is again the lower neighbor note and G the upper, but the latter is incomplete, for the melody skips away in order to bring in the passing note E♭ of the Theme (compare a). It would be incorrect to describe the skip in this figure from G to E♭ as a consonant skip, since it would confuse the correct relations, suggesting that G is not a dependent neighbor note. The turn figure continues over the first three beats of m. 3, then is altered, again in order to bring in a passing note (C) in the Theme (compare a). And, most elegantly, when the melodic goal D on the downbeat of m. 4 is reached, its diminution is still the turn, but that form of the turn which begins on the lower note. Moreover, the composer uses the *chromatic* lower neighbor C♯ to modify D rather than the diatonic lower neighbor C, a note that has just served as ascending passing note. Other chromatic neighbor notes are the E♮ in mm. 2 and 3 and the C♯ in m. 3.

Example 6d gives an analysis of the Theme using the minimal analytic notation introduced thus far—that is, the stem and slur. This provides some interesting information about the organization of the Theme, for with the removal of the diminutions shown above at c are revealed the arpeggiations signified by the abbreviation Arp. (Arpeggiations are discussed in greater detail in the section The Arpeggiation as Motive, below.) It is of interest, however, to point out that the opening note of the Theme, D, is the bottom note of the arpeggiation in mm. 2–3, and occurs again as the goal of the melodic ascent discussed above, falling on the downbeat of m. 4. The connection between these three occurrences of D is indicated by the dotted line in the analysis at d.

In considering Example 6d just a moment longer, it is important to observe that A in the upper voice of the first measure was regarded as a main note in the rhythmic reduction at c, preceded by its upper neighbor B♭. However, its function in the Theme is that of lower neighbor note to B♭;

hence, it appears as a stemless notehead slurred to B♭. The bass note E♭ which accompanies it is also a neighbor note, as is the bass note A which follows in m. 2. In this subtle way the bass reflects the upper voice.

In the second part of the phrase, the bass moves note for note against the upper voice, but the structural configurations in each voice differ. While the upper voice presents an ascending arpeggiation D–F–B♭–D, the bass moves downward stepwise from B♭ to F. Here, and in every real interval of a fourth filled by stepwise motion, two passing tones are adjacent.

Finally, a comparison of the upper voice of the last measure as it appears in the Theme, *a*, and as it appears in the analysis, *d*, reveals that the latter has omitted F in order to show the neighbor note E♭ directly attached to D. This D is shown in the analysis with an eighth-note flag, a symbol not yet introduced and intended only to distinguish this D from the two previous occurrences of that note in the upper voice, pointing up the fact that it appears as the sixth above the bass. It is part of the $^6_4$ formation, which resolves to the $^5_3$ in the traditional manner, thus making D structurally dependent upon C over the dominant harmony and weakening its harmonic support, compared with the previous two occurrences.

Learning to read diminutions correctly is a basic skill of analysis, and the student will be offered many opportunities to develop that skill in the presentations that follow. It is probably not an exaggeration to say that without learning to read diminutions it is not possible to express one's ideas about a tonal composition in a convincing and logical way, using Schenkerian analytic symbols.

Thus far in this section attention has been given to diminutions as they occur in the theme-and-variations genre, since the theme is a given and one can always refer to it to verify the reading of the diminutions in the variations. Now, however, the three following sections will present examples of diminutions in melodic themes where they serve as *motives*. Here the term motive is used in its conventional meaning, to designate a characteristic melodic figure of a composition, one that is repeated and may be transformed in various ways over the span of the work.

The Neighbor Note as Motive

A famous instance of the neighbor note as a motive—one might even say musical motto—is the opening theme of Brahms's *Second Symphony*, shown in Example 7*a*. Three occurrences are labeled there, beginning in the very first measure. In all three, the neighbor note has full metrical (quarter note) value. The opening subject employs all three types of basic structures as motives: the neighbor note, the arpeggiation, and the passing note. These comprise the motivic surface of the subject of this work.

EXAMPLE 7. Brahms, *Second Symphony*, I

In a later section of the same movement (Example 7*b*), we see that the neighbor-note motive is presented first in its original rhythmic form of three even quarter notes, then in three even eighth notes. The integrity of the three-note figure is indicated by the composer's slurs. As a result, the underlying triple pulse of m. 63 changes to a duple pulse (6/8) in the following three measures, and this, in turn, produces the expanded rhythmic pattern shown in Example 7*c*, which reminds us that diminutions have a profound effect upon rhythmic structures in tonal music. Displacement and representation are two terms introduced earlier to characterize general processes involving diminutions. Now it should be evident that rhythmic expansion and contraction are also general musical aspects associated with diminutions.

Example 7 was mainly concerned with the complete lower neighbor-note figure. The next illustration, Example 8, shows, with equal prominence, both a complete upper neighbor figure and a complete lower neighbor figure. The lower neighbor figure consists of G♯ over E♯ attached to A and F♯. These are, of course, chromatic neighbors and must be so, for G♮ and E♮ would strongly imply the function of descending passing notes (Example 8*c*).

EXAMPLE 8. Haydn, *Symphony in D major, No. 104* ("London"), III

The analysis given in Example 8*b* shows how the single pitch A is circumscribed and highlighted by its neighbor notes. And the neighbor notes themselves are given special emphasis through the sforzato on the third beat of the measure. Observe that the last neighbor note B in the motive occurs in m. 3 and is of the indirect type, since it is separated from the first A by the consonant skip upward to D. Meanwhile, the second phrase of the theme (mm. 5–8) features passing notes, as shown in the analysis at *b*. Notice, however, that the leading tone C♯ in the next-to-last measure is also a neighbor note dependent upon D and is slurred accordingly in the analysis.

A curious feature of the theme is the sudden appearance of B on the last beat of m. 6, the first sforzato since m. 3. Is it possible that this is a reference to the upper neighbor note B of the previous music? With the analytical techniques to be attained in the subsequent chapters, the reader will be able to determine easily that this is the case.

As illustrated in Example 8, the neighbor note differs fundamentally from the passing note in musical function, for it always serves as an *adjacency*, whether directly contiguous to the main note(s) or presented indirectly because of an intervening consonant skip. Thus, the neighbor note always relates to another single note (the main note), whereas the passing note is a *connective*, hence joins two notes.

Example 9 offers a beautifully idiomatic instance of the incomplete lower neighbor note as a prefix: an unusual ascending appoggiatura that is a characteristic motive in a famous and beloved work. In the second two-measure group the vertical third E over C♯ is brought in via the double neighbor-note figure F♯–D♯–E and D–B♯–C♯. Again, as in Example 8, the chromatic inflections are essential; otherwise a passing-note function would be implied.

Below the cited passage we give a rudimentary analysis (Example 9*b*). The C♯ on the downbeat of m. 1 is defined as a neighbor note by the harmony. However, it is such a striking event that one could almost imagine it is as

EXAMPLE 9. Chopin, *Prelude in A major*, Op. 28, No. 7

sounding with the upbeat E; indeed, this does happen in the corresponding upbeat to the second phrase in m. 4, where C♯ and E (now an octave higher) occur together vertically. Further interpretation of the structure of this opening phrase would lead to a discussion of analytic matters not yet broached.

When the upper neighbor-note motive of the *Chorale St. Antoni*[14] (Example 10*a*, m. 1) is applied to C three measures later, the result is an incomplete upper neighbor note (D) as suffix. Not only does the upper neighbor motive occur as a short note in the first measure, but it is also immediately repeated as the quarter-note E♭ in the second measure—an expansion of the diminution to full metrical value. And there is a final reference to this expanded neighbor note in the last measure with the motion C–B♭.

EXAMPLE 10. Haydn, *Divertimento in B♭*, II *(Chorale St. Antoni)*

Example 10*b* is an analytic sketch that shows how the relations labeled in Example 10*a* can be more concisely and coherently rendered with the minimal notation introduced thus far. Again, the sketch reveals an underlying regularity: both D and C in the upper voice have consonant filled-in skips attached to them. (Compare Example 137*a*, p. 133.)

The components of the opening or head motive in the Bach solo cello piece shown in Example 11*a* are upper and lower neighbors to G. The rhythmic reduction (Example 11*b*) suggests that the middle note of the second triplet in m. 1 should be read as a passing note, not as the return to the main note G, which would reduce to a very erratic rhythmic pattern. This is one of many instances when upper and lower neighbors of a turn are connected by a passing note, a possibility that was mentioned earlier. Notice that in this figure the first neighbor note, A♭, is indirect—not directly contiguous to the main note. This is shown analytically by the slur in the next reduction, Example 11*c*.

---

14. The *Chorale St. Antoni*, attributed to Haydn, is taken from his *Divertimento in B♭*. Though Haydn's authorship of the chorale itself is uncertain, it will be accepted here for ease of reference when the piece is cited again in Chapter 7 (Examples 135, 136, and elsewhere). Brahms's *Variations on a Theme by Haydn*, Op. 56a, is in fact based on the same chorale.

EXAMPLE 11. Bach, *Cello Suite in C minor*, Gavotte II

In addition to the neighbor-note figure, the other diminution characteristic of the subject here is the consonant skip. Although this skip is suggested by the interval formed between the two neighbors Ab and F, that interval is only incidental, and is not a "real" third as are those formed by the subsequent skips. Some readers will notice that the skips of thirds in Example 11c can be read in two ways: (1) with the upper note as the main note; (2) with the lower note as main note. Once again, it is not possible to discuss this reading—which we believe to be the correct one—without introducing matters extraneous to the discussion at this point.

The complete upper neighbor-note figure is the predominant characteristic motive of Schubert's famous lied *Ständchen* (Serenade), the opening vocal phrase of which is shown in Example 12. In the analysis at *b* several aspects are worthy of comment. First, the tie has been used as an additional symbol for the neighbor-note figure. The signifies that the main note is effective over the span of the figure. The slur from the neighbor to the main note indicates dependency, as usual. Following the two neighbor-note figures in the melody is a consonant skip upward to D. Here the two occurrences of D are associated by means of a dotted line. Most important, however, is the labeling of the melodic G in m. 2 as a lower neighbor note, standing between

EXAMPLE 12. Schubert, *Ständchen* from *Schwanengesang*

two statements of the main note A, one supported by the bass note D, the other by the bass note A. Moreover, the bass note supporting the lower neighbor G is itself an incomplete neighbor note dependent upon the bass note A (V). Thus, we have neighbors as diminutions in the eighth-note triplet figures and also as expanded diminutions, where each component of the figure has the durational value of a full measure (A–G–A). Finally, in the last two measures of the melody, A passes through G to F. Attached to G is the consonant skip down to E, filled in by the passing note F. Here again, we see the small passing note F within the third G–E and, in the same context, the expanded passing note G connecting A to F.

The neighbor-note figure pervades the lied, *Ständchen*. Another occurrence is shown in Example 13. Here, in the coda, the upper voice executes the slow neighbor-note figure A–B♭–A, an enlargement of the original eighth-note triplet figure. In addition, there is a further reference to the opening music with the consonant skip from A to D. An event association of this kind, from the analytical standpoint, is in accord with Schenkerian concepts of motive.

EXAMPLE 13. Schubert, *Ständchen* from *Schwanengesang*

The incomplete neighbor note as prefix or suffix can, theoretically, be either upper or lower neighbor, yielding four possibilities for this species of diminution. However, the incomplete lower neighbor note as suffix occurs very seldom in tonal music. Example 14 shows one of the rare instances—in a chorale both composed and harmonized by Bach. The analytic sketch (Example 14*b*) offers the suggestion that the dissonant incomplete neighbor note C in the soprano (last eighth note before m. 1) is an *anticipation* of the consonant C in the tenor (downbeat of m. 1). Many, if not almost all, such incomplete lower neighbor suffixes can be understood as anticipations in this way.

EXAMPLE 14. Bach, Chorale No. 149, *Nicht so traurig*

In Example 14*b* the upper voice D at the opening is interpreted as a passing note between E♭ and C. In the bass at this point is the reverse motion, a filled consonant skip from C to E♭. The resulting interaction between the two outer voices is called a *voice exchange*, a topic which is covered at greater length in Chapter 6. Here the exchange reinforces the reading of C in the upper voice at *a* as an anticipation.

Example 15 presents an example of incomplete lower-neighbor suffix in a context similar to that shown in Example 14. Again, the neighbor note (D) may be construed as an anticipation and again that reading is supported by the incipient voice exchange marked by crisscrossed double arrows.

EXAMPLE 15. Bach, Chorale No. 291, *Was frag ich nach der Welt*

Example 16 is the final illustration for this section. Its purpose is to demonstrate the reading of complex diminutions and to emphasize the importance of reading them correctly.

EXAMPLE 16. Bach, *French Suite in C minor*, Sarabande

In m. 1 of Example 16a the second beat in the upper voice offers two possibilities for interpretation: (1) the D is a lower neighbor to E♭, or (2) the D is an accented passing tone and the E♭ is attached to it as a neighbor note. As is evident from the labels above the top staff, we have chosen the latter reading, and this is given in full notation in the rhythmic reduction at b, directly below.

Also of interest in Example 16 is the upper voice A♭ in m. 2. This is an indirect neighbor note, separated from the main note G by the consonant skip from G to C. This A♭ is an incomplete upper neighbor of the suffix type. As a motive it is the prototype for the four statements that follow, identified by brackets in the rhythmic reduction. Thus, the correct reading of the diminution in m. 2 reveals the underlying regularity of the upper-voice structure as it expresses the neighbor-note motive. An analytic interpretation of the passage is given at c without comment, but with additional annotations identifying the passing notes and neighbor notes in the bass. Example 16d shows an incorrect reading. The stems are given to the neighbor notes, reversing the relation between neighbors and main notes. As a result, the neighbor-note motive is lost and the stepwise progression of the upper voice from G in m. 1 to B in m. 4 is broken after D.

The Passing Note as Motive

Neighbor notes and passing notes are often closely and organically related in a motive. Example 17 provides an instance. There we see that the thematic motive initially consists of a lower neighbor (F) and a consonant skip from G♭ to E♭. In m. 2 an ascending passing note F fills the consonant skip; then in m. 3 the expanded descending passing note F enters as the characteristic motive of the theme, having evolved from F as lower neighbor and F as ascending passing note in the first two measures. Thus F has functioned both as neighbor and passing note. The unusual bass in m. 3 is sketched at b: both A and C resolve to B♭ in m. 7.

EXAMPLE 17. Brahms, *Intermezzo in E♭ minor*, Op. 118, No. 6

Example 18 shows the passing note in three different contexts and in association with both the neighbor note and the consonant skip in a famous melody by Schubert, the second theme of the first movement of the *Unfinished Symphony*, here played by the cellos. The analytic sketch at *b* presents the motivic components of the theme. These begin with the consonant skip from G down to D and continue with two statements of the lower and upper neighbor notes to G connected by the passing note G, a turn figure. At the end of the third measure two passing notes fill in the consonant ascending skip from D to G. In this motion the F♯ recalls the earlier lower neighbor to G, of course, as indicated by N on the sketch. Thus far the passing note has fulfilled two functions: it has connected the neighbor notes and it has filled in the consonant skip. A function of greater magnitude is then realized in the sixth measure of the example, where G♯ is understood as an expanded chromatic passing note connecting G and A. The G♯ may be regarded as an indirect passing note here, since there is a motion above it to B, which is the upper neighbor of the goal note, A, in the last measure. It is important to recognize that the G♯ is an expanded passing note, while the A which follows immediately and connects G♯ to B is a passing note of shorter span, a traditional diminution of which we have seen a number of examples so far.

EXAMPLE 18. Schubert, *Symphony in B minor, No. 8* ("Unfinished"), II

Example 19*a* displays a theme in which passing notes are combined with neighbor notes and consonant skips. In the first four-measure phrase there is first a skip away from the initial note C and then a descent to D in the upper voice. This D is then supplied with chromatic neighbor-note diminutions in eighth notes. The second phrase continues in eighth notes ascending through passing notes to A (m. 6), then returning to E via F. In the concluding two measures sixteenth-note motion is introduced, carrying a turn around F.

The rhythmic reduction (Example 19*b*) reveals that the melodic contour of the beginning of the second phrase (m. 5) is the same as that of the first. That is, D–G–F–E parallels C–F–E–D. The analytic sketch (Example 19*c*) shows

EXAMPLE 19. Mozart, *Symphony in C major* ("Linz"), K. 425, IV

the structural relations precisely, using the by-now-familiar stem and slur notation (and ties). Since the second phrase offers the greatest complexity, let us begin with it. First, the high A in m. 6 is defined by the harmony as a note dependent upon G, specifically, an upper neighbor to G. It is separated from G by the chromatic passing note G♯, and is therefore a variety of indirect neighbor note.[15] This chromatic passing note is omitted from Example 19c to clarify the relation. Thus, the melodic interval spanned from the D in m. 5 is the fourth, D–G. Filling this interval are the passing tones E–F–F♯.

The sketch in Example 19c shows that the final melodic motion in the theme is the ascent from E to G in the last two measures. There the sixteenth notes form a turn around F, as indicated by stems, slurs, and ties. Shown at *d*, meanwhile, is an incorrect reading—incorrect, because the neighbor note G attached to the ascending passing note F is misinterpreted, with the result that G becomes the main note and F is its lower neighbor, a reversal of the real structural situation. This reduction does not sound like the original at all.

Just as in the case of the neighbor note, the passing note can be direct or indirect. In its indirect form the passing note is not immediately contiguous to one of the main notes it is connecting because the direct connection is interrupted by another type of diminution, either a consonant skip or a

---

15. It must be made clear that A is an upper neighbor to G, not G♯; the latter is a chromatic passing note leading to that upper neighbor.

neighbor note (as in Example 16). The present example (19) provides three excellent instances of this type of passing note, which must be understood in order to construct good Schenkerian analyses. The first instance is the F in the upper voice at the end of m. 6. The rhythmic reduction shows that this F is analogous to E in m. 2, which serves as a passing note connecting F with D. However, F in m. 6 is separated from the main note G because of the neighbor note A appended to G. The slurs in the analytic sketch clarify. The slur from G to E incorporates F as a passing tone, while the slur from G to A shows the dependent neighbor-note relation between the two. The first F in m. 7 (the sixteenth note) is the second instance of indirect passing note, since it is separated from the main note E by the upper neighbor G. Again, the analytic notation clarifies, this time by placing stems on the main components of the concluding motion, E–F–G. The analytic sketch shows D in the upper voice of m. 3 as an expanded passing note between C (m. 1) and E (m. 7). This, then, is the third instance of an indirect passing note in the theme—indirect because D is separated from C by the consonant skip to F.

One of Chopin's beautifully expansive melodic themes is shown in Example 20. It begins with an arpeggiation from F through D♭ down to A♭ on the downbeat of m 2.[16] The first interval of the melody, the third from F to D♭, is filled in by the passing tone E♭. This passing tone is of the *accented* variety, since it falls on the accented beat of the measure, displacing the main note. (The remainder of the discussion is directed to Example 20*b*). Notice that the initial F in the melody is connected by a curved line to the F in the left-hand accompaniment figure. This is to show that the accompaniment doubles the upper-voice components throughout, a fact which is important in helping to explain the unusual and characteristic motive which occurs in the

EXAMPLE 20. Chopin, *Nocturne in D♭ major*, Op. 27, No. 2

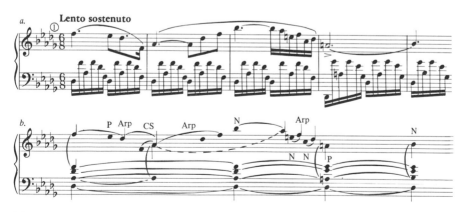

16. Arpeggiations in this and previous examples have not been discussed in order to focus on the main topic. The following section is devoted to the arpeggiation.

upper voice of m. 4. After A♭ is reached in m. 2 the upper voice ascends (through an arpeggiation) to A♭ an octave higher, and the association of the two A♭'s is indicated by a dotted curved line (a modified tie). However, before the high A♭ sounds, its upper neighbor B♭ is brought in and occupies over half the measure. As soon as it resolves on the sixteenth note A♭ a descending arpeggiation unfolds, two notes of which have half-step lower neighbors attached. This half-step motive proves to be in preparation for the striking A♮–B♭ over the next two measures. The A♮ here is a greatly expanded chromatic passing note which connects A♭ of m. 2 with B♭ of m. 5. Since A♭ and A♮ are not adjacent, the passing note is of the indirect type. However, the direct form is given in the accompaniment. In the analytic sketch, notice the curved line from upper to lower A♭ in m. 2. This lower A♭ then moves to A♮ in m. 4 and finally to B♭ in m. 5, expressing the passing-note motion without interruption.

The main purpose of the next example, Example 21, is to illustrate the *consonant passing note* (CP). This is a note that could be simply a passing dissonance above the bass, but is highlighted and given special emphasis by consonant support. Thus, in m. 2 of Example 21, the passing tone G connecting the upper and lower neighbor notes of G is supported by E♭, which makes the interval between upper voice and bass a consonant 10th instead of the dissonant 7th which would have been formed (as G over A♭) had the bass not changed. Similarly, in m. 3 the passing note F in the upper voice is given its own bass note. The F on the downbeat of m. 4 is an indirect passing note that relates back to the main note G on the downbeat of m. 3. Thus, the small motion in the upper voice of m. 3, G–F–E♭, is repeated in expanded form by G (m. 3)–F–E♭ (m. 4), the latter indicated by the stemmed notes.

EXAMPLE 21. Brahms, *Rhapsody in E♭ major*, Op. 119, No. 4

In the opening phrase of the theme of the second movement of Beethoven's Op. 2, No. 1 (Example 22), passing tones fill in the descending

EXAMPLE 22. Beethoven, *Piano Sonata in F minor*, Op. 2, No. 1, II

fourth that begins with the upper-voice C in m. 3. The second of these (A) is another example of a consonant passing note. In general, every enlarged passing note (with metrical value or greater) that has consonant harmonic or contrapuntal support is consonant. The classic Schenkerian case, however, arises within the interval of a fourth, as in Example 22.[17]

Passing notes occur in all voices, of course. Occurrences in the bass are especially important as motivic elements in the High Baroque period. An illustration from Handel's music is given in Example 23. The bass line is set out in continuous eighth notes. When the passing notes are removed in the analytic sketch, we discover an ascending bass arpeggiation from E to B. Notice the different functions the passing note A performs as it connects G and B: first it accompanies the upper-voice neighbor notes F♯ and D♯, then it comes in below the enlarged passing note F♯ in m. 3 as it leads upward to B, the bass note which supplies the major structural support for that F.

EXAMPLE 23. Handel, *Sonata for Flute and Continuo in E minor*, II

---

17. The expression *consonant passing tone*, important in Schenker's writings, will not be extensively used in this volume, since the general relation between passing notes as diminutions and enlarged passing notes has already been described and illustrated.

In the opening of the Handel *Oboe Sonata* movement shown in Example 24, the bass diminutions create a complex and interesting pattern. As we see in the reductions at *b* and *c*, removal of the passing notes in m. 1 reveals the consonant skips attached to bass C and A♭. The bass E♭ resulting from the last of these then connects to F, which in analytic notation (at *c*) is given a flag to indicate its special neighbor-note relation to G.[18] On the other hand, the surface arpeggiations that begin in the second part of m. 2 are attached to a stepwise progression in the bass that spans a fourth from C to G. In both the rhythmic and analytic reductions each note of the stepwise bass is followed by an ascending consonant skip of a fourth—exactly the reverse of the bass pattern in m. 1—unifying the bass progression motivically over the phrase.[19]

EXAMPLE 24. Handel, *Sonata for Oboe and Continuo in C minor,* I

An example of complex diminutions closes this section. It demonstrates the importance of understanding diminutional processes; for what may appear to be a highly irregular surface can always be resolved into a pattern of diminutions, most often into a pattern that results from combining various types of diminutions.

Example 25*a* presents such an irregular surface, on the last quarter note of the first measure. This is the result of the confluence of diminutions at that

18. This interpretation touches upon an important aspect of melodic analysis, and one which cannot be treated extensively and adequately in this context—namely, the matter of properly segmenting and grouping patterns created by diminutions. Here, for example, E♭ is the note related by consonant skip to A♭, and F is the lower neighbor to G. The motion E♭–F–G created by their concatenation is coincidental.

19. The numbers 10–7 between the staffs symbolize a linear intervallic pattern and are placed in Example 24 for future reference. The same applies to Example 31*d*.

point. The rhythmic reduction at *b* shows that the bass note C belongs with the upper-voice note E on the last beat (a IV chord). However, this temporal correspondence does not occur because the accented passing note D comes at the beginning of the beat, displacing C and giving it the duration of a sixteenth note, in accordance with the rhythmic motive of the upper voices at the beginning of the Sarabande. By changing the two accented passing notes F and D to unaccented passing notes in a succession of even eighth notes starting on the downbeat, the rhythmic reduction brings C in on the last quarter note directly beneath E. The additional complicating factor in the original *a* is the final sixteenth-note F in the upper voice, an incomplete upper-neighbor suffix, for this falls together with the sixteenth-note C in the bass, creating a dissonant situation which is momentarily startling.

EXAMPLE 25. Bach, *Partita No. 5 in G major*, Sarabande

The analysis in Example 25*c* places the melodic components of *a* in proper perspective. The bass in m. 1 is a filled-in consonant skip, and the more significant bass progression of mm. 1–2 is represented by the stemmed notes G–G♯–A. The G♯ is an expanded chromatic passing note that also has attached to it a consonant skip, while the intermediate goal of the bass motion is A. The latter proves to be an indirect upper neighbor to G in m. 3: indirect because the lower neighbor F♯ is introduced, resolving to G first. The melodic organization of the first three measures is remarkably regular, despite the fact that each has a different rhythmic pattern. As the analysis shows, each main note is followed by its upper neighbor note. In m. 1 the upper neighbor note itself is supplied with an upper neighbor, the F, which seemed to cause a structural discontinuity. But in reality it does not, because the underlying voice leading (a topic presented in Chapter 2) is unaffected by local temporal displacements.

The Arpeggiation as Motive

Several examples have already been introduced which contain arpeggiations: for instance, Examples 7 (p. 18) and 20 (p. 27). Arpeggiation is such a familiar term that we have not defined it in detail. However, in Schenkerian terms, structural arpeggiation always involves the arpeggiation of a complete consonant harmony. Hence it is distinct from the consonant skip. It may occur in notes of short duration with respect to the metrical organization of a work or in notes of metrical or greater value. Both will be shown in the examples that follow.

Arpeggiations in themes are plentiful, especially in the Baroque and Classic periods, where they are often artfully combined with the other principal diminutions, neighbor and passing notes. Consider Example 26, a famous Beethoven symphony theme. The opening arpeggiation, the characteristic motive of the scherzo, is spanned out over the first three measures, with the upbeat F, arriving at high F on the downbeat of m. 4. The analysis uses the dotted line to show the projection of the low F of the upbeat to the goal F in m. 3. As a subsidiary feature of the arpeggiation, we see the consonant skips following the first two notes.

EXAMPLE 26. Beethoven, *Seventh Symphony*, III

The two subsequent four-measure phrases are also composed of arpeggiations, as shown in the analysis, but these arpeggiations are filled in by passing notes. Like the elements of the opening arpeggiation, each component of these arpeggiations takes up a full measure. While the first arpeggiation terminates on F, the second terminates on G, and the third on A, creating the ascending melodic pattern F–G–A, within which G is a passing tone. For the first time, roman numerals are given as part of the analysis, here to show that the initial F is supported by I, the enlarged passing note G by V, and the final A again by I. Thus, in this theme, although we perceive the arpeggiation to be the characteristic motive, there is a slow underlying melodic progression involving the passing tone. And, of course, passing tones occur in the upper voice in the service of the descending arpeggiations.

Example 27 shows the opening thematic statement of a Chopin waltz. A characteristic motive, the ascending arpeggiation, appears in m. 10 and is interpreted analytically in *b*. It reappears at m. 16, now in descending form. There each occurrence of B is preceded by the upper-neighbor diminution C, harking back to m. 11, in which C participates in the turn around B. There is no arpeggiation of larger scale as in Example 26. Instead, the melody of the consequent phrase descends stepwise to E in m. 16. The corresponding ascending motion from E to B occurs in the bass from m. 10 through m. 14.

EXAMPLE 27. Chopin, *Waltz in E minor* (posth.)

Over the course of this introductory chapter we have pointed out several times that the fundamental types of diminutions do not occur in isolation in well-composed tonal music, but are always combined to form variegated structures. This is illustrated once again by Example 28.

The analysis in Example 28*b* interprets the complete music given at *a*, showing that the overall design consists of three measures of analogous pattern: a descending arpeggiation from the top note through two subsidiary arpeggiations. This is indicated by the large slur containing two smaller slurs. The neighbor note and the consonant skip shown in the analysis are secondary features. The upper voice, which consists of the head notes of the arpeggiations, forms a stepwise progression that ascends from F to B♭ (the stemmed notes at the top). Each of these notes is connected by a dotted line to its counterpart an octave lower, which is always approached by an ascending arpeggiation.

EXAMPLE 28. Bach, *Partita No. 1 in B♭ major*, Allemande

The rhythmic reduction (Example 28*c*) reduces the sixteenth-note motion to eighth-note motion. Here we have a rhythmic texture typical of Bach: a very active surface and a slower-moving pattern that sustains it.

Finally, in Example 28*d*, the arpeggiations are shown in collapsed or verticalized form in a single register above the stationary bass note, B♭, showing in a simple way how the arpeggiations are in the service of the ascending line in the uppermost part, from F to B♭.

As is well known, keyboard music in various periods exploits the arpeggiation in striking and diversified ways. A famous example is provided in Example 29 (compare Example 146, p. 154). Whereas the arpeggiations in the previous example (28) were in the service of an ascending line (thus involving the passing tone), the arpeggiations of the present passage are in the service of a slowly unfolding neighbor-note formation, a turn, as shown on a single staff in Example 29*c*. In Example 29*b* the opening arpeggiation, which is the characteristic motive of the theme, is not the only arpeggiation in the first phrase; there is another and slower arpeggiation of the tonic triad that begins on C, passes through E♭ (m. 2) and arrives at the goal note G on the downbeat of m. 3. This note is then followed by its upper neighbor A♭. The second phrase arpeggiates the dominant triad from G out to D over the first two measures. The lower neighbor F, which corresponds to the upper

EXAMPLE 29. Mozart, *Piano Sonata in C minor*, K. 457, I

neighbor A♭ in m. 4, then enters and completes the turn G–A♭–F–G. Both arpeggiation and neighbor note occur here in expanded form, effecting a dynamic and coherent presentation of the thematic idea.

Example 30 presents the opening of a work that features arpeggiations of various kinds. Indeed, in this beautiful composition, the last of the so-called three-part inventions, Bach assigns a special role to the arpeggiation. It first occurs as the final motive in the three-measure theme, preceded by a pattern that comprises neighbor notes (both small and large) and passing notes, as shown in Example 30b. In the full notation (Example 30a), each metrical beat (dotted-eighth value) of m. 3 seems to consist of an arpeggiation. This strictly metrical reading produces a slow arpeggiation descending through the B-minor (tonic) triad from B to B. The rhythmic grouping within each beat, however, divides it exactly in half: D–B–D, F♯–B–F♯, etc.

EXAMPLE 30. Bach, *Sinfonia No. 15 in B minor*

Example 30c shows the arpeggiation that results from this rhythmic reading: a descent from D to B, with F♯ in the first beat interpreted as a consonant skip. We prefer this latter reading, but the analytic mechanisms required to justify it cannot be presented to the reader at this juncture, and an act of faith is required. The important point here is that underlying the surface arpeggiation is a more fundamental arpeggiation that organizes the structure.

Before leaving Example 30 it behooves us to draw attention to one more aspect: the diagonal arrows that cross between the staffs. One of these lines connects B in the upper voice with B in the bass; the other connects D in the tenor with D in the upper voice. This is an instance of voice exchange, a topic that will be taken up in greater detail in Chapter 2.

As in the previous two sections, on the neighbor note and the passing note, we end this section with an example of complex diminution involving the arpeggiation, occurring at a later point in the same Bach Sinfonia (Example 31).

The cascading arpeggiations in Example 31a contain an underlying stepwise motion in the upper voice which is accompanied by a regular pattern in the bass, but this motion is somewhat concealed. Systematic analysis brings it to the surface, as shown in the successive reductions below the given passage.

EXAMPLE 31. Bach, *Sinfonia No. 15 in B minor*

In Example 31*b* we have a rhythmic reduction which distributes the notes of the arpeggiation evenly over each beat, in accord with the 9/16 time signature. This simplifies and clarifies the arpeggiations greatly; however, there remains the peculiar clash of G over F♯ marked by the asterisk at the end of m. 13. Clearly this results from the imitative design, with the left-hand arpeggiation beginning one metrical beat after the right hand in m. 12, so that the right-hand part finishes first in m. 13. The next reduction, also rhythmic (Example 31*c*), is constructed with this fact in mind.[20] In addition, the arpeggiation on the third beat in mm. 12 and 13 is brought into the lower octave, for reasons that will become clear in a moment. One result of this is that the clash between G and F♯ at the end of m. 13 disappears.

Finally, in Example 31*d*, the analytic sketch shows the descending stepwise line which governs the arpeggiations, one in each measure. The other diminutions and expanded diminutions in this sketch offer a good opportunity to review some of the more recondite types presented in the previous sections. Each stemmed note in the upper-voice line that descends stepwise from B to F♯ has attached to it, in addition to the arpeggiation of a triad, a consonant skip (B–D, A–C, G–B), and—most important—an incomplete upper-neighbor suffix. This neighbor note is of the *indirect* type, for it is separated from the main note in each case by the consonant skip and the arpeggiation. This notwithstanding, its subordinate function with respect to the main note remains clear.

Notice that the composer retains the arpeggiation pattern consistently to the end of the progression, with the final bass arpeggiation A–F♯–D in m. 13. Thus, at the cadence on III in m. 14 the bass does not present a note of the dominant of III, such as A or C♯, although the upper-voice G at that point suggests such a dominant (A[7]) chord. Continuation of the arpeggiation pattern in the bass was of primary concern to the composer, and the conflict between bass F♯ and descant G at the end of m. 13 is a secondary feature that does not affect the structure of the passage.

Exercises

For each of the excerpts construct a rhythmic reduction and an analysis using stem and slur notation. Use ties where applicable. The rhythmic reduction and the analysis should be aligned vertically, following the pattern of the examples in this chapter. Label all diminutions, using the abbreviations N (neighbor note), P (passing note), CS (consonant skip), and Arp (arpeggiation). Comment upon any special or unusual features in the diminutions.

---

20. This procedure effectively eliminates one beat from each measure, converting the 9/16 meter to 6/16.

1. Sample Exercise: Beethoven, *Piano Sonata in G major,* Op. 14, No. 2, I

Solution:

    a. Rhythmic reduction

    b. Analysis using stem and slur notation

Comments:

    1. The rhythmic reduction preserves the arpeggiation in the right-hand part, but loses it in the left hand because of the omission of the unaccented sixteenth notes.

    2. The analysis in stem and slur notation shows that there are three different types of diminutions used in this thematic statement: the consonant skip, the arpeggiation, and the neighbor note.

    3. The neighbor notes in the right-hand part are uniformly half-step incomplete lower neighbors of the prefix type. To maintain the half-step motive, Beethoven introduces the chromatic notes A♯ and G♯, which produce the nonstructural interval of a diminished fourth (D–A♯ and C–G♯).

    4. Beginning in m. 2, expanded neighbor notes come into play: E is upper neighbor to D, C is upper neighbor to B, and A is upper neighbor to G. Similarly, in the bass, the arpeggiation continues in mm. 3–4, but the components of the arpeggiation are neighbors to the previous arpeggiation components. To avoid confusion (i.e., too many N's), these expanded neighbor notes are not labeled in the musical analysis.

2. Chopin, *Waltz in B minor,* Op. 69, No. 2

The E♯ in the upper voice of m. 6 comes from the F♯ in the previous measure and proceeds to E♮ in m. 7.

3. Beethoven, WoO 78

This is a variation on a familiar theme. A correct analysis will reveal the underlying melody in the upper voice.

4. Mozart, *Piano Sonata in G major*, K. 283, I

When constructing the rhythmic reduction listen carefully for the slower motion that underlies the sixteenth-note diminutions in mm. 8–9.

5. Berlioz, *Symphonie fantastique*, II

For the purpose of the exercise only the outer voices need to be represented in the solution.

6. Beethoven, *Piano Sonata in B♭ major*, Op. 22, I

7. Bach, *English Suite in A minor*, Sarabande (ornaments omitted)

8. Schubert, *Impromptu in A♭ major*, Op. 142, No. 2

9. Chopin, *Nocturne in F♯ minor*, Op. 48, No. 2

2

Voice Leading:
Counterpoint and
Figured Bass

Every student of tonal harmony and counterpoint knows how important the concept of voice leading is to those disciplines. A clear understanding of the essentials of voice leading, as well as its ramifications, in the core repertory of tonal music is absolutely basic to the study of Schenkerian analysis, since Schenkerian analytic procedures always give primary consideration to the horizontal dimension of the musical composition. It is of fundamental importance to understand the principles of voice leading that control the motion of the linear components of that dimension. The present chapter undertakes an overview, beginning with voice leading as presented within traditional species counterpoint and concluding with a survey of figured bass notation as it represents the more elaborate voice leading of the free tonal composition.

The study of voice leading is the study of the principles that govern the progression of the component voices of a composition both separately and in combination. In the Schenkerian tradition, this study begins with strict species counterpoint, a pedagogical system devised by Johann Joseph Fux (1660–1741) and diligently studied by Haydn, Mozart, and Beethoven, among others.

The Species Counterpoint Model

The Fuxian system organizes the study of counterpoint according to five categories, or *species*. The work consists of completing exercises that consist of composing a contrapuntal line (or lines) against a given part, the *cantus firmus*, in accord with certain rules that are set out for each of the species. These rules concern voice leading, the shape of the contrapuntal line, and rhythmic features, and are organized to lead the student through the species step by step, introducing fundamental structural aspects gradually. To this day, species counterpoint is regarded by many as indispensable to the serious study of tonal music.

Specifically excluded from all the species is any reference to harmony in the sense of organized harmonic progression, harmonic scale steps (Chapter 5), melodic statements of harmonies (arpeggiations), or patterns such as sequences, which might suggest an underlying harmonic scheme. Voice leading is the primary determinant of tonal motion in the species exercise.

The world of species counterpoint is an abstract and idealized world from which many aspects of the free tonal composition are absent. For example, diminutions play only a limited role, and temporal displacements occur only under the most controlled circumstances (in the suspensions of fourth species). In the material that follows we present a survey of the species in the form of completed exercises with brief comments on their relevance to voice leading.

Example 32 offers a completed first-species exercise in two-part counterpoint by Fux himself. In this species the contrapuntal line (counterpoint) is set against the cantus firmus, one note at a time, under the following basic restraints: First, only consonances (thirds, tenths, unisons, octaves, fifths) are allowed between the note of the cantus firmus (hereafter abbreviated c.f.) and the note of the counterpoint above or below it (above in Example 32). In the examples that follow, these intervals are indicated by numbers between the staffs. The exercise shown in Example 32 begins and ends with the vertical perfect consonances fifth and octave, respectively, while the main part of the counterpoint features the imperfect consonances third and sixth, with perfect fifths formed on the fourth and sixth notes of the exercise—a desirable mixture of imperfect and perfect consonances.

EXAMPLE 32. First-Species Exercise by Fux

The second constraint on first species exercises is: No successive ("parallel") perfect consonances are permitted (unisons, octaves, fifths). This prohibition, simple though it is, has significant implications for voice leading, since it requires the student to find other solutions in case successive (parallel) perfect consonances are impending.

A third constraint affects intervals formed by successive notes of the counterpoint and applies to successive notes of the cantus firmus as well:

Intervals larger than an octave are prohibited. The only dissonances permitted are the fourth, which is regarded as a consonance in this horizontal dimension, and the second, which is the basic building unit for melodic lines, both in species exercises and in free tonal compositions.

Finally, there are guidelines concerning the overall contour of the counterpoint—for example, on the number of consecutive skips in the same direction. Since these have more to do with species conventions and certain general attributes of melodic lines and less to do with voice leading, they will not be discussed here.

In sum, the first-species exercise is based entirely on consonant intervals, with only a single dissonant interval, the second, permitted to occur in the horizontal dimension. Because all the vertical intervals between c.f. and counterpoint are consonances, the counterpoint can skip away to another consonance and need not proceed by step, as is required if the interval formed is dissonant. Thus, in Mozart's exercise[1] using Fux's c.f. with counterpoint below (Example 33), there is a skip away from the fifth in m. 3 instead of stepwise motion suggested by the notehead in parentheses, which would have been within the voice-leading rules for the species, but probably would have led to an unsatisfactory continuation from the melodic standpoint. Again, in the fifth measure from the end, there is a skip away from the consonant tenth instead of the stepwise progression indicated by the authors' parenthesized notehead.[2]

EXAMPLE 33. First-Species Exercise by Mozart (c.f. by Fux)

To sum up, first-species counterpoint rules produce exercises that present entirely consonant interval relations. The dissonance as a determinant of voice leading does not exist in this species.

These first-species characteristics prevail regardless of the number of voices, as shown in Example 34, a first-species exercise in four voices. Notice especially that this four-voice contrapuntal structure is quite neutral with respect to harmonic progression. Indeed, if the succession of verticals were regarded as a harmonic progression there are many ambiguities—as in the C-major triad which follows the D-minor triad at the very beginning and then

1. *Thomas Attwoods Theorie- und Kompositionsstudien bei Mozart* (Neue Mozart Ausgabe, Bärenreiter: Kassel, 1965), p. 43.

2. In modern instruction in species counterpoint, Mozart's use of consecutive skips in the counterpoint of mm. 6–8, outlining a seventh from F to C, would be regarded as problematic.

proceeds to a G-major triad. If the c.f. were a melody to be harmonized, this setting would constitute a poor solution. The reason for this was mentioned above: Species exercises are not at all concerned with harmony; indeed, they avoid any implications of tonal harmony just in order to present voice leading in purified form, uninfluenced by harmonic progression.

EXAMPLE 34. First-Species Exercise in Four Voices by Fux

It is in second species that the dissonance is introduced as an interval between the counterpoint and the c.f., but only under the strictest control. In this species two notes of the counterpoint are placed against one in the c.f. Here the second half note in each measure may form a dissonance against the bass, but the dissonance must be in the form of a passing note: that is, it must be introduced and left by step in the same direction. Example 35 shows a well-constructed second species exercise.[3]

EXAMPLE 35. Second-Species Exercise by Herman Roth

The counterpoint begins on D, forming an octave with the c.f. From this consonance it skips downward to A as the c.f. changes to F. Then on the second half note in this (second) measure the dissonant passing note B♭ is introduced, creating the interval of a fourth against the c.f. The passing note then ascends to resolution on C, which forms a consonant interval (sixth) with the c.f. This voice-leading event is a model for the treatment of dissonance in second species: stepwise passing motion with the dissonance falling on the second half note. (Accented dissonant passing notes and dissonant neighbor notes are not permitted in this species.) The important thing to notice here is that once the dissonance is brought into play its progression is obligatory. If it begins as an ascending passing tone, the motion must continue in an ascending direction; if it comes into being as a descending passing tone, it must resolve by step to a consonance in the descending direction. In m. 5

---

3. Hermann Roth, *Elemente der Stimmführung* (Stuttgart, 1926), p. 76.

another ascending dissonant passing note occurs, and another in the measure following, this one creating a seventh that resolves to a consonant sixth. Consonances, however, are free with respect to progression, just as in first species. Thus, from the C in the counterpoint of m. 3, there is a skip away to G, which forms a third against the c.f. All other things being equal, there is no obligatory resolution (voice leading) for consonances, whereas dissonances *must* resolve by step.[4]

Yet another second-species exercise is shown in Example 36,[5] based on the Fux cantus used in the previous exercises. There, in m. 4, a descending dissonant passing note C appears, introduced by step from the octave in the first part of the measure and resolving by step to the third above the c.f. note G in m. 5. This is a prototype for the 8–7 progression, which is such a common voice-leading event in the free composition. Still in Example 36, the passing note C♯ in the next-to-last measure is a good example of a consonant passing note, for it forms a sixth with the bass. Like the 8–7, the 5–6 voice-leading motion is prominent in many free tonal compositions (Chapter 5). Here it comes about naturally in the context of a strict species counterpoint exercise.

EXAMPLE 36. Second-Species Exercise by Heinrich Bellermann

The most important fact of voice leading learned in connection with second-species counterpoint is that dissonance is fundamentally a passing-note phenomenon and that its stepwise preparation and resolution are obligatory.

In third species the counterpoint sets four notes to each note of the c.f. The c.f. controls the voice leading of the counterpoint according to the following rules: First, passing dissonances may occur on the second, third, or fourth quarter note and must be resolved by consonances in each case. The first quarter note is always consonant. (When the third quarter note carries a dissonant passing note, the accented passing note of the free tonal composition is simulated.) Second, in this species an occasional dissonant neighbor note on the second quarter is allowed. This must be a neighbor note of the complete type, departing from the main note by step and returning to it by

4. In Chapter 4 linear intervallic patterns are introduced as an aspect of voice leading in the free composition. Fixed progression of consonances may be required to complete the pattern.
5. Heinrich Bellermann, *Der Contrapunkt*, 4th ed. (Berlin, 1901), p. 157.

step. Third, parallel perfect consonances are prohibited here as in all the species. Finally, consonances in the vertical dimension are "free": It is possible to skip away from a consonance, provided some guideline for the melodic contour of the counterpoint is not then violated.

Example 37 gives a third-species exercise by Fux, consisting predominantly of stepwise motion in the counterpoint. The first measure contains passing notes on the second and fourth quarters, each coming from and going to consonant vertical intervals. In the second measure there is a dissonant passing note on the second quarter; the fourth quarter also carries a passing note, but it forms a consonant sixth against the c.f. The remaining passing notes occur on the second or fourth quarters in mm. 4, 5, 6, 8, and 10, and as accented passing notes (AP) on the third quarter in mm. 7 and 9. Skips away from consonances occur in four places, which the reader can easily locate. In the third measure, however, there is a skip away from a dissonant seventh. The entire four-note figure there is bracketed and labeled N.C., which stands for *nota cambiata*. Only in the nota cambiata figure is a skip away from a dissonance permitted. The skip must traverse a consonant interval (consonant skip), it must end on a vertical consonance, and it must return by step in the direction opposite to the direction of the skip. All these conditions are met in Fux's exercise. The nota cambiata, then, presents the species counterpoint version of the indirect passing note (Chapter 1). Thus, in m. 3 of Example 37, the second quarter-note D is a passing note between E and C; its direct progression to C is interrupted, however, by the skip down to B, which forms the consonant fifth with the c.f.

EXAMPLE 37. Third-Species Exercise by Fux

Clearly, third-species counterpoint resembles diminutional passages in the free composition, incorporating short passing and neighbor notes. Nothing in species, however, corresponds exactly to the expanded diminutions discussed in Chapter 1, although the dissonant or consonant passing note on the second half note in second species might be regarded as a simulation of an expanded passing note. Since the counterpoint in that species consists only of half notes, there are, of course, no shorter notes that could be regarded as generators of the expanded diminutions. Only in fifth or mixed species would it be possible occasionally to find something that resembled an expanded diminution (neighbor or passing note). However, the notion of diminution and expanded diminution as presented in Chapter 1 is not among the concepts expressed in the species counterpoint exercise, which is concerned with voice leading in small contexts.

Example 38 shows a third-species exercise by Mozart from the Attwood Studies cited above. Mozart's counterpoint differs markedly from that of Fux, while following the rules of the species strictly. There is, for example, a dissonant neighbor note on the second quarter of m. 2, within a neighbor-note figure of the complete type, in accord with the rules of voice leading.

EXAMPLE 38. Third-Species Exercise by Mozart

Like second species, the fourth-species counterpoint consists of two half notes against each note of the c.f. In this species, however, the first half note in the measure may be a dissonance, under the following conditions: The dissonant note is introduced as a consonance on the second half note in the previous measure. The dissonance then resolves downward to a consonance on the second half note in its measure. Taken together, the succession consonance-dissonance-consonance is a suspension formation, and this species is often called the suspension species. Example 39 illustrates.

EXAMPLE 39. Fourth-Species Exercise by Fux

The basic voice leading is not affected by the suspension feature, which is a rhythmic displacement. In Example 39 the C in the counterpoint of m. 3 belongs with the E of the c.f., just as the B♭ of the c.f. in the next measure belongs to D of the c.f. These two displacements are indicated by the diagonal lines.[6] However, the dissonances that are formed as suspensions are subject to the basic rule for this species: stepwise *descending* resolution. In Fux's exercise (Example 39) the only type of dissonant suspension formation represented is the 7–6.[7] Here, again, the consonances are free. Thus, there is a

6. Diagonal lines are also used this way in the Schenkerian analytic notation introduced in Chapter 7.

7. Here we adopt the convention of connecting a pair of figures with a dash to indicate the dependent relationship. The same convention is to be followed in figured bass.

skip away from the vertical third in m. 2 to the sixth which serves as the consonant preparation of the dissonance.

Another type of dissonant suspension is illustrated in Bellermann's exercise (Example 40), the 4–3 in mm. 7 and 8. This exercise also contains two instances of the *consonant* suspension 6–5 (mm. 2,3).[8] The 6–5 pattern has the appearance of a suspension, but the 6 does not require resolution; it just happens to move downward by step to another consonance, 5. It could conceivably move elsewhere. The fact that 5 (the *perfect* fifth) and 6 are, uniquely, both consonances vertically and a step apart melodically also allows the pattern 5–6 to occur (see m. 5). Ascending stepwise motion, tied over the bar, is possible with no other pair of intervals.

EXAMPLE 40. Fourth-Species Exercise by Bellermann

Dissonant suspensions in fourth species are very strictly controlled. Only four types are possible in the counterpoint above the c.f.: 2–1, 9–8, 4–3, 7–6. In the free composition, however, suspensions occur in many different environments. For example, the preparation of the note to be suspended may occur within a dissonant harmony. And suspensions may ascend to resolution, as 7–8 or 9–10. It must also be mentioned here that in free composition a repeated note is equivalent to a tied note in a suspension.

The final species, fifth species (called mixed species), does not introduce any new rules of voice leading, but is concerned with the combination of the various species in counterpoint against the c.f. Accordingly, we omit it from consideration here.

In combined-species exercises, such as Example 41,[9] it is possible to produce structures of some complexity. The c.f. in this example is in the alto voice. Below it are two counterpoints, tenor in second species and bass in first species, while above it in the soprano is a counterpoint in second species. Since the verticals are entirely the result of the voice-leading rules which determine the individual counterpoints (according to the species they represent), they cannot be read as functional harmonies to which one might attach roman numerals. Even in these more complex exercises, the species rules can produce musical abstractions which are generated entirely by

---

8. There are those who may prefer to reserve the term *suspension* only for dissonant suspensions. In this event it might be more accurate to refer to consonant suspensions as syncopations.

9. Heinrich Schenker, *Kontrapunkt*, Part 2 (Vienna: Universal, 1922), p. 184.

voice-leading phenomena represented in the flux of consonance and disso-nance. These exercises, although they are never intended to be musical compositions, serve a very useful conceptual purpose. Precisely because they represent an abstraction that highlights voice leading, they illuminate the greatly expanded phenomena of voice leading in the free tonal composition and reveal the distinctive role of harmony in large and small. There are, moreover, many intersections between strict (species) counterpoint and free composition. For example, just as it is in species counterpoint, the charac-teristic voice-leading motion in the free tonal composition is stepwise.[10]

EXAMPLE 41. Combined-Species Exercise by Schenker

In species counterpoint, moreover, and especially in combined species (where the counterpoints must obey the rules of the species to which they belong, as well as interact correctly with the other counterpoints) we find prototypes of many of the voice-leading patterns idiomatic to the free tonal composition. The 10–10–10 succession between soprano and alto in mm. 2 and 3 of Example 41 is a case in point. (See Chapter 5.)

Figured Bass Notation

The more complex voice leading of free tonal music—especially instru-mental music, with its elaborate rhythmic and chromatic components—still follows the elemental principles of voice leading of the species model, in the sense that it incorporates them. To represent the flux of interacting lines in the free tonal composition, we use the traditional notation known as figured bass.[11] In this notation, the bass is regarded as the fundamental voice to which the others relate. Figures (numbers, signs of alteration, and other symbols) specify the intervals formed by the voices above the bass and, in some cases, the progression of the voices to which the symbols refer. In all cases, a figure represents accurately the local voice-leading situation, indicating required progressions.

In Schenkerian analysis figured bass symbols (figures) are used for the most

---

10. For example, the contrapuntal writing in Bach's *D-major Prelude* (WTC/I, No. 5) closely resembles third species.

11. Schenker's own expertise in the figured bass is well illustrated in his published writings and analyses. The more abstract species counterpoint model of voice leading is perhaps more relevant to the more abstract levels of the tonal work.

part to show surface-level voice leading, the moment-to-moment motion of the lines above the bass. The figures are relatively limited with respect to the aspects of musical structure they represent. They do not show, for example, the registral placement of the voices, nor do they represent, with any degree of accuracy, the durations of the musical elements to which they refer. But they do portray in a concise manner the voice-leading texture as it unfolds in the composition.

This is an analytic use of figured bass—a mode of notation. We are not concernéd with the performance practice of "realizing" figured basses, although experience in that area is a distinct advantage, for it introduces to the musical analyst many refinements in voice leading that occur in the highly developed tonal composition.

In this section we undertake a survey of figured bass notation to prepare the student for the use of figures in the analyses that follow in Parts Two and Three.

We begin with the basic figures $\frac{5}{3}$ and 6. Of these $\frac{5}{3}$ is the most fundamental and designates a vertical consisting of the intervals of a fifth and a third above the bass—that is, a triad. Since the consonant triad is the basic harmony in tonal music, the actual figure $\frac{5}{3}$ is only used for that harmony under special circumstances; a bass note without any figure is understood to be a $\frac{5}{3}$. Example 42 presents a chorale phrase entirely made up of $\frac{5}{3}$'s and 6's. The latter (6) designates a vertical consisting of a sixth above the bass and a third above the bass; that is, the figure 6 always stands for $\frac{6}{3}$. In the chorale phrase of Example 42 the first and third 6's are consonances, because consonant intervals are formed above the bass, in accord with the structure of the underlying scale. The second 6, however, is a dissonance, because the dissonant interval of a diminished fifth is formed between D and G♯. The notes that form this interval therefore have the obligatory resolution indicated by the arrows, as they resolve within the consonant 6 that follows. The voice leading of the consonant $\frac{5}{3}$'s and 6's in the choral phrase is free (of obligatory resolution), just as consonances in the species exercise are free. However, in the regular four-voice texture, which is the norm for tonal music, a complete harmony is required above each structural bass note—almost without exception. This in itself determines voice leading to some extent. Also there are the two well-known guidelines: When changing harmony, 1) preserve common tones or 2) move to the nearest note by step, giving priority to the half step if it is available. Both, in turn, are subject to the prohibition of parallel perfect intervals, which is just as applicable in the free composition as in the species exercise. We can see one of these determinants of voice leading in the chorale phrase of Example 42. In the chord above the third bass note, the tenor F♯ does not ascend to G♯, the nearest note by step, but skips down to B, because B is required to obtain a complete triad; otherwise there would be two thirds and no fifth above the bass. Melodic functions of notes also affect voice leading. For instance, there are two neighbor notes in the bass of the present chorale phrase, F♯ and B. These progress to the notes upon which they are dependent. And, naturally, in a chorale setting such as this, the given melody determines the course of the uppermost voice.

EXAMPLE 42. After Bach, Chorale No. 326, *Allein Gott in der Höh'sei Ehr*

It will be recalled that the numeral 3 is associated both with $\frac{5}{3}$ and 6. If the note above the bass to which the numeral 3 refers is altered chromatically, the appropriate sign of alteration is given in place of the numeral.[12] Thus, in Example 43, $\frac{6}{\sharp}$ below the first bass note in the second measure is the correct notation: ♯ refers to tenor G♯. Altered thirds such as this usually require stepwise voice leading. Here the altered G♯ ascends to A over the next bass note.

EXAMPLE 43. Bach, Chorale No. 287, *Herr, ich habe misgehandelt*

The fifth of the $\frac{5}{3}$ must be figured when it would prevent ambiguity—for instance, if without its presence one might assume that the vertical was a $\frac{6}{4}$. Much more common as a figure is the numeral 5 when it is part of the succession 6–5 or the succession 5–6.[13] Here the figures specify the voice

---

12. This is the notation adopted in the present book. In other systems a sharp may be used to indicate an upward chromatic alteration, a flat for a downward chromatic alteration, regardless of the actual sign of alteration required in the full notation. This notation is convenient in a repeated pattern of figures to show the regularity with which the alteration recurs. Placement of the accidental before or after the figure is another variable. In the musical illustrations in this book, accidentals are positioned before the figured bass numerals. In still another system of notating chromatic alterations, the solidus (/) transecting a figure indicates that the note designated by the figure is to be raised chromatically, while the flat indicates descending alteration. The latter notation is often encountered in editions of Baroque music.

13. See also Chapter 4, Linear Intervallic Patterns, for 5–6 and 6–5.

leading exactly; the fifth above the bass moves to the sixth above the bass. Example 44 provides a familiar instance. In m. 7 the fifth E above the bass moves to the sixth F♯, a connection symbolized by the hyphen between the numerals. The complete array of intervals over the last bass note in the measure is indicated by the figures. In addition to the sixth above the bass, there is a fourth (4) and a third (3). The alteration of the sixth by the sharp in the staff notation is reflected by the sharp before the number 6 in the figured bass. The 5–6 succession is taken up again beginning in m. 11 and stepwise voice leading takes place in all voices. The figure sharp alone on the first beat of m. 12 and the first beat of m. 13 refers to the raised third.

EXAMPLE 44. Beethoven, *Seventh Symphony*, II

The figure $^6_4$ is used when the vertical so designated is not part of a $^{6-5}_{4-3}$ or $^{6-7}_{4-3}$ voice leading (discussed below), that is, when the $^6_4$ is relatively independent. A $^6_4$ of this type is called a consonant $^6_4$. Example 45 presents an instance, the $^6_4$ above the second bass note. As shown at *b*, the replacement of a $^5_3$ containing the same notes as the $^6_4$ does not violate the setting—that is, disrupt the stepwise voice leading or affect harmonic functions. Substitution of $^5_3$ for $^6_4$ such as here will always be a valid test for the consonant as distinct from the dissonant (passing or neighbor) $^6_4$. The very beginning of the Beethoven theme cited above (Example 44) presents another case of the consonant $^6_4$ representing the tonic triad. It is consonant because it does not resolve to another figure in linear fashion (as $^{6-5}_{4-3}$) but is succeeded by the consonant (unfigured) $^5_3$ in m. 3.[14]

While the figures that designate consonant "free" sonorities may be open to more than one interpretation as far as voice leading is concerned (subject

14. Figured bass can refer to any note in a musical texture except the bass itself. Since the bass is given, there is no way (in traditional figured bass) to indicate, for example, that a bass note has undergone chromatic alteration. A frequent mistake among beginners is that they try to do this anyway. As an example, remember: the figure $^6_\sharp$ means that the *third above the bass* is sharped—not the bass itself.

EXAMPLE 45. Bach, Chorale No. 274, *O Ewigkeit, du Donnerwort*

to the prohibition of parallel perfect consonances and the guidelines of common tones and stepwise progression), the figures that represent dissonances are more restrictive. Underlying them is a basic principle of voice leading in tonal music, elemental examples of which we saw in the section of species counterpoint above: *The stepwise resolution of dissonance is obligatory*, with priority given to half-step progression if available and not in violation of the rule against parallels.

From second species, we know the progression 8–7, where the dissonant passing note enters on the second half note above the c.f. Example 46 shows, in m. 8, an occurrence of 8–7 in the context of a free composition. This is indicated by the corresponding figured bass symbols. Here G is a passing note directed toward F♯. However, its direct progression to F♯ is interrupted by the appearance of E♯, a lower neighbor note (appoggiatura) to F♯.[15] In the figures this is referenced by ♯9, the interval which it forms with the bass. It is also accompanied by C♯, which forms a 7th above the bass and is figured accordingly. The figures show the stepwise obligatory ascending resolution $\frac{9-10}{7-8}$. These figures more often occur in the context of a double suspension (look ahead to Example 58, p. 60).

EXAMPLE 46. Beethoven, *String Quartet in D major*, Op. 18, No. 3, I

---

15. The true appoggiatura, of which this is an instance, is an unprepared suspension; it is not present in the preceding harmony.

The figure 7 often (but not always) implies that the fifth and the third are also present above the bass. This is the case in m. 8 of Example 46: When the 7th is led in by the octave the voices below it remain, retaining the $\frac{5}{3}$ figures from the previous arrangement. The continuation of $\frac{5}{3}$ below the figure 7 is shown in the example by the hyphens.

The 7 may occur in a number of voice-leading contexts. When used analytically, it is probably advisable to specify whether the third and fifth are also present. Example 47 shows two 7's, both of which also include the fifth and third and are so figured. In the first of these (last beat of m. 1) the seventh (C♯–B♭) is diminished, hence descends to resolution as shown by the arrow. The other voices (fifth and third) also descend to resolution, closing in on the $\frac{5}{3}$ over D. On the second beat of the following measure a similar voice-leading situation is created: that is, a diminished seventh above the bass (now C over D♯) which descends to resolution. The fifth also descends to resolution against the stepwise bass as before, but the third skips down a fifth, to the fifth of the final $\frac{5}{3}$. Here Bach is observing the traditional rule that prohibits the vertical succession diminished fifth–perfect fifth. Had F♯ descended to E, the result would have been the succession $\frac{C-B}{F\sharp-E}$, that is, the prohibited parallelism.[16]

EXAMPLE 47. Bach, Chorale No. 300, *Warum betrübst du dich, mein Herz*

This is an appropriate time to make an important point about figured bass symbols. Figured bass symbols provide information about the intervals above the bass, with attendant implications about the voice-leading situation, and in some cases they give the actual linear succession of the notes represented by the intervals.

Any information figures may carry about chord type (e.g., "diminished 7th"), harmonic root (e.g., V⁷), or inversion (e.g., I⁶) is entirely ancillary to their main purpose, which has to do with voice leading. Figured bass symbols and roman numerals have, over the years, traditionally appeared together; yet conceptually they are distinct. This distinction will be emphasized in the present section.

Example 48 contains three instances of the figure $\frac{6}{5}$. Here the fifth forms the dissonant interval of the tritone with the bass and descends to resolution

---

16. The reverse succession, perfect fifth–diminished fifth, is unproblematic.

against the ascending stepwise motion in the bass. Arrows show the voice leading in each case. As in Example 46, the rhythmic reduction gives the basic voice leading without the diminutions, which are controlled by the voice-leading patterns.

EXAMPLE 48. Schubert, *String Quartet in A minor*, Op. 29, II

Example 49 also contains $^6_5$'s, in mm. 2–3. In m. 2 the first violin brings in the fifth E as a neighbor note to D♯, to which it resolves. Characteristically, the diminished fifth (tritone)[17] formed as $^E_{A♯}$ resolves stepwise in contrary motion to the third $^{D♯}_B$, as shown by the arrows, following the half-step rule. On the last beat of m. 3 there is again a $^6_5$. This time, however, resolution of the diminished fifth is postponed (to the second beat of m. 4) by a suspension, creating the figures $^{9–8}_{4–♯}$.

EXAMPLE 49. Haydn, *String Quartet in E♭ major*, Op. 76, No. 6, II

The figure $^4_3$ often occurs in a context that features neighbor notes. Example 50, also from one of Haydn's late string quartets, offers an illustration. There in the first two phrases of the theme, the neighbor note is the characteristic motive both in bass and upper voice. Whereas in the $^6_5$'s shown in the previous two examples, the tritone contracted inward to the

---

17. Strictly speaking, "tritone" should only refer to an augmented fourth—that is, to an interval spanning three whole tones. In recent years, however, it has become common practice to apply the term to the diminished fifth as well.

EXAMPLE 50. Haydn, *String Quartet in B♭ major*, Op. 76, No. 4, II

third, here in the $\frac{4}{3}$ the tritone expands outward to the sixth: $\frac{\text{D–E♭}}{\text{A♭–G}}$ and $\frac{\text{E–F}}{\text{B♭–A♭}}$. In both cases the resolution is by half-step, according to the rule.

Example 51 shows a $\frac{\sharp 4}{3}$ on the first beat of m. 3, created by linear motion in one voice, the alto. This is preceded by the $\frac{4}{2}$ over E which, as illustrated at *b*, would normally progress to a 6 above the bass note D. However, instead of remaining on F♯ as expected, the alto voice moves to the passing note G♯. The result, the richer $\frac{\sharp 4}{3}$, is a striking example of the intimate relation between expanded diminutions and voice leading.

EXAMPLE 51. After Bach, Chorale No. 331, *Wo soll ich fliehen hin*

In the figure $\frac{4}{2}$, the bass itself is dissonant. The slow movement of Haydn's quartet, Op. 74, No. 3 (Example 52) provides two instances of it (mm. 1 and 3). There the dissonant tritone (an augmented fourth) involves the bass note A and the inner voice D♯. It resolves, expanded outward, to the sixth, as indicated by the arrows. In m. 2 of the same example, the bass again is a component of the dissonant tritone (more precisely, diminished fifth) formed with the upper voice A. It contracts to resolution on the consonant third $\frac{\text{G♯}}{\text{E}}$ as shown.[18] The third measure of Example 53 also contains normative voice-leading resolutions of $\frac{4}{2}$'s. There the bass note has the melodic function of

---

18. Whether the resolution is outward or inward is, of course, the crucial difference between the augmented fourth and the diminished fifth. The augmented fourth resolves outward to the sixth, while the diminished fifth resolves inward to the third.

EXAMPLE 52. Haydn, *String Quartet in G minor*, Op. 74, No. 3, II

EXAMPLE 53. After Bach, Chorale No. 356, *Jesu meine Freude*

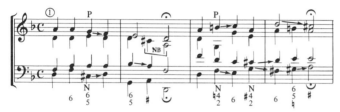

neighbor note and in both cases forms the tritone with a passing note in another voice.

The figure ♯6 designates a raised sixth above the bass, an interval which expands outward by half step to resolution on the octave. This may either be a major or an augmented sixth; the latter is illustrated by Example 52. In m. 8, E♯ forms the ♯6 against the bass G and the two notes resolve outward, as shown by the arrows, to the octave F♯ on the downbeat of the next measure. Sometimes the full notation may be ambiguous with respect to voice leading. Example 54 offers a case in point. In m. 3 of the excerpt the literal figure shows a ♭7 (E♭). However, the voice-leading resolution in m. 5 shows that that ♭7 is really an augmented sixth, for it resolves outward to the octave. Here the E♭ is understood to represent D♯.

EXAMPLE 54. Beethoven, *String Quartet in C major*, Op. 59, No. 3, I

In species counterpoint the suspension is a relatively uncomplicated phenomenon and takes only a few forms. The suspension in free tonal compositions, however, takes many forms. It may be prepared within a dissonance as well as a consonance; the resolution may be quite short in relation to the suspension proper; a dissonance may be present as the suspension resolves; a suspension formation may be double, triple, or even quadruple; the notes suspended need not resolve at the same time; and the bass may change as the suspension resolves. Moreover, unlike suspensions in species counterpoint, suspensions in free composition may also *ascend* to resolution, the most common being the 9–10 and 7–8, with chromatic variants of these.

Before presenting examples of suspension figures, it is essential to make a basic observation about the suspension. It represents a rhythmic delay of a voice-leading connection, a temporal displacement; it does not generate a new voice-leading situation but merely intensifies one that has already been set in operation. This was already suggested in connection with one of the earlier examples (Example 49, p. 55, m. 4) and will be apparent in every illustration that follows below.

In another previously cited excerpt (Example 43, p. 51, end of m. 2) we saw the figures $^5_{4-\sharp}$, the four-to-three suspension, with A resolving to G$\sharp$. The figure 5 appears here to emphasize that the fifth above the bass is present at the time of the suspension, that the suspension formation is not $^{6-5}_{4-3}$. It is not absolutely necessary, however; just a plain 4 would normally mean $^5_4$. Remember that $^5_3$ is the "understood" figure; the 4 here replaces 3 (in this case $\sharp$3, with the 3 understood), and resolves to it. Notice, in the same example, that the alto G$\sharp$ at the end of the second measure (the leading tone) skips away to E at the cadence instead of proceeding to A in unison with the soprano. This is a case where voice leading is momentarily sacrificed in order to have a complete chord at the resolution. (The same thing would not be done if the leading tone were in the soprano.) The alternative (which Bach evidently did not prefer, although it is not incorrect) would be to resolve to a chord with a tripled root and no fifth.

Example 55 contains two interesting suspension formations, in one of which the resolution is much shorter than the suspension proper. At the end of m. 1 the sixteenth-note motion in the alto, C–D, echoes the previous alto motive B–C. The sixteenth-note C in the succession C–D, however, resolves the D which has been suspended over the bass C, forming the 9–8 suspension indicated by the figures, a formation in which the resolution is half the duration of the suspension itself. Similarly, in the second measure of Example 55, E$\flat$ in the alto is suspended above the bass note F$\sharp$ to form a seventh. With the resolution of E$\flat$ to D, the 7–6 suspension formation is completed. Here as in the previous suspension the preparation is far longer than the suspension itself, while the resolution has exactly the duration of the suspension proper. In both cases, the bass makes the suspension formation absolutely clear. In short, durations of the components of the suspension are variable in a free tonal composition.

EXAMPLE 55. Bach, Chorale No. 306, *O Mensch, bewein' dein' Sünde gross*

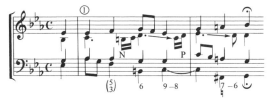

The preparation of a suspension formation in a dissonant context is shown in Example 56. There a triple suspension involving the ninth, raised fifth, and fourth occurs. It is prepared within the dissonant ⁷₅. Every note is suspended except the bass itself. The last measure of a previous illustration, Example 52 (p. 57), also contains a triple suspension. There both ninth and raised seventh resolve to the octave. The dissonant suspended fourth was prepared as the dissonant seventh in the previous measure; hence its resolution to D♯ is the ultimate resolution of that seventh. Similarly, the dissonant suspended seventh is the third above the previous bass note F♯. The resolution of the ♯7 (A♯) brings the leading tone A♯ to rest on the tonic note.

EXAMPLE 56. After Bach, Chorale No. 316, *Christus, der ist mein Leben*

Example 57 illustrates the way in which diminutions may be attached to suspensions before they resolve. On the downbeat of m. 2 the bass changes to E♭, above which D is suspended as a seventh. This seventh resolves to C as the bass moves to F. Before the resolution, however, the double neighbor note ᴇ♭/c is brought in for rhythmic reasons. The E♭ there, a submetrical note, does not resolve the suspended D, but merely embellishes it. If E♭ is taken to be the resolution of the suspension, then the voice leading is placed in jeopardy. Example 57b shows the correct reading of the passage, while c shows what happens when E♭ is regarded as the resolution: namely, a break in the continuity of the upper voice. Specifically, E♭ would then have to be understood as the first and perhaps unique instance of a new kind of passing note: the incomplete passing note!

EXAMPLE 57. Haydn, *String Quartet in F major*, Op. 74, No. 2, II

A famous composition features embellished suspension resolutions at the very outset: the *C-minor Organ Passacaglia* by J. S. Bach, shown in Example 58a. The reduction at *b* shows the chain of suspensions that underlies the beginning of the first variation. The first two are double suspensions, while the last two are triple suspensions. The first triple suspension displaces a $\frac{6}{3}$, the second a $\frac{5}{3}$. Even though the suspended B♮ is notated a second above the bass in m. 3, the figure ♮9 is used. This is because the figure 2 is used only when the bass participates in the dissonance—as in $\frac{4}{2}$, or in the bass suspensions $\frac{5-6}{2-3}$ and $\frac{7-8}{4-5}{2-3}$ illustrated in Examples 58c and 58d.[19]

EXAMPLE 58. Bach, *Passacaglia for Organ in C minor*

---

19. The figure $\frac{7}{2}$ may also be created when the bass incorporates an accented passing note. See Example 59.

Two types of short notes embellish the suspensions in Example 58*a*. In the upper voice the sixteenth note is always an upper neighbor note, and the voice just above the bass brings in the note of resolution one eighth note early (an anticipation), except for m. 11, where that function is taken over by the "alto" voice.

Several other suspensions can be found in the musical excerpts cited earlier in this section. In Example 45 (p. 53), m. 2, the submetrical double suspension $\frac{7-6}{5-6}$ is indicated on the third beat. Normally suspensions formed by short notes such as these are not figured, but here we have extended the notation to this rhythmic level in order to show the detailed voice leading. Brief discussion of other examples follows:

Example 46 (p. 53), mm. 7–8, contains a classic instance of the $\frac{6-5}{4-3}$ double suspension. In contrast to the consonant $\frac{6}{4}$ (Examples 44, p. 52, and 45, p. 53), the $\frac{6}{4}$ here, like all suspensions, depends for its meaning upon its resolution, $\frac{5}{3}$ in this case. The octave in the first violin is also figured here since it prepares the following 8–7 motion.

Still looking back at previous examples, in m. 3 of Example 49 (p. 55) we find the double suspension $\frac{7-6}{5-6}$, prepared within the $\frac{5}{3}$ at the end of m. 2. Both suspended notes resolve to 6, but the motion 5–6 incorporates the chromatic passing note B♯, imitated by the bass E♯ on the last beat of the measure. At the end of the four-measure phrase occurs the double suspension $\frac{9-8}{4-♯}$, prepared within the preceding dissonant $\frac{6}{5}$.

In Example 52 (p. 57), m. 9, the chromatic passing note B♯ in the viola resembles the same chromatic passing note in m. 3 of Example 49 (mentioned above) because it stands between the suspended note and its resolution. This is figured ♯4, since it has full metrical value (quarter note). As is the convention throughout this volume, the hyphen above ♯4 means that the previous figure, 6, continues on this beat as well.

Accented passing notes in the bass and bass suspensions sometimes cause complicated-looking figures to occur, as in Example 59. When the running sixteenth-note motive is passed along to the bass in m. 3, the note that falls on the third (eighth-note) beat is A, an accented passing note. Effectively this throws the vertical interval structure off by one step and creates the figure $\frac{7}{2}$. This changes immediately, however, to $\frac{8}{3}$, as shown on the single staff at the bottom of the example. Thus, $\frac{7}{2}$ is but a momentary displacement of a $\frac{5}{3}$. It is the bass that causes the temporal displacement and the complicated figures. The figures for all such formations resolve to figures exactly one greater. For example, $\frac{5}{4}$ is a displacement (by suspension or accented passing note in the bass) of $\frac{6}{5}$. And again, the general rule is observed: The figure 2 is used when the bass participates in the formation of the dissonance.

At this point we return to three earlier examples to show an interesting and not uncommon feature of voice leading in the free tonal composition: transfer of resolution. Transfer of resolution means that a dissonance is

EXAMPLE 59. Bach, *Trio Sonata in G major*, BWV 1038, II

introduced in one voice, but transferred to another before resolution or at the point of resolution. This occurs frequently with the $\frac{4}{3}$ that contains the tritone between two of the voices above the bass, as shown in Example 46 (p. 53), mm. 4–5. According to the rule of stepwise resolution of the tritone, G in the second violin (m. 4) should go to F♯ instead of A as it does when the bass changes (m. 5). However, the resolution of G is effected when the bass itself takes the F♯ on the downbeat of m. 5: the resolution (indicated by the arrow) has been transferred to the bass. Another instance is shown in Example 48*b* (p. 55), m. 2, where the sixth of the $\frac{4}{3}$, B, is transferred to the bass on the second half note and resolves to C at the beginning of the next measure. In this case the note is transferred before resolution, not at the point of resolution as in Example 4*b*.

A third and final example of transfer of resolution is given in m. 6 of Example 54 (p. 57). The first figure in that measure is $\frac{7}{\sharp}$, the seventh being formed by C against the bass D. On the third beat of the measure, however, the bass takes over the dissonant note C and resolves it to B at the beginning of the next measure. The voice that originally carried the dissonant C, viola, ascends to D as the cello assumes the dissonance, thus literally exchanging notes with it.

The final musical illustration for this section, Example 60, shows at *b* the beginning of an elaborate trio sonata movement by J. S. Bach, a canon over a figured bass. At *a* is a realization of the continuo part in four voices, to show the voice leading that underlies the instrumental parts in the trio sonata. Notice how naturally the upper voice of the realization (Example 60*a*) follows the contour of the lines in the instruments in many places. In a specific sense, the four-voice realization is the basic composition, for it contains all the voice-leading connections expressed by the instruments.

At this juncture all the figures in Example 60 should be familiar to the reader. All the suspensions are prepared within dissonant harmonies, as is

EXAMPLE 60. Bach, *Trio Sonata in C major*, BWV 1037, III

frequently the case in a complex free tonal composition. But two figures in m. 5 deserve special attention. First, the suspended ninth, B, resolves to A as it should, but at the point of resolution the bass changes, giving the succession of figures 9–$\frac{4}{2}$. (Another common situation is represented by the succession 9–6: as the ninth resolves, the bass ascends a third.) Second, the last figure in m. 5, 5, is required here, since $\frac{4}{2}$'s usually resolve to 6's. Bach supplied the figure 5 here to make sure the continuo player would realize the correct intervals.

No attempt has been made in this section to illustrate and discuss all possible figured bass symbols. Instead, we have presented a number of the most common figures and conventions. The central purpose of this section has been to show the relation between figured bass and voice leading, and to introduce figured bass notation for future analytical use. Although a number of the more esoteric figures were omitted from the presentation, the foregoing discussion will enable the reader to determine their structural meaning if and when they are encountered.

Exercises

Since the text did not attempt to present species counterpoint pedagogically, it is not feasible to give species counterpoint exercises here. Instead, we offer selected exercises in figured-bass voice leading.

1. Beethoven, *Piano Concerto in E♭ major*, Op. 73 ("Emperor"), II

Indicate voice leading by adding figured bass symbols below the lower staff. Label all diminutions, including expanded diminutions, in upper voice and bass. Mark all obligatory resolutions of dissonance using arrows, as in the text. There is an interesting voice-leading situation in m. 3. How is the treatment of dissonance to be explained there?

2. Bach, *English Suite in D minor*, Sarabande

Label all diminutions, including expanded diminutions. (Hint: upper-voice F♯ in m. 2 is a chromatic passing tone.) Mark dissonance resolutions by arrows. Supply complete figures below the lower staff. There are unusual voice leadings in the excerpt, notably in mm. 5–6. Is it possible to explain these?

3. Schumann, *Rundgesang* from *Album for the Young*

Supply figured bass symbols, indicate dissonance resolutions by arrows, and label diminutions in the outer voices. There are two ways of figuring the second beat (fourth eighth note) in m. 3; one way is $^5_3$.

4. Purcell, *Dido and Aeneas*, Dido's Lament (orchestral ending)

This famous passage is a study in suspensions and is particularly remarkable for the resolution of suspended dissonances in verticals (marked N.B.) which are themselves dissonances. The bass ostinato figure divides into two parts, from the opening G to D in m. 57, and from B♭ in m. 57 to G in m. 59. Supply complete figures.

5. Schumann, *** from *Album for the Young*

The exercise consists of two discontinuous passages from the piece, the second a variant on the first. Compare them.

6. Handel, *Keyboard Suite in F major*, III (ornaments omitted)

This movement, in D minor, begins and ends on V, and serves to connect two fast movements in the suite. Supply figures and label diminutions in the outer voices. Notice that the inner voices repeat the motive of the upper voice throughout. Recall that a suspension can be brought about by a repeated note as well as by a note that is tied.

3
Compound Melody

The concept of compound melody is intimately associated with the topics of the previous chapters, diminutions and voice leading, and, indeed, can be easily understood only with a working knowledge of both those structural features.

Example 61, drawn from the music of J. S. Bach, portrays very explicitly the idea of compound melody. At *a* is a setting of the first part of the chorale *O Gott, du frommer Gott*. At *b* is the fourth variation on that segment of the chorale, and it is to this that we direct primary attention. There in sixteenth notes the essential voice leading of the upper three voices of the chorale setting begins to unfold. For example, on the first beat of m. 1 the variation melody begins on the inner-voice E♭ of the chorale setting, then arpeggiates upward through G to the top voice C, the second note of the chorale tune. There follows a descending skip to E♭, and the next beat of the measure again begins on a note that belongs to an inner voice, D. Immediately thereafter, however, is a skip in the top voice to B♮, the third note of the chorale tune. On the fourth beat of the measure the variation deviates from the chorale setting, introducing a different bass note, B♭, which carries a $\frac{5}{3}$, in the place of the 6 over B♮ in Example 61*a*.

This variation melody may be regarded as a model compound melody: the melody itself is composed of distinct components of the voice leading, a fact that is demonstrated in Example 61*c*, where the fourth variation is rendered as a succession of verticals in note values corresponding to those of the original chorale setting.

Compound melodic structures differ markedly from the simpler arpeggiations shown in Chapter 1. Whereas the arpeggiation is the projection of a *single voice* through the notes of a consonant triad, compound melody

EXAMPLE 61. Bach, Variations on *O Gott, du frommer Gott*

involves arpeggiation and partial arpeggiation in the more elaborate sense of
Example 61, as conveyors of *two or more voices* over a longer span of music.
Structures of this kind are characteristic and essential to the understanding of
many different kinds of tonal music.

Before leaving the Bach chorale variation example, it is worthwhile to
point out the role of the diminutions in that compound melody. As
highlighted by the label N in Example 61*b*, the lower neighbor-note figure is
the diminution characteristic of this variation. And it is not merely chance
that this figure is the miniature form of the expanded neighbor-note figure
C–B–C at the beginning of the chorale melody itself.

Although the examples that follow (with the exception of Examples 62 and
63) deal with compound melody as it is formed by a group of voices that
includes the soprano or descant,[1] the lower voices may also form a compound

---

1. The term *descant* is sometimes convenient to use in cases where the highest voice is not in
the soprano range (for instance, Example 63), or when description of the voices in vocal terms
does not seem appropriate.

melody. This is the case in much piano music, where an arpeggiated left-hand part will form a compound melody containing the bass and inner voices.

The left-hand texture in Example 62*a* is a case in point. It contains the bass plus two voices above the bass, and expresses the voice leading shown in Example 62*b*. It is this horizontal dimension—the voice leading—that is of greatest interest in the compound melody, the way in which the components of the melody interact to form a coherent and artistic progression over a span of music. Over the length of the present excerpt, in the left hand, we perceive the ascending stepwise bass from A♭ to C through the passing note B♭. The voice just above the bass moves in parallel thirds with it, while the third component of the compound melody remains on E♭ for two full measures, skipping upward to A♭ in m. 3, as the voice above the bass arrives at E♭. Meanwhile, the right hand consists of a compound melody as well, also analyzed in Example 62*b*. Here in the right hand, however, the texture is complicated by the surface polyphony (a fugal subject, mm. 1–2, joined by the beginning of an answer in m. 3). As even this short example demonstrates, what is intended to be but one voice in a polyphonic structure may itself be a compound melody.

EXAMPLE 62. Mendelssohn, *Praeludium IV*, Op. 35

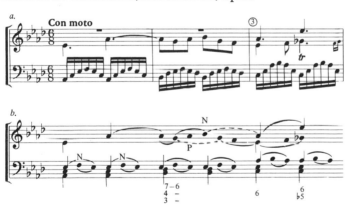

Perhaps the most striking instances of compound melody are to be found in compositions for solo instruments that are essentially single-line instruments, compositions in which the instrument presents a complete three- or four-voice structure in the form of an elaborate compound melody. The works of J. S. Bach for solo violin and solo cello come to mind immediately, of course, and Example 63 offers a relevant excerpt.

Here (Example 63*a*) the descant begins with B♭ on the downbeat of m. 1. On the fourth eighth note the melody skips down to the inner voice D (followed by E♭), and on the last beat of the measure skips again to bring in the bass note G, which leads to the bass note F on the first beat of the second

EXAMPLE 64. Bach, *Cello Suite in G Major*, Menuet II

measure. The skip upward to A that follows reintroduces the descant strand of the voice leading and the downward skip to D again activates the inner voice in this three-voice compound melody. The third measure of the excerpt resembles the first in its voice-leading pattern, while in m. 4 there is an arpeggiation from the bass upward through the inner voice to join the upper voice on G.

In Example 63b the voices are *verticalized* to show the voice-leading connections as though the three voices were literally present at every moment instead of being presented in the form of a compound melody. This shows that a 5–6 linear motion governs the inner voice in mm. 1 and 3, while the suspension figure 4–♯ (G–F♯) represents the voice leading of m. 4.

This example illustrates two major points about compound melodic structures. First, a compound melody always results in a rhythmic displacement of components that "belong together." For instance, the inner voice D in m. 1 of Example 63 belongs to the $\frac{5}{3}$ over the bass note G and is implicit at the outset. However, in the compound melody it does not appear until the fourth eighth note in the measure, while the bass itself does not appear until the very end of the measure! The second major point is this: The component voices of compound melodies always follow the voice-leading pattern; indeed, they are the melodic expression of that pattern, which is contained within a single melodic structure.

As we mentioned briefly in connection with Example 62 (the two-voice fugato in the right hand), fugue subjects are often compound melodies. Example 64b depicts, in analytic notation, the voice-leading structure of the familiar *B-major Fugue* by Bach cited at *a*. The figures below the staff designate the linear 5–6 patterns that characterize the subject. In the first of these the fifth above the bass is present only by implication, an implication verified by the assumed $\frac{5}{3}$ over the bass note B at the beginning (the tonic triad) and by the fully explicit statement of the second 5–6 succession.[2] The bracketed notation at the lower right edge of the example shows the pattern in its most concise and continuous form.

---

2. Notes implied by voice leading are dealt with in greater detail in Chapter 6.

Example 64. Bach, WTC/2, Fugue 23

Although compound melodies play a significant role in the vocal and instrumental music of the Baroque period, with J. S. Bach the undisputed master of the idiom, they also occur abundantly in every other period. Example 65 is the beginning of a familiar composition from the Classic period, the melodic theme of which is a compound melody comprising first three, then two voices. As the rhythmic reduction shows, the descant note G is implicit at the opening, but is approached by an ascending arpeggiation from C and arrives at the end of m. 1, to be followed immediately by a return to the voice which initiated the arpeggiation. In m. 3 the upper voice continues with A, an upper neighbor to the soprano G of m. 1. The reduction at *b* shows that G is implicit in the top voice throughout m. 2, since it is consonant within the voice-leading context at that location. (Implied notes such as these will always be shown in parentheses.) In mm. 3–4, the melody is attached directly to the voice at the top of the compound melody that began with G. There is also a compound structure of a simpler, more consistent sort in the left-hand—a typical example of the so-called Alberti bass.

Example 65. Mozart, *Piano Sonata in C major*, K. 545, I

The opening gestures of Brahms's *D-minor Capriccio* (Example 66) are *partially* compound. That is, there is an initial arpeggiation through the voices, followed by a simultaneous (vertical) statement of the voices involved. In the sketch at *b* the voice-leading pattern is shown entirely in vertical arrangement. In m. 2, the top voice D should have led to C♯, following the

EXAMPLE 66. Brahms, *Capriccio in D minor*, Op. 116, No. 7

half-step resolution of that voice in m. 1. Because of the downward skip, the inner voice A becomes the temporary top voice, and the top voice D resolves in the lower octave to C♯, as shown by the arrow.

Many melodies may be regarded as partially compound, in that they engage more than one voice-leading strand at certain points, but not in a continuous way. The significance of such interactions can only be ascertained with reference to the structure of the particular work involved. Example 67 offers another instance, from the music of Chopin. The melody begins on the inner-voice D♯, which, as shown at *b*, is the octave above the bass that will ultimately move to the seventh through the chromatic passing note C✕. As this chromatic note enters, the sixth above the bass, B, is introduced, leading downward to G♯ in parallel motion with the voice below it. Thus, both voice-leading components are present at the same time, and the compound aspect of melodic structure suggested with the opening skip has vanished.

EXAMPLE 67. Chopin, *Mazurka in G♯ minor*, Op. 33, No. 1

In Example 68 we see a typical Baroque passage in which the solo instrumental part (flute) projects a compound melodic structure. At *a* is the notated form of the opening of the piece, consisting of an instrumental part and a figured bass for the continuo players. The melody, verticalized at *b*, is a bilinear structure with rhythmically distinctive components (the lower consistently a quarter note, the upper distinguished by the dotted-note pattern and the lower neighbor-note diminution). The numerals between the

EXAMPLE 68. Handel, *Sonata for Flute and Continuo in A minor*, I

staffs here designate a linear intervallic pattern (Chapter 5), and should not be confused with figured bass symbols, which are always below the lower staff.

A bilinear melodic structure in a style entirely different from that of the Handel excerpt is shown in Example 69. There the descant note D is introduced by an octave skip that begins on the upbeat and is embellished by an upper neighbor note E♭ and the secondary neighbor note F in small notation (a "grace note"). The melody then skips down to bring in A at the end of the first measure, and this note initiates a long ascending progression (the "alto" voice in Example 69b), terminating on D at the end of the phrase. Even though the D is not present in the upper voice of m. 2, it is implied; and as with most implied notes it is present elsewhere, here as the fifth above the bass in the left hand. Similarly, the F in m. 4 is not literally present in the descant, but is implied in like fashion. It may be apparent to the reader by now that in our discussion of compound melody thus far we have not attempted to say which of the linear components of any of the compound melodies is primary. This determination requires additional analytic refinements which cannot be undertaken here, but which will be presented beginning with Chapter 7.

EXAMPLE 69. Chopin, *Mazurka in G minor*, Op. 67, No. 2

In the preceding examples good use has been made of the technique of verticalizing, to show the alignment of the voices that contribute to compound melodies, without temporal (rhythmic) displacement. This technique, while very useful, is not without pitfalls and should be used with discretion. Consider Example 70a, the opening of Bach's *A-minor Invention*. Thoughtless verticalization here produces the results shown in Example 70b, where the analysis tells us that there is an upper voice that ascends from C to E, passing through D. However, this contravenes a rule of voice leading, for D forms a tritone with the bass G♯ and must *descend* by step to resolution. Furthermore, the reduction at *b* does not really sound like the actual music. The reduction at *c* clarifies. The main upper-voice motion is the stepwise ascent from A to C. Each note in the succession has attached to it a consonant skip of a third. These notes that result from a diminution (the skip) do not represent the underlying voice leading at all, but are ancillary to it. The reduction at *b* has given them the same value as the main voice-leading elements, thus totally confusing the progression and resulting in a violation of a rule (incorrect resolution of the diminished fifth).

EXAMPLE 70. Bach, *Inventio 13 in A minor*

Because compound melodies are sometimes misread by the inexperienced (as demonstrated in Example 70), we are presenting a number of examples in this section of the book for the student to examine carefully. Moreover, not all melodic structures that seem to be compound are such. Example 71 illustrates a common case. The basic motive of the theme of the movement is an ascending consonant skip which is filled by passing notes that connect downward to the next main note of the theme. Thus, the basic melodic structure here is a *single* voice which ascends from C in m. 1 to G in m. 8. In addition, the reduction at *b* reveals a parallel: namely, the consonant skip to G above D in mm. 5–6 corresponding to the consonant skip to F following C in mm. 1–2. However, in mm. 5–6 this consonant skip is filled by passing tones in the ascending direction and intensified by the neighbor note A at the climax in m. 6. One function of the consonant skips is shown in the reduction

EXAMPLE 71. Mozart, *Symphony in C major* ("Linz"), K. 425, IV

at *b*, by the dotted line: the skip to G prepares the definitive ascent to G at the end of the second phrase. (Compare Example 19, p. 26.)

Example 72 (the piano accompaniment only) illustrates in a different way how continuity may be affected by compound melodic structure. The upper voice, which doubles the vocal melody, begins on C♯, suspended over to become a 7–6, with intervening upper neighbor. The melody then skips to the next lower voice in the voice-leading pattern, G♯ continuing with the descending third, G♯–F♯–E. At the beginning of the next melodic phrase is A, and this note is the completion of the passing motion initiated with B in the upper voice of m. 1, as shown in Example 72*b* by the slur—an extended example of the indirect passing note.

EXAMPLE 72. Schubert, *Thränenregen* from *Die Schöne Müllerin*

Example 73, from one of Brahms's violin and piano sonatas, shows how the melodically expressed voice leading of the solo instrument relates to that of the accompanying instrument. The compound melody in the violin is essentially bilinear (as are so many). It begins with the lowest of the upper voices, A, and moves to the next higher voice, on C♯. F♯ enters as still another voice (m. 3, anticipated on the upbeat), and its origin in the voice-leading texture is shown by the curved arrow in Example 73*b*. This F♯ relates to the subsequent E (m. 4) as a neighbor note, but before it proceeds downward to E there is a short inner-voice motion centering on B and C♯ (m. 3). The piano brings E in on the last beat of m. 3, above the bass C♯. The violin, however, does not present this note until the first beat of the following measure, a characteristic rhythmic displacement due to the compound structure.

EXAMPLE 73. Brahms, *Sonata for Violin and Piano in A major*, Op. 100, III

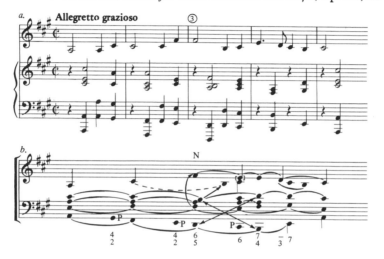

Example 74 (cf. Exercise 16/2,[3] p. 218) shows a compound melody over two four-measure phrases and demonstrates the way in which melodic continuity is effected over that span of music. Again, the compound melody in the upper parts is bilinear and is initiated with the very first motion in the piece, the ascending skip from D to B♭ in m. 1. Following the stepwise descent from B♭ to G (m. 2), there is a return to the lower component of the compound melody, and the phrase ends on C. As shown by the arrow in Example 74*b*, the upper voice G of m. 2 is carried as an inner voice during mm. 2–4, moving to F at the cadence in m. 4. Then, at the beginning of the second phrase (m. 5), that F returns to the upper voice, and the melodic structure of the entire phrase is based upon the voice it represents. This demonstrates a general principle: Although a component of a compound melody may disappear temporarily, it is still represented in the voice-leading pattern, either implicitly (shown by parentheses, as in Example 69*b*, m. 2) or explicitly (by showing the note(s) as they occur in another register).

---

3. That is, Exercise 2 for Chapter 16. This system will be used for exercise references throughout this book. Where there are two or more groups of exercises following each chapter, they will be grouped by letter: in Chapter 12, for example, Exercises 12A/1, 12A/2, etc., and 12B/1, 12B/2, etc.

EXAMPLE 74. Handel, *Keyboard Suite in G minor*, Sarabande

The elements of a compound melody may vary with respect to span and continuity, as illustrated by the theme of the slow movement of Mozart's *A-major Piano Concerto* (Example 75). The first note of the melody, C♯, connects upward to A via the arpeggiation through F♯. On the second eighth note of m. 2 the descending skip to B is a return to the initial voice-leading strand, as shown by the slur in Example 75b. Both voices then proceed downward stepwise in parallel sixths to m. 3. From this point to the end of the phrase, the lower component, which began on C♯, descends stepwise to E♯, while the upper component becomes more fragmentary. As shown in Example 75b, the D in the descant voice of m. 3 implies a resolution to C♯ (parenthesized in the example). Looking over the analysis as a whole, we see that the lower component of the compound melody presents a continuous descending stepwise line, while the upper component has less continuity over this four-measure span of music.

EXAMPLE 75. Mozart, *Piano Concerto in A major*, K. 488, II

When reading compound melodies it is often necessary to distinguish between a *conclusive* motion from one component to another and a *connective* motion. The latter is characteristic of the compound melody.

Example 76 offers a dramatic instance of this. Over the first three measures of this famous theme a large-scale arpeggiation is created, beginning with C and extending to G in the next higher octave. (Compare Examples 29, p. 35, and 146, p. 154.) This is to be understood not as a motion from C to G (except in the most literal sense), but as a connection between C and G, for C returns as a melodic component on the second beat of m. 3, moving stepwise down to its lower neighbor as G moves stepwise up to its upper neighbor in m. 4. In m. 5 G initiates the ascending arpeggiation, passing through B, and connecting to F in m. 7, which serves as lower neighbor to high G, the melodic goal of the second four-measure phrase. Here we have a good example of a greatly extended compound melodic structure, one which underlies an expansive and very dramatic musical subject.

EXAMPLE 76. Mozart, *Piano Sonata in C minor*, K. 457, I

For the two final musical illustrations of compound melody in this chapter we turn to the *B-minor Solo Violin Partita* of Bach, each movement of which is followed by a Double (variation). The running eighth notes of the Double (Example 77*b*) include diminutions of the passing-note and arpeggiation types connecting the basic components of the compound melodic structure (Example 77*c*). Verticalization of successive pairs of notes in m. 3 reveals the descending stepwise pattern shown in the rhythmic reduction at *c*, and this corresponds exactly to the motion in the Bourrée *a* at this moment. Missing from the reduction at *c* is the accented B in the upper voice of m. 1. Although accented and prominent at the surface level, this note is not a component of the compound melody, but is a local consonant skip. The reasoning behind this is one of *consequences*: the high B does not "go anywhere" within the confines of the passage, while the F♯ below it does. However, as with the interpretation of anything incomplete, such judgments are always open to revision pending analysis of the entire composition.

EXAMPLE 77. Bach, *Partita for Solo Violin in B minor*, Bourrée and Double

Example 78, the final illustration in this chapter, presents the first phrase of the Sarabande at *a*, the corresponding music of the Double at *b*, and at *c* a rhythmic reduction of *a*. Again, the Double is an eloquent compound melody, sketching in the voice-leading structure of the Sarabande and adding its own elaborations in the process. For instance, the F♯ in the descant on the downbeat of m. 2 is approached from above by the small motion of a descending third from A in the Double. Moreover, the bass is not completely outlined by the Double in m. 1; instead the melody is creating its own characteristic motives, in particular, the descending third (E–D–C♯, A–G–F♯, etc.). Thus the initial descending third from high A (upbeat to m. 2) is more significant than it first appears to be.

EXAMPLE 78. Bach, *Partita for Solo Violin in B minor*, Sarabande and Double

At the same time, the analysis in Example 78c shows that the opening motive of the theme is based upon upper and lower neighbors to F♯. The second F♯ at the beginning of m. 2 has attached to it a consonant descending skip to D, indicated in the analysis, and the E that follows has a corresponding skip (to C♯) attached to it. D at the end of m. 3 is an indirect passing note that connects E with the parenthesized C♯ on the downbeat of m. 4. As explained above, the parentheses indicate that the C♯ is implied by the voice leading, although not literally present, since the melody skips to the leading tone at the cadence.

This chapter has presented the general idea of the compound melody as it occurs in a variety of periods and styles of tonal music. It has also pointed out some of the most important aspects of compound melodic structures, especially their relation to voice-leading patterns, and suggested their significance with respect to large-scale continuity and other musical matters, such as register. In subsequent portions of this book we will have many occasions to return to compound melody, one of the most important structural features of free tonal compositions.

Exercises

For each of the excerpts construct a rhythmic reduction, using the note values specified. Then make an analysis, using stem, slur, and tie notation. Label all diminutions and supply figured bass symbols. Verticalization may be used provided it elucidates rather than obscures the structure. Comment upon any features of special interest.

1. Sample Exercise: Bach, *Inventio 7 in E minor* (ornaments omitted)

Solution:

    a. Rhythmic reduction in eighth notes

    b. Analysis using stem, slur, and tie notation

Comments:

    1. The compound melody consists of three voice-leading strands. The uppermost of these carries the main melodic motion until m. 5, when the lower component links to the next phrase (D–E).

2. After the upper voice B is reached in m. 3 it is extended in terms of its upper neighbor C (m. 3) and its lower neighbor A (m. 4).

3. Measures 3 and 4 comprise a linear intervallic pattern (Chapter 4) of type 5–10, here enclosed in brackets.

2. Mozart, *Piano Sonata in G major*, K. 283, II

Show the compound melodic structure of the upper part and label diminutions. Only the bass need be represented in addition. Notice that at the beginning of m. 2 the bass and tenor combine to form a compound melody.

3. Handel, *Keyboard Suite in D minor*, Menuetto, Variation 1

Verticalization can be used to good advantage in completing this exercise. Reduce to quarter notes and half notes.

4. Handel, *Sonata and for Flute and Continuo in E minor*, IV

Reduce to eighth notes. The figured bass provides clear clues to the melodic structure.

5. Mozart, *Piano Sonata in C major*, K. 330, II

A word of caution is in order here. Not all skips bring in notes that are part of a compound melody. For example, the F in the upper voice of m. 1 is reached by a local consonant skip from C. There is no continuation from it in the melodic structure. Measures 5 and 6 contain similar consonant skips.

6. Handel, *Sonata for Flute and Continuo in D major*, IV

Verticalize and reduce to quarter notes both in right- and left-hand parts.

7. Bach, *Partita for Solo Violin in D minor*, Gigue

This is a more demanding exercise. In order to understand the compound structure of the solo voice here it is necessary to imagine a bass line, since the bass is only hinted at here and there. Therefore, in the rhythmic reduction, reduce the upper voice to eighth notes and compose a bass in quarter notes, following the beginning given below. This plan can be maintained even when the solo part changes to the sixteenth-note melodic sequence in m. 3.

Beginning of solution to Exercise 7

4

Linear Intervallic
Patterns

A *linear intervallic pattern* is a voice-leading design made up of successive recurrent pairs of intervals formed between the descant and bass (outer voices). Like diminutions, linear intervallic patterns exist over a broad spectrum of tonal music and are not restricted as to musical period, style of genre. Because they are important components of many tonal compositions, it is essential that the student be conversant with their special features so that they may be correctly understood in the context of the complete work. The present chapter undertakes a survey of the major types of linear intervallic patterns, with examples drawn from a number of different sources.

The constituents of a linear intervallic pattern—the intervals formed by the outer voices of a voice-leading design—may be two imperfect consonances (for example, tenths), two perfect consonances (for example, the octave and the fifth), an imperfect and a perfect consonance (for example, the sixth and the fifth), or a dissonance and an imperfect consonance (for example, a seventh and a tenth). The discussion below follows the order just given.

Example 79 presents in open notes a paradigm (model) of the linear intervallic pattern 10–10. Although this pattern is uncomplicated in its archetypal form (Example 79), it may occur in an elaborate setting as part of an actual composition (Example 80). The rhythmic reduction (Example 80*b*) shows the succession of tenths between the outer voices that creates the linear intervallic pattern. The pattern effects a stepwise directed motion in the upper voice from B♭ (m. 20) to F (m. 23), while the corresponding bass motion proceeds from G to D. The upper voice is enriched melodically by the neighbor on the last quarter note in each measure, as indicated in the example. In the full musical context (Example 80*b*), the alto voice also contains an upper neighbor note, and this falls on the second quarter note in each measure. As the pattern begins in m. 20, the tenor voice contains passing-note diminutions that fill in the consonant skips shown as half notes in the reduction. And, finally, the bass itself is supplied with diminutions: a consonant skip filled in with passing notes. Thus, the relatively simple 10–10 pattern is transformed into an intricate musical fabric in which diminutions of two types (neighbor note and passing note) intertwine. Notice, further, that the alto and soprano are in imitation, as are tenor and bass. Imitation is not an uncommon feature of linear intervallic patterns.

EXAMPLE 79. Paradigm of Linear Intervallic Pattern 10–10

EXAMPLE 80. Bach, *The Art of Fugue*, Contrapunctus IV

The linear intervallic pattern determines the voice leading of the outer voices of the passage that it controls, representing directed tonal motion with complete precision and without ambiguity once the pattern has been initiated. This is the essence of the linear intervallic pattern and what distinguishes it from other forms of determinate motion in tonal music generated by other means, the most obvious of which is the harmonic progression (Chapter 5).

The relation of the linear intervallic pattern to the harmonic progression will be examined below. Let us now return to Example 80 to consider an additional aspect of the linear intervallic pattern shown there: its relation to the voice leading as represented by figured bass symbols. The latter are shown below the bottom staff of Example 80b as a succession of 7–6 suspensions. These figures specify completely the vertical and horizontal interval structure of the passage. They do not, however, designate the intervallic pattern formed by the outer voices; that function is performed by the numerals 10–10–10–10. Thus, although figured bass notation is the most general notation, it does not reveal the intervallic pattern formed by the outer voices. The numerical notation of the linear intervallic pattern, on the other hand, refers specifically to the intervals formed by the interaction of bass and descant. It is often advantages to use both notations.[1]

The term sequence is sometimes used, incorrectly, to designate what we call the linear intervallic pattern. Properly speaking, the sequence is a *melodic* pattern in a single voice, which is repeated at different transpositions and in immediate succession, over the span of a passage. Such sequences may occur in connection with a linear intervallic pattern, and, indeed, in all the voices of Example 80 there are sequences. However, the melodic sequence is not a necessary condition for the linear intervallic pattern. There are many instances in the musical literature in which a melodic sequence within a linear intervallic pattern may be terminated, while the linear intervallic pattern itself continues. A striking occurrence of this was given earlier, in Example 31 (p. 36).

As is evident, the numerical notation for the linear intervallic pattern in this case is identical to the figured bass notation. There are three other common instances of this correspondence (5–6, 6–5, 7–6), which, however, cause no difficulty in analytic practice. Before proceeding to an actual musical example, it is important to point out that the linear intervallic pattern 6–6 is not a succession of triads in first inversion. An interpretation of this kind leads to the most mechanical of roman-numerical labeling, which designates as a "harmonic progression" a succession that is not a progression at all. If such a succession were, in fact, harmonic, it would be possible to substitute corresponding $\frac{5}{3}$'s for 6's, resulting in an unacceptable series of root-position triads separated by step, in violation of a basic rule of voice leading (avoidance of parallel fifths) and with no meaningful relationship to functional harmony. The linear intervallic pattern 6–6 is, like all such patterns, entirely linear and is not susceptible to the application of inversion theory.

The paradigm in Example 81 shows a descending 6–6 pattern, whereas the 6–6 in Example 82 is ascending. Both directions are common. An analysis of the 6–6 pattern (Example 82*b*) shows the diminutions associated with its components. Each main note in the upper voice has attached to it a consonant skip and an indirect chromatic passing note which connects it to the next note in the descant. The bass also is elaborated by consonant skips,

---

1. The largest number we will commonly use in designating linear intervallic patterns is 10. The addition of one or more octaves to this and other intervals (compound intervals) is not precisely represented. For instance, in Example 80, the actual distance between descant and bass on the downbeat of m. 20 is a tenth plus an octave (a seventeenth). By comparison, figured bass notation uses no number larger than 9. Also, linear intervallic patterns are usually notated without accidentals, except when the accidental is an integral part of the pattern.

shown as vertical intervals. The apex of the pattern occurs with F in the descant over A in the bass. As the chromatic passing note F♯ enters, in accord with the melodic sequence in the upper voice, the bass changes to A♭, creating an augmented sixth and bringing the passage to conclusion with the octave G, which is the fixed voice-leading resolution of that dissonant interval. Thus, the descant traverses the fifth from C to G, while the bass follows it as far as A, then falls back to G at the conclusion of the passage.

EXAMPLE 81. Paradigm of Linear Intervallic Pattern 6–6

EXAMPLE 82. Beethoven, *Sonata for Piano and Cello*, Op. 5, No. 1, III

It is not possible to generalize about the way in which linear intervallic patterns fit into the larger organization of the musical work. However, in some cases the structural role of the pattern is more immediately apparent than in others. In Example 82, for instance, it is clear that the linear intervallic pattern effects a connection between tonic and dominant harmonies, with the C triad taken to be the tonic at this point. This reading is indicated by the roman numerals appended beneath Example 82*b*. Notice that this harmonic interpretation differs entirely from a reading that would assign harmonic value (Chapter 5) to each of the vertical 6's in the pattern. A similar harmonic interpretation is shown in a previous example, Example 80. There one important structural role of the linear intervallic pattern is evident: it connects the tonic (D minor) triads in mm. 19 and 23.

A succession of 6's often occurs above a stationary bass (pedal point), creating a variant on the 6–6 linear intervallic pattern. Example 83 illustrates this. There the brackets mark sixths formed between viola and first violin, while the figured bass consists of the rather complicated figures that always arise with motion above a pedal-point bass. Here the linear intervallic notation is more meaningful than the figured bass, for it shows the regular progression above the bass in a way that is not evident from the figured bass notation.

EXAMPLE 83. Haydn, *String Quartet in F major*, Op. 74, No. 2, IV

Thus far two patterns composed of imperfect consonances have been illustrated and discussed. Another pattern of the same general type is the succession 10–6, a paradigm for which is given in Example 84. Typically, this pattern gives rise to an incomplete neighbor note in the descant and a consonant skip in the bass. Example 85*b* gives a rhythmic reduction of the music shown at *a*, uncovering the 10–6 pattern with its characteristic combination of upper neighbor and consonant skip as shown in the paradigm.

EXAMPLE 84. Paradigm of Linear Intervallic Pattern 10–6

EXAMPLE 85. Bach, *English Suite in G minor*, Allemande

In the elaborate diminutions at *a* the consonant skip is featured as well, not only in the bass but in both voices above the bass. Here again, one function of the linear intervallic pattern is apparent: that is, it effects a stepwise connection between the tonic (G minor) triad at the beginning of the passage and the dominant seventh at the end, figured $^7_\#$. Here the figured bass shows a chain of 7–6 suspensions, with an initial 8–7 voice leading.

The only possible combination of perfect consonances is the octave and fifth, since two octaves or two fifths in a pattern would create an illegal parallelism. A paradigm of the 8–5 pattern is provided in Example 86. This pattern is interesting because it demonstrates that the pattern can override the normative treatment of a dissonance—the tritone—both horizontally and vertically. First, in the bass, we find a tritone, F–B, created by the second 8–5 in the pattern. However, there is no resolution of B to C as the rules of voice leading would dictate, and as would be the case if this were a compound melody. Instead, this fourth, F–B, is treated just as are all the skips of fourths in the linear intervallic pattern. Meanwhile, over the B we find the note F, creating a tritone (diminished fifth) vertically. This interval is also not resolved as a dissonance, but progresses to an octave just as do the other vertical fifths in the pattern, all of which are perfect.

EXAMPLE 86. Paradigm of Linear Intervallic Pattern 8–5

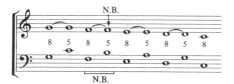

In the illustration of 8–5 in an actual piece (Example 87), there is a harmonic element as well as the purely linear aspect represented by the linear intervallic pattern. The seventh chord over bass F is a secondary dominant to II,[2] and this is followed by the harmonic progression V–I. Here we have a clear example of a linear intervallic pattern associated with a truly harmonic progression. (See also Examples 91 and 92.)

There are three combinations involving a perfect and an imperfect consonance, The first of these is the 5–6, a paradigm for which is shown in Example 88. In the 5–6 pattern the bass remains stationary while the descant ascends one step; then the bass ascends one step, and so on. Without this temporal displacement, which brings in the sixth, the pattern would consist of parallel ascending fifths, contravening the voice-leading syntax of tonal music.

---

2. Throughout this book, the notation [V] means that the chord in question is a secondary (applied) dominant to that which follows it; see Chapter 5.

EXAMPLE 87. Schubert, *Erste Walzer*, Op. 9, No. 6

EXAMPLE 88. Paradigm of Linear Intervallic Pattern 5–6

Many beautiful passages are constructed with the 5–6 pattern, which is often motivic. Perhaps one of the most remarkable of these is shown in Example 89, the beginning of Chopin's *Eb-minor Prelude*. The initial voice-leading motion is 5 6; the sixth is then suspended over to become a seventh, as shown by the numbers between the staffs. In m. 3 the linear intervallic pattern takes shape with C♮ (a passing note), replacing the neighbor note Cb in the upper voice and initiating the stepwise ascent to F in

EXAMPLE 89. Chopin, *Prelude in Eb minor*, Op. 28, No. 14

m. 5. Here again, as in Example 86, the diminished fifth at "N.B." is not treated as a dissonance, but as another fifth in the pattern; in other words, the linear intervallic pattern overrides the rule governing its resolution. The score at *a* has the form of a compound melody comprising three voices and probably was modeled after the solo violin and solo cello works of J. S. Bach. The inner voice here, as in all three-voice versions of the 5–6 pattern, follows the bass in parallel tenths. And, again, one role of the pattern in the music is evident: it connects the tonic triad in m. 1 with the (minor) dominant triad in m. 5.

The linear intervallic pattern 6–5 exists in two principal forms, both displayed in three-voice paradigms in Example 90. The first of these, at *a*, may be regarded as a variant on the descending 6–6 shown in Example 81 (p. 86), with each sixth becoming a fifth just by the stepwise motion in the descant over the sustained bass. The second pattern, at *b*, is perhaps encountered more often in the tonal literature. There the upper voice descends by step, just as in the first pattern; the bass, however, proceeds alternately by step and skip, skipping down a consonant third as the descant descends a step and returning by ascending step to form the fifth. In the three-voice version, the inner voice moves in parallel tenths with the bass. Chromatics often occur in the bass of this pattern, hence the parenthesized sharps in paradigm *b*.

EXAMPLE 90. Two Paradigms of Linear Intervallic Pattern 6–5

Example 91 illustrates the 6–5 intervallic pattern in a composition and relates to Example 90*b*, with its characteristic bass motion. The reduction (Example 91*b*) reveals the pattern clearly, divesting it of the diminutions in the music shown at *a*. These comprise the descending arpeggiation in the first violin and the consonant skips both in the viola (currently the lowest part) and in the second violin. Three of the fifths (mm. 13, 14, and 16) are preceded by verticals that have harmonic value as secondary dominants (in $^6_5$ position). However, the penultimate fifth (m. 15) is diminished and so, therefore, is the triad formed by the three voices; as such, it cannot have a secondary dominant. Instead, the upbeat to m. 15 contains a $^6_3$ rather than a $^6_5$ (see the figured bass below *b*).

EXAMPLE 91. Haydn, *String Quartet in B♭ major*, Op. 76, No. 4, III

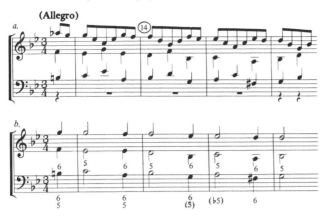

Example 92 shows a dramatic symphonic passage based upon the linear intervallic pattern 6–5. At *b* the compound melodic structure of the upper voice of *a* is presented, to indicate the continuity of the uppermost voice: the larger motion from B to A. Like so many linear intervallic patterns, this one incorporates a variety of features. In addition to the sixteenth-note diminutions and compound melody of the descant (the highest voice), there are two voice exchanges, each denoted by a pair of double arrows. There will be more on the subject of voice exchanges in Chapter 6. Here we point out only that each of the ascending thirds in the bass (from E to G and from D to F♯) is a filled-in consonant skip; that is, E remains the effective bass note in m. 48 and D the effective bass note in m. 50, as indicated by the "5" of the 6 5 pattern.

EXAMPLE 92. Haydn, *Symphony in G major, No. 92* ("Oxford"), I

The linear intervallic pattern 5–10 is yet another one combining perfect and imperfect consonances (Example 93). In this pattern the bass proceeds by

EXAMPLE 93. Paradigm of Linear Intervallic Pattern 5–10

step, while the descant first moves downward by step from fifth to tenth, then skips up a third to gain the next fifth over the stationary bass note.[3] The relation between this linear intervallic pattern and the ascending 10–10 is evident.

In Example 94, from one of the masterworks of Western music, the 5–10 pattern combines with the 6–5 to produce a cohesive and compelling passage. Again, the linear intervallic patterns connect two harmonic points, tonic and dominant, as indicated below the lower staff. Shown more clearly in *b* is the ascending bass that spans an octave from D to D. In the original excerpt *a*, this progression is enriched by lower neighbor-note diminutions. The fact that linear intervallic patterns are often associated with other special features was mentioned above. Here the linear intervallic pattern carries a canon between soprano and tenor, the characteristic motive of which is the consonant descending skip. This intricate passage, a combination of two patterns, ends when the ascending octave line in the bass is completed at the end of m. 19.

EXAMPLE 94. Bach, *The Art of Fugue*, Contrapunctus I

The reverse of the 5–10 pattern, 10–5, may be regarded as a variant on the descending 10–10 pattern in Example 79 (p. 84). As shown by the paradigm in Example 95, the descant forms a stepwise descent while the bass consists of successive consonant skips of a third.

---

3. In notating linear intervallic patterns, as mentioned in an earlier footnote, interval numbers larger than 10 are usually reduced (hence 5 instead of 12 in the present example).

EXAMPLE 95. Paradigm of Linear Intervallic Pattern 10–5

In a passage from one of Haydn's late string quartets (Example 96*a*), we see in the reduction that the characteristic consonant skip in the bass is filled in by an expanded passing tone. This is considerably harder to see at *a*, for here the motion within each measure is displaced by the diminutions within each beat.

EXAMPLE 96. Haydn, *String Quartet in G minor*, Op. 74, No. 3, I

The final category of linear intervallic patterns, and perhaps the one most amply represented in tonal music, combines dissonances with imperfect consonances. The major types are the 10–7, the 7–10, and the 7–6. We begin with the 10–7, shown in paradigmatic three-voice form in Example 97. This resembles the 10–5 pattern shown in Example 95; here the bass skips down a fifth, while there the bass skipped down a third. The third voice is included in the model to show what so often happens in the free composition: the inner voice creates a complete succession of vertical $^7_3$'s.

EXAMPLE 97. Paradigm of Linear Intervallic Pattern 10–7

The outer voices of the passage from the *Jupiter Symphony* cited in Example 98*a* are imitative (almost canonic). The diminutions here are in the service of the linear intervallic pattern 10–7, as indicated in the rhythmic reduction. The dotted lines in this reduction show that B♭ in the descant is effective over the first two measures, during the stepwise descent to C. Similarly, A♭ is effective in the descant of the next two measures, during the descent to B♭. In m. 143 the 10–7 pattern is replaced by the 10–6 pattern. However, the latter already occurred within the previous 10–7 pattern, as indicated by the parenthesized 6's. Involved here is registral displacement, a topic that will be discussed and referred to at various points in the book.

EXAMPLE 98. Mozart, *Symphony in C major*, K. 551 ("Jupiter"), I (woodwinds omitted)

The Bach passage in Example 99 is similar to the Mozart passage in Example 98 in that the diminutions conceal the fact that the structural voice-leading note of the descant is effective over the change of bass. This is shown in simplified form in Example 99*c*, where the descant notes D♭, C, and B♭ are assigned the value of a whole note to stress that they are each effective for an entire measure. This is an instance of compound melody, a clear bilinear structure. In Example 99*b* the connection from the upper-voice D♭ of m. 20 to G in the inner voice at the end of that measure is negotiated by a completely stepwise motion. The same connection is effected in m. 21 (from C down to F) and in m. 22 (from B♭ down to E). In this rhythmic reduction the sequential aspect of the complete music is preserved. Correspondingly, the essential organization of the passage, as based upon the linear intervallic pattern 10–7, remains unchanged at the surface of the music in Example 99*a*. There, however, the passing note A♭ within the third beat of m. 20 is taken up one octave, as is its counterpart G in the next measure. This is another case of registral displacement.

One final aspect of the passage shown in Example 99 deserves comment. Since the seventh in m. 22, unlike its predecessors, remains unresolved, it is

EXAMPLE 99. Bach, *Inventio 5 in E♭ major*

reasonable to assume a voice-leading resolution to A♭, even though A♭ is not literally present in the upper voice on the downbeat of m. 4 of the example. This is an instance of an implied note, hence the parentheses (see remarks accompanying Examples 65, p. 71, and 75, p. 77).

Of all the linear intervallic patterns, the 7–10 is perhaps most frequently represented in tonal music. Unlike the previous patterns, this one begins with a dissonance. Accordingly, it requires an initiating motion from a consonance. In the paradigm given in Example 100 this initiating motion is 5–6. The upper note of the consonant sixth (A) is then suspended over as the bass moves down by step to form the first seventh of the pattern. Thereafter the bass proceeds by descending skip of a fifth followed by ascending skip of a fourth (a cycle of fifths) against the descant, which descends in uninterrupted stepwise motion. The three-voice form of 7–10 shown in the paradigm incorporates an inner voice which moves in a direction parallel to the descant, forming sevenths against the bass by suspension and completing the chain of sevenths indicated in the figures below the lower staff. The linear intervallic pattern then ends, with the inner voice resolving upward instead of suspending (at N.B. in Example 100).

EXAMPLE 100. Paradigm of Linear Intervallic Pattern 7–10

A beautiful compositional instance of the 7–10 pattern is shown in Example 101, from a work by Mozart. The reduction at *b* displays the pattern in numerical notation. Here the initial bass skip from F to B♭ corresponds to the ascent from C to D♭ in the descant so that the first seventh in the pattern is prepared as a consonance, here a tenth, compared to the sixth in Example 100. Thereafter the pattern proceeds exactly as it does in the paradigm, with typical bass motion by fifth and fourth. With the final bass fifth the inner voice resolves upward, creating the $\frac{5}{3}$ vertical. In Example 101*a* the basic inner voice and descant are supplied with the same diminutions, which create an imitative surface. The bass is elaborated by quarter-note octave skips until the pattern breaks on the second beat of m. 98, where the rhythm changes to eighth notes. Typical of other linear intervallic patterns examined thus far, this one describes a path from tonic to tonic, as shown by the roman numerals below the lower staff in Example 101*b*.

EXAMPLE 101. Mozart, *Piano Sonata in F major*, K. 494, I

The linear intervallic pattern 7–6, the next-to-last type to be illustrated in this chapter, is closely related to the 7–10. As shown in the paradigm, Example 102, the bass descends uninterruptedly by step in parallel with the descant, in place of the characteristic fifths and fourths of the 7–10 pattern. Here the pattern has been extended to close on the octave C. The break in the pattern is effected by not suspending the descant note, but instead by resolving it upward by step (compare Example 100).

EXAMPLE 102. Paradigm of Linear Intervallic Pattern 7–6

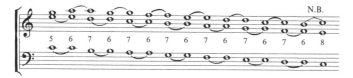

Once again, Bach's *The Art of Fugue* offers an eloquent musical illustration of the 7–6 pattern (Example 103). The reduction, Example 103*b*, presents the four voices associated with the pattern and retains essential features of each. Comparing this reduction with the score at *a* we see that the stepwise bass motion at *b* is elaborated at *a* first by incomplete upper neighbor notes (mm. 45–46), then by consonant skips (mm. 47–49), both in approximate imitation of the tenor, which also descends by step in the reduction. The latter is true as well of the top two voices, which in their original form (at *a*) are supplied with distinctive diminutions: the soprano with a filled-in consonant skip of a third, the alto with a filled-in consonant skip of a fourth. At the end of the third full measure of the excerpt (m. 47) these melodic sequences break off, but the linear intervallic pattern 7–6 continues through the next measure (m. 48). Then a new form of 7–6 begins in which the dissonant seventh is prepared by a tenth brought in by consonant skips in both soprano and bass (upbeats to mm. 49, 50). The figured bass symbols below the lower staff in Example 103*b* show the rich texture created by the motion of the tenor voice, in parallel tenths with the soprano. (The downward motion of the tenor from the fifth to the fourth above the bass (mm. 45–47) creates the figure $\genfrac{}{}{0pt}{}{(6)}{4}{3}$, as opposed to the plain $\genfrac{}{}{0pt}{}{6}{(3)}$ that would result if the tenor were to ascend to the sixth.)

EXAMPLE 103. Bach, *The Art of Fugue*, Contrapunctus IV

As a final introductory example of the linear intervallic pattern and as an illustration of the intricate musical shape such patterns may assume, we offer, first, a paradigm of the pattern 8–10 in Example 104. Here we see the essentially nonharmonic character of the linear intervallic pattern in extreme form. Extracting the octave components of the pattern yields the bass pattern C–D–E–F, each supporting a $\genfrac{}{}{0pt}{}{5}{3}$. A progression of this type is not only meaningless from the standpoint of harmonic progression, but it violates a basic rule of voice leading (parallel fifths and octaves). The same situation

EXAMPLE 104. Paradigm of Linear Intervallic Pattern 8–10

obtains if the tenths component (bass notes G–A–B–C) is detached from the pattern. Only the complete pattern achieves a coherent and correct large-scale motion—in the paradigm a connection from one form of C-major triad at the beginning to another form of the same triad at the end. The linear components of the pattern can be read from the paradigm: descant and inner voice move in parallel by descending step followed by ascending third. The bass has the succession descending fourth–ascending fifth.

The excerpt from Mozart's *C-minor String Quintet* is drawn from the third movement, entitled by the composer "Minuetto in Canone" (Example 105). The analytic reduction at *b* shows the outer voices behaving as they do in the paradigm (Example 104), with the soprano moving by descending second–ascending third, the bass by descending fourth–ascending fifth.

EXAMPLE 105. Mozart, *String Quintet in C minor*, K. 406, III

In m. 22 of Example 105*a* a chromatic lower neighbor note, C♯, breaks the sequential pattern of the bass. As shown in Example 105*b*, however, this abrupt change does not affect the underlying linear intervallic pattern, the bass of which moves by descending (stemmed) fourths.

A feature of this particular movement which makes the linear intervallic pattern harder to distinguish is the double canon in the top four voices. One canon takes place between the two violins, the other between the two violas; comparing one with the other, we see that the violin canon is an elaboration (contraction) of the canon in the violas. Notice the initial violin motive, consisting of an arpeggiation that spans an octave followed by a descending step (that is, Eb–[G–Bb]–Eb–D) and the way it is paralleled by the first viola (mm. 17–18), likewise second violin and second viola (mm. 18–19), and so on. The figured bass symbols appended to Example 105a highlight a further detail of rhythm and voice leading, namely, the series of 4–3 suspensions between alternating pairs of instruments (in parallel octaves) and the bass.

The linear intervallic pattern in Example 105b carries a progression that moves from I to III (in the key of Eb) and, because of the dominant preceding III, effects a modulation from the one diatonic harmony to the other. (Compare Example 101, where such a modulation does not take place.)

To sum up, many features of linear intervallic patterns have been discussed in connection with the paradigms and the corresponding examples from free compositions. We have stressed the fact that the linear intervallic pattern owes its origin to voice leading: each pattern is a determinant of linear progression and establishes a coherent and uncomplicated framework for directed motion. The complete musical setting of the linear intervallic pattern, however, can be quite elaborate and its complicated diminutions may even conceal the underlying pattern to some extent, as in the example just discussed. Furthermore, the linear intervallic pattern is often associated with secondary structural features of considerable interest, such as the voice exchange (Chapter 6).

The essence of the linear intervallic pattern is stepwise motion. And stepwise motion is present even in the bass when it moves by fifth and fourth as in the 7–10 pattern, where each component of the bilinear structure forms a stepwise line (Example 97, p. 93). Thus the linear intervallic pattern represents in the most concise and intensive way the basic voice-leading motion of tonal music.

Although the components of a linear intervallic pattern may sometimes have harmonic value (as in Example 87, p. 89), the pattern is essentially either without harmonic meaning or the harmonic reading is a secondary feature, subsidiary to the pure voice-leading impetus that drives the design toward a goal. Failure to recognize this has caused misunderstandings in the past and continues to do so. A classic case is the pseudo-seventh chord created entirely coincidentally as a result of the pattern 10–10, as in Example 106. There, on the second beat of the first full measure, a vertical $\frac{7}{5}$ arises as a

EXAMPLE 106. Bach, Chorale No. 296, *Nun lob' mein' Seel' den Herren*

result of the 10–10 pattern between alto and bass. The seventh does not resolve as a dissonance, however, because it is not a true seventh chord; instead, it is the product of passing notes in all the moving lines.

If there is a harmonic function of the linear intervallic pattern, it is as a *connector* of harmonies: in other words, harmonic importance (if any) resides in where the pattern begins and where it ends. A linear intervallic pattern may effect a connection between two statements of the same harmony (as in Examples 80, p. 84, and 101, p. 96) or between one harmony and another (as in Examples 82, p. 86, 89, p. 88, 94, p. 92, and 105, p. 98). This is, of course, only one aspect of how a linear intervallic pattern may operate; again, it is not the main one, which is melodic in nature. Finally, applications vary with individual works, as is the case with all the structural features introduced in Part One.

It is possible, however, to make one general observation about linear intervallic patterns. These patterns, however intrinsically interesting and beautiful they may be, never serve as primary structural constituents but are always in the service of some musical element of larger scale. The basis for this observation will be made clear in subsequent portions of this book as the concept of structural levels emerges.

Exercises

For each excerpt construct a rhythmic reduction, according to the note values specified. Label all diminutions. Comment on the function of the pattern over its full span, if possible.

1. Mozart, *String Quartet in A major*, K. 169, II

Reduce to quarter notes and eighth notes. The inner parts may be condensed to whole and half notes and the entire passage can be represented on two staffs. The passage is unusual since it begins on a chromatic harmony, ♮III in D major, the main tonic. (There are two patterns.)

2. Bach, *English Suite in G minor*, Prelude

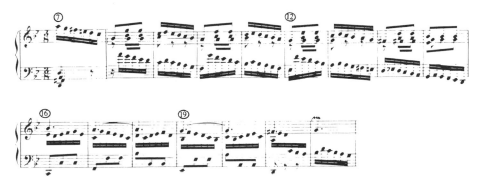

Reduce to quarter notes and eighth notes. A beginning to a solution is suggested below.

Beginning of solution to Exercise 2

3. Beethoven, *Sonata for Piano and Cello*, Op. 5, No. 1, I

Reduce to half notes and quarter notes. (Hint: On the third quarter note in m. 212, C is still effective in the top voice of the piano.)

4. Haydn, *Symphony in G major, No. 92* ("Oxford"), I (strings only)

Reduce to quarter notes and half notes. Example 92 (p. 91) shows the measures immediately preceding the exercise excerpt (mm. 47–50). These also contain a linear intervallic pattern.

5. Handel, *Sonata for Flute and Continuo in E minor*, II

Reduce the long linear intervallic pattern that begins in m. 5 to quarter notes and eighth notes.

5
Harmonic Relations

The subject of harmony in all its ramifications is a vast one; yet the essentials as they relate to Schenkerian analysis are relatively few in number. We assume, however, that the student has mastered the elements of harmony in the practical sense through the completion of exercises and in harmonic analysis. As is the case with the other chapters in Part One, the present chapter provides both a partial review and a reorientation directed toward the development of analytic concepts introduced in the later chapters within the context of Schenkerian analysis proper.

Harmonic Relations

In Schenkerian analysis, the harmonic component goes beyond consideration of individual chords, their intervallic structures, and various functions, to a consideration of harmony in the large as it governs long spans of music. This is the most significant aspect of harmony in Schenkerian terms. An illustration from the writings of Schenker serves well to elucidate the concept.

Example 107 is taken from Schenker's essay on Mozart's *G-minor Symphony*, K. 550 (No. 40). One of a series of analytic graphs, it shows the harmonic organization of the first movement of the work from the beginning up to m. 166 (the reprise). The outer voices of harmonies of largest scale, notated as whole notes, comprise the succession I–III–V–I. Both III and V are preceded by their own dominants, designated by the abbreviation "sec. V," for secondary dominant (see below), on the example. Other ancillary but important structures are shown—for example, the protracted 5–6 motion that ends in m. 101.

EXAMPLE 107. Schenker, "Mozart: Sinfonie G-Moll," *Das Meisterwerk in der Musik*, Vol. 2, App. 7 (1926).

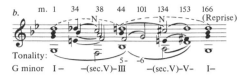

To be sure, an abstract analytic graph such as this is far removed from the surface of the music. It was never intended to be shown apart from the other graphs in the series, which present the analysis of the work in all its details, and it is used here only to demonstrate the Schenkerian concept of large-scale harmony, which will emerge in a practical and natural way in the course of constructing analyses later on. Example 108 is still a further distillation of the harmonic structure shown in Example 107. It represents the basic succession of consonant diatonic triads that forms the cohesive progression which binds the long span of music together. While the upper voice maintains the common tone D, the bass arpeggiates the tonic (G minor) triad, moving from I to V through III. When V is reached (in m. 153 in the music), there is a return to I. The outer voices thus represent a projection of the tonic triad—a basic Schenkerian concept and the essence of large-scale harmonic structure.

EXAMPLE 108. Further Reduction of Example 107 (I–III–V)

The terms *key* and *modulation* are used by Schenkerian analysts, but with specific reservations. For instance, the B♭ triad in m. 44 of Example 107 may be considered as the tonic triad of the key of B♭ and the progression that immediately precedes it may be regarded as a modulation from G minor to B♭.[1] This is certainly correct, in the local sense. But, with respect to the overall organization of the movement, which is governed by the tonic (G minor) triad, the B♭ triad is still III (mediant) and the D-major triad is still dominant. It is a question of focus and scale.

The term *modulation* in the sense of an arbitrary change of key is foreign to the Schenkerian orientation. Although Schenker used the term, especially in his earlier writings, he came to prefer the term *tonicization*, which refers to the establishment of a diatonic triad as a temporary tonic. Thus, in Example 107, the mediant (III) is tonicized by the progression that begins in m. 34.

---

1. In graphs c) and d) of Schenker's analysis, this is, in fact, shown as a modulation and change of key.

Harmonic Functions of Diatonic Triads

The main triads within the diatonic key are the tonic and dominant. The remaining diatonic triads function in relation to them as tonic substitutes (VI and III), dominant substitutes (the leading-note triad, VII), or dominant preparations (II, IV, VI), depending upon context. The triads IV and III often have special functions. Example 109 shows two common functions of IV: at *a* it serves to connect two forms of the tonic, and the two notes that it does not hold in common with the tonic are neighbor notes (see below, under Harmony and Diminutions); at *b* IV is shown in its function as dominant preparation, and again the moving notes are neighbors (three in this case).[2] An important large-scale function of III has already been illustrated in Example 108. There the bass of III, B♭, stands between I and V (G and D) as a component of the arpeggiation of the tonic triad. In this function, III is often referred to as a *third-divider*, since it divides the fifth determined by tonic and dominant into two thirds.

EXAMPLE 109. The Subdominant in Relation to I and V

The correct determination of harmonic function is sometimes crucial in understanding diminutions, as illustrated in Example 110. A question arises in connection with the third vertical in m. 1: in reducing this to quarter notes in all voices, which of the tenor eighth notes should be omitted, B or C♯? Example 110*b* omits tenor C♯, producing a $\frac{5}{3}$ with the roman numeral II, while Example 110*c* omits B, yielding a 6 with the designation VII. To the trained ear, the alternative at *b* sounds wrong, whereas *c* sounds correct. This is because II as shown at *b* does not have a proper harmonic function; it sounds as though it will serve as a dominant preparation, but the following chord is the tonic again. The VII[6] at *c*, however, serves the correct harmonic function, linking two forms of I by a dominant substitute.

---

2. The subdominant in a more expanded harmonic role, as the governing harmony of a section of a movement or of a movement of a multimovement work, requires special attention and will not be discussed here.

EXAMPLE 110. Bach, Chorale No. 367, *Befiehl du deine Wege*

Harmonic Progressions

In Chapter 4, Linear Intervallic Patterns, the question of true harmonic progression was raised several times. Indeed, linear intervallic patterns comprise a large class of structural events *not* determined by harmonic relations.

The basic large-scale harmonic progressions are two in number: I–V and V–I. And of course these connections also occur in the small. In general, the intervals of harmonic bass progression (supporting root-position triads) are the intervals of the consonant triad: the major and minor third (minor and major sixth), and the perfect fifth (fourth). Bass progression by second occurs in the case of the dominant preparations. In such progressions, the bass may have a strong melodic (stepwise) role (see Harmony and Diminutions, below).

Harmony and Voice Leading

The interaction of harmony and voice leading has already been discussed in several ways, especially in Chapter 2. In progressions over short spans of music as well as in the large, such as the organization shown by Schenker in Example 107 (p. 104), voice leading and harmony are inseparable. The classic case is the dominant seventh chord. In the species-counterpoint model of voice leading (Chapter 2) we see the seventh introduced as a passing dissonance, a phenomenon entirely of voice-leading origin. In the figured bass model, which is closer to free composition, the seventh is a vertical formation, a chord, in its own right. It has been absorbed by the dominant triad.

Although the basic harmonic structure of the tonal composition consists solely of the consonant diatonic triads I and V, often with the inclusion of III in the minor mode, harmony at the level of detail (chords) is considerably more variegated. In addition to the entire array of consonant diatonic triads, there are various types of seventh chords, including the diminished sevenths, chords that arise as the result of suspensions, and chords that result from linear motions (neighbor and passing notes) that do not fit into any of the previous categories.

A special type of chord, and one of considerable importance, is the secondary dominant, mentioned above in connection with Example 107, a chord which functions as a dominant with respect to some diatonic triad other than the tonic. It is a temporary dominant, emulating the main dominant in the key. There are many instances among the prior examples in this chapter; a single short illustration here will suffice to review the idea.

Example 111 shows the first phrase (five measures) of a Bach chorale setting. On the last beat of m. 2 a $\frac{5}{3}$ is introduced which contains a chromatic (neighbor) note, F♯. This chord is the dominant of the dominant, a secondary dominant, symbolized here and elsewhere in the present volume by enclosing brackets. It does not proceed immediately to its "tonic," but instead moves up to a $\frac{6}{5}$ over bass F♯, passing through the 6 chord over bass E. The $\frac{6}{5}$ over bass F♯ is an inversion of the secondary dominant *seventh* of the dominant triad, a logical extension of the preceding secondary dominant triad over bass D. The phrase then cadences on a G-major triad, the dominant triad. Since this is established as a new temporary tonic at the end of the phrase by the cadential motion II–V–I (in G), we notate the chord symbols accordingly to show a modulation to the dominant. It is important to recognize that the final D-major triad in Example 111 is a *modulating* dominant, since it establishes a new tonic, whereas the D-major triad that ends m. 2 is a *secondary* dominant that brings in the dominant triad, which is still under the direct control of I (C major).

EXAMPLE 111. Bach, Chorale No. 298, *Weg, mein Herz, mit den Gedanken*

The topic of inversion comes up naturally in connection with harmony and voice leading. A roman numeral is correctly applied to a vertical other than a $\frac{5}{3}$ if the harmonic function of the vertical is the same as that of its parent triad. The rule of substitutability is operable here: to test whether an inversion has the same function as its parent triad, substitute the parent triad in the context. Even though voice leading may be disrupted, it should be possible to determine if the harmonic relation holds. An interesting case is the cadential $\frac{6}{4}$, often called, incorrectly, the "I^6_4" and regarded as the second inversion of the tonic triad. Example 112a shows a typical context in which this type of $\frac{6}{4}$ arises. The cadential dominant is delayed by neighbor notes in the descant and the voice below it. In this example, we have placed a secondary dominant (in first inversion) before the $\frac{6}{4}$, and this works perfectly well, because the neighbor notes E and C of the $^6_4$ are expanded diminutions displacing notes of the dominant triad, which is the effective harmony here at the cadence. Thus, the reduction shown in Example 112*b* is a reasonable representation of the music in Example 112*a*, whereas the reduction in Example 112*c* sounds wrong because it is incorrect with respect to harmonic relations. The C triad in fundamental position has no harmonic function in the progression. And, in general, the rule of substitutability fails when it is applied to $^6_4$ chords of this cadential type (and others as well).

EXAMPLE 112. The Six-Four

Harmony and Diminutions

In Chapter 1 the notion of an expanded diminution, a neighbor or passing note with full metrical value (or greater), was introduced. Such notes become "chord" notes, members of triads or seventh chords. (It was for that reason that we excluded the term "nonharmonic" from the discussion there.) The examples of Chapter 1 therefore include many illustrations of the relation between harmony and diminutions, which will not be enumerated here. Instead, we turn our attention to the opening section of a famous chorale setting by Bach and giving special attention to the melodic functions of the chords.

Example 113 gives a roman-numeral analysis of the harmonic relations in the chorale setting. Two of the chords (verticals) have no roman-numeral designation, however. These are the second vertical in m. 5 and the second vertical in m. 6. Both are entirely of linear origin. The first, in m. 5 (cf. Example 106, p. 99), connects the first inversion of a secondary dominant with its parent chord. The second, m. 6, is a passing "linear" chord. It serves as a voice-leading corrective, since it stands between what would otherwise be parallel fifths between soprano and alto.

EXAMPLE 113. Bach, Chorale No. 296, *Nun lob' mein' Seel' den Herren*

The melodic functions of the individual chords are indicated by the symbols P and N in Example 113. In m. 1, III fulfills a common role, the setting of the descending passing note, scale degree $\hat{7}$, while the IV that follows it completes the passing motion to scale degree $\hat{5}$, which is set by the tonic triad. In m. 3, the II is not only a dominant preparation, but also incorporates the passing note D in the soprano and the passing F in the bass. The second phrase, which begins in m. 5, brings in a secondary dominant to VI. The entire measure, in fact, is consumed by the secondary dominant, since the second vertical is a passing chord. (See Example 106.) The remaining melodic functions can be read from the example.

Conclusion

An understanding of harmonic relations is basic to Schenkerian studies. Even though not all considerations of harmonic organization are explicitly represented in a Schenkerian analytic graph, harmonic relations contribute substantially to many decisions in the analytic process.

In particular, it is important that we know how harmonic connections are effected, how harmonic relations interact with voice-leading and melodic functions, and, most important, to realize that harmonic relations are basic to the study of form, as will become apparent beginning with Part Two.

Exercises

All the preceding exercises for Chapters 1, 2, and 3 may serve for the analysis of harmonic relations. The exercises for Chapter 4 may be used, but advisedly, since linear intervallic patterns, in the main, are not harmonically determined—although they may connect or otherwise interact with structural harmonies.

6

Some Common Secondary Structural Features

The purpose of this section is to introduce the student to certain common secondary but important musical features that need to be taken into account when carrying out a Schenkerian analysis. Here, as in the case of the linear intervallic patterns introduced in Chapter 4, it is not possible to say in a general way how these features are to be interpreted with respect to other aspects of the musical work which are both more elemental and of longer range, for such analytic interpretation depends upon a number of variables and must be made with regard for the characteristics of the individual composition. Suggestions regarding the interpretation of these features will be made, however, as the examples are discussed.

Specifically, this section deals with three features of tonal composition: the voice exchange, melodic substitution and implied notes, and octave displacement (register transfer), in the order just given. In addition, subsidiary melodic lines are discussed briefly.

Voice Exchanges

The voice exchange, in one form or another, is frequently found in the music of a wide variety of composers. Indeed, instances have already appeared in previous examples (14, on p. 22, 15, on p. 23, 30, on p. 35, and 72, on p. 75), but with minimal comment. In this section the voice exchange will be examined with greater thoroughness and in greater depth.

The voice exchange is a pattern that involves two and only two voices, a pattern in which the voices literally exchange their pitches. The simplest type of voice exchange is shown in Example 114, from the beginning of the adagio introduction to Beethoven's *Second Symphony*. There the descant and bass

110

effect an exchange. The descant descends from F♯ to D while the bass ascends from D to F♯ over the same time-span. Thus, when the pattern is completed, the bass carries the initial note of the soprano, F♯ (two octaves lower, of course), and the soprano carries the initial note of the bass, D. Each voice has traversed the same interval, the major third between D and F♯. This type of exchange creates the outer-voice interval succession 10–8–6, indicated within brackets in Example 114 since it will rarely be necessary to represent the exchange numerically this way in an analysis, and the numbers are used only for explanatory purposes here. The notation for the exchange is the intersecting double-headed arrow configuration shown in Example 114. In the 10–8–6 exchange, the middle note is always of the same type, here E, the only case in which the same note can simultaneously be an ascending and a descending passing note! As to what the functions of the exchange are in this particular context (Example 114), one is apparent: the exchange highlights the interval of the major third from D to F♯ and it emphasizes the melodic note F♯.

EXAMPLE 114. Beethoven, *Second Symphony*, I

Although it was stated above that no general observations can be made about the function of the voice exchange over the broad range of individual works that comprise the corpus of tonal music, two fundamental aspects of the 10–8–6 voice exchange are of considerable significance to the analysis of musical structures via the Schenker approach. First, the exchange projects a single interval, the third, over a short time span, and in an unambiguous voice-leading setting. If this interval is taken to represent a harmony—the D-major (tonic) triad in Example 114, for instance—then we see, in miniature, a model of the Schenkerian concept of *prolongation*: the preservation of a single harmony over a time span. The concept of prolongation is introduced in Chapter 8 as it pertains to the construction of Schenkerian analyses. The foregoing brief discussion should be regarded only as an elementary preparation for that concept.

The second fundamental aspect of the 10–8–6 voice exchange of interest is this: the exchange is a replacement process involving two voices. Each voice takes over the voice-leading function of the other. This is evident in Example

114, where descant F♯ at the onset of the pattern becomes bass F♯ at the end of the pattern and bass D at the onset of the pattern becomes descant D at the end. The bass then leads to G on the downbeat of m. 2 while the upper voice pursues its voice-leading destination, C♯, creating, on its way, the suspension indicated by the figures below the lower staff. This aspect of the voice exchange is especially significant when a dissonant interval is involved, as in the common tritone exchange, discussed below in connection with Example 121.

Voice exchanges, like other patterns, may be enriched by diminutions, and those diminutions may conceal, to some extent, the underlying exchange. Example 115 provides an instance. At *a* the lower voices move in eighth notes against the sixteenth-note triplets in the descant. The analysis at *b* reveals, however, that when the diminutions in the upper voice are taken into account there is a slightly concealed voice exchange of the 10–8–6 type underlying the melodic motive at the beginning of the theme of this movement.

EXAMPLE 115. Haydn, *Piano Sonata in E major*, Hob. XVI/22, II

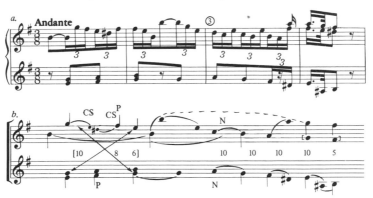

Example 116 shows a similarly elaborate 10–8–6 exchange at the beginning of a thematic statement. Not only do intricate diminutions ornament the basic voice-leading pattern here, as is evident in the complete music at *a*, but within that basic pattern, the 10–8–6 exchange C♯–A↔A–C♯, there is another exchange, D–B↔B–D. The elements of this internal exchange consist of a neighbor note and a passing note, which interchange, as shown in Example 116*b*. Here the prolonged harmony is the tonic (A major) triad, and it seems clear that the melodic note brought to the fore by the exchange is the first note of the descant and the last note of the bass, C♯, the third of the tonic triad. The subsequent arpeggiation out to E in m. 2 of the excerpt cannot be interpreted without study of more of the music of this composition.

EXAMPLE 116. Mozart, *Piano Sonata in D major*, K. 576, II

A second common type of voice exchange is the 10–10–6–6 (or 6–6–10–10) exchange. Example 117 provides an instance in the music of Handel. At *a* is the complete music, including Handel's figures. The upper part (flute) is a bilinear melodic structure, while the bass is a single line doubled at the octave below. At *b* the exchange is shown, the typical 10–10–6–6 pattern, which involves an interchange of note pairs. Thus, the note pair C–B in the upper voice becomes the note pair C–B in the bass, while the note pair A–G in the bass becomes the note pair A–G in the upper voice, producing the outer voice intervallic succession 10–10–6–6. On the second beat of m. 5 the pattern begins again, with C–B in the upper voice against A–G in the bass. However, the complete exchange does not occur, because the bass changes to F♯–B on the last beat of the measure, breaking the pattern.

EXAMPLE 117. Handel, *Sonata for Flute and Continuo in E minor*, II

Example 117c offers an analytical interpretation of the Handel passage. Because of the harmonic organization of the passage, the components of the 10–10–6–6 exchange are not all of equal structural significance. The notes C and A are expanded diminutions, neighbor and passing notes, while B and G are members of the tonic triad. Thus, the upper voice is not a true fourth, but a third expanded to a fourth by a prefix neighbor note.[1]

A voice exchange may be associated with a linear intervallic pattern, as in Example 118, from Schubert. The basic voice leading of the passage, which is distributed among the instruments at *a*, is brought together in simplified form at *b*, revealing the 10–10–6–6 exchange. If this exchange is compared with the one shown in Example 117, it will be seen that it is the inversion. Here the note pairs in the bass form an ascending fourth, while the corresponding pattern in the upper voice of Example 117 was a descending fourth. And each note pair in the upper voice of Example 118 is an ascending second, whereas the corresponding note pairs in the bass of Example 117 were descending seconds.

EXAMPLE 118. Schubert, String Quartet in B♭ major, Op. 168, III

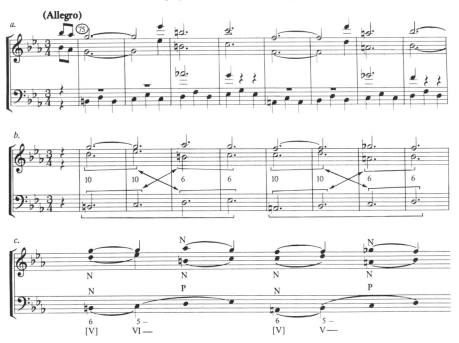

---

1. In fact, in some cases the upper voice of an exchange of this type is best regarded as a succession of two note pairs (seconds) which do *not* combine to form a larger interval (fourth or third).

Example 118*c* shows, analytically, the harmonic location of this passage in the movement as a whole: the progression from VI to V with intervening secondary dominants. However, the linear intervallic pattern 6–5 is also essential here. As shown by the analysis, each 5 in the 6–5 pattern is extended by an ascending third in the bass and the neighbor-note formation in the upper parts. Thus, the passage combines a harmonic progression with a voice exchange and a linear intervallic pattern.

Example 119 shows a passage that features the 6–6–10–10 voice exchange, reversing the pattern of the previous examples. The note pairs are designated by brackets labeled a and b in the example. Here the bass has the characteristic fourth (descending this time), while the descant has the note pairs forming seconds. The exchange is in the service of a progression from I to V, as shown by the roman numerals at *b*. Interestingly, the passage ends with a 6–8–10 exchange.

EXAMPLE 119. Haydn, *Piano Sonata in C major*, Hob. XVI/21, III

EXAMPLE 120. Mozart, *Piano Sonata in D major*, K. 311, II

A second and final instance of the 6–6–10–10 exchange is provided in Example 120, from the theme of a movement of a Mozart piano sonata. Here the exchange, in mm. 3 and 4, centers around notes of the tonic triad. The characteristic fourth is in the bass, and proves to be a structural third from D to B, while the upper voice has the note pairs forming seconds, here with the meaning of neighbor-note patterns. To take the analysis just one step further, it is not difficult to understand the bass from the end of m. 2 through the first beat of m. 4 as an arpeggiation of the tonic (G major) triad.

We have seen examples of the 10–8–6 exchange, which always involves the consonant interval of a third. An exchange may also operate within a dissonant interval, as shown in the next two examples, both from Beethoven's *Eighth Symphony*.

In Example 121 there is an exchange in m. 3 between the upper voice and the voice above the bass. Each of the two voices spans the diminished fifth, creating the exchange E–Bb↔Bb–E. The effect of the exchange is to emphasize the melodic note Bb in the upper voice on the downbeat of m. 4. As the rhythmic reduction in Example 121*b* makes clear, this Bb is an indirect passing note that relates back to the first note of the theme, C. Secondary motions that interrupt the direct connection from C to Bb are the two arpeggiations (C–A–F and E–G–Bb) shown at *b*. The ultimate resolution of Bb, which is the dissonant seventh of V⁷ here, is, of course, to A, and that occurs on the downbeat of m. 7, not included in Example 121.

EXAMPLE 121. Beethoven, *Eighth Symphony*, I

In the recapitulation of this movement the composer introduces another exchange following the diminished-fifth exchange shown in Example 121. At m. 200 of Example 122 is the passage that corresponds to m. 3 of Example 121, the diminished-fifth voice exchange. As soon as Bb is attained in the upper voice on the downbeat of m. 201 two inner voices exchange over another dissonant interval, the seventh: C–Bb↔Bb–C. This new exchange

EXAMPLE 122. Beethoven, *Eighth Symphony*, I

intensifies the restatement of the important B♭ in the upper voice and serves as an example of the special importance that the voice exchange may have in a composition, in this instance by dramatizing the expanded passing note, B♭, which relates back to C in m. 1.

To conclude this introduction to voice exchanges, we present four examples of particularly interesting occurrences of that structural feature, drawn from three different periods.

In Example 118c (p. 114) it was seen that a linear intervallic pattern may combine with a voice exchange in structuring a passage. Another instance is displayed in Example 123a from a famous keyboard work by Bach. At b we see the ascending linear intervallic pattern 10–6, which connects the upper-voice C on the upbeat to m. 43 to the G on the downbeat of m. 46, while the bass follows in stepwise ascending motion. The voice exchange occurs as each 6 is reached in the linear intervallic pattern. However, the pattern of voice exchanges is broken on the second beat of m. 45: F♯–A in the upper voice is answered by A–A, not A–F♯, in the lower voice. Since F♯ is bound to stepwise resolution to G, the occurrence of F♯ in two voices almost simultaneously would strongly suggest parallel octaves.

EXAMPLE 123. Bach, *Italian Concerto*, I

One other aspect of Example 123 should be mentioned. The lower component of the voice exchange does not occur entirely within a single octave register because the second note is always displaced by an octave. This is because the bass on the downbeat of each measure is then replicated an octave higher on the second beat of the measure, just as the exchange begins. On the last eighth note in the measure, the bass returns to its original register, creating in m. 43 the tenth F–D in place of the third F–D and in m. 44 the tenth G–E in place of the third G–E. The subject of octave displacements will be addressed below.

An extraordinary instance of a 6–8–10 exchange is shown in Example 124, from a late Brahms piano composition. Here the exchange involves a consonant third, as usual, but in this context a dissonant harmony, a diminished seventh chord, is extended by the exchange. This, in turn, causes a curious reversal of relations. The diminished seventh chord stands at each end of the exchange pattern, while the passing chord in the middle is a consonant harmony; the first is equivalent to a $^6_3$ over bass E, the second to a $^5_3$ over bass B♯ (= C).

EXAMPLE 124. Brahms, *Intermezzo in E major*, Op. 116, No. 6

In Example 125, from Brahms's *Requiem*, a passage is shown that incorporates a chain of voice exchanges. In the first of these, bass and soprano interchange in the 6–8–10 pattern operating within a half-diminished seventh chord. At m. 26, this pattern is reversed, producing the 10–8–6 pattern. In both exchanges the passing chord is a $^6_4$. Then, at the end of the passage, in m. 27, bass and alto interchange, again forming the 6–8–10 pattern. As shown by the roman numerals below the lower staff, the exchanges are in the service of the harmonic progression II⁷ V.

EXAMPLE 125. Brahms, *Requiem*, III (chorus only)

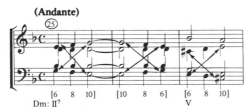

Example 126 presents an exchange that resembles the 10–10–6–6 exchange, in that it involves note pairs. Here however, the note pairs, although linear seconds, as in the 10–10–6–6, form vertical intervals that combine

EXAMPLE 126. Mozart, *Symphony in E♭ major*, K. 543, I

dissonances with consonances. The first, an augmented fourth, resolves outward to a sixth, while the second, a diminished fifth, contracts to a third (tenth), following normative voice leading.

Implied Notes

In the free composition, a note may be implied although not actually present in the music. This is possible because of the completion of a voice-leading connection, the continuation of a linear intervallic pattern, the completion of a voice exchange, or by the completion of a component of a compound melodic structure (as a special case of a voice-leading connection).

The implied note may be regarded as effective in the melodic structure. Whether it is consequential is another matter, one that can only be determined in a particular musical setting. Two questions are important in this regard. First, does the implied note complete a significant structural motion? Second, does the implied note initiate a significant structural motion? We will refer to these questions in connection with the examples to be presented below.

An implied note was shown earlier in Example 28 (p. 34), where the seventh, A♭, in m. 1 was resolved to an implied G at the beginning of m. 2. In this case, as in many others, the voice-leading resolution of dissonance strongly articulates the implied note. In that example and elsewhere in the present volume, the implied note is enclosed (appropriately) in parentheses.

Example 127 presents a situation in which the harmonic progression determines an implied note: the progression from V to I in mm. 9–10 at the beginning of the second section of the piece. This causes an A to be implied on the downbeat of m. 10, which is significant since it is this A and the concomitant 5–6 voice-leading motion that initiates a long ascending line in the subsequent music (not shown). Here the assumption of an implied note is

EXAMPLE 127. Bach, *English Suite in F major*, Menuet II

definitely consequential; the ascending melodic structure does not begin abruptly and unexpectedly on B♭ in m. 10, but on the A firmly anchored within the tonic triad.

A somewhat different situation is given in Example 128, where two notes are implied. In the bass of m. 3 there is a descent from B♭ to G, which supports a sixth chord. The normal resolution of this sixth chord, in which the bass would continue stepwise to F, does not take place, however. Instead, the bass skips to D. Thus, in the voice-leading scheme, F is implied and D is substituted for it. In general, *substitution* and *implication* are often associated in free compositions. In m. 4 of Example 128 are another implied note and substitution. There in the upper voice, F at the end of m. 3 should have proceeded by step to E; instead, it skips away to C♯, the leading note, at the cadence. The C♯ is therefore a substitution for E.

EXAMPLE 128. Handel, Air from *Keyboard Suite in D minor*

Example 128 also provides a lucid illustration of local melodic motion. Beginning in m. 5 the bass descends by step from dominant (A, preceding measure) to tonic (D, m. 6). This essential structural motion in the bass is accompanied by tenths in the descant, beginning on B♭. At the conclusion of the motion the upper voice arrives on F over bass D, and this note is the continuation of the melodic structure that was in effect at the cadence in m.

4. The subsidiary function of the upper voice in m. 5 is shown by the brackets surrounding B♭–A–G in Example 128*b*.

As indicated above, compound melodic structures may bring into play implied notes. Example 129 illustrates. At *b* is a rhythmic reduction that verticalizes the components of the compound melody, showing that the upper-voice D at the end of m. 1 would have progressed naturally to C on the downbeat of m. 2. However, only the lower component of the bilinear structure fulfills its voice-leading commitment, moving to E♭ on the first beat of m. 2. The melody then ascends to pick up C on the last eighth note of the measure, and this is the actual statement of the note that was implied on the downbeat of the measure, as shown by the tie in Example 129*b*.

EXAMPLE 129. Bach, *Little Prelude in C minor* from *Six Preludes for Beginners*, BWV 934

Furthermore, the seventh, G, that enters in the inner voice in m. 2 (Example 129*b*) is prepared by an implied A♭ at the beginning of the measure. The implied G in the upper voice of m. 4 corresponds to the implied A♭ in m. 2. In m. 4, however, the G is even more strongly implied by the preceding A♭, which moves in parallel sixths with the voice below it. This implied G is especially important, since it effects stepwise melodic continuity, preparing the seventh, F, which follows.

Example 130 shows two implied notes, with accompanying substitutions. First, in mm. 3–4 the upper voice ascends from F♯ to C, a diminished fifth, while the bass moves in contrary motion to the upper voice, beginning on C. Clearly this is a diminished-fifth voice exchange, which would be completed if the bass ended on F♯. However, the bass skips away to D on the downbeat of m. 4. This D is to be understood as a substitution for the expected F♯ in the voice exchange, as shown in Example 130*b*.

The second implied note in Example 130 occurs in m. 7, where B♭ in the descant, instead of descending by step to A, skips down to join the inner voice on D, the substitution. The implied A is consequential, for it is the first melodic note of the B section which follows, as indicated in Example 130*b*.

EXAMPLE 130. Haydn, *Symphony in D major, No. 104* ("London"), II

Thus, of the two implied notes in Example 130, the first is less consequential than the second.

As a final illustration of implication and substitution, Example 131 offers a passage from a work by Chopin. The upper voice, which begins on G, proceeds slowly downward, with diminutions (neighbor notes, passing notes, and consonant skips). On the downbeat of m. 7 an $\frac{8}{6}$ is reached, and this is followed by $\frac{7}{5}$. However, the upper voice, which should fulfill its voice-leading commitment by moving from D to C, skips to F♯, a substitution. At that point in Example 131*b* the expected C appears within parentheses as an implied note. This is the C that continues the slow stepwise descent, and it resolves on the B♭ that comes in as part of the final flourish in thirty-second notes in m. 8. Here, the implied note plays an important role in the melodic structure, since it provides the essential link that completes the stepwise progression begun in m. 5 on G.

EXAMPLE 131. Chopin, *Nocturne in C minor*, Op. 48, No. 1

Although implied notes and substitutions are not features of every work, it is important to understand them as an aspect of voice leading in the free composition and to be able to interpret them analytically in a significant way when they arise. In general, however, when no structural consequence ensues as a result of an implied note, there is no particular reason to give it special attention.

Register Transfer

In Chapter 18 the notion of register transfer is presented within the context of full-scale Schenkerian analysis. We introduce the topic here in an elementary way, since registral changes are so common in almost all music. The occurrence of an important structural element in a new register and the return to the register of origin are both events of great significance.

Register transfer denotes change of octave, or the placement of a note in a different octave (including a return to its original register from some other register).[2] In the simplest case there is a direct shift, as in the two instances shown in Example 132. In the first of these, indicated by the dotted slur and the abbreviation RT in Example 132*b*, the register transfer explains the origin of the descant note B on the second quarter note of m. 1: it comes from the inner voice. Similarly, in m. 2 the high D, is a transferred inner-voice note. As a result of these successive register transfers, the upper voice at the end of the phrase is one octave higher than at the beginning. Example 132 is used here only to demonstrate registral relations. It is not always necessary to indicate direct shifts of register, as here, since the registral relations can easily be read from the score and do not require analytic interpretation.

EXAMPLE 132. Haydn, *Symphony in G major, No. 92* ("Oxford"), III

---

2. In Chapter 12 the Schenkerian term *coupling* is introduced in relation to register transfer.

In Example 133 a register transfer occurs from the inner-voice A in m. 4 to the upper-voice A in m. 5. From this A an arpeggiation then descends to the C of m. 6, a restatement of the upper-voice C of m. 4. As indicated by the stems in the graph, this C resolves to B, which, in turn, descends to A. At this juncture (m. 7) the final gesture of the phrase connects A to G an octave higher, a register transfer effected by stepwise motion. In this case, the interval involved is a seventh (A–G), representing the descending second which would have resulted had A remained in register in m. 7. In retrospect, the high A in m. 5 is a preparation for the cadential G in the same register in m. 8.

EXAMPLE 133. Haydn, *Symphony in G major, No. 100* ("Military"), III

Example 134 contains register transfers involving both the octave and the

EXAMPLE 134. Schubert, *Moments musicaux*, Op. 94, No. 6

seventh. The first transfer occurs in m. 2 and is shown by the dotted slur at *b*. Measure 6 contains the transfer involving the interval of a seventh. There neighbor note D♮ is presented an octave higher as well as in its original register. In this example, as in many others, changes of register are intimately connected with compound melody. Here the register transfers create a melodic structure that is partially compound (Chapter 3).

The previous examples illustrated register transfers of a note of an inner voice to a note of the upper voice. The final example in this chapter, Example 135, shows a transfer of longer range involving the upper voice alone. As shown at *b*, at the end of the first four-measure phrase the upper voice has arrived on B. In the three measures that follow (mm. 5–7), the upper voice ascends stage by stage until it arrives at B an octave higher on the downbeat of m. 8, concluding the register transfer.[3] Two details within the ascending passage (mm. 5–7) are worth mentioning. First, there is a small register transfer from F♯ in the inner voice to E in the upper voice in mm. 5–6, indicated by the dotted slur. This reading reveals the voice exchange 6–6–10–8 shown by the crossed arrows in Example 135*b* and serves as a reminder that the various features discussed in the foregoing section often occur in combination, requiring careful study of the ways in which they interact.

EXAMPLE 135. Haydn, *String Quartet in G major*, Op. 76, No. 1, III

---

3. The means by which this transfer is effected is disregarded here; the general procedure is called *overlapping*.

Exercises

Of the three features presented in the text of this chapter, exercises are given only for voice exchanges and register transfers. Additional instances of implied notes will be provided in subsequent examples and exercises.

1. Beethoven, *Sonata for Piano and Cello*, Op. 5, No. 1, I

Reduce to quarter notes and verticalize upper parts. Identify the voice exchange by the customary numerals.

2. Beethoven, *Thirty-two Variations in C minor*, Theme

Using stem and slur notation construct an analysis that shows the basic progression of the upper voice clearly and the register transfer of its goal note. Indicate the voice leading by figured bass symbols.

3. Mozart, *Symphony in C major*, K. 551 ("Jupiter"), II

The excerpt is the beginning of the second theme of the slow movement of the symphony. Identify the exchanges and the diminutions (expanded) which they incorporate.

4. Mozart, *Symphony in Eb major*, K. 543, III

Register transfer is a prominent feature of the melodic theme here. Identify the elements that are transferred and label all diminutions in the upper voice.

5. Mozart, *Symphony in G minor*, K. 550, IV

As in Exercise 4, the thematic excerpt here features register transfer in the upper voice. Label diminutions in the outer voices only.

Part Two

Reductions
of Small to Moderate
Dimension

7
Basic Axioms

Structural Levels

Any analytic method based on Schenker's writings must have as its cornerstone the concept of structural levels. Of these, the one most commonly associated with Schenker is that which often seemed to concern him least: namely, the *background*. Here Schenker viewed every well-composed tonal piece as being reducible to one of essentially three patterns, all based on the tonic scale and triad (these will be covered in the following section). While these patterns and the ability to recognize them are important, so are the details and the working-out of motivic and thematic ideas. These occur at the *middleground* and *foreground* levels—as the terms suggest, closer to the surface of the composition. The progression from background to foreground moves from the basic idea to its realization; conversely, analysis involves the progressive reduction of a finished work to its fundamental outline. Foreground events are taken directly from the piece itself, one or more levels of middleground are derived from the foreground, while the final stage of reduction represents the background. In broadest terms, the closer we get to the background, the more similar any two pieces are likely to appear; obviously, the more detail we introduce, the more differences we are likely to find.

Models of Fundamental Structure

By its simplest definition, tonal music is "music in a key." If a piece is in a given key, it will communicate that fact by intelligibly involving the tonic scale and triad as a frame of reference. This concept lies at the heart of Schenker's work. It translates into our very general expectation that a tonal piece will somehow begin and end with an assertion of the tonic harmony.

131

For Schenker, it also translates into a basic rule of melodic motion: that within a minimally complete unit (say a thematic statement) such motion will take place to, from, or about a member of the tonic triad. Eventually, and usually within the theme itself, one triadic degree in particular—third, fifth or eighth—will assert itself as the *primary tone (Kopfton)*,[1] and a descending *fundamental line (Urlinie)* from this primary tone to the tonic will be traceable over the span of the piece or movement. In many cases this fundamental line is reflected in the profile of the theme itself, a fact which Schenker viewed as profoundly significant—a testimony to the organic nature of a well-composed tonal work. In terms of the structural levels set forth above, the fundamental line belongs to the background. Chapters 7–12 will deal not so much with the fundamental line proper, but with its reflection and reinforcement at the middleground and foreground levels.

The bass, on the whole, is easier to interpret than the melody. Since a tonal piece or movement normally begins and ends on I (the beginning, of course, can be more complicated), and since the end is signaled by an authentic cadence in the tonic key, we can see that the bass at the background level will be framed by the outline I . . . V–I. In between the initial I and the final V–I, we often find III as an intermediate resting place in addition to (or instead of) the more usual secondary goal of V. This is, of course, the rule in minor keys (where III is the relative major), but it can and does happen in major keys as well (chiefly as the nineteenth century progresses). The result is the large-scale succession I–(III–)V–I, or a broken tonic triad (incomplete if the third is missing). Because of this last feature, Schenker called this progression *arpeggiation* (literally "breaking") *of the bass (Bassbrechung)*, or *bass arpeggiation*.

The combination of fundamental line and bass arpeggiation constitutes the *fundamental structure (Ursatz)* of a tonal composition, and represents the background level of the analysis. Graphically, the fundamental structure is presented in either whole notes or half notes (usually beamed). What these note values have in common is the open notehead; therefore the term *open note* will be used when referring to these values generally (see Example 136*a*). Lesser values used in conjunction with open notes indicate middleground events leading to or from the background notes. The scale degrees of the fundamental line are labeled by arabic figures with caret marks (for example, $\hat{3}$–$\hat{2}$–$\hat{1}$ for the descent from the third degree of the scale), while the bass has the customary roman numerals below. Either two staffs or one may be used, depending on the amount of detail one intends to supply. Characteristic features associated with each type of fundamental structure, which Schenker

---

1. Schenker's word *Kopfton* is translated in *Free Composition* (FC) as "primary melodic tone." We prefer the term *primary tone*, except where ambiguity might result. The word *Kopfton* is also used in its literal translation, "head note," in connection with linear progressions (Chapter 19).

EXAMPLE 136. Forms of the Fundamental Structure

summarizes in the abstract (FC, Figs. 1–11, 14–19, and elsewhere), will be introduced as we move on to specific examples.

It is important to realize that the open notes, when used as graphic symbols in a Schenkerian analysis, are not intended to represent actual durations as in standard music notation. The open notes signify that the pitches with which they are associated are members of the fundamental structure.

Fundamental Structure in Thematic Statements

In this section we take the first step in applying the fundamental structures (outlined in Example 136) to actual music. This is easiest to do with small units at first, such as thematic statements which are likely to be familiar to the reader. Three such statements, each depicting a different fundamental structure in microcosm, are cited in Example 137.[2]

The notation in Example 137 takes the outline of the fundamental structure and superimposes it on the original music. In so doing, we arrive at a simple version of what Schenker calls the *Urlinie-Tafel* (literally, "fundamental-line chart"), a comprehensive graph combining two different kinds of notation, rhythmic and analytic (see the following section), and combining structural levels.[3] Though this is a bit of a simplification, rhythmic notation is generally associated with the foreground, analytic notation with the middle-ground and background levels.

EXAMPLE 137

a. Haydn, *Divertimento in B♭* (*Chorale St. Antoni*)

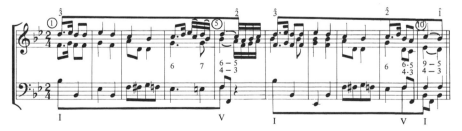

---

2. Example 137c, outlining a descent from $\hat{8}$ to $\hat{1}$, will be expanded upon in Chapter 13.

3. See especially the comprehensive graphs in *Five Graphic Music Analyses* (FGMA).

b. Mozart, *Sonata in A major,* K. 331, I

c. Bach, Chorale No. 20, *Ein' feste Burg ist unser Gott*

In the present example (and elsewhere where only an excerpt is involved) any structural profile that appears complete is only a miniature replica of the fundamental structure; as such, this replica (depicted by careted numbers and roman numerals applied to the beamed notes) belongs to the middleground level. (The melodic component of this middleground event is a specific type of *linear progression,* a topic which will be explored in Chapter 19.) At the same time, the *type* of structure represented may occur over the entire length of the piece or movement—in which case it becomes the fundamental structure, thereby belonging to the background. The aim of Example 137, once again, is to illustrate the three basic types of fundamental structure, each in a context that can be easily grasped.

Rhythmic versus Analytic Notation

In an elementary way, the reductive process—simplification through stages—has already been introduced and used in Part One. In dealing with this matter we used two kinds of music notation: *rhythmic notation,* where notes are assigned value according to temporal placement or duration (in other words, traditional music notation); and *analytic notation,* where the value of a note depnds upon its relative melodic and harmonic importance.

The analytic note values used in Part One were restricted to the stemless note (or notehead) and the stemmed note (both filled notes). Notes of greater significance were assigned stems, and linear motions leading to or from these notes were slurred. In short, the vocabulary of symbols basically consisted of the notehead, the stem, and the slur.

Analytic notation appropriate to the background, or fundamental, structure has been introduced earlier in this chapter. (For practical purposes, "background," "background structure," and "fundamental structure" usually refer to the same thing.) This level of analytic notation uses the open note, which we will not be using at present (since we are, right now, dealing with dimensions considerably smaller than the complete work or movement which the fundamental structure is supposed to represent). It also uses the beam, to connect notes belonging to the fundamental line on the one hand, and to connect notes of the bass arpeggiation on the other.

Groups of filled notes (as opposed to open notes) may also be beamed together, to denote middleground-level replicas of fundamental structure (as in Example 137), or to highlight significant stepwise melodic motions other than those of the fundamental line. Although we leave open notes in abeyance until Chapter 10, we shall be using the beams earlier, for the reasons explained above.

The simplified comprehensive graph, the kind shown in Example 137, is a useful device for showing an overall outline. It is, in other words, an *analytic overlay*, and will be of special value in connection with later discussions of musical form (Chapters 16 and 17 in particular). Inclusion of much middleground detail while the complete surface of the piece is present, however, can becoming confusing; for that reason it is preferable, once the basic outline is determined, to depict one's analysis in stages.

A first level of reduction can be done in rhythmic notation, as was frequently the case throughout Part One. Essentially, this involves omitting diminutions and assigning their durational values to more basic components. To illustrate, a rhythmic reduction of the *Chorale St. Antoni* (Example 138a) is obtained (from Example 137a) in the following way: By omitting the neighbor note E♭ and its doubling at the lower sixth G, the upper voices become D over F and have the value of a half note. Measure 2 cannot be

EXAMPLE 138. Haydn, *Divertimento in B♭* (*Chorale St. Antoni*)

reduced further. The bass of m. 3 becomes quarter-note F followed by quarter-note G, with the removal of passing tones F♯ and F. From the upper voice of m. 4 the passing note D is omitted and the following four sixteenth notes collapse into two eighth notes, with the component voices now verticalized as E♭ over C followed by D over B♭. In this way we have begun to set aside what can readily be seen as surface detail, the submetrical diminutions reviewed in Chapter 1.

The diminutions described above (the neighbor notes and passing notes) are easy to accept as "ornamental," as belonging to the lower structural levels, because these notes are of short duration and unaccented. But the duration and/or metrical placement of a note can just as often work contrary to a correct analysis, and it is most important that the student recognize this fact early and keep it in mind. An appoggiatura or suspension always occurs in a relatively stressed position and frequently occupies more time than its resolution, yet it is from the resolution that the dissonant note derives its meaning. To graph these without their resolutions would make no sense, regardless of the temptations posed by accent or duration. In particular the cadential $^6_4$ chord, because of its favored rhythmic position and its quality of borderline consonance, can be a typical opportunity for error; remember that it is not a true I chord but a double appoggiatura to V. On this point look at Example 137a, m. 5, and compare it with the same measure in Example 138.

Although foreground events may be notated analytically as well as rhythmically, and although the rhythmic reduction contains material belonging to the higher structural levels, it is nonetheless true that rhythmic notation by itself cannot *describe* or *delineate* anything beyond the foreground level. Therefore, as a matter of convenience, the rhythmic reduction may be thought of as a foreground sketch (or graph: the terms *sketch* and *graph* are interchangeable). The rhythmic reduction need only occur as a first step; for the more experienced it is a stage which can often be bypassed. It does, however, clarify harmonic and melodic outlines, and thereby makes the next stage, in analytic notation, easier.

To illustrate, the first two passages from Example 137 are graphed in Examples 138 and 139 respectively, first in rhythmic, then in analytic notation. The latter concentrates on (but is not necessarily limited to) the outer voices, and starts with the symbols already introduced in Part One and reviewed at the beginning of the present chapter: the symbols are, once again, the stemless notehead, the stemmed filled note, and the slur. To these we add the beam for significant linear motions. Again, the more important notes (points of departure or resolution) are stemmed, and motions to or from these notes are indicated by slurs. Stemmed notes may themselves be slurred or beamed together, as appropriate. (Recall that at this point we are not concerned with the fundamental structure of an entire work; therefore open

EXAMPLE 139. Mozart, *Sonata in A major*, K. 331, I

notes are not needed.) In general and above all, there are *no unattached notes*. Everything must be accounted for, whether by beam, slur, or tie.[4]

Since they highlight the stemmed and beamed middleground components, the bottom graphs in Examples 138 and 139 can rightly be called middleground sketches. The reading for the Haydn excerpt (Example 138; review Example 10, p. 20) is clear: D is the primary tone, initiating a line proceeding to C in the first phrase and, after retracing its steps, to B♭ in the second. Once the overall thrust of the passage is recognized, everything else becomes subordinate in varying degrees. The initial E♭ (m. 1) has already been eliminated in the first reduction, but E♭'s remain in mm. 2 and 4. Traditional harmonic analysis would not consider these notes secondary, as they are both harmonized; in context, though, the harmonized E♭ is still a neighbor to the D.

The reading of the Mozart theme (Example 139) is more complex: at first glance one might question the choice of E over C♯ as the primary tone. After all, the downbeats of mm. 1–3 neatly show C♯–B–A in parallel tenths with the bass. Giving primary emphasis to this line, however, would ignore the fact that the A in m. 3 is harmonized by a dissonant chord whose justification is not complete until the downbeat of the next measure (at which point the soprano is back on C♯). On the other hand, the correctness of assigning the primary tone to E is verified in a number of subtle ways. Notice the pattern of ascending thirds: C♯–E, B–D, and then A–B–C♯—the last stretched over a longer span of time and filled in with a passing note, but an ascending third nonetheless. Also, look back at the score (Example 137a) at the expressive "breath" which would be taken before the last eighth note (E, then D) in

---

4. A fine but important restriction on the application of slurs is that steps and skips should not be mixed under a single slur. Rather, these are dealt with by slurs within slurs, as in the melody of Example 138b (first phrase) and in the bass lines of Examples 138 and 139.

each of the first two measures, and then at the artful way Mozart recapitulates the descent from E to B in the diminutions of m. 4.[5]

Examples 138 and 139 introduce a new analytic symbol: the diagonal line. Its use in standard notation is to trace voice leading; in analytic notation it means something quite different. Here the diagonal indicates that the outer parts it connects belong together structurally, as if they were the outer voices of an underlying harmonic or contrapuntal progression. These voices can be verticalized in a subsequent reduction, or they can at least be thought of in that way. Example 140, drawn from the Haydn theme, depicts a common cadential formula, II⁶–V–I. In the melody, C and A together constitute an interval belonging to the V chord, even though on the surface C is harmonized by the inverted II. The fact that C is the higher of the two notes give it aural prominence, while V is the more essential of the two chords.[6] In mm. 1–2 of the Mozart (Example 140*b*) the two positions of I and V are respectively combined via their extremities into two single chords, illustrating the general principle (to which there are many exceptions) of looking to the higher melody note and to the lower bass note when all other factors are equal. These factors are not all equal in the two succeeding measures, where harmonic and contrapuntal senses indicate A rather than F♯ as the controlling bass note. Example 140*c* shows why.

EXAMPLE 140

a. Haydn, mm. 9–10

b. Mozart, mm. 1–2

c. Mozart, mm. 3–4

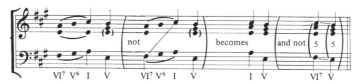

---

5. Schenker (FC, Fig. 157) reads the D in the upper voice of m. 4 as a descending passing tone at the middleground level.

6. It must be emphasized that II functions as a prefix to V and is therefore subordinate to it. In tonal syntax, the meaning of the cadential progression V–I is clear, as is II–V–I. However, II–I would not qualify as a satisfactory cadence. (A simple demonstration at the keyboard will bear this out.)

Exercises

Construct a rhythmic reduction and middleground analytic sketch for each of the following passages, using Examples 138 and 139 as a guide, and observing the hints given.

1. Sample Exercise: Beethoven, *Sonata in E♭ major*, Op. 7, II

Solution:

   a. Rhythmic reduction

Comments:

   1. In line with the general process of rhythmic simplification, a quarter note replaces the eighth note and rest. It would be possible to go still further and use a half note to fill out the remainder of the measure.
   2. As in Example 138 (p. 135), appoggiaturas are represented by their resolutions only.
   3. The lower octave doubling of the bass is normally omitted from a graph.

   b. Middleground sketch

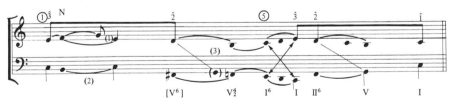

Comments:

   1. Although G is the highest note of the passage and a note of the tonic triad, there is no stepwise descent leading from it. In the present context, G is an extension of the neighbor-note relationship E–F. Later in the music it acquires greater significance.

2. Immediately repeated notes are generally omitted at the middleground level.
3. In this progression, the resolution of the leading tone is omitted, resulting in a chromatic descent in the bass. Roman numerals in brackets denote secondary dominants.

2. Schubert, *Impromptu in B♭ major*, Op. 142, No. 3

Basic rhythm: half notes. Concentrate on the outer voices, especially the compound melody in the right hand. Compare the last two measures of each phrase with regard to melodic detail. (As a hint, think of the last three half notes of each phrase as belonging together. This holds for the analysis of the compound melody as well as the bass progression.)

3. Mozart, *Piano Sonata in B♭ major*, K. 333, III

First reduce to quarters or larger units. Compare with Example 139 (p. 137). You should find, as in Exercise 2, essentially one controlling note per measure in both melody and bass, with more detail required at the cadence.

4. Mozart, *Piano Sonata in C major*, K. 545, III

Basic rhythm: quarter and eighth notes. Diagonals between soprano and bass are appropriate in several places (review the last section of this chapter). The second beat of m. 5 combines the upper neighbor to $\hat{5}$ with the $\hat{4}$ of the descending line. Although the left hand has a rest on the upbeat to m. 1 (likewise the upbeat to m. 5), it should be apparent that a tonic harmony is implied; accordingly, the bass note C should be inserted in parentheses in those two places.

5. Schubert, *Impromptu in G♭ major*, Op. 90, No. 3

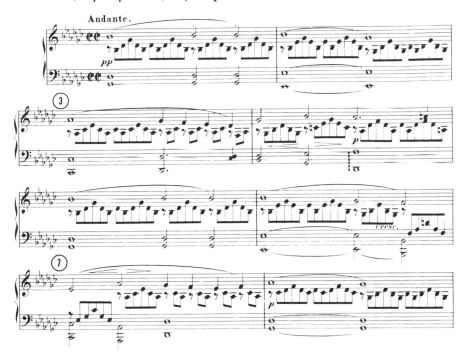

Basic rhythm: whole notes and breves.

8

The Concept of
Prolongation

In Schenkerian analysis the concept of *prolongation* is basic. Prolongation refers to the ways in which a musical component—a note (melodic prolongation) or a chord (harmonic prolongation)—remains in effect without being literally represented at every moment. Of the two main categories of prolongation, melodic and harmonic, the latter is easier to grasp. Essentially, a given harmony is prolonged so long as we feel it to be in control over a particular passage. A simple instance can be seen in mm. 1–2 of Example 138 (p. 135) where the subdominant prolongs the two tonic chords. In m. 3 we can still sense the influence of I, while II⁶ (m. 4) prepares the dominant. The prolonged harmonies in this first phrase are therefore I (mm. 1–3) and V (mm. 4–5).

Additional examples of harmonic prolongation are given in Example 141; in each case the reasoning should be evident from context. Thus in Example 141*a* the first phrase begins and ends in I; scarcely can it be conceived as prolonging anything else. The second phrase changes direction midway, as indicated by the bass progression F♯–G♯–A, hence the shift from motion initiated by I (and prolonging I) to motion directed toward V (thereby prolonging V). In contrast, Example 141*b* as a whole prolongs I, with an intervening II–V that can be taken as an internal prolongation of V (see Exercise 1 at the end of this chapter for a correlation of the melodic and harmonic prolongations in this excerpt).

In Example 141*c* each measure is self-contained. The progression of m. 1 prolongs the tonic harmony. Measure 2 then prolongs VI; and the fourth measure prolongs V. The third measure is somewhat more complicated. The initial dominant 7th chord (G⁷) does not progress to I, but to a secondary dominant 7th of IV (hence the parenthesized roman numeral IV below the

142

EXAMPLE 141

a. Bach, Chorale No. 356, *Jesu, meine Freude*

b. Mozart, *Piano Sonata in B♭ major*, K. 333

c. Chopin, *Prelude in C minor*, Op. 28, No. 20

staff), and the progression is then completed with the arrival of I on the last quarter note in the measure.[1]

Melodic prolongation, meanwhile, builds upon the concept of diminution as discussed in Part One: namely, a melodic motion that maintains the *effect* of a given note despite the fact that this note is not literally present all of the time. There are three main types of melodic prolongation:

---

1. When the entire third measure is correctly understood to be a self-contained progression like the others, it then becomes evident that the upper-voice note on the last quarter must indeed be E♭ of the tonic triad—not E of a secondary dominant to IV, as it appears in some editions. In a larger sense, however, this measure is preparatory to the one following, and the I that it prolongs functions less as a tonic than as a subdominant of V. In other words, though mm. 3 and 4, taken individually, prolong I and V respectively, the two taken together unmistakably point to V. This larger prolongation is shown in parentheses in Example 141c. The fact that the composer placed a single slur over both these measures (as opposed to two slurs for mm. 1 and 2) reinforces this last interpretation.

1. Motion *from* a given note, normally a *descending* diatonic scale segment or arpeggiation (where the prolongation *follows* the note that is prolonged);

2. Motion *to* a given note, normally an *ascending* diatonic scale segment or arpeggiation (where the prolongation *precedes* the note that is prolonged);

3. Motion *about* a given note, most frequently by means of upper and/or lower neighboring tones (which may in turn be prolonged themselves).

The specifications, given above, as to which is the prolonged note in each type of prolongation, are all subject to exception, depending on either the larger melodic structure or the harmonic prolongation currently in force. Type 1 in particular is often modified by the latter consideration, as in Example 138 (p. 135). There it would have been incorrect to read the soprano line of mm. 2–3 as prolonging E♭, owing to the concurrent harmonic prolongation of the tonic (B♭) triad. The crucial factor is that E♭ is not a structural member of that chord, but rather an upper neighbor to the chord tone D. In general, the prolonged *note* should belong to the prolonged *chord*. (In the case of the dominant, and sometimes II or IV, this can include the seventh as well as the triadic degrees 1, 3, 5, and 8.) As a companion illustration we offer a hypothetical revision of the beginning of the *Chorale St. Antoni* (Example 142; compare Example 137a, p. 133), in which E♭ (though still a neighboring tone in the larger sense, as per Type 3 above) is correctly graphed as the prolonged note in mm. 2–3. What changes the situation is the

EXAMPLE 142. Hypothetical Revision of *Chorale St. Antoni*

new underlying harmony that goes from IV to V instead of immediately back to I. This motion from IV to V establishes V as a temporary goal in the hypothetical example, resulting in a prolongation of the dominant harmony of sufficient length to accommodate the line descending from E♭ which prolongs that note as an expanded neighbor note.

Exercises

a. Indicate:

    1. the overriding linear progression;
    2. the overriding harmonic progression;
    3. subsidiary melodic prolongations.

b. Incorporate the above in a middleground sketch.

1. Sample Exercise: *Mozart, Sonata in B♭ major,* K. 333, I

Solution

    a. It may be helpful first to sketch the passage in plain noteheads (with slurs). The pattern of broken chords in the left hand can be represented by the bass line alone. It is generally best to keep the left hand in the bass clef and the right hand in the treble, even when the score does otherwise.

        1. Overriding linear progression: F–E♭–D ($\hat{5}$–$\hat{4}$–$\hat{3}$). The highest active degree of the tonic triad is the fifth, F. The G thereby becomes an upper neighbor, initially appearing as a grace note (performed on the beat as if it were the first of four sixteenths, but not written that way—an interesting reflection on the relationship of notation to structural meaning), then recurring in the latter half of m. 1. The F on the downbeat of m. 2, though an appoggiatura, actually completes the neighbor-note figure F–G–F, and can be understood as the fulfillment (rhythmically displaced) of a broken tonic chord. A diagonal line drawn between the left hand's B♭ and the second F will show this interpretation graphically.

2. Overriding harmonic progression: circular progression beginning and ending on I.

3. Subsidiary melodic prolongations:

(a) The first prolongational line begins with the upbeat to m. 1 and extends over the bar into that measure. As mentioned under 1 above, the topmost *structural* note is F, and that is the note which is prolonged.

(b) The parallel figure leading to m. 3 prolongs F locally with the descending line of a sixth. (Compare the notation of the upbeat to m. 3 with the upbeat to m. 1.)

(c) Looking at all of m. 2, again leading into m. 3, we can trace a more substantial line from E♭ to A (see under *b* below). This line prolongs E♭ over the span of mm. 2–3. As the dominant seventh, E♭ belongs not only to the II chord in m. 2, but to the V of m. 3, hence the diagonal connecting this E♭ with the bass note F.

(d) The third A–C, presented linearly as an upbeat to m. 4, is stated vertically as a double appoggiatura on the downbeat. The upbeat figure can be viewed as a very small prolongation of the lower neighbor to $\hat{3}$.

b. Middleground sketch

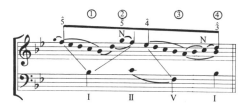

The following condensed version incorporates the unfolding symbol (compare Examples 148, p. 160, and 149, p. 161). Look ahead to exercises for Chapter 11 for further examples.

2. Schumann, *Aus meinen Thränen spriessen* from *Dichterliebe*

Your melodic analysis should take into account both the vocal and piano lines, which double each other until the cadence. Be sure to differentiate the initial motion to A from the more definitive one at the close of the excerpt.

3. Haydn, *Piano Sonata in C major*, Hob. XVI/35, I

The motion to and from high C (m. 1) is a consonant skip (a variety of diminution; see Chapter 1), and should be regarded as a foreground event only.

4. Haydn, *Piano Sonata in C major*, Hob. XVI/21, I

Although the overall profile of this Haydn theme is much the same as that of the preceding, the pattern of internal prolongations is considerably more complex. In particular, comment on the use of register transfer in the prolongation of F over mm. 2–3.

5. Beethoven, *Sixth Symphony*, I

The task here is a common one: to use analytic notation to distinguish the descent at the cadence from those earlier lines that cover the same ground. Though for present purposes the labeling $\hat{5}$–$\hat{4}$–$\hat{3}$ is allowable, it must be noted that a study of the movement as a whole yields $\hat{3}$ as the primary melodic tone. (See FC, Fig. 145/5.)

6. Beethoven, *Seventh Symphony*, I

A first reduction of the top voice is already present in the doubling below it, and should give you a hint as to the true melodic progression in mm. 64–65 and 68–69. The pedal A through the downbeat of m. 69 illustrates the basic notion that the last statement of the descending line is the definitive one.

9

Prolongation
of the Primary Tone:
Initial Ascent

Despite the importance of the descending line at all structural levels, we frequently find motion in the opposite direction occurring in conjunction with it—that is, prolongational motion listed under type 2 in the previous chapter. When a motion such as this occurs at the beginning of a theme or work, and when it leads directly to the primary tone, it acquires special significance; if stepwise and ascending it is called an *initial ascent* (*Anstieg*).

A good example of an initial ascent occupies the first half of an eight-measure theme by Handel (Example 143) which, like the Haydn theme in the same key (Example 137*a*, p. 133), inspired Brahms to write a set of variations. The complete ascent is from B♭ to F, but with considerable emphasis on D midway. To ascertain that F, not D, is the primary tone, we look for a descending line from that note. Though this does not occur immediately, we can pick up a stepwise progression beginning with the E♭ in m. 6 that continues in a straightforward way thereafter. As a result, the ascent and descent balance each other in length (not a usual occurrence); the breadth of each, moreover, allows for various diminutional prolongations within the larger linear motion. These include the two neighbors about D in mm. 1–2, and the ascending line from C (itself prolonged in turn) to E♭ in mm. 5–6. Though the line does go on to F in m. 6, the strength of the resolution from E♭ to D on the downbeat of m. 7 leads to the reading of that particular F as an upper neighbor to E♭, and E♭ as the prolonged note. The larger motion, from F (mm. 3–4) through E♭ (m. 6) to D (m. 7), makes aural as well as logical sense (look ahead to Example 144). As mentioned in Chapter 8, consideration of the larger melodic structure can supersede the normal "rules" of melodic prolongation.

EXAMPLE 143. Handel, *Leçon in Bb major*, Air

A properly executed analytic graph can make evident at a glance what can often be cumbersome to explain. Prolonged notes are stemmed, prolongational motions slurred, and slurs within slurs denote subsidiary motions within larger ones. At times it is also appropriate to use arabic numerals to highlight a succession of intervals between voices when those intervals form a significant pattern (see Linear Intervallic Patterns, Chapter 4). For instance, a series of parallel tenths or sixths in a uniform direction usually means that a single harmonic and/or melodic prolongation is in force. In the present graph (Example 143*b*) we have drawn attention to the parallel sixths in mm. 5–6. Included in this ascending progression is the soprano prolonging Eb above a rather neutral bass; the latter acquires meaning when A, its last note, links with the F which began the fifth measure. The result is an overall bass motion from F to A prolonging V; putting soprano and bass together yields a root-position V[7], as is shown in Example 144. (Notice the use of the diagonal line and the figure 7 in Example 144*c*.)

EXAMPLE 144. Handel, *Leçon in B♭ major*, Air

Exercises

Graph the following excerpts using analytic notation. In each one, pay special attention to the initial ascent leading to the primary tone, along with any internal prolongations you may find.

1. Schubert, *Impromptu in A♭ major*, Op. 142, No. 2

(See Exercise 1/8, p. 40)

2. Beethoven, *Piano Sonata in F minor*, Op. 2, No. 1, I

The first B♭ (m. 4) is a neighbor note to the returning A♭ rather than a passing note to C. The reason for this lies in the need for the outer voices of m. 4 to resolve inward; the second A♭ (m. 5) is the note that begins the ascent. At the end of the passage (mm. 7–8), C is prolonged melodically (the notes that follow should be slurred from that C and not stemmed) while the prolonged harmony shifts from I to V.

3. Beethoven, *Piano Sonata in C minor*, Op. 10, No. 1, I

Notice the ways in which this opening resembles—and differs from—the preceding exercise. How is the change of register at m. 9 prepared in the preceding measures?

4. Beethoven, *Piano Sonata in C minor*, Op. 10, No. 1, II

The primary tone here is C (3̂). In mm. 5–7 the main melodic motion, C–D♭–C (3̂–N–3̂), is "covered" by upper-octave doublings of the right hand's lowest voice (see Chapter 18). How do the melodic thirds in mm. 1 and 3 differ from those in mm. 5–6? Finally, comment on (and let your sketch show) the composer's treatment of the neighbor-note motive over the course of the passage.

10

Prolongation
of the Primary Tone:
Arpeggiation

Like the prolongational line, the *arpeggiation* normally prolongs its topmost structural note. Special rank is given to the *first-order arpeggiation*, which ascends through the tonic triad to the primary tone, thereby performing a function analogous to the initial linear ascent. Like the latter, the first-order arpeggiation is frequently extended or embellished by internal prolongations, that is, by foreground diminutions.

The excerpts in Examples 145 and 146 (the latter an updated version of Example 29, p. 35) begin with first–order arpeggiations. The first is decorated only by the consonant skips below C and E. In the second example the arpeggiation of the tonic is followed by a similar treatment of the dominant seventh—in Schenker's own word, a "parallelism." In both excerpts, as at the beginning of any extended work, the background is initiated but goes no further, hence the "hanging beam" attached to the primary tone (indicating that the fundamental line will be resumed later on). Notice also how open notes (see "Models of Fundamental Structure" in Chapter 7) not only differentiate the background from the surrounding material, but also allow for a wider range of notation for middleground events. At the same time, the student should be cautioned that open notes and careted scale-degree numbers tend to be overused by the inexperienced. Open notes are strictly reserved for the fundamental structure (fundamental line plus bass arpeggiation) of the entire piece or movement, while careted numbers identify the descending tones of the fundamental line. When placed in parentheses, these numbers may also be attached to restatements of notes of the fundamental line (such as the second labeling of $\hat{5}$ in Example 146), or to relevant descending middleground lines (such as the descent from $\hat{5}$ to $\hat{1}$ in Example 145). Above all, scale-degree numbers are only for melodic events, *not* for bass lines.

EXAMPLE 145. Mozart, *Piano Sonata in C major*, K. 309, I

EXAMPLE 146. Mozart, *Piano Sonata in C minor*, K. 457, I

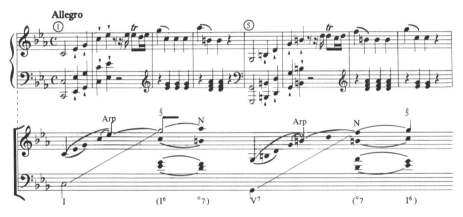

Example 147 shows a self-contained musical form, with a first-order arpeggiation that occupies most of its sixteen-measure length. This arpeggiation does not occur in a simple way, but comes about as the result of a series of leaps from a recurring low A♭, culminating in the octave above that note on the downbeat of m. 14. The descent to D♭ that follows is accomplished in less than one-fourth the time. Despite this temporal imbalance, the upper A♭ remains the primary tone (that is, $\hat{5}$ in the key of D♭), and the ensuing descent from $\hat{5}$ to $\hat{1}$ is still the melodic background, or fundamental line. While we shall comment more on this last point in a moment, notice that the left hand quotes a miniature version of the $\hat{5}$–$\hat{1}$ descent at every cadence (mm. 4, 8, 16), underscored each time by a rhythmic pattern unique to this motive. Surely it was no accident that Beethoven saw fit to do this.

EXAMPLE 147. Beethoven, *Piano Sonata in F minor*, Op. 57, II

Ascending motion in general, whether linear or arpeggiated, is part of the natural rise and fall inherent in any complete musical statement. It creates a feeling of expectation, of tension, which the descending motion will presumably resolve. In the case of an initial ascent or first-order arpeggiation, the goal is the primary tone itself; the fundamental line that follows is, of course, the ultimate prolongation. Remember also (see Chapter 8) that prolongational motion can precede as well as follow the note that is prolonged.

However, a logical question arises when the initial ascent or arpeggiation is of such proportion that it dwarfs what is supposed to be the fundamental line of the piece. This can happen particularly in small forms, such as the example just discussed. In part the answer lies in a correct determination of the primary tone—and the ability to do this comes with experience. It also lies in the initial gesture itself, which should maintain sufficient interest and continuity to keep up the feeling of expectation that it should create. Moreover, a well-composed piece is likely to give clues, linking details both to one another and to the fundamental structure. In Example 147 the fundamental line is foreshadowed, not only by the remarkable motivic correspondence already mentioned, but by the initial emphasis on a lower-octave replica of the primary tone. In addition, the motivic correspondence is dramatically highlighted in m. 6, where the bass A♭ is introduced by its chromatic upper neighbor B♭♭, designated by N.B. in Example 147.

Exercises

Graph the following excerpts, with special attention to the first-order arpeggiation that begins each one. Use Examples 145 and 146 as a guide regarding the use of open notes.

1. Haydn, *Piano Sonata in G major*, Hob. XVI/27, I

The opening of this theme is an arpeggiation in spite of the diminutions, such as the passing notes and turns in m. 1. The motion between D and high G (mm. 3, 5, 6–7) is once again a consonant skip (compare Exercise 8/3), though embellished by passing-note and neighbor-note diminutions (the latter in small notes).

2. Mozart, *Piano Sonata in D major*, K. 311, I

Compare Exercise 1.

3. Beethoven, *Fourth Piano Concerto*, II

This passage essentially comprises a first-order arpeggiation to scale degree $\hat{8}$ (mm. 1–7) followed by a linear descent from $\hat{8}$ to $\hat{1}$ (mm. 7–13). Some hints on tracing the arpeggiation follow: E and G are contained in m. 1, the latter prolonged by the descending broken chord. The neighbor-note figure B–C is an inner voice in mm. 2–3 (a downward stem on B would be appropriate), likewise mm. 4–5. The same relationship is also articulated an octave higher: the filled-in diminished fifth in mm. 3–4 prolongs the neighbor note C, whose resolution to B does not occur until the piano entrance on the downbeat of m. 6. Although on the surface the orchestral portion appears to be a monophonic succession of octaves, your sketch should (as always) indicate the basic harmonies implied (specifically, I–II–V). In contrast, the piano's octave descent should be relatively easy to see, although there are two readings possible for the span between E and B (mm. 7–9). Also, why is the definitive G in m. 11 and not in m. 12?

4. Chopin, *Mazurka in G♯ minor*, Op. 33, No. 1

The content of the opening statement is complete in the first eight measures. Literal repetitions of entire passages, such as occur in mm. 9–12, may be indicated by measure numbers, but need not be graphed more than once. (The very beginning of this piece was cited in Example 67.)

5. Chopin, *Mazurka in C♯ minor*, Op. 63, No. 3

This example begins with a mixture of skips and steps; the stepwise motion fills in the third C♯–E. Because of the skips that precede and follow this stepwise progression, the overall motion is still classed as an arpeggiation. The descent from G♯ needs study also: though it spans an octave, it begins on scale degree $\hat{5}$ (not $\hat{8}$!), and not all of its notes are equal. The right-hand melody is paralleled by the top voice of the left hand through the downbeat of m. 8 but not thereafter, suggesting that the descent from E to G♯ is subordinate to the line that precedes it. The main portion of the descent, G♯–F✕ –F♯–E (mm. 5–7) contains one chromatic degree, which should normally not be stemmed, since it is not part of the basic diatonic structure.

11

Introduction
to Musical Form;
Unfolding
of Intervals

It is understandable that our excursions into complete musical forms will be confined to short ones first. The variation "theme" is ideal in this respect, for while it is the basis for a larger work or movement (an aspect to be discussed in Part Three), it can also stand as a composition in its own right. By the very nature of the variation process, coupled with the common practice (at least through the early nineteenth century) of keeping the variations in the tonic key, we can expect that the background structure of the theme will be maintained and reinforced by its subsequent treatment. Conversely, we can look to the variations and coda (if any) in cases where a reading of the theme is in doubt.[1]

The variation themes presented in their entirety in Examples 143 (p. 150) and 147 (p. 155) are both in *binary form*: two sections, normally of equal length, each within repeat signs. A modification of this pattern is the so-called rounded or extended binary form, in which the second section may be longer, begins with contrasting material, and concludes with a reminder of the first section. Thus the rounded binary is a middle stage between a two-part and a three-part (*ternary*) form; in the latter the initial (A), contrasting (B), and recapitulatory (A) sections are more nearly equal in length.

The Haydn and Mozart excerpts cited first in Example 137 (p. 133) constitute the respective A sections of two very similar forms. The first is possibly ternary, or perhaps rounded binary without repeats; the second is definitely rounded binary. We shall first look at the remainder of each; then, in the next chapter, at each as a whole.

---

1. For example, the coda of the first movement of Mozart's *A–major Piano Sonata*, K. 331, confirms E as primary tone—if confirmation is required (see Example 139, p. 137).

The B section of the Haydn (Example 148) divides neatly into two four-measure phrases. The first, a line ascending from F to D accompanied by the progression V–I, prolongs the goal harmony I. The second, a line descending from E♭ to A, is accompanied by a progression back to and prolonging V.[2] In both cases the prolongation precedes the harmonies being prolonged. By the principles outlined in Chapter 8, the sixth F–D prolongs D ($\hat{3}$), while the descending diminished fifth prolongs E♭ (the upper neighbor to $\hat{3}$, also active in the first section). Thus the prolonged melody notes fit in, as they should, with the corresponding prolonged harmonies. (Remember that the seventh is allowed as a structural member of the dominant chord.) However, notice that in this example the *interval* spanned by each prolongational line is structurally relevant also: that is, F–D belongs to I, while E♭–A belongs to V (more precisely, V[7]).

EXAMPLE 148. Haydn, *Divertimento in B♭ major (Chorale St. Antoni)*

This last phenomenon can be understood as the linear *unfolding (Ausfaltung)* of an interval which could conceivably be verticalized in a later stage of reduction.[3] Such an interval always proceeds from or to another interval, which may be either vertical or itself unfolded. It is symbolized graphically by an upward stem on the lower note, a downward stem on the upper note, and a crosswise beam connecting the two (Example 149). The upper note's downward stem permits it to take an upward stem as well, plus any other analytic symbol that may be appropriate. It is also possible to incorporate the open note into the unfolding if it intersects with the background structure: here the open note and hanging beam on D signify the reactivation of the primary tone, while the flag on E♭ identifies another kind of special function, in this case the prolonged neighbor note. (Schenker used the flag in a variety of situations to highlight melody and bass notes of significant intermediate

2. Schenker (FC, Fig. 42/2) reads the melodic line as reaching all the way to E♭, and reads the entire middle section as a prolongation of V[7].
3. See Example 154a (p. 167) for the detailed stepwise motion that the unfolded interval succession incorporates.

EXAMPLE 149. Haydn, *Chorale St. Antoni*: Unfolding

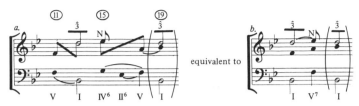

value; earlier, we used this symbol briefly in Examples 6, p. 15, and 39, p. 47). As can be seen by proceeding from Example 149*a* to 149*b*, the unfolding symbol enables us to keep track of voice leading.[4]

The B section plays a parallel role in the Mozart theme (Example 150), stressing once again the primary tone (5̂) and its upper neighbor, though the prevailing texture and prolongational techniques are different. The section begins with a single voice in the right hand, moving basically in octaves with the top of the left (common in much good piano music), tracing the pattern E–F♯–E. In mm. 11–12 the melody becomes compound and presents C♯–D–C♯ (over A–B–A), as shown in the graph. This, of course, is a restatement and enlargement of the first melodic motive of the theme. When the soprano sustaining E drops out in the latter part of m. 12, it is replaced by the E that emerges in the top voice of the left hand, intensified by the chromatic passing tone D♯ that precedes it.

EXAMPLE 150. Mozart, *Piano Sonata in A major*, K. 331, I

By returning to the opening (A) material, the process of recapitulation obviously gives coherence to any musical form. However, in a well-composed piece, there is always in addition some final gesture that enhances the

---

4. Use of the unfolding symbol by students tends to be excessive at first, and for that reason it is not being emphasized at this point. The exercises below provide some elementary practice in this area, which will be examined in greater depth early in Part Three (Chapter 20).

meaning of the whole. This gesture may take the form of a coda several measures long, or it may be very small indeed; either way its essential function is the same. In practical terms, the final gesture provides an opportunity to check the correctness of an analysis, since we can normally expect some confirmation of the primary tone, along with the reintroduction of noteworthy details which surrounded it during the course of the piece. Thus the *Chorale St. Antoni* ends with a reminder of the primary tone together with its upper neighbor, the latter reinforced harmonically by the applied dominant to IV which precedes it (Example 151). By the same token, we find in the Mozart a return to E ($\hat{5}$) prior to the final $\hat{2}$–$\hat{1}$ of the fundamental line (Example 152). In the latter example there is yet a more remarkable feature: the motion from F♯ to high A on the upbeat to the final measure. Although this embellishment of the neighbor note F♯ seems but a small detail, its significance grows when we realize that its path has already been established by the diminution in m. 10. More important, notice how this little flourish literally puts a cap on the motion of a third, focusing attention on a germinal motivic idea, summarized in Example 153, which shows its multiple occurrences throughout the theme.

EXAMPLE 151. Haydn, *Divertimento in B♭ major* (*Chorale St. Antoni*)

EXAMPLE 152. Mozart, *Piano Sonata in A major*, K. 331, I

EXAMPLE 153. Mozart, *Piano Sonata in A major*, K. 331: Motivic Thirds

Exercises

As introduced in Example 149, the unfolding symbol is applicable where a segment of the melodic line covers an interval within the currently prolonged harmony, and where this interval proceeds to or from another interval (either vertical or unfolded). Unfolded intervals are most characteristically thirds and sixths, but not exclusively so: the diminished fifth, for example, is a likely candidate for unfolding if the prolonged chord is a dominant seventh (Example 149).

The opening sections of the following Bach chorales are intended as an introduction to the use of the unfolding symbol. For each chorale excerpt, provide *two graphs in analytic notation*: a) without the unfolding symbol, fairly detailed, with all chords labeled; b) using the symbol where appropriate, with bass and roman numerals reduced to show only the prolonged harmony that accompanies each unfolding.

1. Sample Exercise: Bach, Chorale No. 55, *Wir Christenleut'*

Solution

Comment:

Although at first glance it would seem logical to read the ascending third in mm. 3–4 analogously to the two descending thirds that precede it, such a reading would imply an incorrect resolution of the seventh.

equivalent to

As a consequence, we have interpreted the E of m. 2 as an upper neighbor prolonging D, rather than a step in the ascent to F♯.

2. Bach, Chorale No. 172, *Sei gegrüsset, Jesu gütig*

The remarks above regarding the resolution of the seventh apply in this exercise: namely, the first C (downbeat of m. 2) resolves back to B♭ before proceeding on to D (m. 3). Unfoldings apply only in mm. 1–2; mm. 3–4 contain an ascent to 5̂ and a middleground descent to 3̂.

3. Bach, Chorale No. 233, *Werde munter, mein Gemüte*

Unlike the first three notes in m. 1, the restatement of the filled-in third in m. 3 should *not* be represented as an unfolding. Why?

4. Bach, Chorale No. 317, *Herr, wie du willst, so schick's mit mir*

This excerpt consists of an initial ascent to $\hat{3}$ followed by a middleground descent to $\hat{1}$. Both of these involve unfolded thirds.

12

Fundamental Structure
in Complete Units

As defined in Chapter 7, the fundamental structure of a musical composition comprises both the fundamental line and the bass arpeggiation that accompanies it. Taken as a whole, the fundamental structure represents the background level of an analysis, and as such is written in open notes. In setting the background apart from the middleground and foreground, the following generalities must be kept in mind:

1. Though its profile will likely be reflected on at least one structural level closer to the surface, the fundamental line as such descends to the tonic (scale degree $\hat{1}$) only once.

2. The status of the fundamental line at any given time is determined by the highest currently active degree of the tonic scale. (Usually this means that some kind of prolongation is in force.) A note of the fundamental line is considered "active" until it has appeared for the last time.

3. The final $\hat{2}$–$\hat{1}$ of the fundamental line is accompanied harmonically by the final authentic cadence.

4. The open notes showing the fundamental structure should be used sparingly. This includes the bass as well as the fundamental line.

Example 154 shows the application of these principles to the Haydn and Mozart themes discussed above, presented so as to emphasize the parallel roles played by their respective beginning, middle, and final sections. In addition to illustrating the proper use of open notes, these two sketches employ some new notational devices. The doubly curved slur, applied to either the bass line or the roman numerals below it (or both), is a symbol Schenker employed to denote progression to the dominant by way of II or IV (or perhaps a secondary dominant). As a rule, it is superimposed upon whatever conventional slurs would ordinarily be applied. (The way the doubly curved slur crosses the conventional slur, as for example between the E♭ and F in the bass line of 154a, is characteristic.) Also used here are arrowheads, which clarify the meaning of the diagonal lines when necessary. Remember that the plain diagonal in analytic notation means something else. The single arrowhead indicates either voice leading or a transfer of register (Chapter 18), while the crisscrossed diagonals with arrowheads at each end point out an exchange of voices. And although the inclusion of detail is always a flexible matter—as with the careted numbers in parentheses (see Chapter 10)—the correct use of analytic notation allows it to be done without obscuring the fundamental structure. Consistent and correct use of analytic notation also enables others trained in Schenkerian analysis to read and understand your graphs and to evaluate them thoughtfully.

EXAMPLE 154

a. Haydn, *Chorale St. Antoni*

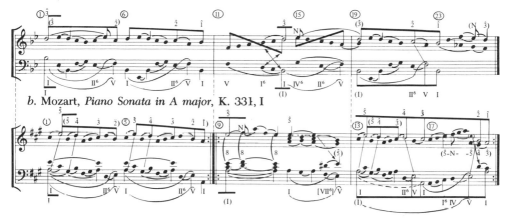

b. Mozart, *Piano Sonata in A major*, K. 331, I

Coupling of Registers

The third movement of Mozart's *A-major Sonata*, K. 331, is a large form, the rondo (Chapter 23). However, the theme of the movement, called the refrain in rondos, is a rounded binary form. This theme can be viewed as a study in the systematic use of register transfer (Chapter 6), the relation Schenker called *coupling* (*Koppelung*), denoted graphically by the dotted slur. (The dotted slur may also be used to show the reappearance of a specific melody or bass note in the *same* register.) In the present instance, Example 155, the use of coupling is especially thorough, as evidenced by the fact that the pattern of the entire fundamental line, 3̂–2̂–1̂, is traceable from both the octave and double-octave above middle C. The opening first-order arpeggiation spans this octave plus a third below, the high B before the first repeat sign is duplicated at the lower octave just before the recapitulation, while motion down to A can be found in both registers in the recapitulation. The fact that the recapitulation retraces the descent from C before proceeding to A causes an *interruption (Unterbrechung)* in the fundamental line; as a result the overall $\hat{3}$–$\hat{2}$–$\hat{1}$ assumes the more specific profile, $\hat{3}$–$\hat{2}$ || $\hat{3}$–$\hat{2}$–$\hat{1}$, the actual "interruption" symbolized by the double vertical line.

EXAMPLE 155. Mozart, *Piano Sonata in A major*, K. 331, III

However, the two representations of the above pattern are not equal. Schenker's principle of *obligatory register* (*obligate Lage*) dictates that the fundamental line should present itself within a single octave. The latter constitutes the primary ("obligatory") register of the work, while other registers, introduced through coupling, remain subordinate. In the present example, the lower version of the fundamental line is the definitive one. There are distinct clues pointing to this conclusion: lower C appears first, while the lower B and A round out the final cadence. A subsequent reduction of Example 155 would therefore indicate the lower $\hat{3}$–$\hat{2}$–$\hat{1}$ as the fundamental line and perhaps go no further. Yet it is frequently desirable to retain middleground (and even foreground) elements in a background sketch, especially if there are special circumstances surrounding the piece. The interplay of registers in the "alla Turca" theme is a perfect case in point.

Exercises

A. Each of the following contains at least one instance of coupling in the melody and sometimes in the bass as well. Using Example 155 and Exercise 1 as models, make a middleground sketch of each passage. Indicate each coupling by a dotted slur.

1. Sample Exercise: Haydn, *Piano Sonata in E♭ major*, Hob. XVI/28, I

Solution

Comments:

1. The repeated descending fifth in the middle register (mm. 1–4) is harmonically strongest at the beginning, while the descending fifth an octave higher (mm. 6–8) is strongest at the end. In this respect they complement each other. Complementation also exists in the way the right hand's parallel thirds at the beginning of the passage are replaced by parallel sixths at the end.

2. The arrows here indicate register transfer, and in this case result in *overlapping* (*Übergreifung*: literally, "reaching over"), a phenomenon to be discussed in Chapter 18. In the meantime, the details of voice leading in mm. 4–6 should be studied before proceeding further. Look again at both the score and the graph.

3. Notice how the doubly curved slur is used. For review, see Examples 154 and 155 plus the appropriate remarks in the first part of this chapter.

2. Bach, *English Suite in G minor*, Gavotte I

3. Mozart, *Piano Concerto in D minor*, K. 466, II

4. Beethoven, *Piano Sonata in F major*, Op. 10, No. 2, I

Despite the middleground lines descending from C, the primary tone in this passage is A (3̂). This is the kind of decision one makes after looking over an entire movement; sometimes it is not wholly evident in the theme alone. (Exercise 8/5 is very similar in this regard; see also Schenker's graph of the present work in FC, Fig. 101/4.)

5. Beethoven, *Fifth Piano Concerto*, II

This theme is developed melodically in two distinct registers. (See also Exercise 2/1.)

B. Each of the variation themes quoted below may be treated as a self-contained form containing a complete statement of one of the fundamental structural types. Omitting the possibility of a descent from scale degree $\hat{8}$ for the present, these include the descent from $\hat{3}$ or $\hat{5}$ as given in Example 136 (p. 133). Using the guidelines in the first part of this chapter, make a combination middleground and background sketch of each theme, and indicate whether its sectional form is binary, rounded binary, or ternary. Label all special features, such as initial ascent, arpeggiation, and coupling.

1. Beethoven, *Nine Variations on "Quanto è bello l'amor Contadino"* (Paisello)

The differences between the second and third eight-measure groupings are so slight that you may substitute a pair of repeat signs in your graph. Be sure to take this fact into account in your determination of the musical form of this theme.

2. Haydn, *Piano Sonata in A major*, Hob. XVI/30, III

This theme and the variations that follow together form the final segment of a one-movement work. Despite the two-voice texture, the implied harmonies should be indicated in your analysis, just as if three or four voices were present. One clarification: the diminished fifth (such as G♯–D in the third measure) normally implies V_5^6 rather than root-position VII. The clarity of the melodic progression overall should influence (and facilitate) your interpretation of the descending runs in the latter half of each section, a task which will still require some careful thought.

3. Mozart. *Six Variations on an Allegretto*, K. Anh. 137

The first four measures of this theme are similar in content to those of the A-major Mozart theme of Example 137*b* (p. 134). A parallel reading of the next phrase, however, finds a missing note in the penultimate measure. In cases such as this, where the harmony conforms but the expected melody note is avoided, we normally place the note in question within parentheses (recall Chapter 6). Notice also that each half of the piece concludes with the melody in a higher register.

4. Mozart, *Ten Variations on "Come un agnello"* (Sarti), K. 460

The primary melodic tone of this piece may be $\hat{3}$ rather than $\hat{5}$. Why?

5. Beethoven, *Six Easy Variations on an Original Theme*

The primary tone of this theme is established in and by the outer sections.

6. Mozart, *Twelve Variations on an Allegretto*, K. 500

The treatment of register here recalls the *alla Turca* theme of Example 155 (p. 168). A comparison with the latter will be of help in solving the present exercise.

13

The Harmonized Chorale

Formal Aspects

"From Hymn Tune to Teaching Tool" might be an apt title for a history of the harmonized chorale over the past three centuries.[1] Its universal acceptance as a model for the study of Western harmony is surely no secret to any music student; however, the matter of just how the chorale relates to the "real world" of freely composed instrumental and vocal music is all too often left to chance. As a result, what is studied in traditional harmony courses runs the risk of remaining in a vacuum. While the chorale may well deserve its special place in the curriculum, its larger musical role must be understood in order for it to be truly useful.

Certain features set the harmonized chorale apart from other types of music. Its texture is uniform: four voices in four vocal ranges (allowing for an occasional instrumental bass). It is highly compressed in time. And while its harmonic pace is relatively rapid (a chord change on virtually every beat), its melodic pace (also moving chiefly with the meter) is relatively slow. In form the chorale differs from other genres in that thematic recapitulation occurs far less frequently, as witness the prevalence of the *bar form*, ||:A:|| B. A typical chorale in bar form is shown in Example 156.

EXAMPLE 156. Bach, Chorale No. 42, *Du Friedensfürst, Herr Jesu Christ*

---

1. Strictly speaking, the term *chorale* refers to the melody alone; what we normally call a chorale is actually a chorale harmonization (setting), or harmonized chorale. Though the chorale settings of Bach are by no means the only ones, they are the ones most widely studied, and for that reason will be the source for the chorale material in the present chapter.

The asymmetrical design of the bar form is partly offset by the fact that chorale phrases, determined as they are by the text, can normally be expected to occur in pairs—as they do in Example 156. Just the opposite can happen, though: that is, an odd number of phrases repeated an even number of times (twice, to be specific, with the harmony varied and the second time), resulting in the pattern AA'. Such is the case with a celebrated chorale from the *St. Matthew Passion* (Example 157), known variously as *Nun ruhen alle Wälder*, *O Welt, ich muss dich lassen*, and *Ich bin's, ich sollte büssen*. This chorale, whose melody initially resembles that of Example 156, is analyzed by Schenker in *Five Graphic Music Analyses* (FGMA, pp. 32–33). The technique of restating a melody with a different harmonization occurs in extended form (scheme AA'BB') in Example 158.

EXAMPLE 157. Bach, Chorale No. 117, *Nun ruhen alle Wälder*

EXAMPLE 158. Bach, Chorale No. 142, *Schwing' dich auf zu deinem Gott*

At the same time, there remain numerous chorales in which opening material does reappear at the end. In Example 159 we see two complete ternary forms: *a*, with the A section repeated, in other words ‖:A:‖ BA; *b*, with no repeats, and therefore simply ABA. Also not uncommon are the varieties of incomplete recapitulation shown in Example 160: *a*, first phrase only; *b*, second phrase only; *c*, final phrase strongly resembling, though not identical to, the first. The last of these suggests that, even in chorales, there are likely to be thematic and motivic similarities lying beneath the surface.[2]

EXAMPLE 159

    a. Bach, Chorale No. 41, *Was mein Gott will, das g'scheh'*

    b. Bach, Chorale No. 141, *Seelen-Bräutigam*

EXAMPLE 160

    a. Bach, Chorale No. 356, *Jesu meine Freude*

---

2. More can possibly be said about Example 160. In *a*, phrase 5 can be read as an extended version of phrase 2; and in *c*, the reference to the opening in the final phrase is rhythmically offset and does not begin immediately after the penultimate fermata.

b. Bach, Chorale No. 22, *Schmücke dich, O liebe Seele*

c. Bach, Chorale No. 118, *In dich hab' ich gehoffet, Herr*

Techniques for Reduction

A chorale setting moving in basic, even note values already resembles a reduction from a more detailed surface. Put another way, a rhythmic reduction of a typical free composition (as in Examples 138*a*, p. 136, and 139*a*, p. 137) will tend to resemble a chorale setting. The chorale's compactness and relative clarity provide a good first opportunity to see the fundamental structure of a complete composition virtually at a glance.

Determination of the primary tone of a chorale melody, as in any type of composition, takes a certain amount of practice. While the basic premise remains the same—that we look first to the highest active degree of the tonic triad—we look for some kind of melodic emphasis as well. In a chorale, where melody notes proceed generally at an even pace, sheer recurrence of a pitch can be one indication of its possible importance. Though not a strong index by itself, recurrence of a pitch (and the durational emphasis resulting from this recurrence) can be a deciding factor in cases where all other factors are equal.

This matter of emphasis is demonstrated in Example 161. Two chorales, presented in the same key to facilitate comparison, have very similar melodic profiles. Both operate within the lower portion of the tonic scale, and both have the fifth as top note. The difference lies in the role played by this top note: in 161*a* motion to and from E takes place only once, and within the space of just one measure (m. 4). Elsewhere the melody peaks at C♯, and does it so frequently that one cannot help but regard the third as the primary tone.[3] Example 161*b*, on the other hand, stresses the third less and the fifth more, shifting the balance of attention to the higher note, which is reached by a first-order arpeggiation over the first five measures.

EXAMPLE 161

a. Bach, Chorale No. 141, *Seelen-Bräutigam*

b. Bach, Chorale No. 159, *Als der gütige Gott*

The analytic graphs in Example 162 parallel the overlays in Example 161 and reflect the differences between them. The motion leading to the primary tone, for instance, is an initial (linear) ascent in the first chorale (review

3. Another case where the third is the primary tone despite the fifth being the highest note is shown in Schenker's analysis of *Ich bin's, ich sollte büssen* (FGMA, pp. 32–33), the chorale included here under an alternate title as Example 157.

Chapter 9), an arpeggiation in the second (Chapter 10).[4] And the role of the fourth scale degree, though it is prolonged similarly by an unfolding in each chorale, differs as a consequence of whether the third or fifth is the primary tone: in the first, D is graphed as an upper neighbor to $\hat{3}$; in the second, as step $\hat{4}$ of the fundamental line (and, as such, a large-scale passing note). Further details are clarified by means of the unfolding symbol (review Chapter 11 with its exercises), the diagonal line (end of Chapter 7), and in general by the consistent use of analytic note values.

EXAMPLE 162
  a. Bach, Chorale No. 141, *Seelen-Bräutigam*

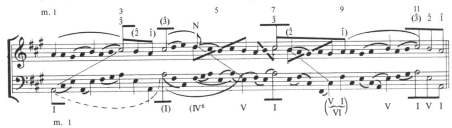

  b. Bach, Chorale No. 159, *Als der gütige Gott*

The Chorale and the Octave Progression

We now turn to some instances where scale degree $\hat{8}$ functions as an active melodic note and therefore may be the primary tone, a phenomenon which probably occurs more frequently in chorales than elsewhere. The chorale *Ein' feste Burg ist unser Gott*, quoted previously in part (Example 137c, p. 134), is here shown in its entirety alongside another chorale which closely resembles it (Example 163). The two not only share the same original key and melodic range, but use an identical melody for their respective final phrases; this melody is especially significant because it summarizes and retraces the descent from $\hat{8}$ to $\hat{1}$ (a feature indicated by the careted numerals $\hat{8}, \hat{7}, \hat{6}, \hat{5}$, enclosed in parentheses).

---

4. The distinction between linear motion and arpeggiation requires some thought when the arpeggiation is embellished internally. In the second chorale in Examples 161 and 162 there is a stepwise ascent from A to C♯ but not from C♯ to E (the D in m. 3 functions as a neighboring tone to C♯ rather than as a passing tone); as a result the entire motion from A to E is classed as an arpeggiation.

EXAMPLE 163

   a. Bach, Chorale No. 20, *Ein' feste Burg ist unser Gott*

   b. Bach, Chorale No. 46, *Vom Himmel hoch, da komm' ich her*

In general, the existence of scale degree $\hat{8}$ as primary tone depends on two criteria: that $\hat{8}$ be sufficiently emphasized melodically, and that $\hat{7}$ and $\hat{6}$ be sufficiently supported harmonically.[5] If, for whatever reason, scale degree $\hat{8}$ is

---

5. There are a number of ways for these criteria to be filled. Some prolongation of $\hat{7}$ (melodic, harmonic, or both) is desirable, but difficult in major keys; in minor keys, where the seventh in descent is not a leading tone, this becomes much easier. Schenker's own discussion (FC §§42–44) focuses on the role of $\hat{5}$ as resting place, stating that this scale degree should be harmonized by V. One consequence of this condition is what Schenker calls a *double arpeggiation of the bass* (FC, Fig. 11), that is:

$$\hat{8}\text{-}\hat{7}\text{-}\hat{6}\text{-}\hat{5}\text{-}\hat{4}\text{-}\hat{3}\text{-}\hat{2}\text{-}\hat{1}$$
$$\text{I-} \qquad \text{-V} \qquad \text{V-I}$$

judged not to be the primary tone, then the upper portion of the scale reverts to the middleground. Schenker's term for this is difficult to translate;[6] for our purposes, "initial descent" will suffice. Despite the obvious parallel to the initial ascent, the initial descent is less common and on the whole less important.[7]

A good example of an initial descent from scale degree $\hat{8}$ occurs in the well-known Christmas carol *Joy to the World* (Example 164), where the rate of harmonic change is noticeably slower (and the harmonic changes are less varied) than in a true chorale setting. While one could argue that scale degree $\hat{8}$ is clearly heard as the melody's top note, it is plain that the steps between $\hat{8}$ and $\hat{5}$ are merely passing notes over a tonic harmony; this contrasts with the full support given the slow descent from $\hat{5}$ to $\hat{1}$ over the last seven measures.

EXAMPLE 164. Handel, *Joy to the World*

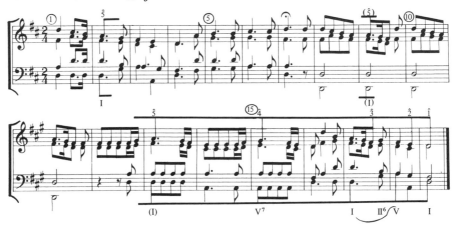

The simplicity and familiarity of the example above provide an opportunity to review and expand upon some of the fine points of sketch technique. In translating the rhythmic notation of Example 164 to analytic notation, one might begin as in Example 165a. This first graph retains every note of the outer voices except for those that are immediately repeated; in addition, immediately repeated passages (such as mm. 8–9) are stated only once. Analytic note values are tentatively assigned according to the interpretation shown in the initial overlay; in ascending order these are: 1) the plain filled notehead; 2) the stemmed filled notehead; 3) the stemmed open notehead. This last note value is used for the fundamental line and bass arpeggiation; the use of beams (optional for the bass) further highlights the fundamental structure as a whole.

---

6. *Leerlauf*, literally "empty run." Oster's translation reads "unsupported stretch" (FC, p. 20).

7. Though the present discussion centers on the initial descent from $\hat{8}$, it must be mentioned that an initial descent may also begin on scale degree $\hat{5}$—that is, when $\hat{4}$ is not supported harmonically (see FC, §37)

EXAMPLE 165. Handel, *Joy to the World*

The graph shown next (Example 165*b*) is more concise, with refinements an experienced analyst might make directly. For one, the first seven measures are now summarized by a high D in the soprano over a tonic harmony: in other words, the identical starting and ending points of the passage make what happens in between them parenthetical. Implicit in this reduction is revised interpretation of the melodic line (Example 165*c*), showing a descending octave followed by an ascending fourth, both prolonging D. What in Example 165*a* was regarded as the primary tone $\hat{5}$ is now seen as part of that descending octave. However, since the primary tone is sufficiently emphasized thereafter, deferring its introduction graphically will not change the overall outcome of the analysis. Another improvement in the second graph is the use of the unfolding symbol for the successive thirds in mm. 12–15.

Again by way of review and reinforcement, some discussion is needed concerning the placement of scale degree $\hat{3}$ in the fundamental line. As happens frequently, the third of the tonic scale here makes its last appearance over a cadential $^6_4$ chord, and is therefore actually part of a double passing-note formation dependent upon V. Although it is often necessary to accept this contrapuntal support of $\hat{3}$, it is preferable to have this scale degree supported harmonically by a root-position tonic. Thus while the F♯ on the downbeat of the penultimate measure is more visible on the surface, the F♯ in the measure preceding is more sound structurally. These observations, detailed in Example 165*d*, have a wide range of application, including the Haydn and Mozart themes cited in Chapter 7 (Examples 137*a* and *b*, pp. 133–34, 138, p. 136, and 139, p. 137).

So far we have seen scale degree $\hat{8}$ in two guises: as the primary tone itself (Example 163), and as the top note of an initial descent to a primary tone further down the scale (Example 164). A third possibility, illustrated by Example 166, shows it stemmed but unnumbered, at the upper end of a consonant skip filled in by step: in other words, a diminution (Chapter 1). For this interpretation to be valid, a lower degree of the tonic triad (here $\hat{5}$) should be readily perceptible as the primary tone, through emphasis on that note itself and on the linear descent that follows.

EXAMPLE 166. Bach, Chorale No. 6, *Christus, der ist mein Leben*

a. Score with analytic overlay

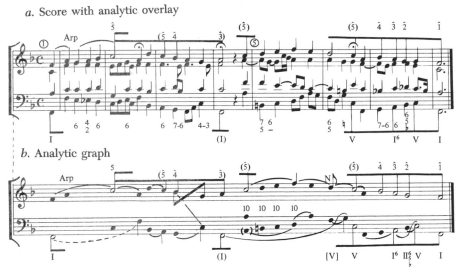

b. Analytic graph

Exercises

For each of the following, a) comment on the form of the chorale, using the designations A, B, C (along with A′, B′, C′), as appropriate; b) analyze the chorale setting harmonically, using figured bass and roman numerals; c) make a comprehensive middleground and background graph, as in Example 162 (p. 180). Hints concerning the fundamental structure are given in each case.)

1. Bach, Chorale No. 217, *Ach Gott, wie manches Herzeleid*

Initial ascent to $\hat{3}$.

2. Bach, Chorale No. 159, *Als der gütige Gott*

What first appears to be an initial linear ascent to $\hat{5}$ over the first five measures is actually a first-order arpeggiation. This is because the C in m. 3 is clearly a neighboring tone reverting back to B rather than a large-scale passing note to D.

3. Bach, Chorale No. 41, *Was mein Gott will, das g'scheh'*

Although the initial phrase moves immediately toward C major, the home key of this setting is A minor. Your graph should show a fundamental line of $\hat{3}$–$\hat{2}$–$\hat{1}$ in that key. *See Example 159a (p. 177).*

4. Bach, Chorale No. 118, *In dich hab' ich gehoffet, Herr*

Straightforward descent from $\hat{5}$. *See Example 160c (p. 178).*

5. Bach, Chorale No. 48, *Ach wie nichtig, ach wie flüchtig*

Initial ascent to $\hat{5}$.

6. Bach, Chorale No. 22, *Schmücke dich, O liebe Seele*

First-order arpeggiation to $\hat{8}$. *See Example 160b* (p. 178).

7. Bach, Chorale No. 44, *Mach's mit mir, Gott, nach diener Güt*

Initial ascent to $\hat{8}$. Compare this chorale and the one preceding with Example 166 (p. 184)—notice the difference in emphasis upon scale degree $\hat{8}$.

8. Bach, Chorale No. 356, *Jesu, meine Freude*

In this famous chorale, the descent from $\hat{8}$ to $\hat{5}$ is not in the tonic scale. This leads us to conclude that $\hat{5}$, rather than $\hat{8}$, should be read as the primary tone. *See Example 160a* (p. 177).

9. Bach, Chorale No. 24, *Valet will ich dir geben*

Here the primary tone is clearly $\hat{8}$, embellished by the third above. The position of scale degree $\hat{7}$, prolonged in mm. 6–7, is stronger than is usual for the major mode.

10. Bach, Chorale No. 47, *Vater unser im Himmelreich*

This final chorale exercise is longer than most of the foregoing, and lacks any clear thematic repetition. However, there is an approximate resemblance between phrases 1 and 6, phrases 2 and 5, and phrases 3 and 4, which produces a symmetry not encountered in earlier examples. Moreover, these six phrases are of exactly equal length.

If we read $\hat{8}$ as the primary tone, then we can draw a large-scale coupling from the end of phrase 1 (m. 2) to the end of phrase 3 (m. 6). This is followed by a prolongation of the upper neighbor, E (mm. 7–8), and by a prolongation of scale degree $\hat{7}$ (mm. 9–10). Notice that scale degree $\hat{6}$ *in the tonic key* (compare Exercise 8) is not reached until the downbeat of m. 11.

14
Elaborated Chorales: Instrumental Preludes and Studies

Though elements of chorale texture pervade the whole of tonal music, there is one class of composition whose relationship to the chorale is especially close. This kind of piece consists of a series of broken chords (a common form of compound melody—Chapter 3); putting the chords in block form makes it kinship with the chorale self-evident. Passages of this type exist everywhere, and arpeggiated studies are the mainstay of the technical literature for virtually every instrument. The music of Bach and Chopin comes to mind as a source of particularly fine examples, of which some of the best known will be discussed in the present section.

In approaching this kind of composition, it is first necessary to establish the number of structural voices. The norm is four as expected, though a fifth voice may be present part or all of the time. As a case in point, the C-major Prelude from *The Well-Tempered Clavier, Volume I* (hereafter WTC/I) keeps a five-voice structure throughout.[1] The part immediately above the bass

EXAMPLE 167. Bach, WTC/I, Prelude 1

---

1. Schenker analyzes this Prelude in FGMA, pp. 36–37.

initially looks like a doubling of the soprano, but even from the first few measures (Example 167) we see that it does not remain as such. Consequently, there are no voices to eliminate from the first reduction, and continuing the pattern becomes a straightforward matter.

A parallel reduction of the next example requires more decisions. In the right hand (Example 168*a*) an arpeggiated pattern is stated at successive octave levels, while the composer's accent marks point to the structural soprano voice (in other words, to the "true" melodic line). Obviously only one complete pattern is needed for each chord: normal procedure is to choose one in a moderate register. Thus derived, the four upper voices can be further streamlined by bringing the bottom voice of the right hand up an octave (Example 168*b*). Doing this in effect trims the number of upper voices to three, except when the chord requires four. As for the left hand, the doubling of the bass at the lower octave is omitted from this and any subsequent graph.

EXAMPLE 168. Chopin, *Etude in C major*, Op. 10, No. 1

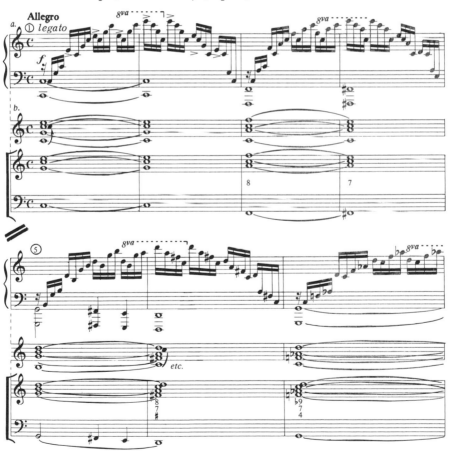

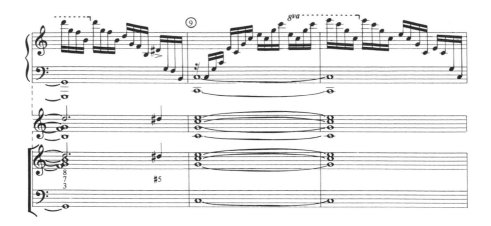

In reduced form, these two passages (Examples 167*b* and 168*b*) show a strong resemblance, which becomes still more evident in analytic notation (Example 169). However, the pacing of harmonic changes is twice as slow in the Chopin excerpt: roughly one every two measures as opposed to one per measure in the Bach. In terms of the chorale model, pieces of this sort represent varying levels of rhythmic augmentation: in the first (Example 167) we can intuitively equate two measures with one measure of a chorale in 4/4 time; in the second (Example 168) four measures are needed to fill the same space. Such observations are especially useful from a performance standpoint, as they lead to a broader grasp of phrase and period structure.

EXAMPLE 169.
    a. Bach, WTC/I, Prelude 1

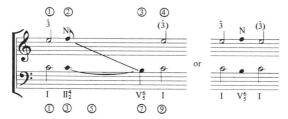

    b. Chopin, *Etude in C major*, Opus 10, No. 1

A companion to the two preceding examples is Chopin's first prelude, also in C major (Example 170). The basic pulse is now the quarter note, one per measure, with regular phrases of eight measures divisible into antecedent and consequent portions of four measures each. The rhythmic reduction (Example 170*b*) makes several simplifications. Each measure is divided evenly into two eighth notes (replacing the dotted pattern of the original), while the harmonic content of each chord is represented by three voices in the right hand.[2] Eliminating the lower doublings allows the bass to be transposed up an octave, thus normalizing the distance between soprano and bass. Additional chord tones originally in the left hand are added in parentheses.

EXAMPLE 170. Chopin, *Prelude in C major*, Op. 28, No. 1

---

2. This arrangement results in parallel octaves (between the right hand's lowest voice and the bass) at those places where one triad moves directly to another (as for example mm. 3–4). An alternative would be to reduce the number of right-hand voices to two when the harmony is a triad.

The figured bass symbols in Example 170*b* are intended to underscore the linear aspects of the eighth-note motion and, in particular, to show the pervasive 5–6 motivic pattern. This pattern also occurs in the chromatic form ♯5–6 at critical points, such as mm. 13, 14, 16 (in connection with $^6_4$), and elsewhere. (A review of the last part of Chapter 2 may be helpful at this time.)

As with the two other pieces, the primary tone is E ($\hat{3}$). Here, however, the primary tone is not so clearly established at the outset; in fact, it occurs directly over a root-position tonic only at the very final chord, presumably after the fundamental line has already run its course. (This last-minute "reminder" is a Chopin trademark, and at the very least can be taken as a sign that the composer wanted that melody note to linger in the listener's mind after the piece was over.) The more subtle ways in which the primary tone asserts itself are discussed below.

The first eight-measure phrase (Example 171*a*) begins with an arpeggiation whose goal, E, is turned into an appoggiatura by the harmonic change at m. 5. Despite the local change of chord, it is still possible to interpret the E as an extension of the tonic harmony—that is, provided later events justify this interpretation. This is shown by the diagonal line in Example 171*a*, which conceptually implies the alternative temporal alignment shown in Example 171*b*.

EXAMPLE 171. Chopin, *Prelude in C major*, Op. 28, No. 1: Diagonal Relation

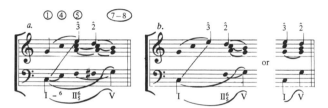

The second phrase retraces the arpeggiation from G to E, but with the E on a surer footing harmonically—as the tonic $^6_4$ concluding the phrase is a point of rest rather than a cadential $^6_4$ chord requiring resolution. As a result, the relationship depicted in Example 172 is easier to grasp.

EXAMPLE 172. Chopin, *Prelude in C major*, Op. 28, No. 1: Diagonal Relation

In the third phrase, beginning m. 17, it is the starting point that is structurally important: that is, the first-inversion IV harmonizing F (Example 173*a*). Justification for this departure from the rules of prolongation (remember that normally the top note of an ascending line is the one prolonged) is twofold: first, F connects logically as an upper neighbor to the note that ends the preceding phrase (it is also foreshadowed in m. 15); second, notice the abrupt downward shift in register, in both hands, at the end of the

EXAMPLE 173. Chopin, *Prelude in C major*, Op. 28, No. 1

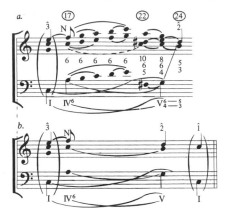

sequence. As a result of these changes in register, the next stage of reduction can omit the passage between mm. 17 and 21 (Example 173*b*).

The beginning of the final phrase (m. 25) marks the definitive return of the tonic, which remains as a pedal point through the end. Despite the static harmony (the essential content of the phrase is simply the resolution of the final authentic cadence, indicated in parentheses in Example 173*b*), there are important thematic elements here: the reappearance of the initial 5–6 gesture of the first and second phrases, plus a small-scale replica of the fundamental line (bracketed in Example 174).

EXAMPLE 174. Chopin, *Prelude in C major*, Op. 28, No. 1

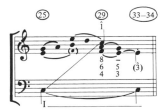

Exercises

The pieces in this group should each be graphed at least twice, as follows:

> *a*. Rhythmic reduction, with consistent doublings eliminated. The result should approximate a four-voice chorale texture, with either two voices on each staff (see solution to Exercise 1 below) or the upper voices all on the top staff (see Example 170, pp. 191–2). Figured bass symbols, with an emphasis on voice leading, should be added between or below the staffs.

b. Middleground-background sketch (background in open notes). In addition to substituting analytic for rhythmic notation, this sketch should aim at being more concise than sketch a. Surface diminutions should be eliminated, and inner voices need not be included all the time. (The instructor and/or the student may wish to do this in more than one stage.)

1. Sample Exercise: Chopin, *Waltz in A♭ major*, Op. 42

Solution:

   a. Rhythmic reduction

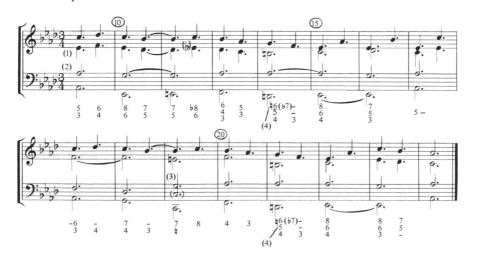

Comments:

1. The alto in this four-part structure is derived uniformly from the lower portion of the right hand. There are two notes per half measure; consistently the first lies a semitone below and acts as an appoggiatura to the second. (Compare with the soprano of Example 170b (pp. 191–2), which is not so consistent.)

2. The tenor begins with the doubling of the root in m. 1. Its path is clear until m. 17, where choosing C rather than F would result in parallel octaves with the soprano.

3. Correct voice leading of the tenor from D♭ in the preceding measure calls for C in m. 19; at the same time, continuation in this manner would result in parallel octaves with the bass in mm. 21–22. The solution as shown is perfectly permissible; in general, it is more useful for a reduction to show the true voice leading than to adhere to a specified number of voices at all times.

4. In mm. 13 and 21, the notation ♮6(♭7) in the figured bass refers to the function of the chord contained in these two measures: a diminished-seventh chord built on the leading tone to E♭ (V). The use of the cadential $^6_4$ (with the resulting voice leading from B♮ to C) is the reason for the composer's choice of this spelling rather than C♭.

Solution (continued):

b. Middleground-background sketch

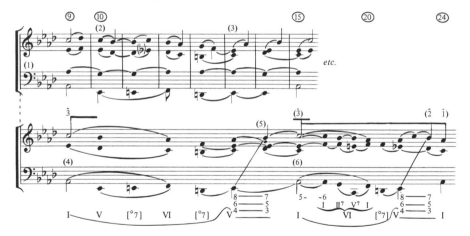

Comments:

1. This first system sets the pattern for an intermediate reduction of the sort suggested in the directions for this group of exercises. This graph (to be completed by the student) presents the material of sketch *a*, translated into analytic notation. In this way we can show in detail some of the decisions that are reflected in the finished solution.

2. After determining the primary tone (clearly C in this case), the next step in analyzing the melody is to indicate, by means of stems, those notes which are structural members of the chords that accompany them. Since only the structural tones are included in the final sketch, these stems are no longer needed there.

3. The series of skips from middle E♭ suggests a compound melody in mm. 13–15. Accordingly, these skips are verticalized in the final sketch. Once we do this, we then see that the F in m. 12 is part of the same inner voice as the E♭ that follows it.

4. The tenor part, mostly routine, has been omitted here.

5. Upon closer examination, we find this ascent from A♭ to be a product of an implied overlapping (look ahead to Chapter 18 and Example 185, p. 220). The true resolution of A♭ downward to G (made explicit in the tenor part) is shown as a small note in parentheses.

6. The background of this passage remains C over A♭ ($\hat{3}$). The descent to $\hat{1}$ is not final and should thus be depicted as a middleground event.

2. Chopin, *Etude in A♭ major*, Op. 25, No. 1

The background in this passage is $\hat{3}$–$\hat{2}$ (see FC, Fig. 40/10). At the middleground level it is complicated by the following: a first-order arpeggiation from E♭, and downward transfer of register at the close.

3. Chopin, *Etude in C minor*, Op. 25, No. 12

Scale degree $\hat{3}$, the primary tone of this piece, undergoes a change of mode in the course of this passage—from $(\flat)\hat{3}$ over I to $\natural\hat{3}$ over I♮, though this does not happen directly. Such mixtures of mode applied to notes of the fundamental structure belong not to the background, but to the first level of middleground (FC, §§102–103, Figs, 28, 30). One way of thinking about this problem is to regard the notes of the fundamental structure as background and the accidentals as middleground; in that way we can justify the use of open notes for both versions of the scale degree in question. Sketch *a* of your solution should begin in the same manner as Example 168 (p. 189). The details of mm. 5–6 may need some comment: there the chord progression should be read as II moving to an altered V over a tonic pedal; melodically we have a middleground statement of scale degree $\hat{2}$ proceeding to $\hat{1}$ on the downbeat of m. 7. What must be recognized is that the soprano's E♭ in m. 6 is an upper neighbor to $\hat{2}$ and *not* a restatement of $\hat{3}$.

4. Bach, *Twelve Short Preludes*, No. 1

This otherwise straightforward four-voice study is complicated by register transfer (the subject of Chapter 18) in three places: (1) the overlappings on the fourth beats of mm. 1 and 2 respectively (that is, the tenor of the third beat, through the upward skip of an octave, becomes the soprano of the fourth beat); (2) the descent of a seventh from G to A over mm. 3–6, which should be read as a registrally transposed second; (3) the compensating upward transfer of middle F in mm. 9–10 (see Chapter 12 and remarks on obligatory register). The primary tone is $\hat{3}$. In sketch *b* of your solution, an unfolding symbol would be an appropriate device for connecting B to F over mm. 7–14.

5. Bach, WTC/I, Prelude 2

Solution (Continue for entire piece.)

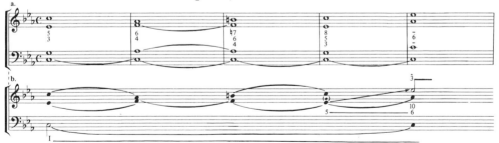

6. Chopin, *Trois nouvelles Etudes*, No. 2

Solution

Though the choralelike texture of this study is what concerns us at present, its formal aspects pertain to Chapter 15. As a hint in interpreting the passage beginning m. 17, G♯ should be thought of in terms of its enharmonic equivalent A♭, and E major should be analyzed as ♭VI instead of ♮V.

15

Musical Form and
Fundamental Structure:
"One-Part" Forms

In this section we begin to explore the relationship between the Schenkerian concept of fundamental structure and musical form as it is commonly discussed. The difference between the two is that the conventional notion of musical form emphasizes matters of surface texture, while the Schenkerian view looks beyond to the deeper aspects of tonal structure. For example, all three pieces cited in Chapter 14 are conventionally classed as one-part forms. At the background level they share the same fundamental structure, showing an overall fundamental line of $\hat{3}$–$\hat{2}$–$\hat{1}$, yet they differ in what happens between the initial $\hat{3}$ and the final $\hat{2}$–$\hat{1}$. Despite the lack of textural contrast within each piece, each one reveals the fundamental structure in a different way; in no case is the term "one-part form" an adequate description by itself.

A common variant of the descent from $\hat{3}$ is the pattern:

$$\hat{3}\text{–}\hat{2} \ \| \ \hat{3}\text{–}\hat{2}\text{–}\hat{1}$$
$$\text{I–V} \qquad \text{I–V–I}$$

The double vertical line denotes an *interruption* (see Chapter 12 and Example 155, p. 168); the pattern as a whole can informally be called the "interrupted $\hat{3}$–$\hat{2}$–$\hat{1}$." Pieces of this type begin with the combined melodic-harmonic motion $\genfrac{}{}{0pt}{}{\hat{3}\text{-}\hat{2}}{\text{I-V}}$, then follow with a second beginning which retraces and completes the opening gesture, perhaps with some elaboration. A suitable illustration is the Chopin *C-major Prelude* (Example 175; review Example 170, p. 191). Though at the deepest structural level one can say that $\hat{3}$ and I remain active through the interruption (Example 175*b*), the more detailed picture (Example 175*a*) can, for practical purposes, serve as a final level of reduction. It must again be mentioned that Schenker understood musical form in a deeper sense than simply to call a piece such as this a "one-part form"—the very existence of the interruption suggests a division into at least two parts.

201

EXAMPLE 175. Chopin, *Prelude in C major*, Op. 28, No. 1

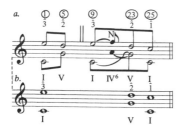

We now turn to some examples in which no interruption takes place. This is the case with the opening prelude of *The Well-Tempered Clavier*, where instead of an interruption we have successive couplings of scale degrees $\hat{3}$ and $\hat{2}$ respectively (Example 176).[1] The term "one-part form" would more aptly apply to this piece. Not so, however, with the Chopin *C-major Etude* (Example 177).[2] As this piece is longer, the contributing factors are more complex, and space permits only the inclusion of the graph here. To summarize, the opening sixteen measures conclude on I rather than V, and with a reassertion of scale degree $\hat{3}$ in the melody. Measures 17–48 continue to prolong $\hat{3}$ (now over VI), and the inverted dominant at the end of m. 48 (harmonizing the upper neighbor to $\hat{3}$, not $\hat{2}$) is clearly felt as a transition rather than a point of rest. Thus the interrupted pattern fails to materialize.

EXAMPLE 176. Bach, WTC/I, Prelude 1

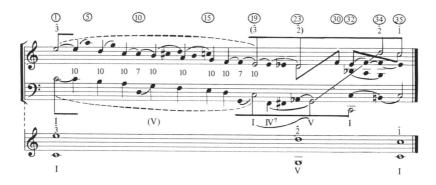

---

1. See FGMA, pp. 36–37; FC, Fig. 49/1. This example happens also to illustrate the principle of obligatory register, introduced together with the concept of interruption in Chapter 12 (again in connection with Example 155). Unlike the Mozart *alla Turca*, the definitive fundamental line in the present example is in the higher rather than the lower of the two registers involved.

2. Schenker presents a more detailed graph in FC, Fig. 130/4. His labeling of the passages from mm. 1–16, 17–48, and 49–79 as a_1, b, and a_2, respectively, shows that he actually viewed the piece as a three-part form.

EXAMPLE 177. Chopin, *Etude in C major*, Op. 10, No. 1

This point of rest (missing in Examples 176 and 177 but present in Example 175) is accomplished by means of the *divider* (*Teiler*), Schenker's term for the chord (normally V) that immediately precedes and defines the interruption. The double vertical line in the graph denotes the actual interruption, while the preceding V harmonizing $\hat{2}$—the divider—makes the interruption possible. The stronger the harmonic motion toward the divider, the more clearly the interruption will be perceived. The raised leading tone F♯ to bass G in m. 6 of the Chopin prelude (Example 170, p. 191) functions toward this end, though the brevity of the passage in relation to the piece as a whole (notice the measure numbering in Example 175) works somewhat against it.

In another Chopin prelude, No. 3 in G major, a combination of factors makes the interruption more apparent (Example 178). First, the well-articulated right hand makes it plain where one musical sentence ends and another is about to begin. Second, the harmonic progression toward the divider is strengthened by the repeated use of the secondary dominant in mm. 7 and 9. In Example 178a we present the first eleven measures of the right hand intact, accompanied by a reduction of the left hand to whole notes. The first measure of the latter is not reduced; the pattern shown there is maintained throughout the piece with only slight variation. What seems at

EXAMPLE 178. Chopin, *Prelude in G major*, Op. 28, No. 3

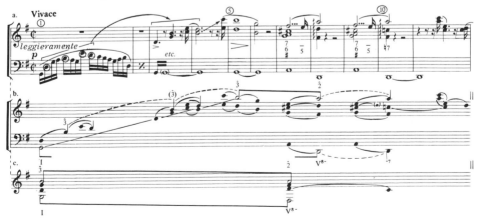

first to be only an accompaniment turns out to be significant thematically: notice how the circled notes in m. 1 are echoed in rhythmic augmentation by the right hand in m. 3.

Example 178*b* is a first reduction in analytic notation. It emphasizes interpretation rather than elimination of detail, with one exception: in the secondary dominant introduced in m. 7 and repeated in m. 9, the F♯ acts as an appoggiatura to E and in the graph is replaced by the latter alone. This is the correct approach in general, even in cases such as this where the duration of the appoggiatura dramatically outweighs that of its resolution. Though the primary tone, $\hat{3}$, is presented in two registers prior to m. 5, the fact that it is the primary tone is not made clear until then. The alignment of Example 178*c* with 178*b* emphasizes the principles of melodic and harmonic prolongation: $\hat{3}$ over I in mm. 1–6, $\hat{2}$ over V in mm. 7–11.

It must be remembered that all of the pieces cited in the present section represent what are commonly called one-part forms. Viewed at the middleground and background levels, these forms often become something else: interrupted patterns such as Example 175 suggest two parts rather than one, while Example 177 tends toward a tripartite structure. On the other hand, Example 176 remains true to one-part form at all structural levels. Further and more varied examples of one-part forms will be found in the exercises.

Exercises

Solutions for this group of exercises should follow the general pattern established for those of the preceding chapter, with a concise middleground-background graph the final goal. Now, however, the first reduction may be in either rhythmic or analytic notation (see Exercise 14/1, p. 195, sketch *a* and the first system under *b*); your choice should depend on the piece and the degree of difficulty posed by surface details. Actually, it would be helpful to sketch at least the beginning of the piece both ways before proceeding to the final graph.

1. Bach, *Twelve Short Preludes*, No. 12

The following, with a fundamental line descending from scale degree $\hat{8}$, qualifies as a one-part form both superficially and structurally (see remarks beginning this chapter). The descent of the fundamental line is paced fairly evenly until it reaches $\hat{5}$; the latter undergoes a relatively lengthy prolongation from mm. 6–12. In contrast, scale degree $\hat{4}$ (last beat of m. 12) is of brief duration. Notice the extensive use of compound melody in both staffs.

Solution (beginning):

   a. First reduction
       Rhythmic notation (meter simplified)
       Analytic notation (barlines optional)

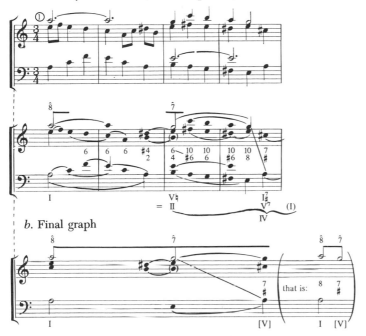

   b. Final graph

2. Bach, *Inventio 8*

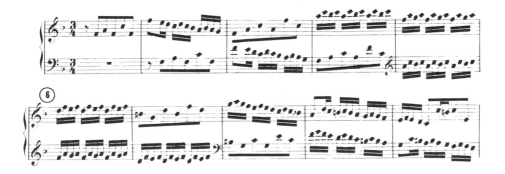

On a small scale, this two-part invention involves two problems to be discussed more specifically in Part Three: namely, problems posed by registral expansion (Chapter 21) and imitative counterpoint. The primary tone, found in its highest register in m. 4, is preceded by an elaborate first-order arpeggiation and is then prolonged in various other ways through m. 20. Tracing the line in this highest register leaves us at scale degree 1̂ in m. 24; harmonically, however, a proper conclusion is not reached until the end of the piece.

Solution (first reduction, beginning):

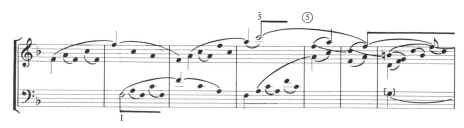

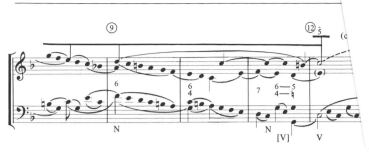

3. Chopin, *Prelude in E minor*, Op. 28, No. 4

As we have emphasized in the text, many pieces conventionally classed as one-part forms have structural divisions pointing to two parts or more—hence the quotation marks for the term. One way for such division to take place is through the interruption (see Example 175); in the present case the interruption is in a descent from $\hat{5}$ rather than $\hat{3}$. Here, after the first prolongation of $\hat{4}$ (mm. 9–12), there is a return to the opening gesture of the piece and a new prolongation of $\hat{5}$. Some questions to be answered are:

1. Why does the initial prolongation of $\hat{4}$ *not* begin with the A in m. 4? (Look at the overall motion, B–A–G♯ in mm. 1–8.)
2. How does the composer's choice of I^6 as support for scale degree $\hat{5}$ lessen the break caused by the interruption? (Look for a connection from the divider, $\frac{\hat{4}}{V^7}$, to the resumption of $\frac{\hat{5}}{I^6}$.)
3. What happens to the fundamental line from scale degree $\hat{3}$ onward?
4. In how many guises do you find the neighbor-note motive B–C–B? (Notice how this motive is reinforced by the extremes of register in m. 17, and that the resolution of the high C in that measure is registrally displaced.)
5. Is the chord in m. 23 spelled according to its function? Explain.

16

Musical Form
and Fundamental Structure:
Two-Part Forms

By its simplest definition, two-part form normally means that there are two sections roughly in balance with each other temporally. The most common two-part form is binary form, represented by the scheme ‖:A:‖:B:‖, or simply AB if there are no repeats. If only the A section is repeated the result is a bar form, typified by many of the chorales cited in Chapter 13. The rounded binary form, ‖:A:‖:BA:‖, comes closer to being a three-part form, and for that reason discussion of it will be deferred to the next chapter.

In exploring the relationship between the formal division inherent in binary form and the Schenkerian notion of fundamental stucture, we begin with two selections from Chapters 9 and 10. These are Handel's *Air in Bb* (Example 179a) and the variation theme from Beethoven's Op. 57 (Example 179b). In the former, the entire A section is occupied with the initial ascent to scale degree $\hat{5}$ while the B section takes the fundamental line from $\hat{4}$ downward. In the latter, the first-order arpeggiation is not completed until well into section B; in the A section the primary tone is represented only by the first note of the arpeggiation, in the larger scheme of things an inner voice. The Beethoven example is also atypical harmonically in that the A section both begins and ends on the tonic; the normal pattern is a progression to V in major keys, to III or V in minor keys.

EXAMPLE 179
    a. Handel, *Leçon in Bb major,* Air

208

b. Beethoven, *Piano Sonata in F minor*, Op. 57, II

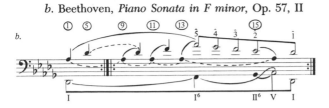

The most characteristic binary forms occur in Baroque instrumental works, particularly movements based on dance forms. The suites of Bach for keyboard and for solo strings are as a group the most useful source; however, these tend to be laden with complexities at the middleground and foreground levels which cannot be completely explored at the present time. The Sarabande from the *First French Suite*, shown with analytic overlay in Example 180*a*, is instructive on several counts. The background structure shares with those in Example 179 the predominance of scale degree $\hat{5}$, and as in those earlier examples the descent from the primary tone takes place during the second half of the movement. Though not central to the topic of this section, the middleground (Example 180*b*) bears examination for its use of unfolded thirds and coupling of registers (review Chapters 11 and 12).

EXAMPLE 180. Bach, *French Suite in D minor*, Sarabande

The descent from $\hat{5}$ is by no means the only type of fundamental line to occur within the context of binary form. Another D-minor Sarabande, from the *Second Suite for Unaccompanied Cello* (Example 181), illustrates how the third of the scale can function as primary tone in a similar situation. In comparing this movement with the preceding example, notice how the harmonic designs differ: in Example 180 the A section moves from I to V under a melodic prolongation of $\hat{5}$, while in Example 181 the opening section progresses instead toward the relative major, allowing scale degree $\hat{3}$ to remain as one of the two tones common to both I and III.

EXAMPLE 181. Bach, *Cello Suite in D minor*, Sarabande

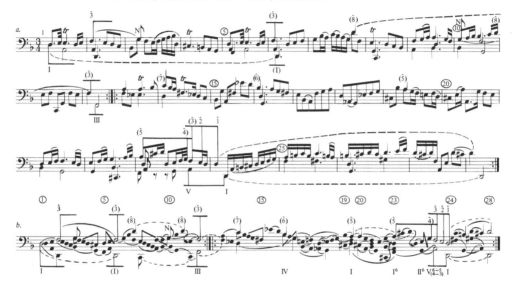

At the same time, the middleground in Example 181 is complicated by a descent from scale degree $\hat{8}$. Although it would be possible to read this descent as the fundamental line, the emphasis given scale degree $\hat{8}$ does not seem sufficient to establish it as the primary tone, especially given the way the opening section is framed by scale degree $\hat{3}$. Another point to consider is that F recurs continually in the same register as an inner voice during those times when the focus of melodic activity is on the upper portion of the scale.

In the Courante from the same suite (Example 182), scale degree $\hat{8}$ is asserted at the very beginning, and it is stressed no less than any of the lower triadic degrees. These facts, combined with a difference in the harmonic plan (motion to V by the end of the first section) make the octave descent convincing as the fundamental line of this movement. Overall, the linear and harmonic outlines fit Schenker's model (see the last part of Chapter 13): a progression from $\hat{8}$ over I to $\hat{5}$ over V, followed by a descent from $\hat{5}$ to $\hat{1}$ over a second arpeggiation of the bass. Moreover, this division in the fundamental structure matches the partitioning of the binary form.

EXAMPLE 182. Bach, *Cello Suite in D minor*, Courante

Exercises

The exercises in this group should take a somewhat more telescoped view than those preceding. Using the format of Examples 180–182, begin by tentatively marking the score with an overlay of the fundamental structure; then proceed to a middleground-background graph.

1. Handel, *Keyboard Suite in E major*, Air

This well-known air is a good, concise example of binary form. However, the relation of foreground to middleground and background makes the piece not quite so simple as it first appears to be. (For example, what do you hear as the main melodic progression from m. 1 through the downbeat of m. 3, despite the higher notes that come at the very beginning? Why is the primary tone $\hat{5}$ and not $\hat{8}$? Hint: Review Chapter 14 and look ahead to Chapter 18 [cover tones].)

2. Bach, *Suite No. 3 for Orchestra in D major*, Air

Despite the repeated use of A as the highest triadic degree, this always happens in the context of a linear progression toward F♯. Consider also the strong initial assertion of F♯ as a melody note, plus the fact that none of the occurrences of A is supported by the tonic triad, and it becomes evident that $\hat{3}$, rather than $\hat{5}$, is the primary tone. In completing the exercise, take into account the continuation of the inner voice, and the number of times the linear progression from A to F♯ is articulated in the descant (its final occurrence, mm. 17–18, is varied through a change of register).

Solution (beginning): (Continue for entire piece.)

3. *Notebook for Anna Magdalena Bach* (anonymous), March

4. Johann Philipp Kirnberger, *Dance Pieces*, Bourrée

5. Johann Mattheson, *Pièces de Clavecin*, Sarabande (F minor)

6. Bach, *Cello Suite in G major*, Menuet II (G minor)

> For the present, this movement should be regarded as a self-contained binary form, though actually it is the middle portion of a large ternary form (see Part Three). Measures 1–4 were the subject of Example 63, p. 70.

7. Corelli, *Sonata da camera a tre*, Op. 4, No. 5, Allemanda

17

Musical Form
and Fundamental Structure:
Three-Part Forms

As in the preceding two sections of the text, our concern here will be not just with the categorization of musical form, but with the relationship of the surface aspects of form to the deeper aspects of fundamental structure. From this point of view, the rounded binary form, ||:A:||:BA:||, can be discussed together with the simple ternary form, ABA or ||:A:|| BA (the latter commonly called "song form"). The distinguishing feature of both rounded binary and ternary forms is the middle, or B, section. This section must differ in some immediately perceptible way from the A sections on either side of it; at the same time, a desire for coherence persuades us that there should be a definable relationship between these two bodies of material.

The fact that a three-part form begins and ends with essentially the same music virtually guarantees that the fundamental structure will be presented intact in the outer portions. This leaves the middle section with the role of reinforcing or enhancing the structural profile rather than just restating it. In some cases this is done straightforwardly through continued prolongation of the primary tone over a tonic harmony moving to the dominant—as in the Haydn and Mozart themes with which we began Part Two, sketched in their entireties in Example 154 (p. 167). Example 155 (p. 168), on the other hand, shows the B section completing the downward coupling of scale degree $\hat{2}$ begun in the opening, over a harmonic progression from III to V.

Predictably, the richer examples of three-part form occur in the music of the nineteenth century, as witness the songs and piano pieces of Schubert, Schumann, and Brahms. One illustration is the intermezzo cited in Example 183. While this piece contains some specific complexities which will be relevant to the next topic (Chapter 18), it also shows clearly what concerns us presently: that is, how the sectional form of a piece is mirrored in the larger tonal structure. The primary tone and its upper neighbor are stated right at the beginning, and it is these two notes which connect the outer and middle sections. Of course, F♯ (5̂) is common to both I and III, the prolonged harmonies in the A and B sections respectively. While the "covering" of this note in the middle section (one of the matters to be discussed in Chapter 18) may temporarily shift attention elsewhere, the emphasis given to its upper neighbor, G, is unequivocal.

EXAMPLE 183. Brahms, *Intermezzo in B minor* Op. 119, No. 1

Another composition in three-part form is given in Example 184. As is the case with many other songs, the extensive use of compound melody is a complication at the foreground level; however the middleground is far simpler than that of Example 183 (which will be discussed in greater detail in Chapter 18). Both works demonstrate how the neighboring tone—in particular, the upper neighbor to the primary tone—tends to be featured in a three-part form. In Example 183, though the middle section continues to prolong the primary tone, its temporary placement in an inner voice makes its upper neighbor more visible by comparison. In Example 184 the corresponding note gets more weight, as it is prolonged over the duration of the section—from the C on the downbeat of m. 25 to the F on the third beat of m. 32. The accompanying prolonged harmony is II[6], though in a larger sense V takes precedence as the harmonic goal of the passage.

EXAMPLE 184. Schumann, *Du Ring an meinem Finger*, from *Frauenliebe und Leben*

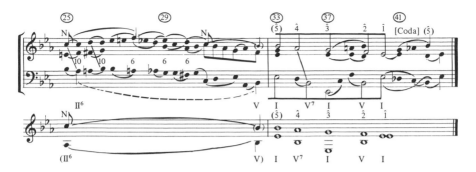

The specific form in both species is ternary, with the first A section twice the length of the second (equivalent therefore to the scheme ‖:A:‖ BA).[1] The two examples show two different ways in which the middle section can be set apart: in the Brahms there is a distinct separation at the sectional boundaries (including a transitional passage at the end of the B section), while in the Schumann there is a tempo change.

As a general trait, we can expect ternary form to show more contrast and more balance between the A and B sections than we find in rounded binary form; indeed, the latter can be considered a three-part form only marginally. Both are involved in the compound (or "large") ternary form (typified by the minuet and trio), and as factors in the evolution of sonata form. These larger forms are among the topics to be discussed in Part Three.

Exercises

For each of these pieces, begin by determining whether its form is ternary or rounded binary, and by informally identifying the fundamental structure. Pay special attention to the role of the middle section: the relationship of its main melodic prolongation(s) to the fundamental line, and that of its main harmonic prolongation(s) to the bass arpeggiation. A graph showing at least two stages of reduction (see Examples 183 and 184) is desirable.

---

1. This description must be qualified as follows: first, the fact that the middle section of Example 183 involves a written-out repeat paralleling that of the opening section. Meanwhile, in Example 184, the opening section is in itself a three-part structure. As shown in Example 184*b*, this section can be divided into three eight-measure progressions from tonic to dominant. The melodic material of the second eight measures does not return in the final section. At the same time, the statement regarding the length of the opening and final sections is exactly true: twenty-four measures for the former, twelve for the latter (owing to the four-measure coda).

1. Schubert, *Ihr Bild*, from *Schwanengesang*

Two special features of this song are the unison writing and mixture of mode, which respectively begin and end the outer sections. Analysis of mm. 1–8 should yield the progression $\frac{\hat{3}-\hat{2}}{\text{I-V}}$ which is continued in the ensuing measures thus: $\frac{\#\hat{3}-\hat{2}-\hat{1}}{\text{V -I}}$. Notice that at no point in the song does the raised form of scale degree $\hat{3}$ have full harmonic support—and for that reason (in addition to the obvious fact that the song is in Bb minor) the flatted form takes precedence structurally.

2. Handel, *Trio Sonata in Bb*, Gavotte

As in any Baroque solo or trio sonata, the bottom staff is intended to be the left-hand portion of a keyboard part (usually doubled by a string or wind instrument). Realization of the figured bass, though not necessary for analytic purposes, may be undertaken for purposes of review and/or performance. The middle section is especially notable in its use of melodic diminutions.

3. Chopin, *Prelude in F♯ major*, Op. 28, No. 13

This prelude is atypical in that it has a fully developed three-part form. It is also noteworthy for its use of cover tones, specifically in the middle and final sections (look ahead to Chapter 18; mm. 29–34 are cited in Example 192). The parallel octaves between the soprano and the top of the left hand enable us to read an implied continuation of the soprano in m. 8, which may be graphed in parentheses. Notice the wealth of detail in this piece: the compound structure of the left hand; the way the meter effectively changes from 6/4 to 3/2 when the right hand drops out in m. 8; the grace note linking the two A♯'s when the right hand reenters. Of larger structural importance is the use of descending motion toward the primary tone, contrary to the rule of prolongation established in Chapters 8–10.

4. Mozart, *Minuet in D major*, K. 94

5. Schumann, *Nachklänge aus dem Theater*, from *Album for the Young*

6. Schumann, *Ich kann's nicht fassen, nicht glauben*, from *Frauenlieben und Leben*

7. Schumann, *Ich grolle nicht*, from *Dichterliebe*

8. Chopin, *Mazurka in G minor*, Op. 67, No. 2

18

Register Transfer and Displacement

As we saw in Chapter 12, and in several subsequent places (Examples 176, p. 202, 180, p. 209, 182, p. 211, and 183, p. 215), it is possible for notes of the fundamental structure and/or their neighboring tones (as in Example 183) to be presented in more than one register. This process, coupling, is obviously one form of register transfer—one that occurs at a level of middleground very close to the background. In contrast the present section will deal with the by-products of register transfer at or near the foreground level. These are precisely the sort of details that give a musical work its individual character; at the same time, such details tend to make the fundamental structure less apparent.[1]

The terms *transfer* and *displacement* are linked by the basic fact that the latter is usually the result of the former. If an inner voice, say the alto in a four-part structure, moves up an octave while the soprano remains stationary, it is likely that the alto will temporarily displace the soprano as the highest voice (Example 185a). Register displacement, as a result of register transfer, can also happen when motion by step is inverted into a seventh (Example 185b) or compounded into a ninth (Example 185c). In addition, a displacement of the soprano can occur simply when an inner voice is doubled

EXAMPLE 185. Examples of Register Displacement

---

1. Relatively simple examples of register transfer, without interpretation in terms of the fundamental structure, were given in Chapter 6.

(Example 185*d*); this can of course be reviewed as a verticalized form of the octave transfer.

Two specific devices involving register transfer and displacement are *overlapping (Übergreifung)* and the *cover tone (Deckton)*. Literally, the first of these is a "reaching over"[2] of an inner voice to a higher position, and can occur either polyphonically or as compound melody (the latter is more frequently the case). The simplest kind of overlapping is shown in Example 186*a*: two descending seconds separated by the interval of a third, yielding a neighbor-note figure as the net effect. Example 186*b* extends this pattern to form an ascending line, while Example 186*c* results in the arpeggiation shown by the stemmed notes.

EXAMPLE 186. Overlapping

There are several features common to every overlapping, as summarized below:

> 1. The role of register transfer is either explicit (Example 187*a*) or can be discerned with the addition of a hypothetical extra voice (Example 187*b*).

EXAMPLE 187. Overlapping

> 2. The succession of notes in the uppermost position alternates among the two or more structural voices in sequence.
> 3. Each voice makes a stepwise descent as it displaces the previous top voice.
> 4. The overlapping process tends to be a foreground event, while the composite top "voice" belongs to the middleground. The latter may conform to one of the patterns in Example 186 or it may be a combination from among these basic types; in either event, it requires interpretation and must be placed in context.[3]

Some relevant passages from the literature are presented in Example 188, together with graphic analyses which, at this juncture, should be self-explanatory.

---

2. This is the translation of *Übergreifung* in FC.

3. Earlier we saw an example of overlapping in the solution to Exercise 12A/1. Here a sequential use of register displacement at the foreground level was used to effect a coupling of registers at the middleground level.

EXAMPLE 188

a. Beethoven, *Fifth Symphony*, I

b. Schubert, *Eighth Symphony*, II

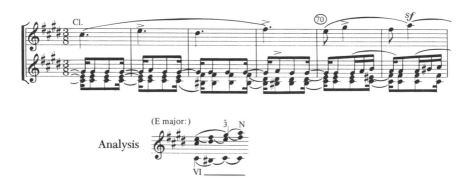

c. Schubert, *Das Wandern*, from *Die schöne Müllerin*

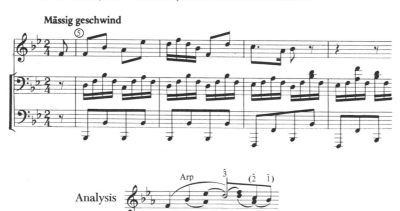

d. Beethoven, *Piano sonata in E♭ major*, Op. 81a ("Les Adieux"), I

The cover tone, like the overlapping, is formed by an upward transfer or doubling of an inner voice and the displacement of the soprano by that voice (Example 185*d*). It differs from overlapping in that the main thread of melodic activity remains with the displaced voice while the voice that does the displacing functions as a "cover," hence its name.[4] The central issue in dealing with cover tones is this: what appears to be a cover tone in a small context may turn out to be more important in a larger one, while conversely what at first appears to be the primary tone of a piece may actually be only a cover tone.

For example, the beginning passage cited in Example 189 contains three voices in the right hand; what appears to be most significant locally is the moving voice centered around D. Either the F♯ or the B above it may be a cover tone depending on what happens in the rest of the movement. If the primary tone is in fact D, then both F♯ and B may be considered cover tones.

EXAMPLE 189. Bach, *French Suite in B minor*, Menuet

---

4. Schenker's own discussion of the cover tone (FC, §267) is perhaps briefer than it should be.

In another instance (Example 190) we find what appears to be a succession of cover tones: first B, then G♯, then E–F♯–G♯.[5] This succession, which takes place over an octave descent prolonging G♯ through a 10–10 linear intervallic pattern, can be called a "covering progression"—a term which seems appropriate even though Schenker does not use it.

EXAMPLE 190. Beethoven, *Piano Sonata in E major*, Op. 109, I

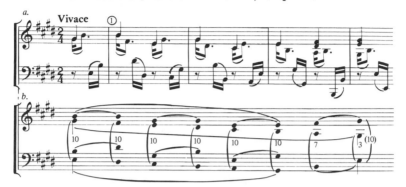

Essentially, like the overlapping, cover tones themselves belong to (or near) the foreground. However, cover tones can very readily impinge on the deeper structural levels. This is because they enter into the very basic decision as to the identity of the primary tone and, consequently, the shape of the fundamental line. A classic case is Chopin's *C-minor Prelude* (Example 191), cited earlier in Example 141c, p. 143. This choralelike piece is in two sections, the second of which is repeated and followed by a single C-minor chord. The A section begins and ends on scale degree $\hat{5}$, over a harmonic progression from I to V. The B section, on the other hand, shows scale degree $\hat{3}$ in the next higher register, prolonged by means of a descending line. The question as to which of these scale degrees is the primary tone can be answered by the following considerations:

1. If $\hat{3}$ were the primary tone, then there would have to be a clear ascending motion to that note. The skip from G to E♭ is insufficient by itself: to be an arpeggiation it would have to pass through C, and it does not.

2. The descent from E♭ in m. 5 is in parallel octaves, resulting from the doubling of an inner voice at the octave above, as shown in Example 191b.

3. It is therefore possible to read the descent from E♭ as a succession of cover tones (that is, a covering progression), below which we find the primary tone G.

5. Schenker (FC, Fig. 90), interprets this passage somewhat differently.

EXAMPLE 191. Chopin, *Prelude in C minor*, Op. 28, No. 20

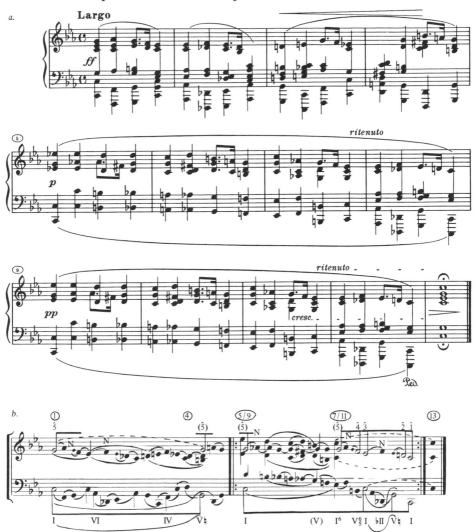

These observations are reflected in the accompanying graph (Example 191*b*), which sets $\hat{5}$ as the primary tone. The covering progression beginning at m. 5 is shown with the aid of downward stems; it consists of the notes Eb–D–C, with a subsidiary line of a third prolonging D (that is, D–C–Bb). This covering progression disappears at the point where the fundamental line begins its descent, although there is a clear reminder of it in the final C-minor chord. Meanwhile, the details of the descent from $\hat{5}$ require some examination. In the passage where this occurs (mm. 7–8, 11–12) $\hat{4}$ has the foreground duration of a sixteenth note. However, it is the fifth above the bass of the $^6_5$, and here, and in general, voice-leading rules of dissonance

resolution take precedence over duration. Scale degree $\hat{3}$ follows $\hat{4}$ immediately, prolonged by its upper neighbor F as suffix. The subsequent $\hat{2}$ is
preceded by its upper neighbor E♭ and supported by the cadential dominant
harmony.

Before proceeding further, it must be mentioned that cover tones need not
occur at the beginning of a piece (as in Examples 189 and 190), nor need they
be as pervasive as in the example just discussed. Also classed as cover tones
are the higher scale degrees that frequently appear at the very end of a work
or movement. In this category belong, for example, the reassertion of scale
degree $\hat{3}$ in the coda of the *Chorale St. Antoni* (Example 151, p. 162) and the
top voice of the rolled chord at the end of the first Chopin prelude (Example
171, p. 193). In both of these cases, by no means unusual, the cover tone has
the same pitch as the primary tone, but it comes after the fundamental line
has completed its descent. The same can be said for both the vocal conclusion
and coda of *Du Ring an meinem Finger* (Example 184, p. 216) and the way
they each return to scale degree $\hat{5}$. A cover tone of this same general type can
also duplicate scale degree $\hat{1}$ at the upper octave: that is, the goal of the
covering progression $\hat{7}$–$\hat{8}$ over the final $\hat{2}$–$\hat{1}$ of the fundamental line. A simple

EXAMPLE 192

a.

b. Chopin, *Prelude in F♯ major,* Op. 28, No. 13 (left hand simplified)

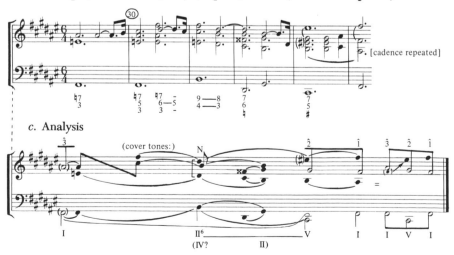

harmonic and contrapuntal model is given in Example 192*a*, followed by a specific passage showing its use, the close of Chopin's *F♯-major Prelude* (Example 192*b*). The cover tone feature that corresponds to the model in Example 192*a* is shown in Example 192*b*. The complete analysis appears in Example 192*c*, and this shows by means of an arrow the projection of an implied inner voice F♯ to a position an octave higher (the transfer of register). This F♯ descends to D♯, which is read as a neighbor note to E♯ in m. 33 (compare *b*). By this elaborate means the descent of the fundamental line A♯–G♯–F♯ is concealed, as it were, by the succession of cover tones that lies above it.

We conclude Part Two with a more detailed look at the Brahms Intermezzo (Op. 119, No. 1) first cited in Example 183, p. 215. Here, in Example 193, we have graphed at *a* the first eight measures of the opening section and at *b* the first fourteen measures of the middle section. Each of these continues with a second segment of equal length, the analysis of which will be left to the student (see Exercise 1).

EXAMPLE 193. Brahms, *Intermezzo in B minor*, Op. 119, No. 1

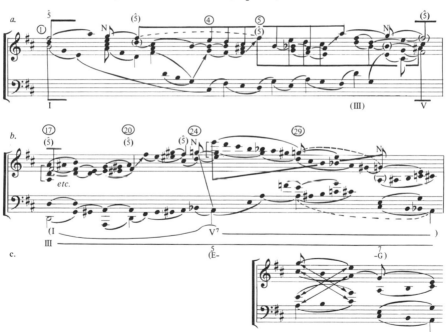

The first problem to be solved is the unusual subposition of thirds in mm. 1–3. These can best be understood by dividing the harmony in each measure into two chords, of which the first is verticalized.

More to the point of the present topic is the extent to which register transfer from an inner voice is used in this piece, in the form of both overlapping and cover tones. In Example 193*a* we see how overlapping can serve to maintain a given note: that is, in the way the second descending line from F♯ begins (m. 5) before the first one has finished. In Example 193*b* the emphasis is on cover tones: first, the motion centering around A (mm. 17–20); second, the descending line from high E (mm. 24–27). Both of these explicitly double an inner voice: the first covers the primary tone, F♯; the second covers and eventually joins with the upper neighbor note G. The latter is then transferred down an octave (mm. 27–29) depicted graphically as a large unfolding. The return of the theme of the middle section at m. 31 (not shown here) coincides with the resolution of the unfolded interval (E–G) to the primary tone F♯ (recall Example 183*b*).

Other aspects of this intermezzo combine with the foregoing to make it an extremely rich source for reflection and comment. The attention given to F♯ and G is carefully balanced between two registers until m. 62, where the fundamental line begins its definitive descent (shown in Example 183*b*); and at the conclusion of this descent we find a covering progression terminating with G–F♯. Looking back at the beginning of the piece and at Example 193*a*, it seems fitting that the notes G and F♯ are the focus of the register transfer leading to the reassertion of F♯ as the primary tone in m. 5.

The qualities of symmetry and balance come through in some smaller details as well. In Example 193*c* we see a double voice exchange (E–G↔G–E and A–C♯↔C♯–A), stated in both the higher and lower registers, with one pair of voices repeated, the other retrograded. This is, of course, a diatonic version of mm. 27–30. Looking back to Example 193*b*, we see that this passage can be analyzed from the standpoint of polyphonic imitation as well as voice exchange: that is, from the covering progression of mm. 24–26 to the alto of mm. 27–28 to the bass of mm. 29–30, and from the bass of mm. 27–28 to the alto of mm. 29–30.

Exercises

In the following pieces or excerpts, identify instances of register transfer and/or displacement, including (but not limited to) specific devices such as overlapping, cover tones, and covering progressions. Since all of these are middleground events, your graph should emphasize that level. This is in contrast to exercises for Chapters 15–17, where emphasis was on the background structure.

1. Brahms, *Intermezzo in B minor*, Op. 119, No. 1

Following Example 193, analyze a) mm. 9–16 and b) mm. 31–42. Refer to the score and graph in Example 183.

2. Bach, WTC/I, Prelude 7

3. Haydn, Symphony No. 101, III

4. Schubert, *Valses sentimentales*, Op. 50, No. 19

5. Handel, *Keyboard Suite in G major*, Air

The emphasis on scale degree $\hat{3}$ suggests that it is the primary tone, despite the involvement of higher triadic degrees from the very outset. The two-measure opening theme begins with an initial descent from $\hat{5}$ to $\hat{3}$, which is followed almost immediately by the introduction of scale degree $\hat{8}$ as a cover tone. At the foreground level, the composer's use of the incomplete neighbor note merits discussion, particularly as it relates to the third beat of m. 1.

Part Three

Reductions of Larger Dimension

19
Review and Refinement: Structural Levels and Linear Progressions

We begin this chapter with a reaffirmation of the basic Schenkerian principle introduced early in Part Two: that various aspects of large-scale structure are often mirrored in the small, and that seemingly small gestures can turn out to be more significant than they first appear to be.

Already we have seen one remarkable illustration in the slow movement of Beethoven's Op. 57 piano sonata (Example 147, p. 155), where at the close of each half of the variation theme (mm. 7–8 and 15–16) the descending fifth in the bass is filled in by step. The filling-in of a skip by stepwise motion is one of the basic types of melodic diminution (see Examples 1 and 2, pp. 8–9), and it is possible, as here, for the bass temporarily to assume a melodic role. The unusual feature of this particular example, however, is the degree to which the diminution is emphasized. First, its rhythm is unique within the context of the variation theme: that is, the dotted-sixteenth/thirty-second-note figure appears in the bass at the cadence points and nowhere else. Second, the diminution occurs not before, but after the downbeat of each closing measure; the arrival of the bass on the tonic is delayed as a result, and the listener's attention is drawn to it all the more.

Of course, there is a reason for drawing attention to the descending fifth at the foreground level: it replicates the fundamental line. Another noteworthy example, also from the piano music of Beethoven, involves the "Lebewohl" motive that begins the introduction to the "Les Adieux" sonata, Op. 81a, cited in Chapter 18 (Example 188*d*, p. 223). The motion G–F–E♭ prolongs G at the outset; if G (scale degree $\hat{3}$ in the key of E♭) turns out to be the primary tone, then this descent from G to E♭ can be read as a replica of the fundamental line. That G ($\hat{3}$) is the primary tone seems indeed to be the case, owing to the way in which G, its upper neighbor A♭, and the stepwise descent

of a third from G, are emphasized variously throughout the first movement.[1]
To illustrate in part, we cite the opening of the Allegro (Example 194).
Comparing the score, *a*, with the reduction, *b*, we see, first, a middleground-
level reinforcement of the neighbor-note motion A♭–G (mm. 17–21), followed
several measures later by a stepwise descent from G (m. 30) to E♭ (m. 35).[2]
However, the nonconclusive harmony supporting E♭ causes us to look
further, to the temporary resting place on F (m. 40). The larger melodic
progression over these measures (mm. 30–40) can thus be expressed as
G(–F–E♭)–F: an incomplete statement of the descending third containing a
complete statement as subordinate.

EXAMPLE 194. Beethoven, *Piano Sonata in E♭ major*, Op. 81a ("Les Adieux"), I

Finally, there is the descending third formed by two conjoined seconds in
m. 41, marked by N.B. in Example 194*b*. This last statement of the
descending third—in an inner voice, transposed, without internal diminutions
—clearly takes place at the foreground level. By comparison, the earlier
statement in the original key (mm. 30–35) is middleground, but still close to
the surface; the larger, incomplete motion G–F (mm. 30–40) represents a
deeper level of middleground. The way in which this motive is announced at

1. Schenker's graph in FC, Fig. 119/7, of the introduction and exposition, is relevant to this
   aspect of the work.
2. The space between mm. 21 and 30 gives considerable attention to the B♭ above G (cover
   tone), thereby foreshadowing the role of B♭ in the second theme.

the opening of the piece (recall Example 188*d*) could well lead one to expect that it might have a larger structural significance. By something more than mere chance, this expectation is fulfilled, thus relating large and small.

The reflection of the fundamental line at the middleground level (recall Chapter 7, "Fundamental Structure in Thematic Statements") is a specific variety of *linear progression*. As the term implies, a linear progression is a stepwise succession of notes. Although the fundamental line is always descending, a linear progression may occur in either direction, and need not span the same interval as the fundamental line. Normally each note of a linear progression is harmonized. This last fact distinguishes the linear progression from the stepwise diminution, and places it generally within the realm of the middleground. (Diminutions, of course, are always foreground.)

Linear Progressions in the Upper Voices

Every linear progression in an upper voice is prolongational; the general rule (recall Chapter 8) is that prolongational lines, whether ascending or descending, prolong their topmost structural note. Recall also that "structural" means, essentially, that the note in question is in agreement with the underlying harmony. What this means, in turn, is that the interval spanned by a linear progression will be a component of a harmonic function relevant to the context. The test for the validity of a linear progression rests, therefore, on whether the interval between its starting and ending points agrees with the harmonic goal of the passage. Linear progressions that replicate the fundamental line can readily be seen as fulfilling this requirement (as for example the descending fifth in Example 145, p. 154); however, a linear progression may also legitimately span an interval of a different size whose significance is more local, as indicated above.

The latter situation is depicted in Example 195, where in two instances a stepwise descent of a sixth is accompanied by a harmonic progression from tonic to dominant. The passage graphed at *a* shows this happening at the foreground level (the score for the excerpt can be found in Exercise 9/3, p. 152), while at *b* the phenomenon is middleground in scope; of the two, only the latter can properly be called a linear progression. The schematic[3] shown at *c* applies equally to both passages (the difference in structural level notwithstanding), and illustrates Schenker's point (see FC, §203) that linear progressions in the upper voices actually involve motion at a deeper level from one voice to another.

Although, as remarked above, linear progressions usually prolong the topmost note, in certain situations a progression may best be regarded as a

---

3. This term can be used to refer to any graph that presents only the most essential features of a passage or composition.

EXAMPLE 195

a. Beethoven, *Piano Sonata in F minor*, Op. 2, No. 1, I

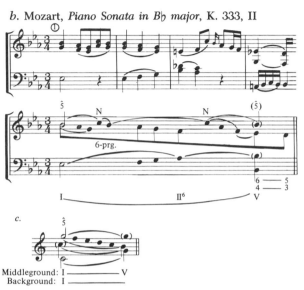

b. Mozart, *Piano Sonata in B♭ major*, K. 333, II

prefix-type prolongation of the goal note of the progression. Example 265 (p. 315) presents an instance. There the fifth-progression that begins on C in m. 9 has as its goal F in m. 19. This F, which is $\hat{1}$ locally, represents the primary melodic tone $\hat{5}$. As a component of the fundamental line it therefore takes precedence over the head note of the linear progression, C. In general, determination of the priority of head note or tail note of a linear progression is not arbitrary, but depends upon the role of the progression in the middleground and background levels. Ultimately, middleground melodic and harmonic structures adjust to fit the background, either explicitly or implicitly, since it is the background structure which governs the entire composition.

Linear Progressions in the Bass

Linear progressions in the bass are fundamentally different from those in the upper voices. Schenker, however, labeled both alike by the word *progression* (Zug), prefixed by the size of the interval spanned. The compound word in German is succinct and convenient to use, although its English equivalent is less so. A linear progression of a sixth, for example, would be labeled *Sextzug* in German, while in English it would be called a sixth-progression. When used as a label in a graph, this expression is abbreviated to 6-prg., following the practice in FC. Such labeling is useful, though not absolutely necessary.

With respect to linear progressions in the bass, the crucial distinguishing factor is that the interval spanned by such a progression cannot correctly be verticalized under normal circumstances. A look at what is probably the most common linear bass progression, the descending fourth, will demonstrate why this is so (Example 196).[4] As we see here, the motion from C down to G supports a harmonic progression from I to V♮, while the intervening harmonies derive their strength from the downward pull of the bass line.[5] In the alternative form of the tonic–dominant progression, the ascending fifth, this downward pull obviously does not exist—although, as in the bass line of Example 195*b*, such a lack can be compensated for by a change of register. In

EXAMPLE 196. Chopin, *Etude in C minor*, Op. 10, No. 12 (left hand simplified)

----

4. A complete analysis of this composition appears in FGMA, pp. 54–60; an essentially similar but less detailed graph of this particular passage is given in FC, Fig. 73/1.
5. In this regard it is interesting to note that the word *Zug* incorporates the notion of "pull" or "thrust," a connotation which is lost in translation.

either case, it can be seen that while the tonic and dominant *notes* can coexist within a single vertical, the harmonies which they support cannot. Thus the difference between the two main categories of linear progression, upper voice and bass, resides in the simple fact that the bass supports, while the upper voices are the ones supported.

Dissonant and False Linear Progressions

Earlier, in discussing linear progressions in the upper voices, we mentioned that as a rule the interval spanned by a linear progression should be in agreement with the harmonic goal of the passage in question, and that a linear progression spans an interval between two notes of a single harmony. If we include the dominant seventh in the class of basic harmonies, as we have done thus far, it follows then that a linear progression can span a tritone or a seventh as well as one of the triadic intervals. These two additional classes of interval, because of their special properties, merit special attention.

Examples of stepwise lines spanning tritones (specifically in the form of diminished fifths) can be found in previously cited passages: in the descant of Example 194, mm. 17–20 (p. 236) and in Example 148, mm. 15–18 (p. 160) (represented alternatively as an unfolding in Example 149). Another instance similar to the latter can be found in the solved Sample Exercise 8B/1 (p. 146). All of these are at or near the foreground level, and thus their status as linear progressions is at best questionable.

A true middleground progression of a diminished fifth is depicted in Example 197. The excerpt cited at *a* covers the distance from the last chord of the A section of a rounded binary form,[6] through the entire B section, up to the resumption of the opening (A) material in m. 49. Over the length of the passage, through m. 48, we can trace an ascending diminished fifth-progression that begins in the "alto" voice of m. 32 and changes register in m. 33. That this progression originates in an inner voice and concludes in the descant reinforces what we have earlier mentioned as a basic attribute of linear progressions in the upper voices: namely, that the interval of progression is actually an interval between two different structural voices.[7] (In the schematics given in Example 195c and 197c, the stemming of the starting and ending points of the linear progressions is intended to reflect this fact.) Example 197 also hints at another matter of concern: the capacity of the

---

6. This rounded binary form becomes, in turn, the outer portions of a large ternary form (see Chapter 23). Consideration of the scherzo and trio as a whole led to our designation of $\hat{3}$ (and not $\hat{5}$) as the primary tone.

7. Schenker's statement on the subject (FC, §203) is as follows: "The descending linear progression always signifies a motion from the upper to the inner voice; the ascending linear progression denotes a motion from the inner to the upper voice."

interval of a second to be transformed via register transfer into a seventh, and conversely the possibility that an interval presented as a seventh may in reality be an inverted second. In the graph at *b*, the beamed third-progression A–G–F♯ in the descant participates in the same change of register as does the diminished fifth-progression that begins in the inner voice. The interval A–G is consequently expressed as a seventh rather than a second.

EXAMPLE 197. Beethoven, *Piano Sonata in D major*, Op. 28, II

The likelihood that a seventh may in fact be a registrally transposed second extends to those situations where the seventh is filled in by stepwise motion. In such cases the line spanning the seventh must be reinterpreted as an expanded form—or *composing-out (Auskomponierung)*—of a single step.[8] The opening of Mozart's *G-minor Symphony*, K. 550 (Example 198) provides an illustration. In Example 198*b* we present three interpretations of the melody of mm. 1–9 given at *a*. As can be seen, reading the descending

8. The composing-out of a second may also be accomplished by the stepwise motion of a ninth, as in the bass of Example 194, mm. 17–20.

foreground lines from B♭ (mm. 3–5) and A (mm. 7–9) at face value does not yield a satisfactory result, since the intervals B♭–C and A–B♭ are not components of the underlying harmonies. The interpretation offered at 2 translates the sevenths into seconds, suggesting that B♭ is the primary tone of the passage. This, however, is not in accord with the large-scale reading of the entire passage, shown in Example 198c, where D is clearly the primary tone. Part 3 of Example 198b shows the correct solution: The upward skips of sixths, here represented as downward skips of thirds, are consonant skips; the motion by second (seventh) is entirely secondary.

EXAMPLE 198. Mozart, *Symphony in G minor*, K. 550, I

The graph in Example 198c uses one set of slurs for the consonant skips and another for the succession of seconds expressed as sevenths. The sevenths arise through the motion which returns from the consonant skips to the main components of the beamed descending line. Viewing the passage as a whole (review the score at a), we find that the notes D, C, and B♭ continue their stepwise progression through F♯, with a change of register in m. 9. (The continuation of this progression without the registral change is shown by the notes in parentheses, which happen actually to be present in the full score through doubling.) The result is a linear progression of a sixth (sixth-progression) at the middleground level.[9] Unlike the foreground descents of a seventh, this is a true linear progression, whose interval (the sixth D–F♯) is contained in the goal harmony V. The reassertion of scale degree $\hat{5}$ at the end of the passage explicitly presents the interval spanned by the linear progression—that is, D–F♯—within a single vertical. The essential nature of the linear progression—that it exists as a bridge between two structural voices—is thereby emphasized. In fact, one can say that a linear progression prolongs, not just its starting or ending note, but the interval between the two.

Example 199 is more to the point, since here the progression of a seventh (E–F) takes place at the middleground level, and is thus more likely to be confused with a true linear progression. This progression, a displaced neighbor-note formation, is a *false* (or illusory) linear progression (FC,§§205–7), a face that is made clear when the voice "corrects itself" registrally in m. 20, thus bringing the neighbor note F (m. 21) back into the same octave as the opening E. The result is an octave doubling of the neighbor note between voice and piano.

EXAMPLE 199. Brahms, *Es hing der Reif*, Op. 106, No. 3

---

9. This is shown with far less detail in FC, Fig. 89/3.

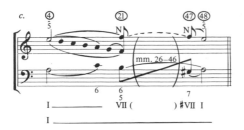

Regarding the details of this false linear progression, some remarks are in order. In the first reduction (Example 199*b*) we have drawn attention to the sequential use of two types of diminution: the consonant skip and the neighbor note. The latter derives special significance due to its importance at the deeper structural levels. Notice also that the first appearance of the neighbor note, on the motivically important pitch F, lies a sixth above the tonic, and forecasts the succession of vertical sixths in the outer voices that accompanies the descending line. A telescoped view of mm. 4–25 is shown in the schematic at *c*, which in addition shows how the conclusion of the passage connects with the onset of the recapitulation (mm. 47–48, not shown in Example 199*a*). The intervening measures (26–46) are not shown, since they contain a complicated prolongation not relevant to the present topic.

Although there is some question as to whether there is such a thing as a genuine linear progression of a seventh (as opposed to the false progression delineated in Example 199), Schenker does allow for its existence (FC, § 215).[10] In his discussion, Schenker makes the point that in a true seventh-progression, the "harmonic intervals" within the seventh (the fifth and third, particularly the latter) are emphasized along with the outer notes. (Clearly, Schenker is here invoking the concept of harmonic relevance—something which we have emphasized throughout this discussion.) The least contro-vertible instance of a seventh-progression is a descending line prolonging scale degree $\hat{4}$ (as neighbor or passing note to $\hat{3}$) over a harmonically prolonged dominant. Such an instance occurs in a passage cited by Schenker (FC, Fig. 62/4), from the development section of the "Les Adieux" sonata. This passage, graphed by Schenker in rhythmic notation, is shown in analytic notation in Example 200. (The components of sonata form wil be discussed in Chapter 21; for the present, compare Example 200 with the opening of the exposition cited in Example 194, p. 236.) What makes the linear progression in this example especially convincing is the fact that much of the stepwise motion takes place in the form of unaccompanied whole notes (see mm. 73–74, 77–78, 81–82, 85–86).

---

10. At the same time, Schenker's remarks elsewhere (FC, §177; see also Oster's footnote *13), shed some doubt as to how deeply Schenker believed in the seventh-progression as a true linear progression.

EXAMPLE 200. Beethoven, *Piano Sonata in E♭ major*, Op. 81a ("Les Adieux"), I

Exercises

The first three exercises in this section should be quite easy to complete. The remaining exercises, however, become more challenging to the analyst and require special attention. We suggest that barlines be included in the first sketch, but omitted from the second.

1. Mendelssohn, *String Quartet in D major*, Op. 44, No. 1, III

While sketching the complete two-phrase segment given here, consider whether both phrases present a linear progression in the upper voice.

2. Mozart, *Symphony in D major*, K. 385, II

Watch out for m. 5 in reading the linear formation in the upper voice.

3. Tchaikovsky, *Romeo and Juliet, Overture Fantasy*

The rhythm of the chordal voices above the bass is simpler than in the complete and elaborate orchestral version. The analytic graph should show clearly the melodic structure of the upper voice and the line that descends in the alto part below the upper voice (played by the horn). Is this a linear progression?

4. Beethoven, *Second Symphony*, II

A solution for mm. 52–55 is given below the passage to be analyzed. The unfoldings in mm. 54–55 of this sketch provide a hint for the analysis of the music that follows.

5. Mozart, *Symphony in C major*, K. 551, I

This passage occurs near the beginning of the development section of the first movement. (See Chapter 21.) It contains two linear formations in the upper voice: one that ends in m. 139 and a second that begins at that point. In reading the second one, pay particular attention to the change of foreground pattern that begins at m. 145. This signals a change in the progression of the upper voice.

6. Bach, *Inventio 1 in C major*

After analyzing this passage, consider the opening music of the invention as a supplementary but related exercise. What special kind of linear progression occurs in the upper voice over the first three measures?

7. Bach, soprano aria from Cantata 61, *Nun komm der Heiden Heiland*

In this more difficult passage implied notes and register transfer play a significant role in the determination of linear progression. (Do not overlook the soprano clef.)

20
Review and Refinement: Unfolding, Register Transfer, Overlapping, Motivic Structures

Register Designations

In the remainder of this section it will be convenient, if not essential, to be able to specify the precise register in which certain pitches occur—especially those involved in register transfers. While there are many systems of registral designation in use, we have chosen the system employed by Schenker (for example, in FGMA), to coincide with his published analyses.

A summary of the system is provided in Example 201. As can be seen, each octave is demarcated by a pitch of type C. Reading from left to right, every pitch from the C notated in the sixth space below the bass staff (contra C) up to the next C is written as a capital letter followed by the subscript 1. From C on the second leger line below the staff (great C) up to C in the second space, every pitch is written as a capital letter with no subscript or superscript. From C in the second space up to middle C, lower-case letters without subscript or superscript are employed. Beginning with middle C (whether notated on the leger line above the bass staff or on the leger line below the treble staff), each octave is designated by a lower-case letter followed by a superscript. It is this range which will be of greatest use in the material that follows.

EXAMPLE 201. Register Designations

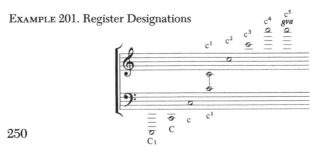

In the earlier parts of this book, capital letters without subscripts or superscripts were used to name pitches in a general way, without designating a particular register of occurrence. We will continue to use this method whenever specific register is not pertinent to the discussion. If there is ever a possibility of confusion with the registral designation for pitches in the second bass octave (from great C up to C in the second space (c)), the word *bass* will be inserted to indicate that the bass register is referenced, not just the letter name. For example, "bass D" means D on the third line in the bass clef.

Example 202 gives some registral designations for pitches notated in treble and bass clefs, so that the reader can see how the system is applied. For example, E♭ in the fourth space of the treble clef is designated e♭², since it lies within the octave governed by c².

EXAMPLE 202. Sample Registral Indications

Unfoldings of Small Scale

The unfolding as a type of prolongation was first introduced in Chapter 11. It is taken up again here in greater detail, since it occurs in many different ways and has many different functions in tonal compositions. An example from a familiar piece will serve to reintroduce the concept of unfolding.

Example 203 shows the first phrase of this famous aria sung by Tamino. It begins with the skip from b♭¹ to g². From g² there is then a stepwise descent back to b♭¹, and this comprises the first unfolding, labeled (1) in Example 203*b*. Specifically, the interval unfolded is the sixth G–B♭ above the bass E♭, composed out by a complete stepwise, diatonic motion. In the fourth measure of the excerpt, as the bass changes to B♭, b♭¹ in the upper voice is led to a♭¹, then skips out to f². From this note there is an unfolding in to a♭¹, again by step, paralleling the first unfolding. Finally, in the last measure of the excerpt, a♭¹ in the upper voice is led to g¹, in accord with normal resolution of the dissonant seventh. Since the upper component of the unfolding, f², cannot be left hanging, as it were, an appropriate implied resolution is shown in the sketch at *b*. This implied e♭² is, of course, the first note of the very next vocal phrase (not shown).

EXAMPLE 203. Mozart, *Dies Bildnis ist bezaubernd schön*, from *Die Zauberflöte*

At the middleground level over the span of the phrase it is clear that the three foreground unfoldings prolong a descending third-progression in the upper part (g²–f²–e♭²), accompanied by another descending third-progression (b♭¹–a♭¹–g¹). Foreground unfoldings are often in the service of linear progressions in this manner, as will be seen in subsequent examples.

Notation of the unfolding was described in Chapter 11. The endpoints of the unfolding are supplied with stems in reverse directions, the upper note receiving the down stem. A beam then connects the initial and final stems. In the case of the composed-out (stepwise) unfolding, the beam is broken so as to leave the stepwise motion intact, as in Example 203. Reversal of stem direction permits double stemming to show middleground formations, also shown in Example 203*b*, whenever this is desirable. Double stemming is not obligatory, however, but depends upon the context in which the unfolding occurs and what middleground motion is to be shown.

Because an unfolding is a horizontalization of a voice-leading intervallic succession, we rarely have occasion to deal with a single unfolded interval. Rather, unfoldings usually come in pairs, triples, quadruples, and so on, to form longer prolongational patterns. Thus, in Example 203 the three unfoldings represent a horizontalization of this vertical succession:

$$g^2 \quad f^2 \quad e\flat^2$$
$$b\flat^1 \quad a\flat^1 \quad g^1$$

Both voices of an unfolded interval succession may move by step, one voice may remain stationary while the other moves by step, or one voice may move by skip. In either case the voices proceed in accord with the rules of voice leading. If an analysis presents a series of unfoldings that violate principles of tonal voice leading, then it must be incorrect. An example would be a succession of unfolded perfect fifths or octaves.

The tritone and the augmented sixth are the only dissonant intervals that can be unfolded. An unfolded second is illogical, since a horizontal second is either a neighbor note or passing note formation. And a horizontal seventh commonly represents a change of octave of one of its members (register transfer).

A further and important limitation on unfoldings is the following: each component voice of the unfolding pattern must have its own complete and coherent progression and must have a clear structural role at the foreground and middleground levels.

Example 204 employs analytic notation to illustrate in schematic form typical unfoldings and certain common ramifications. Before discussing this example, it is appropriate to ask in what way a series of unfoldings differs from a bilinear compound melody. The answer is that a bilinear compound melody is a type of melodic structure characteristic of an entire work, as in many of Bach's compositions. An unfolding series, on the other hand, is only one of several prolongational features in a work. The distinction will become clear in the musical examples that follow.

EXAMPLE 204. Some Characteristic Unfoldings

a. basic pattern
b. unfolded 6ths
c. unfolded 3rds
d. simultaneous completion
e. with register transfer: a^2 replaces a^1
f. basic pattern
g. with register transfer f^2 replaces f^1
h. further interpretation of *g*

i. basic pattern
j. unfolding between soprano and alto
k. elaboration of *j*
l. one voice skips
m. unfolded version
n. unfolding between bass and tenor
o. 3rds may be read incorrectly

Example 204*a* gives a basic and simple succession consisting of parallel sixths between the two upper voices. At *b* these intervals are unfolded and shown in analytic notation. The sixths are changed to thirds at *c* and unfolded. Now the upper voice forms the line E–D–C, instead of C–B–A as at *b*. At *d* we see two unfoldings, from E in to C and from B out to D. Here, however, the voices end simultaneously with C over A instead of the horizontalized C down to A as at *c*. The possibility of mixing horizontal and vertical modes of occurrence within the unfolding pattern greatly enriches its musical potential.

Special attention is directed to Example 204*e*. There the unfolding begins as in the previous two illustrations, but ends in a radically different way: the lower component of the unfolding completes itself not on a^1, as before, but an octave higher, on a^2, an instance of register transfer combined with unfolding.

Example 204*f* shows a new basic pattern, one which involves the augmented fourth dissonance. This dissonance is highlighted by the register transfer of F at *g*, with f^2 replacing f^1. Since these schematic examples are so short, they are subject to a variety of interpretations with respect to some imaginary middleground structure. Example 204*h* shows one way in which the previous example *g* might be interpreted: the unfolding prolongs the interval C–E. We have not taken the further step of determining which of those two notes is primary at the middleground level.

A final basic pattern is shown at *i*, this one involving three different types of intervals: the perfect fifth, the diminished fifth, and the minor third between the two upper voices. At *j* is a series of three unfoldings between those voices, clearly projecting the descant motion g^2–f^2. A more elaborate situation is presented at *k*, where each unfolding is supplied with a different kind of diminution. In particular, notice that the consonant skip attached to the descant f^2 does not alter that note's role in the unfolding pattern.[1]

Although many unfoldings are horizontalizations of stepwise progressions, it is possible for an unfolding pattern to include a skip in one of the component voices, as illustrated in Example 204*l*. There the alto skips from E to G, and the same motion occurs in the unfolded version shown at *m*. The soprano voice, however, moves by step. In general, if both voices skip or if there are many skips involved in a pattern that comprises two voices, it probably should not be read as an unfolding succession, but as some other type of prolongation. The experienced analyst will have no difficulty in making an appropriate decision in such cases.

One tends to think of unfoldings as occurring only in the upper voices. However, there are many beautiful instances of unfoldings in the lower parts. Example 204*n* offers a hypothetical series of unfoldings of that type. It begins

---

1. In addition to the unfolding symbol, the slur has been used in Example 204*j* to connect the arpeggiated and passing notes more effectively, a useful procedure in a more complicated analytic sketch.

with an unfolding from bass c up to tenor g. The next bass note, d, which is approached via the chromatic passing note c♯, then unfolds up to tenor f, which is retained as bass B♭ enters. The voice-leading pattern then continues note against note.

Finally, just as there are false linear progressions (Chapter 19), there are false unfoldings. The pattern given in regular notation at the beginning of Example 204*o* might be read as a series of unfolding thirds. However, this would be misleading, in the sense that it is incorrect. In a true unfolding, both components have linear continuity. But in the example at hand only the lower component completes itself as C–D–E (against the exchanging bass motion). The thirds are formed by consonant upward skips, which exist at the extreme outer surface of the foreground and do not create a continuous pattern. Were they true structural thirds there would be some coherent terminal element, the lack of which is indicated by the question mark at the end of Example 204*o*.

Two musical examples will serve to indicate the various prolongational roles that unfoldings carry out in tonal music. The first of these, Example 205, from the end of the last of Bach's *Three-Part Inventions*, illustrates the role of unfoldings in prolonging the descent of the fundamental line. At the end of m. 31 the unfolding from g² down to b¹ takes place, and this is answered by the unfolding from a♯¹ out to f♯² in the next measure. This F♯ is the head note of a subsidiary linear progression attached to scale degree $\hat{2}$ of the fundamental line, which enters in the penultimate measure (m. 37). Before f♯² progresses to e² in m. 36, however, it unfolds down to d² on the first beat of m. 34. This large unfolding, f♯²–d², is answered in mm. 35 and 36 by the unfolding from c♯² out to e². The latter note is the next component of the linear progression from f♯², as indicated by the beam. Still further unfoldings at the foreground level in mm. 36 and 37 prolong the descending linear progression in the upper

EXAMPLE 205. Bach, *Sinfonia 15 in B minor*

voice, accompanied by parallel unfoldings in the lower parts. Thus, the unfoldings are attached to the middleground linear progression in each case and are elements of the foreground—even the large unfolding f♯²–d². (The large-scale arpeggiation shown in the sketch beginning in m. 33 will not be discussed here since it is not germane to the present topic. See Example 30, p. 30.)

In considering Example 206 it will be advantageous first to examine the schematic graphs at c and d, which show the regular pattern that underlies the elaborate music of this passage. The simplest version is that shown at d, which comprises a linear intervallic pattern following the 10–7 paradigm. At c the vertical thirds of the upper voices of d are unfolded, with inward and

EXAMPLE 206. Chopin, *Nocturne in C minor*, Op. 48, No. 1

outward directions in alternation. Example 206*c* also interprets the series of unfoldings analytically, to show the descending linear progression g^2–f^2–eb^2, which controls the last three unfoldings. The first unfolding, from ab^2 in to f^2, is in the service of the neighbor note a♭.

The analytic sketch in Example 206*b* shows how the unfoldings are stretched out in an improvisational manner characteristic of Chopin, with expanded passing notes filling in the first and third thirds. A further complication occurs in mm. 2–3, where the head note of the second unfolding, eb^2, connects downward to c^2 through the descending passing note d^2 as it completes the unfolding out to g^2.

Unfoldings of Larger Scale

In the previous section, unfoldings of small scale were discussed. The term *small scale* is applied to an unfolding that occupies a relatively short duration. Each of the unfoldings in the examples of the preceding section (with one exception, to be mentioned below) is of that type. A *series* of unfoldings of small scale, however, may occupy a relatively long time span, as in Example 206 (Chopin). The single large unfolding shown in the previous examples is that in Example 205 (Bach), where $f\sharp^2$ at the fermata in m. 32 unfolds inward to d^2 two measures later on the downbeat of m. 34.

Example 207 shows an unfolding of moderate scale as a prominent feature of an opening theme. The primary tone c^2 presents itself unequivocally and is furnished with consonant skips above and below. This is followed by the dramatic leap down to e^1 at the end of m. 1 and the motion from e^1 to f^1 via the neighbor note g^1 in m. 2. With f^1 in m. 2 the unfolding begins, terminating on d^2, as indicated in the analytic sketch in Example 207*b*. The unfolding is then completed with the upper component moving from d^2 to c^2 in m. 3, while the lower component remains stationary on f^1.

EXAMPLE 207. Mozart, *Piano Sonata in C major*, K. 330, II

Example 208, from Bach, shows an unfolding that spans some four measures. It begins with f♯^{1} in m. 16 and ends with d♯^{2} on the second beat of m. 19. The second unfolding in the series is from e^1 in m. 20 out to g^1 in the same measure. The definitive setting of g^1 does not occur, however, until m. 21, as shown by the stem, since there g^1 is supported by the dominant of III.

EXAMPLE 208. Bach, *Sinfonia 15 in B minor*

Example 208c, a schematic, shows the basic voice leading that underlies this rather complicated series of two unfoldings. The entire passage lies within the control of the mediant harmony, and the upper voice consists of a complete neighbor-note figure, f♯^{1}–g^1–f♯^{1}. Example 208d shows how the two upper voices are horizontalized, with f♯^{1} unfolding out to d♯^{2}, completed by the unfolding from e^1 out to g^1.

Since the analytic sketch in Example 208b shows an ascending stepwise progression that connects f$\sharp^1$ (m. 16) with d$\sharp^2$ (m. 19), the question may arise as to why this is not correctly regarded as a linear progression, rather than an unfolding. There are several reasons for this, but the most important is that the terminus, d$\sharp^2$, is not a stable pitch within the controlling harmony, III. This is clearly apparent in the basic voice leading of Example 208c, where D$\sharp$ is located within the vertical $\sharp$6. Thus, regarded as a linear progression, the melodic structure from f$\sharp^1$ to d$\sharp^2$ does not project a stable interval at the middleground level, but instead an interval which is dependent upon the interval E–G to which it progresses.

In other instances where it might be essential to draw a distinction between a linear progression and a large-scale unfolding, the criterion of harmonic or contrapuntal support for each component of the linear progression could be applied. If this is met *and* if the head note and the terminus of the progression fit properly into the stable middleground, then the structure is correctly called a linear progression. Such problems occasionally occur in interesting situations in advanced analytic studies.

The final demonstration of unfoldings of larger scale is presented in Example 209. A 10–7 linear intervallic pattern supports the descant unfolding from a$\flat^2$ in to f^2, which spans three measures. The sequel e^2 out to g^2 then occurs entirely within m. 10. Thus, the upper component of the unfolding carries the large-scale stepwise motion a$\flat^2$–g^2. As indicated in the sketch at *b*, the goal of the unfoldings, g^2, is simultaneously the beginning of a linear progression, the first two notes of which (g^2 and f^2) are shown.

EXAMPLE 209. Handel, Courante from *Suite in F minor*

The examples of unfoldings given in this section comprise only a minute sample of this basic prolongational type. Of particular interest to the student of advanced Schenkerian analysis are the unfoldings of larger scale. As with other types of prolongations these must be studied very carefully in order to understand how they work within the tonal structure, that is, within the middleground. And almost always they incorporate some other feature of interest. For instance, the first unfolding in Example 208, from f♯¹ to d♯², is completely composed out in a stepwise progression, while Example 207 includes a voice exchange, and Example 209 involves a linear intervallic pattern.

Register Transfers (Couplings)

The concept of register transfer and the associated notion of coupling were introduced in Chapters 6 and 12, and subsequently discussed in Chapter 18. The term *register transfer* covers the general situation of change of octave of specific note.[2] *Coupling* is a term normally used when two registers (octaves) are linked by a structural motion (skip) at a particular juncture in the music, one that often corresponds to an important moment in the formal arrangement—for example, at the end of a section. Couplings typically involve components of the fundamental structure (background) or elements directly related to them (middleground elements).

In general, a change of register is an event of the utmost significance when it involves an element of the fundamental line, since it may be a signal for further prolongation or, on the contrary, a signal for closure. Furthermore, once registral relations (couplings) have been established in the composition it is possible to refer to these in very subtle and artistic ways and to develop progressions which incorporate register in a structural way and not merely as an arbitrary decorative factor. Some indication of these features is provided in the following musical illustrations.[3]

An instance of local octave coupling is shown in the short composition by Schubert in Example 210. The work, in simple binary form, has two correspondingly different middleground structures, shown at *b*. In the first section the primary tone 3̂ (f♯²) is introduced via a subordinate middleground linear progression that descends from a² to f♯². In the first foreground gesture a¹ is coupled to a² through the arpeggiated diminished-seventh chord. This horizontal relation is represented vertically at *b*. In the second phrase of the first section, beginning at m. 5, the linear progression again begins its descent, but breaks off at m. 7 to cadence on scale degree 1̂ in the upper voice. The sketch at *b* clarifies: the f♯² expected in m. 8 occurs as f♯¹, and this is based on the octave coupling established at the beginning of the piece. That is, at the end of the section there is a return of the primary tone to the register in which it originated (from a¹).

---

2. A type of register transfer which effects displacement (overlapping) was discussed in Chapter 18. This topic is reintroduced in the following section.

3. Beginning in this section we sometimes present score and analytic material separately, rather than aligned, since by now the reader is accustomed to associating the sketches visually with the fully notated score.

EXAMPLE 210. Schubert, *Deutsche Tänze*, Op. 171, No. 3

The second section of the piece is strikingly different from the first. The upper voice begins on f♯², the melodic note expected at the end of the first phrase. As indicated by the dotted slur, f♯² derives from f♯¹ by coupling. While the linear successors of f♯² are not subjected to further transfer of register, the components of the other line in the upper parts are. This is shown clearly in the graph at *b*. Beginning with d² at the end of the first section, there is a descending linear progression spanning the sixth from d² to f♯¹. The second note of the linear progression, c♯², leaps up a seventh to connect with the third element of the progression, b², and so on, until g² appears in the upper voice in m. 15 as the seventh of V. This dissonance then resolves as g¹–f♯¹ in the lower octave, to complete the linear progression. The upper octave here continually refers to the octave in which the primary tone f♯² was first presented (m. 4). The primary tone 3̂, however, literally occurs only in the lower octave, as f♯¹, at the end of the composition, although f♯² is strongly implied at the end, indicated by the parentheses that enclose it in the sketch at *b*. In the elaborate foreground diminutions, the two elements of the bilinear melodic structure are clearly differentiated: The diminution of the uppermost element (e.g., in m. 10) consists of an appoggiatura followed by a descending arpeggiation, while the lower element has associated with it a double neighbor-note figure.

The concept of obligatory register, that is, the notion that the fundamental line belongs primarily in a single register, was introduced in Chapter 12. In Example 210 the obligatory register is the register of the primary tone, f♯². However, there is no stepwise close of a fundamental line from the primary tone; the primary tone alone governs the structural upper voice of the piece.

Example 211 shows the end of one of the extraordinary compositions by Bach for solo violin. Here, as in Example 205 and many of Bach's works, unusual and unexpected events occur at the very close of the piece. Example 211*b*, an analytic interpretation of the score shown at *a*, indicates that scale degree $\hat{4}$ of the fundamental line e² has been reached on the downbeat of m. 28. However, just at that moment there is a sudden motion out to b². Example 211 shows that this b² (m. 29) begins a linear motion that descends from b² to f♯², upper neighbor to e² ($\hat{4}$). The subsequent return of e² in m. 30 completes the stepwise motion initiated by b² in m. 29 and brings in $\hat{3}$ (d²), which finally resolves the dissonant $\hat{4}$ that begins the passage. Here we have an instance of what in Chapter 18 was called a covering progression: the line from b² to d², which divides into the fourth b²–f♯² to which is appended the third f♯²–d². It should be clear to the reader at this point that this line is not a linear progression, but a subsidiary foreground motion attached to the middle-ground f♯², which is upper neighbor to scale degree $\hat{4}$ of the fundamental line. Its function is to delay (prolong) the descent of the fundamental line, by "covering" the dissonant e² of the fundamental line.

EXAMPLE 211. Bach, *Partita in B minor for Solo Violin*, Sarabande

Finally, as the dotted slur in Example 211 shows, the crucial note b² in this final prolongation originates by coupling from a♯¹ within the dominant-seventh chord, a remarkable instance of the rich musical resources provided by register transfer.

Like Example 211, Example 212 illustrates a progression that originates with a register transfer from an inner voice. At m. 17 a linear progression emanates from the primary tone $\hat{3}$ (e^2) and descends as far as g♯^{1} in m. 25. At that juncture, as shown in Example 212*b*, c♯^{2} is understood (implied) in the upper voice above bass C♯; its voice-leading origin is the inner-voice B♯, the end of a descending line which has been following the upper voice in parallel sixths from the beginning. Beginning in m. 26 there is in the foreground an ascending stepwise connection from g♯^{1} out to the superimposed c♯^{2}. The latter, in turn, is the beginning of a stepwise subordinate line that slowly returns to g♯^{1} in m. 31, the same note that accompanies e^2 in m. 17. (Thus, the linear progression of a sixth may be understood as the horizontalization of the initial interval formed between the two upper voices.) At the very end of Example 212*b* the coupling g♯^{1}–g♯^{2} is shown. The latter note is the main melodic note of the new section, which is initiated by the coupling.

EXAMPLE 212. Chopin, *Waltz in C♯ minor*, Op. 69, No. 3

It is well known that the importance of register has a long tradition in tonal music—especially in keyboard music, where change of register is so idiomatic. The previous example, from Chopin's music, is only one of many. Example 213, from Bach's *D-minor Invention*, illustrates the role of register as

EXAMPLE 213. Bach, *Inventio 4 in D minor*

it relates to the obligatory register of the fundamental line, as well as the referential function mentioned at the beginning of this section.

Example 213*b* is an analysis of the music shown in Example 213*a*. It shows the bilinear subject of the invention, with a¹ on top in the initial presentation, prolonged by its upper neighbor, bb¹, and by a descent through a third to f¹ in m. 3. Thus, the first statement of the subject involves "soprano" and "alto" voices. The second involves "bass" and "tenor" in mm. 3–4, while the third engages two voices that lie an octave above soprano and alto. It is this third presentation that is the definitive one, in the sense that it is the statement of the primary tone in what proves to be the obligatory register. The coupling a¹–a² shown at *b* has a number of ramifications for the subsequent music, one of which is illustrated in Examples 213*c* and 213*d*. At m. 38 the upper voice returns to a¹ over the dominant harmony to complete a section of the piece. Just before it does so, however, there is a striking reference to the obligatory register, with the appearance of a² in the upper voice of m. 36. This note is flagged in the analysis at *d*. In a very specific sense this reference to the primary tone in its basic structural register is an interpolation here, for the note b¹, which introduces a¹ in m. 38, is already implied in the voice leading, as shown by the parentheses in the sketch.

The remainder of Example 213 shows the coupling a¹–a², which restores the primary tone to its obligatory register. As soon as a² arrives, the descent of the fundamental line begins, as indicated in the sketch, *d*. Before the completion of the coupling, however, a¹ is prolonged by the expanded neighbor note b♭¹, which unfolds in to e¹ before returning to a¹ in m. 41. This neighbor motion is motivic, deriving from the upper component of the subject itself, as shown in Example 213*b*.

Overlappings

The melodic prolongation known as overlapping was first introduced in Chapter 18 in connection with register transfer and displacement, and various types of overlapping were illustrated schematically in Examples 186 and 187 (p. 221). The reader may wish to review these now before we undertake a further examination of overlapping and the various roles it plays in the tonal composition.

Essentially the overlapping results from the superposition of an inner voice, either an inner voice that is literally present or one that is implied by the harmony and voice leading. In many cases it is not necessary to trace the inner-voice origin of the overlapping voice. It is essential, however, to understand how a series of overlappings works in the context of a prolongation of larger scale at the middleground level and the nature of the structures created by the series.

As illustrated in Examples 186 and 187, a series of overlappings may create (perhaps simulate is a better word) a stepwise motion, an arpeggiation, or a neighbor-note formation. It is not always the case, however, that a series of overlappings will create a structure of longer range. Instead, each overlapping note may resolve locally as its note of resolution is covered by the next overlapping note. No coherent structure of longer range is then formed. The overlapping series, however, is in the service of some middleground motion and is supported by a coherent bass and/or harmonic progression which makes the goal of the series clear. The following two examples illustrate.

Example 214*a* presents the climactic passage from a well-known song by Schubert, and Example 214*b* provides an analytic interpretation. Before examining the series of overlappings in the upper voice, let us first consider the bass and harmony. The progression begins on the tonic, with bass e♭¹. This is followed by ♭VI (the submediant in the parallel minor mode), which leads (as dominant prepration) to V in m. 58. The dominant then moves to the tonic, but the tonic is supplied with a ♭7, propelling it ahead to IV at the apex of the phrase. In m. 63 the subdominant returns to V, which cadences on the tonic harmony at the end of the phrase in m. 65. As part of this progression there is a two-octave coupling from e♭¹ down to E♭, as indicated by the dotted slur in Example 214*b*.

EXAMPLE 214. Schubert, *Du bist die Ruh'*

Against this relatively uncomplicated bass and harmonic progression the upper voice presents a more elaborate structure. Within the middleground (large-scale) unfolding from b♭¹ out to g² is a series of overlappings. The chromatic note c♭¹ enters as upper neighbor to b♭¹ (a reference to the beginning of the song). As c♭¹ moves to b♭¹, d♭² overlaps, and as it resolves to c♭², e♭² overlaps. The final overlapping in the series is negotiated by g² in m. 59, and this completes the middleground unfolding, which began with b♭¹ at the beginning of the passage. The climactic a♭² in m. 60 couples down to a♭¹ in m. 62 and a stepwise descent to e♭¹ ensues, as shown in the graph.

Thus, we have here a series of unfoldings in the service of a middleground unfolding. This series itself does not build a long-range structure, however. If we were to assert such a structure as a component of the music here it would be a very strange one, indeed, for it would consist of an ascending whole-tone scale, which was not part of the musical vocabulary at the time Schubert composed this song!

Example 215 is drawn from the beginning of the development section of a symphonic movement by Mozart. Here, as in the previous example, let us first consider the bass motion of the passage. As shown, in Example 215*b* this consists of a straightforward linear progression from c¹ to g¹ (I–V) followed by a close on the tonic in m. 41.

EXAMPLE 215. Mozart, *Symphony in C major*, K. 425, II

The upper voice shows a connection from the middleground note g¹ in m. 37 up to the primary tone c² in m. 41, the melodic goal. The intervening melodic motion is created by the series of overlappings, indicated by the flagged notes in *b*. To what extent does this series of overlappings constitute a coherent substructure in its own right? From the notation in the sketch at *c* it would appear that the flagged overlapping notes form a stepwise succession from c² to f². However, since these notes form a series of parallel octaves with the bass, ameliorated to some extent, of course, by the sixths, the stepwise succession is not supported by voice leading with the respect to the bass.

Example 215*d* presents a better reading of the upper voice: it accompanies in parallel sixths the linear progression of a fifth in the bass. In this reading, the overlapping notes are ancillary and belong to the immediate foreground, with no long-range implications.

Motivic Structures

In Part One it was shown that the basic types of diminutions—neighbor notes, passing notes, and arpeggiations—are the components of melodic motives. Implicit in those earlier discussions was the idea that motives can extend beyond the immediate foreground to other levels of structure. This was touched upon again in Chapter 7, and was reintroduced in greater detail in Chapter 19.

We now wish to emphasize two interrelated aspects of the motive from the Schenkerian point of view: 1) concealed forms of a thematic motive as components of melodic structures and 2) expansions (enlargements) of motives at higher levels of structure. Both are very important and interesting, and we will have more than one occasion to refer to them in subsequent chapters, for they are significant features of many tonal compositions.

Example 216 shows the first section and the beginning of the second section of a Schubert dance in binary form. The most prominent foreground motives are marked by brackets labeled *a* and *b* in Example 216*b*. These consist, respectively, of complete lower and upper neighbor-note formations, and are associated by virtue of the fact that they have the same rhythm. A third motive labeled *c* also plays a role in the motivic structure of this piece, as will be shown.

EXAMPLE 216. Schubert, *Deutsche Tänze*, Op. 33, No. 10

The extent to which motives *a* and *b* pervade the melodic structure is truly remarkable. In m. 5 motive *a* appears twice in succesion, a form of enlargement, combines with motive *b* as the first three eighth notes in the descant of m. 7 and, in incomplete form, occurs in the bass of mm. 6–7, as F–E. In the second section of the piece, the descant continues to develop the motives, with motive *b* appearing in the expanded form indicated by the bracket. And at the cadence on V in mm. 11–12, the augmented-sixth chord incorporates both motive *a* (in the inner voice) and motive *b* (in the bass). Motive *c*, which originally appeared as a¹–g♯ in the inner voice of mm. 2–3, is now stretched out in the inner voice of mm. 9–10 in reverse order, as g♯–a.

In Example 217*b* we find three forms of a basic motive in a context of small span. Motive *a*, consisting of the lower-neighbor figure c²–b¹, is completed by the return to c² in m. 4 of the excerpt (Example 217*a*). This form of the motive is marked *a¹*. The motive marked *a²* is, of course, the complete neighbor-note figure prolonging the inner voice c², which, in turn, prolongs the primary tone e².

EXAMPLE 217. Chopin, *Mazurka in A minor*, Op. 59, No. 1

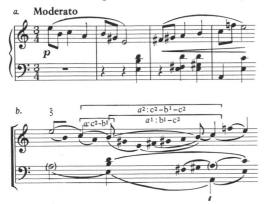

The final example in this section, Example 218, is but one of a multitude of similar occurrences in the tonal repertory in which a motive of small scale is expanded to become a middleground structure that governs a long span of music.

EXAMPLE 218. Haydn, *String Quartet in D major*, Op. 76, No. 5, II

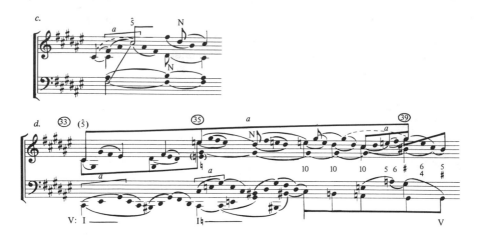

At Example 218*a* the opening motive of the first theme, an ascending arpeggiation f♯¹–a♯¹–c♯² is designated as motive *a* in Example 218*c*. (The other characteristic motive of the first theme, the upper neighbor-note figure, is included in Example 218, but will not be discussed.) In the closing theme of this movement in sonata form (Chapter 21), the descant projects an enlargement of this ascending arpeggiation, transposed: c♯¹–e²–g♯². This structure is beamed in Example 218*d*, which is a detailed sketch of the entire passage. However, the motive also occurs in other forms. Most obviously it occurs in the cello in mm. 33–34, where it has the rhythmic shape of the original motive. This is then imitated in the viola in mm. 35–36, but with E♮—exactly the form that is unfolding slowly in the descant. This same form occurs at the very end of the progression, filled in by passing tones, in first violin mm. 38 and 39, summarizing the large-scale descant motion of the passage.

Exercises

A. *Unfoldings of Small Scale*

Sketches in analytic notation should be carefully drawn for both exercises, with written comments on the analyses. Both exercises involve elaborate diminutions at the foreground level.

1. Bach, *Suite in C major for Solo Cello*, Courante

This excerpt, although short, is challenging. The voice leading can be read in terms of arpeggiations connecting the two basic components, bass and upper voice, and in terms of unfoldings between those voices. The primary tone, $\hat{3}$, does not arrive until m. 7, right at the cadence.

2. Mozart, *String Quartet in G major*, K. 387, I

In this long passage from the development section of the first movement, the bass line provides a firm underpinning and a clear sense of direction. The first unfolding is in first violin, m. 68. The unfoldings continue in the elaborate figures which begin in the viola in m. 70 and then are exchanged between second and first violins. These unfoldings also include local octave couplings, which can be indicated in the graph. Sketch the accompanying voices in as simple a way as possible: a single statement may stand for all the repeated notes.

B. Unfoldings of Larger Scale

1. Mozart, *Piano Sonata in F major*, K. 280, III

The change of foreground here does not mean that the progression of the upper voice is completed.

2. Bach, *English Suite in F major*, Menuet II

As shown in Example 127 (p. 120), a¹ is implied on the downbeat of m. 10. The 5–6 motion which ensues is the beginning of an ascending linear progression which pauses on e² in m. 17. It is at this juncture that the unfolding occurs. Be sure to take into account register transfer in mm. 17–18. The primary tone of this piece is 3̂ and the obligatory register is f² (m. 10). With this information it should be possible to specify how the middleground of the passage relates to the fundamental structure.

This exercise should be completed using the full score, since many piano reductions are misleading with respect to the upper voice (first violins), in the sense that the notation does not coincide with the aural experience. A start is given below. Why is this an unfolding and not a linear progression?

3. Beethoven, *Seventh Symphony*, I, Introduction, mm. 32–43

C. Register Transfer

1. Beethoven, *Piano Sonata in E♭ major*, Op. 7, II, mm. 78–90

> This excerpt is taken from the coda of the movement. In Exercise 7/1, a sample exercise, the primary tone is given as 3̂. This information will be helpful in interpreting the registral relations among the components of the upper voice in this closing music.

2. Schubert, *Valses sentimentales*, Op. 50, No. 2

> A coupling occurs at the beginning of the second part of this binary form. How does this affect the middleground structure?

3. Beethoven, *Piano Sonata in E♭ major*, Op. 7, III

The exercise comprises the first section of the movement. The primary tone is $\hat{5}$ and the obligatory register is the register of origin, bb¹.

D. Overlappings

1. Schubert, *Deutsche Tänze*, Op. 33, No. 5

Overlappings are prominent at the beginning of this binary piece in D major. The primary tone $\hat{3}$ arrives in m. 4.

2. Brahms, *Intermezzo in Bb major*, Op. 76, No. 4, mm. 21–32

This is a challenging exercise, drawn from a complicated later piano composition by Brahms. The passage comprises the middle section of a ternary form. The middleground descant structure is a linear progression that descends from eb². This structure is prolonged at the foreground level by overlappings from m. 21 to m. 27 and by unfoldings thereafter. The beginning of an analytic sketch is provided.

E. Motivic Structures

1. Beethoven, *Bagatelle in D major*, Op. 33, No. 6

Study the motives of the foreground level and discover any concealed repetitions of motives. In the sketch of the given music, be sure to represent registral relations and note how they contribute to the middleground structure.

2. Beethoven, *Piano Sonata in F minor, Op. 2, No. 1*, III

The descending-third motive is enlarged. What type of prolongation occurs in the immediate foregound?

3. Mozart, *Piano Sonata in B♭ major*, K. 333, II

The descending-third motive (first three notes) is presented in enlarged form twice. Discovery of the second one is dependent upon a correct reading of the thirty-second-note diminutions in m. 4. (See Example 195*b*, p. 238.)

21

Sonata Form
and
Structural Levels

The Design of the Sonata Form

Most musicians would agree that the sonata form is the most important large-scale design in tonal music, with many beautiful instances, such as the first movement of Beethoven's *Eroica Symphony*. Complete agreement on other aspects of the sonata form might be difficult to reach, however. For example, the historical development of the form is not yet completely understood. The form is most prominent during the Classic period in the music of Haydn, Mozart, and Beethoven, but the prototype of the form as it occurs in their works is assumed to be found in the sonatas of Carl Philipp Emanuel Bach, Haydn's immediate predecessor. Is the form a large-scale binary form or a large-scale ternary form? This question is often posed. Is the form determined by contrasting melodic themes or by contrasting harmonic units ("keys")? And finally, is there really an entity called sonata form at all, since many works that are supposed to exhibit that form usually depart from it in some significant way?

We attempt to answer these questions, beginning with the last. In general, the outlines of sonata form are followed by many works in the Classic period, especially first movements of instrumental sonatas and symphonies. However, each such work, unless it is completely trivial or stereotyped, has its own characteristic prolongations, from the level of foreground diminutions through the middleground structures that govern long spans of music; hence, each work is unique. It is for this reason that we combine in the title of this section the notion of sonata form, as a general design, and the concept of structural levels, the content of which breathes life into the abstraction known as sonata form. This is the essence of the Schenkerian concept.

The sonata form, in its broadest outlines, is presented schematically in

Example 219, which also provides a frame of reference for answers to the remaining two questions posed above. First, is the form binary or ternary? The large sections are designated as ABA in Example 219, commonly called exposition, development, and reprise (recapitulation). Thus, the form appears to be ternary. With the repetitions indicated, however, it resembles a rounded binary: ||:A:||:BA:||. Both types are represented in the tonal repertory. The rounded binary form, with repetition of development and reprise, is characteristic of Haydn, Mozart, and early Beethoven. Beethoven's later sonata forms tend to omit that repetition. However, many find it convenient and convincing to regard the sonata form as a three-part form, with exposition, development, and reprise comprising the distinct parts. This is the view adopted in the present text.

EXAMPLE 219. Summary of Sonata Form in Major and Minor Modes

A:

[Slow Introduction] Exposition

||: Theme (Group) 1/Transition (with modulation)/

| Major: | – – –V I– – – | – – –V of V |
| Minor: | – – –V I– – – | – – –V of III |

B:

Development

Theme (Group) 2/Closing Theme :||: Episodic sections/Retransition/

| Major | V– – – | – – –V | | V |
| Minor: | III– – – | – – –III | Various "keys" | V |

A:

Reprise

Theme (Group) 1/ Transition (no modulation)/Theme (Group) 2/

| Major: | I | I– – – | I |
| Minor: | I– – – | I– – – | I |

[Coda or Codetta]

Closing Theme :||

| Major: | I– – – | | I |
| Minor: | I– – – | various "keys" | I |

The remaining question regarding a thematic as compared to a harmonic basis for distinguishing the sections of a sonata form can be answered unequivocally with reference to Example 219. The main feature that determines sections is harmonic in nature. The exposition in major begins in tonic and ends in dominant, as shown in the summary, while the exposition in minor begins with the tonic harmony and ends with the mediant. The development section does not permit generalization with regard to its harmonic content, hence the rubric "various 'keys'." The reprise, however, is controlled by a single large-scale harmony, the tonic, as indicated, while the coda or codetta is developmental in nature, moving within "various keys" but always ending on the tonic. The thematic content of the exposition of the sonata form can be quite complicated at the foreground level, consisting—for example, in many of Haydn's sonata-form movements—of variegated thematic configurations. Indeed, the term "exposition" refers to the statement of melodic themes which are then "developed," and ultimately recur in the reprise. Of course, these traditional terms say nothing about large-scale continuity at the middleground level in the Schenkerian sense and are thus of limited utility to the analyst.

Before undertaking a step-by-step analysis of a complete sonata form, a few more comments on Example 219 are in order.

The movement may begin with a slow introduction, as does the famous example of Beethoven's *Pathétique Sonata*, Op. 13. The exposition, however, firmly establishes the tonic key, within which a single theme or group of themes is set forth, designated theme 1. Usually a transitional passage follows, and this passage often incorporates a modulation—to V in major or to III in minor (although there is an exception to this rule in our very first example of sonata form; see Example 224, p. 282). Theme 2, prolonging V or III, is then presented. Often this theme bears an interesting structural relation to theme 1 at the middleground level, to be the subject of a later discussion in this chapter. The closing theme, which may be very brief, continues to express the dominant harmony in major or the mediant harmony in minor. With the repetition of the exposition, theme 1 is thrown into relief once again, but now in a new context, since its middleground structure will engage those of theme 2 and the closing theme. Thus, the repetition of the exposition is not trivial, for the first theme (group) is heard in a different way, just because so much has transpired musically since it was first stated. This aspect of repetition in the sonata form is usually ignored.

Following the exposition is that very special section known as the development, often episodic in character, improvisational, or even fragmentary, and often difficult to analyze for continuity with respect to the point of departure—the end of the exposition—and the point of arrival—the dominant harmony at the end of the retransition that prepares the return of theme 1 in the reprise. It is not possible to make any general statement about the structure of the development. However, many developments carry middleground motions of large scale and effect linear continuity between exposition and reprise. Two examples are given below.

The development of the first movement of Beethoven's Op. 14, No. 1 is sketched in broad outlines in Example 220. Against the bass, which prolongs the dominant harmony by means of a large-scale upper neighbor C (m. 65), the descant prolongs $f\sharp^2$ through a descending third: $f\sharp^2$ (m. 38)–e^2 (m.

EXAMPLE 220. Beethoven, *Piano Sonata in E major*, Op. 14, No. 1, I

65)–d♯² (m. 81). The inner voice descends from b¹ to f♯¹ in the retransition, and the prolonged dominant harmony resolves to tonic at the beginning of the reprise, with d♯² in the descant moving to e¹ in the inner voice, as shown.

Example 221, from a late and well-known work by Mozart, reads the upper-voice motion as a large-scale unfolding from g² in to b♭¹, a motion which is completed over the subdominant harmony at the beginning of the reprise, with g² moving to f² while b♭¹ moves to a¹. This example also illustrates an exception to the general harmonic design of the sonata form, since the reprise begins with the subdominant harmony rather than with the tonic.[1]

EXAMPLE 221. Mozart, *Piano Sonata in C major*, K. 545, I

Two aspects of the reprise are often of interest in the analysis of sonata forms: theme 2 and the transition. Theme 2 as it relates to theme 1 will be discussed below. The transition in the reprise is interesting because it must adjust to the new tonal situation: Whereas the transition in the exposition carries a change from tonic to dominant, the transition in the reprise remains within the tonic, with corresponding adjustments in the middleground structure.

In the early sonata forms theme 2 was often simply a transposition of theme 1 in the exposition. Thus, when both themes returned in the reprise, unity of melodic structure was effected as well as unity of key, since theme 1 and theme 2 were then identical. This procedure persisted in certain later sonata forms—for example, in the first movement of Beethoven's *Les Adieux Sonata*, Op. 81a, cited in Chapter 19, and in the first movement of Haydn's

---

1. Similar exceptions are to be found in abundance in the music of Schubert—for example, in the *Piano Sonata in A minor*, Op. 164, I.

Symphony in D major, Hob. I/104. It is not generally realized, however, that the tradition of the replication of theme 1 by theme 2 persisted in subtler ways in a number of sonata forms, through motivic structures at the middleground level (Chapter 20) which are revealed by Schenkerian analysis. Theme 2 may present a middleground structure that is very similar to that of theme 1, or, in some cases, a structure that is virtually identical. These relations then become explicit in the reprise, which is the unifying section of the sonata, since (as in the earlier sonatas) both themes are based upon the tonic harmony. Most obviously, theme 2 often has the same primary tone as theme 1, but the relation of similarity may well penetrate deeper into the middleground structure as well. In the analyses that follow we will have occasion to consider thematic relations of this kind.[2]

An Exemplar of Sonata Form

Because this section of the text is the first to deal with music of relatively long duration, we present a somewhat detailed analysis in short segments and discuss the relations between component levels of structure. The composition to be studied is the third (last) movement of Beethoven's *Piano Sonata in C minor*, Op. 10, No. 1.

The movement is in sonata form, with a short development section of eleven measures and a coda of twenty-one measures. The coda itself is developmental, in the sense that foreground motives are transformed. Indeed, the term *development* applied to the middle section of the sonata form is misleading because it may suggest that melodic development cannot occur in other sections of the form, whereas a well-composed work begins to "develop" immediately, with transformed repetitions (including concealed repetitions) of motives, extensions to the middleground structure, and so on. This will be made evident in the analysis that follows.

Each of the ensuing series of examples, beginning with Example 222, depicts a distinct unit of the form. Barlines are retained to facilitate reference to the complete score,[3] and almost all the foreground detail is included. This graph may be regarded as typical of a working sketch, akin to the overlays introduced in Part Two. Since we wish to emphasize the interaction of structural levels as they create form, major foreground features (motives, etc.) as well as middleground motions are shown. Although elements of the fundamental structure are presented as beamed open notes, in the usual manner, the purpose of the sketch is not to give a synoptic view of the entire movement, in terms of fundamental structure, but a more detailed view of the component levels within the discrete sections of the movement.

---

2. Of course, the topic that is broached here deserves far more extensive treatment, but that is true of many aspects of sonata form touched upon in this section.

3. It is not feasible to reproduce the complete scores for the sonata movements discussed in this section. All are from standard works to which it is assumed the reader has access.

Beethoven, Piano Sonata in C minor, *Op. 10, No. 1, III: Exposition*

Theme 1 consists of two parts. The first of these (Example 222) opens with a middleground arpeggiation from c^1 out to g^1 in m. 2. Attached to the arpeggiated notes are the foreground neighbor-note motives labeled α (alpha) and β (beta). As will be seen, these motives pervade the movement in various guises and at various levels. In m. 3 a third foreground motive is introduced by the descant: the ascending third c^1–d^1–$e\flat^1$, marked δ (delta). Remarkably, each of these notes carries a rhythmic diminution of motive beta, while, at the same time, the motive appears, in stretched-out form, as c^2–b^1 in the alto and as $a\flat$–g in the bass. With the arrival on V in m. 5 the second phrase of theme 1 begins, now presenting the arpeggiation of the dominant triad. This proves to be a preparation for the expanded arpeggiation that ascends all the way to g^2 in m. 7, the primary tone. This foreground arpeggiation contains the middleground unfolding from b out to $a\flat^1$, which completes itself on g^2 (the primary tone) over c^1 on the downbeat of m. 8. With the resolution of $a\flat^2$ to g^2, motive beta is formed, while the resolution of b^1 to c^2 creates an expanded (and incomplete) form of motive alpha.

EXAMPLE 222. Beethoven, *Sonata in C minor*, III: Exposition, Theme 1, First Part

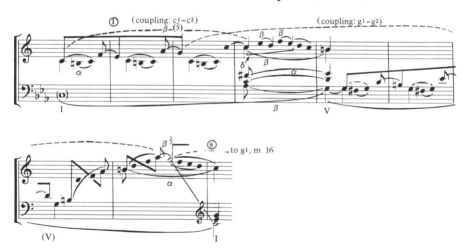

Also shown in Example 222 are the leapfrog couplings from c^1 to c^2 and from g^1 to g^2, which gradually expand the registral scope of the theme.

While the first part of theme 1 is a harmonically closed form in itself, moving from tonic to dominant and back to tonic, the second part of theme 1 (Example 223) occurs above a stationary bass. The motivic subtleties are extraordinary. Not only does motive alpha appear undisguised in the immediate foreground of the opening descant figure, but it also appears in stretched-out form in mm. 9–10, as indicated on the graph. Moreover, the unfolding from f^3 in to b^2 in m. 9 strongly implies the completion on $e\flat^3$ over

c^3, thus combining alpha and beta motives. Perhaps the most significant occurrence in this part is the establishment of a new register, represented by f^3. This event looks far ahead in the music to the climax and end of the development (Example 232, p. 286), where f^3 is directly association with f^1 of theme 1's opening beta motive.

EXAMPLE 223. Beethoven, *Sonata in C minor*, III: Exposition, Theme 1, Second Part

The transition (Example 224) undoes the upward registral shifts of the descant of theme 1, arriving in m. 14 on c^1, the original register of the descant. The conclusion of this transition then presents a slightly concealed ascending arpeggiation (m. 14) which, of course, strongly refers to the opening middleground motion of theme 1. The primary tone then appears in the upper voice at the end of the transition as g^1, the register in which it will resume its course as the main melodic note of theme 2, which is forthcoming. It is perhaps worth noting that the ascending arpeggiation of m. 14 is prepared in mm. 12 and 13 by the upward motions from c^3 to $e\flat^3$ and from c^2 to $e\flat^2$.

EXAMPLE 224. Beethoven, *Sonata in C minor*, III: Exposition, Transition to Theme 2

The transition contains multiple occurrences of the alpha and beta motives, all indicated in the sketch, Example 224. Indeed, the successive

downward couplings from c³ to c¹ incorporate the alpha motive each time, thus expanding it over some three measures.

As suggested in the general discussion of sonata form above, the transition from theme 1 to theme 2 often involves a modulation. In fact, this is usually the case for a movement in minor, where theme 2 is in the key of the mediant (III). Here, however, the composer does not modulate in the transition, but moves directly from I to V. In the reprise the transition will return unchanged, for it leads directly to the tonic harmony upon which theme 2 is based in that final section.

As is evident in Example 225, the melodic component of theme 2 is markedly different from that of theme 1. Here we have an arpeggiation outward from b♭ to g¹, with the latter representing the continuation of the primary tone, 5̂. In m. 22 a sharp accent highlights c² in the upper voice, where a pair of unfoldings is initiated to conclude the first part of theme 2. As is the case with second themes (or theme groups) in sonata forms in general, the structural meaning of the theme depends not only upon its occurrence in the exposition, where it is juxtaposed with theme 1 but based on a different harmony (either V or III), but also and more importantly upon its occurrence in the reprise, where it, like theme 1, is based upon the tonic harmony. At that location in the form complete unity is achieved, and the relations between the two "contrasting" themes become fully evident. Hints at their connection begin with the second part of theme 2, however.

EXAMPLE 225. Beethoven, *Sonata in C minor*, III: Exposition, Theme 2, First Part

In the second part of theme 2 (Example 226) the melodic component occurs in the bass. Here the foreground is that of theme 2, but the middleground arpeggiation clearly replicates that of theme 1. In the upper voice of this part, the most important events are the coupling from g¹ to g².

EXAMPLE 226. Beethoven, *Sonata in C minor*, III: Exposition, Theme 2, Second Part

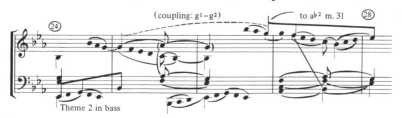

When g^2 is attained, a linear progression of a descending third, g^2–eb^2, ensues, melodically closing this part of the theme. (The corresponding section in the reprise is interpreted in a different way, because of the middleground and background structures effective at that point in the music.)

At the beginning of the third part of theme 2, shown in Example 227, a startling development occurs in the bass. Whereas the previous part began with a bass figure that incorporated aspects of theme 1 and theme 2, as explained, now we find theme 1 in the bass undisguised, presenting the middleground arpeggiation from eb up to bb, with foreground alpha and beta motives. As the bass statement of theme 1 completes itself in mm. 29–30, with the final beta motive, the upper voice brings in the alpha motive eb^2–d^2–eb^2, followed by the onset of the beta motive that just concluded theme 1 in the bass: c^3 over ab^2. The sketch shows that this motive takes up the entire measure (m. 31), with ab^2 descending stepwise in a dramatic gesture to ab^1 before ending on g^1 on the downbeat of m. 32. This is an excellent and very explicit example of a motivic expansion, one that involves octave coupling, a type of prolongation introduced at the very beginning of the composition.

EXAMPLE 227. Beethoven, *Sonata in C minor*, III: Exposition, Theme 2, Third Part

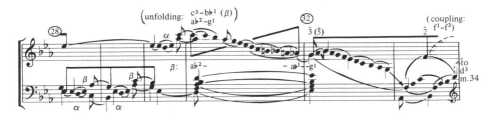

With the arrival of g^1 in m. 32, there is further registral extension downward to the tenor register before f^2 comes in as the continuation of g^2 in m. 33. This connection is shown by a beam in Example 227, while the comma at the end of the beam marks an interruption of the complete motion to eb^1.

Indeed, the motion to eb^1 never does occur, for in the fourth part of theme 2, shown in Example 228, the descant ascends from d^3 through eb^3 (a passing

EXAMPLE 228. Beethoven, *Sonata in C minor*, III: Exposition, Theme 2, Fourth Part

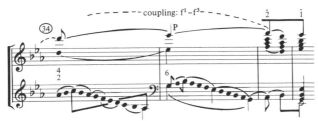

tone!) to f³. The latter completes the coupling from f¹ in m. 33. It must be emphasized that eb³ in the descant of m. 35 is not the continuation of f¹ in m. 33—a potential misreading, which would render eb³ some kind of lower neighbor—but is, instead, an ascending passing note in the motion d³–eb³–f³, which is in the service of the coupling f¹–f³. The bass that articulates the ascending third is ab–G–Eb.

The closing theme of the exposition (Example 229) features a neighbor-note figure which has the rhythm of the beta motive and the melodic shape of the alpha motive. Here, especially, the meaning of this theme will become clear only in the reprise. There bb² in the uppermost voice will become g², the primary tone 5̂, and the emphatic d¹–eb¹ of mm. 38–39 will become b–c¹, the literal alpha motive of theme 1, in register.

EXAMPLE 229. Beethoven, *Sonata in C minor*, III: Exposition, Closing Theme

At the middleground level, the closing theme presents the descending third (3̂–2̂–1̂), a closure in the lower register that was avoided in theme 2, part 4, by the coupling f¹–f³ discussed above.

The exposition ends with a very short codetta, the counterpart of which in the reprise is greatly expanded. At the middleground level is the coupling eb¹–eb³, as shown in Example 230, while the foreground presents alpha and beta motives in combination. Also present in the upper voice are g¹ and g², the registers in which 5̂ was first stated in theme 1. The ascent through two octaves from eb¹ to eb³ is not trivial. This upper register is the topmost register in the movement and is very beautifully set as a goal of motion in the short development that follows.[4]

EXAMPLE 230. Exposition, Codetta

---

4. Those familiar with all of Op. 10, No. 1 will realize that this high register is of the utmost significance to the other two movements as well. It is appropriate for the finale to refer to it.

Beethoven, Piano Sonata in C minor, *Op. 10, No. 1, III: Development*

In comparison with the exposition, the development is relatively short, consisting of the two parts shown in Examples 231 and 232.

EXAMPLE 231. Beethoven, *Sonata in C minor*, III: Development, First Part

EXAMPLE 232. Beethoven *Sonata in C minor*, III: Development, Second Part

Motive alpha is in the foreground throughout the development, whereas motive beta emerges only at the end to effect the middleground melodic connection back to theme 1 in the reprise. We will return below to the latter feature.

The most important large-scale motion in the development is the bass unfolding g–B, which spans mm. 47–54. The goal of the unfolding, B, is, of course, the bass of V, which returns the harmonic motion to the tonic at the beginning of the reprise. But more than that, the status of B as the goal of the unfolding reflects the function of that pitch at the foreground level, within the alpha motive, as it continually refers to the tonic C.

The upper voice of the development is at first rather inactive, centering on bb^1, with a small excursion in mm. 50–51 where the soprano db^1–c^1 follows the bass f–e. However, the voice below the descant, which carries the foreground alpha motive, ascends from eb^1 (m. 47) to f^1 (m. 52). This f^1 is then transferred to f^2 (m. 52), and f^2 couples upward to f^3 via the arpeggiated diiminished seventh chord. This melodic apex pitch f^3, supported by the bass B, the goal of the large-scale unfolding, prepares in a very specific way for the return of theme 1. Just as B resolves to C to initiate the return of the alpha motive within theme 1, so f^3 returns to f^1 in m. 57 to initiate the return of the beta motive of theme 1. Thus bass and descant goals of motion in the development are perfectly positioned to reintroduce theme 1, not only in its harmonic setting but with specific reference to its melodic profile, the middleground ascending arpeggiation of the tonic triad.

A summary of the voice leading that underlies the development is provided by Example 233. In the harmonic sphere the large-scale motion is represented by the open bass notes E♭–G–C. The overall bass motion from the exposition to the reprise, of course, encompasses the complete arpeggiation of the tonic triad, expressing the harmonic succession I–III–V–I, a phenomenon characteristic of sonata forms in the minor mode. At the middleground level the straightforward bass succession of the development becomes more complicated. Within the expansive unfolding g–B, discussed above, occurs the subsidiary but significant motion from III to IV. With the arrival on IV the upper voice moves out to f² and begins its upward course to the climactic f³ in m. 54. Thus, the subdominant, in its harmonic role as dominant preparation, clearly signals the direction toward V. An additional complication, at least with reference to textbook norms of progression, is caused by the role of B as the terminal bass note of the development. The reason for this was set forth above: The pitch B has an essential motivic role in this composition and is not merely the "leading note." However, in the analytic sketch, Example 233, the final bass note of the development is shown as G within parentheses in order to emphasize the harmonic presence of the dominant in the bass at that important point in the music.

EXAMPLE 233. Beethoven, *Sonata in C minor*, III: Development—Summary of Voice Leading

Example 233 also shows essential motion of the upper voices as they move through the development and connect to the beginning of the reprise at m. 57. The top voice at the outset, b♭¹, passes downward through a♭¹ over IV in m. 52, is suspended over V in m. 54, and finally comes to rest on g¹ within the tonic triad at the onset of the reprise. However, the most striking event in the development is the superposition of f² at m. 54, a pitch that emanated from the inner voice e♭¹ at the beginning of the development.

Beethoven, Piano Sonata in C minor, *Op. 10, No. 1, III: Reprise*

Because theme 1 in the reprise is identical in all respects to its counterpart in the exposition, there is no need for a separate sketch of it. The transition returns intact, as well, and leads, as before, to the dominant with the primary tone $\hat{5}$ in the descant. This, then, is the situation at m. 73, just before the entrance of theme 2. Far from being a routine transposition of theme 2 in the exposition, theme 2 in the reprise introduces a number of striking transformations.

To begin with, the first part of theme 2 (Example 234) is in C major, not in C minor, as might be expected. Interpreting the middleground of this part with respect to the background, g^1 is read as representative of the primary tone, $\hat{5}$. The other components of the melody, c^2 and e^2, are prolongational with respect to $\hat{5}$. This places the high point of this part of the theme, a^2 in m. 79, in quite a different perspective; as shown in the sketch, it is the upper neighbor note to g^1, a relation that involves an octave coupling, as indicated.

EXAMPLE 234. Beethoven, *Sonata in C minor*, III: Reprise, Theme 2, First Part

In the second part of theme 2 (Example 235) the bass again presents a melody that has the foreground of theme 2 and the middleground of theme 1, as in m. 24 of the exposition. Above this is the coupling from g^2 down to g^1, again, the two registers in which $\hat{5}$ was first stated in theme 1. With the completion of this coupling, the melodic bass arpeggiation repeats, but this time in minor and slightly enlarged by the passing note f on the downbeat of m. 84. The change to minor is subtly prepared in the upper voice by the neighbor ab^1, which brings in g^1 to complete the coupling. This, of course, forms the beta motive, just as did the motion a^2–g^1 in the upper voice of mm. 79–81.

EXAMPLE 235. Beethoven, *Sonata in C minor*, III: Reprise, Theme 2, Second Part

The close association of themes 1 and 2, which was strongly suggested in the exposition, now becomes very explicit in the second part of theme 2 in the reprise, as remarked above. This association becomes even stronger in the

third part of theme 2, when, as shown in Example 236, theme 1 appears in the upper voice, arpeggiating upward from c² to g² (5̂). Theme 1 has now literally replaced theme 2.

EXAMPLE 236. Beethoven, *Sonata in C minor*, III: Reprise, Theme 2, Third Part

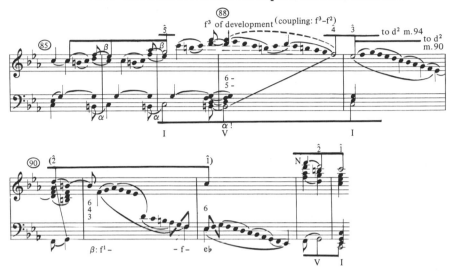

Following the first statement of theme 1 in mm. 85–87, a repetition of it begins, with the leap from c³ up to f³ in m. 87. Now, this climactic note, f³, refers directly back to the climax of the development, m. 54, where it had the same bass support, B, and dominant harmony. Its resolution here, however, is quite dramatically different: After coupling downward to f² it resolves to eb² on the downbeat of m. 89, completing the expanded beta motive. Here the beta motive is part of the fundamental structure, for the progression f²–eb² represents scale degrees 4̂ and 3̂ of the fundamental line, as indicated by the open notes.

Scale degree 3̂ of the fundamental line is thereupon prolonged through a descending linear progression of a third, as we see in mm. 89–91. Although this might momentarily be taken to be the descent of the fundamental line to scale degree 1̂, the bass prevents the motion from being definitive, for it brings in f in m. 91 and f leads to eb at the beginning of m. 92, so that the 1̂ in m. 92 is harmonized by I⁶ rather than by I. The real close of the fundamental line (properly supported by V–I) then follows in mm. 93–94. Interestingly, the f³ that occurs on the downbeat of m. 93 is an upper neighbor to 3̂ in m. 89; although locally it appears in isolation it actually belongs to the middleground (since it is attached to the background element 3̂), and, of course, serves as a final reminder in this section of the special note f³.

With respect to the fundamental structure, the movement is now complete. However, the musical discourse continues in developmental fashion to reveal relations among thematic components that were only suggested in the exposition. Thus, in Example 237, the upper voice g^2 is clearly a reference to the primary tone, while the skip down to b in m. 95 introduces the alpha motive—in its original register. The bass figure accompanying this motive is G–A♭, a replica of the alpha motive, which also suggests the beta motive of theme 1 because of the pitches involved. It is interesting that the composer has changed the closing theme precisely at this point in order to bring in A♭ in the bass. Had this final form of the closing theme followed that of the exposition exactly (m. 39), the bass would have been G–A.

EXAMPLE 237. Beethoven, *Sonata in C minor*, III: Reprise, Closing Theme

Most unexpected, however, is the appearance of the enigmatic delta motive in the descant of m. 96: c^1–d^1–$e♭^1$ (Example 222, p. 000). It will be recalled that this motive occurred in theme 1 directly after the characteristic arpeggiation motive. Thus, although theme 1 contained the germ of the closing theme, the connection was not revealed until the reprise. Here, of course, the delta motive echoes the final third of the fundamental line, as indicated in Example 237 by the careted numerals within parentheses.

The coda begins in m. 100 (Example 238), considerably expanded with respect to the form it took in the exposition (mm. 43–45). As indicated in the sketch, the alpha and beta motives occupy the foreground. Here attached to C and E♭ of the tonic triad, they are a compressed repetition of the motivic forms in the opening figure of theme 1: c^1–b–c^1–f^1–f^1–$e♭^1$.

EXAMPLE 238. Beethoven, *Sonata in C minor*, III: Reprise, Coda, First Part

Following this is an extraordinary passage based upon ♭II, a "Neapolitan in root position," which carries a transposition of theme 2 (Example 239). Here the head note of the melodic theme is clearly f¹, because of the conclusion of the passage in m. 114, and the structural role of that note can only be understood in the context of the middleground, which is summarized in Example 240.

EXAMPLE 239. Beethoven, *Sonata in C minor*, III: Reprise, Coda, Second Part

EXAMPLE 240. Beethoven, *Sonata in C minor*, III: Summary of Coda, First and Second Parts

This sketch shows the upper voice of the coda as it presents C and E♭ in three successively higher registers. In the last of these, the note-pair c³–e♭³ is stretched out, filled in by the passing tone d♭³, and accompanied a sixth below by e♭²–f²–g♭². With the unfolding from e♭³ in to g♭² (mm. 104 6) the latter note assumes the leading role in the foreground, as upper neighbor to f¹, which arrives in m. 107 as the head note of theme 2. In m. 112 g♭¹ again appears in the upper voice as a neighbor note, but is reinterpreted enharmonically as f♯¹ in m. 113 and resolves *upward* to g¹ in m. 114, a reference to the primary tone of the movement in its original register. Thus, the middleground structure of the first two parts of the coda consists of the thematic arpeggiation of theme 1, with f¹ a passing tone filling in the top third of the arpeggiation. This passing tone is temporarily stabilized by the D♭ triad, introducing an element of ambiguity—that is, of indeterminate structural direction—typical of many codas. With the attainment of g¹ in the upper voice of m. 115, over bass G, the ambiguity disappears and resolution to the tonic triad at the beginning of the last part of the coda is forthcoming.

Although the final part of the coda, shown in Example 241, which is based on the tonic pedal C, does not exhibit any degree of harmonic activity, there are many interesting melodic motions, all recalling foreground features of the preceding music. Once again, and for the last time, the characteristic figures of theme 2 and theme 1 are associated, with the latter answering the former twice. Theme 2 ends with the beta motive ab^1–g^1 (mm. 116 and 118), while theme 1 also ends with that motive f^3–e^3. After the second appearance of the latter motive there are successive downward couplings which return the beta motive to its register of origin, f^1–e^1.

EXAMPLE 241. Beethoven, *Sonata in C minor*, III: Reprise, Coda, Last Part

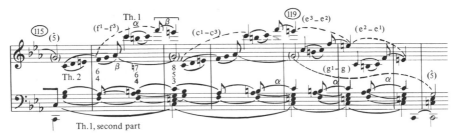

Here the highest statement of the beta motive of theme 1, f^3–e^3, recalls the apex of the development, with respect to register (Example 232, p. 286) and the C-major presentation of theme 2 in the reprise (Example 234, p. 288), with respect to mode.

Finally, the voices above the bass in Example 241 refer back to the inner voices of the second part of theme 1, shown in Example 223 (p. 282). Both passages carry the alpha motive in incomplete form, but in the coda it returns in the register of origin, as b–c^1.

This detailed presentation of a movement in sonata form, the first work of large scale to be discussed in the text, is intended to demonstrate the analytical procedure, including graphic representation of the analysis, with emphasis upon the interpretation of foreground and middleground structures. The work, even though one of Beethoven's early compositions, is especially rich in motivic associations, some of which exist at the surface level, while others are somewhat more concealed, thus providing many opportunities to draw attention to the interaction of foreground and middleground. We have not paid special attention to the fundamental structure, which can be read easily from the examples, except when it was important to the interpretation of the middleground.

Example 242 provides an overview of the form of Beethoven's Op. 10, No. 1, III, indicating the three main sections with their themes and subparts. Controlling harmonies and harmonic progressions are given together with measure numbers for convenient reference to the score as well as the preceding analytic graphs.

EXAMPLE 242. Beethoven, *Sonata in C minor*, III: Summary of Form

Exposition: I–III

Theme 1: I (C minor)		Transition: I–V♮	Theme 2: III (E♭)				Closing Theme and Codetta (III)
Part 1	Part 2		Part 1	Part 2	Part 3	Part 4	
1–8	8–12	12–16	16–24	24–28	28–33	34–37	37–45

Development: III–V

Part 1	Part 2
46–52	52–56

Reprise: I

Theme 1: I	Theme 2: I♮–I♭			Closing Theme: I	Coda: ♭II–V♮–I(♮)		
	Part 1	Part 2	Part 3		Part 1	Part 2	Part 3
57–73	73–81	81–85	85–94	94–100	100–6	106–15	115–22
(same as Exposition)							

Additional Examples of Sonata Form

The sonata form is sometimes called first-movement form because many first movements of multimovement instrumental sonatas, symphonies, and chamber works exhibit that basic design. This designation, however, is misleading, since the form can occur in any movement of a multimovement work. Examples 222–42 gave a detailed analysis of a sonata form that occurs as the final movement of a piano sonata. Of the two additional examples to be presented in this section the first is a second movement and the second is a first movement.

Both are movements from piano sonatas by Haydn which have been selected for several reasons, foremost among which is that the relations among structural levels are relatively uncomplicated, hence suitable to the pedagogical purpose of this chapter. Secondly, and perhaps of equal interest, both offer development sections in which the thematic configurations of the expositions undergo transformations in their original order, an unusual situation.

In the set of examples devoted to the first of these sonata movements, from Haydn's *Piano Sonata in E major*, Hob. XVI/22, we use a method of presentation that differs from that in the previous set of examples. Here, again, the analytic sketches display the musical structure section by section. However, instead of one sketch for each section there are two sketches vertically aligned. The upper of these is a measure-by-measure working sketch with most of the foreground detail and quite a bit of analytic interpretation of structure. The lower sketch is a refinement of the upper, often omitting or simplifying components in order to show the middleground more clearly. This procedure is intended to be a model for the completion of the exercises associated with this chapter.

Haydn, Piano Sonata in E major, *Hob, XVI/22, II: Exposition*

The opening melodic gesture of the movement, Example 243, has two elements: the statement of the primary tone $\hat{5}$ with upward coupling b¹–b² and the voice exchange spanning the third from E to G. Of the two positions of the primary tone, b¹ is selected as the main register, because of the subsequent behavior of the fundamental line.

EXAMPLE 243. Haydn, *Sonata in E major*, II: Exposition, Theme 1 and Transition

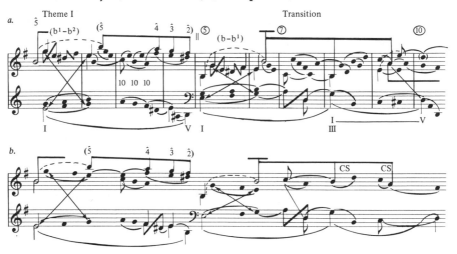

The first phrase of theme 1 is completed with a middleground linear progression of a fourth from b² to f#² ($\hat{5}$–$\hat{4}$–$\hat{3}$–$\hat{2}$) and a bass motion from I to V, creating an interruption form. In m. 3 the upper voice extends downward momentarily to c², flagged on both graphs, which originates as upper neighbor to the primary tone, b¹.

The second phrase of the theme begins as did the first, but an octave lower. Beginning in m. 7, where theme 1 merges with the transition, is a typically Haydnesque elaborate descant foreground, which is only partially interpreted in Example 243 at *a*. In complicated situations such as this the maxim is: Work from the bass up. The correct solution is shown at *b* in the example. Bass notes a and d support c², which forms the seventh above d. On the downbeat of m. 8 bass g supports b to resolve the dissonant seventh. The change to bass B in m. 8 supports the upward motion to d², while bass C on the first beat of m. 9 supports a¹ primarily, although it literally comes together with c². The latter note must be a consonant skip, as shown at *b*. It can only be a purely local event in the immediate foreground, for it has no voice-leading successor. An interesting secondary feature of mm. 7–9 is the upper-voice pattern c^2–b^1–a^1, which is more than a hint at an enlarged repetition of the same succession in m. 3.

Taken as a whole, the transition effects a modulation from I to III, ending on V of III, with d^2 implied in the upper voice. (Looking ahead to Example 244, we see that this d^2 is stated literally as the primary tone of theme 2, where it is also mirrored in the upper octave as d^3.) The arrival of d^2 is prepared by superposition in m. 9, during which time the harmony moves toward V of III. The note a^1, which represents the continuation of the main primary tone b^1, is thus submerged, and when the harmony changes to III in m. 12 (the second measure of theme 2, shown in Example 244), it comes to rest on the tonic note of III, G, here stated as g^2.

EXAMPLE 244. Haydn, *Sonata in E major*, II: Exposition, Theme 2

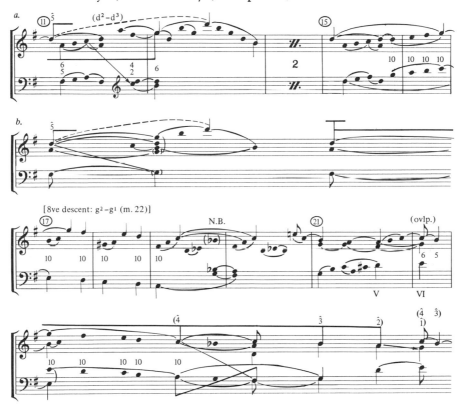

Theme 2 presents two facets in the upper voice. The first is the statement of the primary tone d^2 and the octave coupling to d^3, which incorporates the ascending arpeggiation of III. The second is the prolongation of d^2, which begins in m. 15. There d^2 proceeds upward by step to g^2, accompanied by the bass in tenths, so that the bass ends on e^1, a seventh above the note of origin, f♯. From g² in m. 16 a stepwise line begins, shown at *a*, and this ends on g¹ in the inner voice at m. 22. The refined analytic sketch at *b* shows how this motion fits into the middleground structure: The motion from g² to c² (m. 19) is a foreground succession that follows the bass motion from e¹ to a. At m. 19 c² is the middleground element that connects back to d² in m. 15, as shown by the beam. This c² is prolonged at the foreground level by the motion down to a¹—through the unusual chromatic note b♭¹—which is accompanied by an unfolding third in the bass. Notice that the foreground detail changes markedly just at m. 19, singling out c² from the preceding notes in the stepwise descent from g². Thus, at the middleground level the upper voice consists of a linear progression of a fourth from d² to a¹. At the conclusion of this progression in m. 21, there follows the "special" measure, m. 22, a deceptive progression to VI (of III). This special measure has more than local significance, for it refers back to the opening of theme 1: specifically, to the primary tone b¹ of m. 1 and the upper neighbor c² of m. 3.

Before leaving theme 2, it is perhaps worthwhile to mention that the ascending third in the immediate foreground of m. 11 and elsewhere clearly derives from the ascending thirds in the bass and tenor of theme 1 and thus relates to the exchange feature of that theme.

The closing theme, shown in Example 245, begins by repeating m. 21 of theme 2 and the beginning of the special measure. The latter, however, proves to be the onset of a very beautiful 6–6–10–10 exchange prolonging c², as shown at *b*, an expansion of the upper neighbor figure c²–b¹. In m. 26, at the end of the exchange pattern, the middleground notes c² and b¹ are covered momentarily, a slight diversion in the foreground. Similarly, the concluding motion $\hat{2}$–$\hat{1}$, which closes the middleground linear progression of a fifth that began in m. 11, is concealed by the elaborate foreground diminutions.

EXAMPLE 245. Haydn, *Sonata in E major*, II: Exposition, Closing Theme

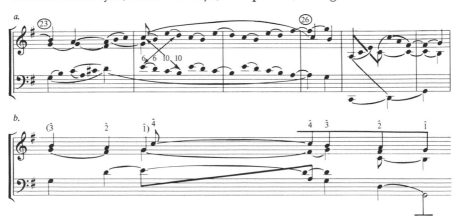

Haydn, Piano Sonata in E major, *Hob. XVI/22, II: Development*

It was remarked above that the development presents the themes of the exposition in order. Thus, the section begins with theme 1 in the mediant, continuing the harmony at the close of the exposition (Example 246). The primary tone of theme 2 and the closing theme, d^2, is projected upward to d^3 in m. 30, which initiates the linear progression that ends on a^2 in m. 32, interrupted briefly by the motion from e^2 down to c^2 in m. 31 accompanied by tenths (thirds) in the bass.

EXAMPLE 246. Haydn, *Sonata in E major*, II: Development, First Part

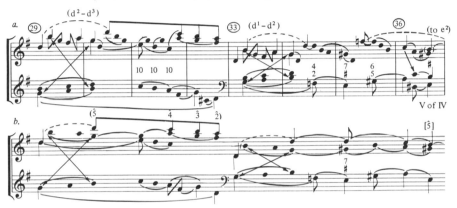

A basic structural disjunction exists naturally in sonata forms in minor in which the mediant is the harmonic foundation of theme 2, as it is in this work. This is because the mediant has a quasi-independent status with respect to the main tonic (here E minor). The most critical factor is the fifth of the mediant triad, the only tone that the mediant does not share with the tonic, for it must be reconciled with the tonic, so to speak, at some point and cannot remain an isolated and independent element. This can be done in a number of ways. For example, in simple tonal music, the fifth of the mediant often moves up to the tonic note through the chromatic passing note just above it, the leading note, which is set by the dominant triad. This effectively brings the mediant back within the tonic orbit and negates its independent status.

The mediant–tonic situation just described pertains, of course, to the movement under consideration. It is represented especially strongly in the melodic upper voice, since the fifth of the mediant, d^2, is the primary tone of theme 2 and the controlling note in the descant at the beginning of the development. Haydn makes the necessary adjustment in an ingenious and artistic way in the next section of the development, which corresponds to the transition in the exposition, mm. 33–36. As shown in Example 246, the transition begins by repeating the beginning of theme 1, just as in the exposition. However, the entrance of the bass passing note f in m. 34 signals a change of direction, and when it arrives on e in m. 35, supporting a harmony of dominant seventh type, that direction is clearly toward A minor. Now, it is at this point that the primary tone d^2 loses its independent status, for it progresses as seventh above bass e to c^2 over bass a. The motion does not end there, however, for the phrase terminates on the dominant of A minor (IV), as indicated by the roman numerals at *a*.

Indeed, IV is strongly prepared to become a harmonic area within the development, but it never achieves that role. Instead, in the next four measures of the development (Example 247), which correspond to theme 2 of the exposition, a linear intervallic pattern takes command and negates the implied harmonic direction toward IV.

EXAMPLE 247. Haydn, *Sonata in E major*, II: Development, Second Part and Retransition

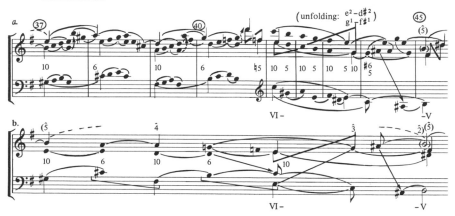

Example 247*b* shows how the final two sections of the development return to V of E minor at m. 45. The linear intervallic pattern of mm. 37–41 is a 10–6, as indicated. This pattern carries the descant from b^1 to a^1 (m. 39) and then to g^1 in m. 40. (Disregard the registral displacements at the foreground level in Example 247*a* for the present.) This g^1 is then stretched out over some four measures, its middleground statement occurring definitively only at the end of m. 43.

This expansion of g^1 occurs within the section that corresponds to the transition of the exposition, here designated the retransition (mm. 41–45). It is worth studying in a bit more detail, since it combines a number of features introduced earlier in the text and represents a rather intricate interaction of elements at the foreground and middleground levels. The structure of largest scale in the retransition is the unfolding e^2–g^1 in Example 247*a* (mm. 41–43). This unfolded interval is completed by $f\sharp^1$ over $d\sharp^1$ at the cadence in m. 45, where V is attained. In the more abstract graph at *b*, these unfolded sixths are registrally compressed into thirds. In mm. 41–43, the diagonal line connects the bass note e with g¹ to indicate that these notes belong together as the final tenth in the 10–6 pattern.

The picture at the foreground level, Example 247*a*, is somewhat more complicated. First, the 10–6 intervallic pattern involves registral couplings beginning in m. 37. As a result of these successive couplings the unfolding begins on e² in m. 41 and spans the sixth in to g¹ in m. 43. This lower element, which is the main note being prolonged in middleground, then resolves to f♯¹ in m. 45, and the upper note, e², completes the unfolding immediately afterward on d♯².

The inward unfolding in mm. 41–43 incorporates the linear intervallic pattern 10–5 at the foreground level, with the bass beginning on c². In Example 247*b*, this C is shown as an inner voice above the bass e, by analytic verticalization to compress the structure and reveal its intervallic underpinning. Considered from the harmonic standpoint the unfolding expresses the dominant preparation VI.

The chromatic note A♯ plays a crucial role both in the upper parts and in the bass in the cadential measure 44, since it strongly implies b¹, which, of course, appears immediately thereafter as the primary tone at the opening of the reprise. (In the bass of m. 44, A♯ has the secondary function of alleviating parallel fifths: g¹ over C moving to f♯¹ over B.)

An interesting feature of the second part of the development is the middleground upper-voice structure, which, as shown in Example 247*b*, simulates the linear progression $\hat{5}$–$\hat{4}$–$\hat{3}$–$\hat{2}$, which will be the first middleground progression in the forthcoming reprise. Since this motion is partly supported by a linear intervallic pattern, it is not represented as a beamed linear progression, however. Its presence gives additional and significant melodic content to the end of the development, nevertheless, since the descending fourth prefigures an important feature of the next section, hence is a unifying factor.

Haydn, Piano Sonata in E major, *Hob. XVI/22, II: Reprise*

In the reprise, themes 1 and 2, shown in Example 248, bear a strong resemblance to one another at the middleground level. Theme 2 begins with the primary tone in obligatory register and coupled to b², just as in theme 1. Moreover, the coupling passes over e², which has bass support g¹ in both cases. As indicated in the earlier discussion of the sonata design above, this similarity of profile is far from unusual in the form. It provides a measure of melodic unity that would be lacking if the second theme had a middleground entirely different from that of the first theme. In this case the association of the two themes is dramatized by two modifications that take place in the reprise, with respect to the exposition: (1) theme 1 is not repeated in the lower register; (2) there is no transition from theme 1 to theme 2.

EXAMPLE 248. Haydn, *Sonata in E major*, II: Reprise, Theme 1 and Theme 2 (beginning)

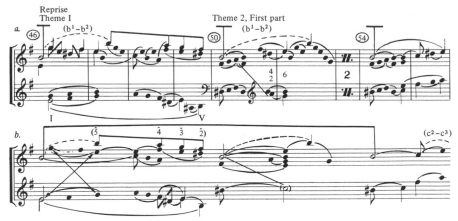

The second part of theme 2 (Example 249) introduces additional unifying elements. Most striking of these is the upper-voice motion that begins with c^2 in m. 56. As shown at *a*, this is a pattern in parallel tenths which ends on g^2 in the upper voice, then begins anew in m. 58 in the lower register. In mm. 60–61 it completes the progression to $\hat{2}$. What makes this unusual is that the motion C–B–A–G in the upper voice exactly repeats mm. 2–3 of theme 1 in the exposition. That is to say, the second part of theme 2 is derived from the consequent phrase of theme 1. The observant reader will quickly see that Haydn has taken special care to begin the second part of theme 2 in the reprise on c^3. Had this been a simple transposition of theme 2 in the exposition, the upper voice of the second part would have begun on e^2, with quite a different outcome.

EXAMPLE 249. Haydn, *Sonata in E major*, II: Reprise, Theme 2 (ending) and Closing Theme, Part 1

The closing theme begins with the special measure 61, which introduces g^1 in the upper voice covering what would otherwise have been a cadential e^1. This g^1 then couples upward to g^2, a note that refers back to the exchange at the opening of the movement. In the analytic sketch at *a* the ensuing motion is almost entirely uninterpreted. In fact, the verticalization in mm. 63–65 is somewhat misleading, for the uppermost parts belong to the immediate foreground and are solely decorative. A more lucid picture of the progression here is provided by *b*, which shows the descending motion of a sixth from g^2 to b^1, the primary tone. The linear intervallic pattern here, 6–5, culminates in $d\sharp^1$–e^1, and it is there that the close of the fundamental structure begins.

A comparison of the last section of the closing theme of the exposition with its counterpart in the reprise is instructive in terms of Schenkerian structural levels. As shown in Example 245 (p. 296), the exchange prolongs c^2 in the upper voice and e^1 in the bass. In m. 26 c^2 becomes $\hat{4}$, and this is followed by the descent to g^1 and the close on the mediant triad. In the reprise (Example 250) the situation is quite different. Now the exchange prolongs a^1 in the upper voice over c^1 in the bass. Here a^1 is $\hat{4}$ in the fundamental line. At the end of the voice exchange, with $f\sharp$ in the bass, $d\sharp^2$ covers a^1. The "special" measure, m. 67, follows, and a^1 does not move to g^1, as expected, but to b^1. At the same time scale degree $\hat{3}$ in the fundamental line appears in the bass, as g. The final two measures bring in $\hat{2}$ and $\hat{1}$, as shown in Example 250*b*. The very last measure is of special interest because it has the rhythm of the special measures and because it resolves a to g in the tenor, the direct resolution which was diverted in m. 67.

EXAMPLE 250. Haydn, *Sonata in E major,* II: Reprise, Closing Theme (end)

To complete the discussion of the second movement of the Haydn *E-major Sonata,* Example 251 gives a summary of its form. It is evident that this is considerably less elaborate than the form of the third movement of Beethoven's Op. 10, No. 1 summarized in Example 242 (p. 293).

EXAMPLE 251. Haydn, *Sonata in E major*, II: Summary of Form

Exposition: I–III
Theme 1 and Transition   Theme 2   Closing Theme
1–10   11–22   23–28

Development: III–V
Part 1   Part 2 and Retransition
29–36   37–45

Reprise: I
Theme 1   Theme 2   Closing Theme
               Part 1   Part 2   Part 1   Part 2
46–49   50–55   56–60   61–65   65–69

Haydn, Piano Sonata in C major, *Hob. XVI/21, I*

Like the previous work discussed, this piano sonata was composed in 1773, when Haydn was 41 years old. The first movement, to be analyzed here, is in a fast tempo (allegro) and exhibits the classical sonata form. However, like all the mature sonata forms by Haydn, it contains unusual features not included in the paradigm given in Example 219 (p. 277). For instance, the third part of theme 2 is in G minor, the minor form of the dominant harmony in the key of the movement, C major.

Since the reader has now been guided through two sonata forms of large scale, one by Beethoven, one by Haydn, he or she may find it valuable at this juncture to work independently through the final example, section by section, before reading the corresponding analysis in the text. This would comprise a preliminary exercise in preparation for those given at the end of this chapter. It would also be advantageous to analyze some of the sections, if not all, before reading the text presentation. With this in mind, we provide a guide to the sections of the movement in Example 252, together with the analytic sketches of those sections as presented in the text.

EXAMPLE 252. Haydn, *Sonata in C major*, I: Guide to Form

Section	Measures	Example
Exposition		
Theme 1	1–6	253
Transition	7–18	254
Theme 2, Part 1	19–27	255
Part 2	27–36	256
Part 3	36–44	257
Closing Theme	45–57	258

Development		
First part	58–78	260*a*
Second Part	78–88	260*b*
Third Part	88–95	260*c*
Reprise		
Theme 1	96–101	none
Transition	102–12	none
Theme 2	113–37	261
Closing Theme	137–49	262

Haydn, Piano Sonata in C major, *Hob. XVI/21, I: Exposition*

Theme 1, shown in Example 253 (and earlier the subject of Exercise 8/4, p. 147), consists of a six-measure phrase whose upper voice traverses a descending linear progression of a fifth. As can be seen from the score, the foreground features the suspension figure 4–3 over the first four measures, changing in m. 5 to a diminution consisting of consonant skips and neighbor notes. This reflects the division of the phrase into four measures plus two measures, which corresponds to the descent from $\hat{5}$ to $\hat{3}$ and from $\hat{3}$ to $\hat{1}$, as shown in Example 253*b*. These six measures comprising theme 1 can thus be viewed as a closed form, a complete piece in itself and a miniature expression of a fundamental structure, such as those first introduced in Part Two.

EXAMPLE 253. Haydn, *Sonata in C major*, I: Exposition, Theme 1

In addition to the linear progression of theme 1, the elegant unfolding in mm. 2–3 from f^2 into b^1 is worthy of mention: a foreground unfolding in the service of a middleground passing tone (f^2).

The transition to theme 2 (Example 254) begins by repeating the first four measures of theme 1 an octave lower, thus completing the linear progression of a third in m. 10 on e^1. At that point the bass introduces a new motive, which consists of the lower-neighbor figure and the arpeggiation up to the inner voice. The arrival on b♭ in the "tenor" of m. 11 signals the large upper-voice neighbor note a¹ in m. 12, which is rhythmically related to the suspension figures of theme 1, as can be ascertained from the full notation of the score. After the upper voice returns to g¹ in m. 14, that note is prolonged by the superposition of e² and the subsequent third descending to c² in m. 16 in parallel sixths with the now covered descant. In m. 16 c² is thrust down to the inner voice c♯¹, which introduces the foreground arpeggiation figure—an imitation of the ascending arpeggiation of theme 1—that completes the prolongation of g¹ and leads to the close of the linear progression 4̂–3̂–2̂. The transition thus ends with 2̂ in the upper voice, an interruption form. Notice that this is not a modulation to the dominant, as G major is not established as its own tonic.

EXAMPLE 254. Haydn, *Sonata in C major,* I: Exposition, Transition to Theme 2

Following the transition, which progresses (but does not modulate) to V, we have theme 2 beginning on the same dominant, as is apparent in Example 255. The status of temporary tonic then gradually accrues to the dominant by virtue of the appearance of emphatic secondary dominants and, most significantly, by the action of the cadential V of V in m. 27 at the end of the first part of the theme.

EXAMPLE 255. Haydn, *Sonata in C major,* I: Exposition, Theme 2, First Part

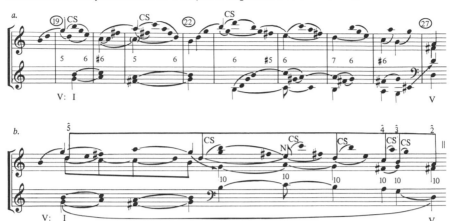

The middleground melodic structure of the first part of theme 2 can best be seen in Example 255*b*. There, somewhat concealed by covering voices and other foreground events, is the middleground progression $\hat{5}$–$\hat{4}$–$\hat{3}$–$\hat{2}$. In the first four measures d² ($\hat{5}$) is prolonged by a subsidiary linear progression of a descending third and decorated at the immediate foreground by the covering voice that centers on g². The second phrase of this part of theme 2 is five measures long, an unusual expansion of the norm of four measures.

Example 255*b* shows clearly how this comes about. The primary tone of the theme, d², is first prolonged by a complete upper neighbor-note figure d²–e²–d², and each element occupies exactly one measure. The fourth measure in the phrase contains the two passing notes c²–b¹, and the terminal note a¹ occupies the last measure. Thus, the linear progression of four elements is stretched out over five measures.[5]

The main middleground line of the second part of theme 2, shown in Example 256*b*, is extremely lucid. It begins with an extension of scale degree $\hat{2}$ over V of V; then the primary tone of theme 2, $\hat{5}$, is restored in m. 29 via the ascending arpeggiation, reminiscent of theme 1. At the foreground level, d² is mirrored an octave higher by d³, which returns to d² in m. 31. This is followed by two subsidiary descending third-progressions and, finally, by the descent to g¹ in m. 36, which completes the linear progression of a fifth from d² and closes this part of the theme.

---

5. Measure groupings of this kind are obviously an aspect of rhythm, and were always given consideration by Schenker in his own analyses, just as he gave attention to the rhythm of diminutions. While we have attempted to draw attention to rhythmic features of the music, beginning in Part One, it has not always been possible to offer detailed discussions of rhythmic organization in this introductory textbook, since we have wished to emphasize pitch organization as it is expressed in the general Schenkerian concept of structural levels.

EXAMPLE 256. Haydn, *Sonata in C major*, I: Exposition, Theme 2, Second Part

As the third part of theme 2, the *minore*, begins (Example 257), the first two parts have completed a binary form, with fundamental line:

$$\hat{5}\ \hat{4}\ \hat{3}\ \hat{2} \parallel \hat{5}\ \hat{4}\ \hat{3}\ \hat{2}\ \hat{1}$$
$$\text{I---V}\qquad\text{I----I}$$

It was mentioned earlier that the third part of theme 2 is unusual, and indeed it is. By converting the major dominant triad to a minor triad, the main tonic, C major, is momentarily rendered quite remote. (In fact, a radical change such as this is much more typical of the episodic forms that are discussed in Chapter 23.) Within this *minore* section the descant arpeggiates from g^1 up to d^2 ($\hat{5}$), and then d^2 is prolonged by a descending linear progression of a sixth down to $f\sharp^1$, at which point it is restated in the upper voice. There follows a foreground motion of a third down to b^1, which restores the major mode. The closing theme ends in a curious cadenza-like way based upon the seventh c^2 above the dominant, represented as an unfolding in Example 257*a* and, more simply, as a stationary seventh in 257*b*.

EXAMPLE 257. Haydn, *Sonata in C major*, I: Exposition, Theme 2, Third Part

This seventh remains unresolved until the entrance of b in m. 47 of the closing theme, Example 258. The note b¹ on the upbeat in m. 45 is understood to be a passing tone between c² and a¹, as indicated in the sketch. The closing theme itself is relatively simple, and can be read easily from Example 258*b*. Scale degree $\hat{3}$ in the long line is attained in m. 47, as b¹. This has attached to it two descending third-progressions, the second of which, beginning in m. 55, is definitive, closing the line down to g¹. This note is $\hat{1}$ within the dominant and $\hat{5}$ within the main tonality, a role that it assumes immediately with the repetition of the reprise.

EXAMPLE 258. Haydn, *Sonata in C major*, I: Exposition, Closing Theme

Other aspects of the closing theme can be seen in Example 258*b*. Especially beautiful are the references to the primary tone of theme 2, d², and its echo, d³, in m. 53, as well as the thematic arpeggiations formed in mm. 53–55.

Haydn, Piano Sonata in C major, *Hob. XVI/21, I: Development*

As just pointed out, with the return to the exposition, the last melodic note of the closing theme, g¹, is restated, as g², and becomes the primary tone of theme 1 (and the entire movement). After the repetition of the exposition, however, the development begins with d², the primary tone of theme 2, over the dominant harmony. This note, d², remains the controlling upper-voice component throughout the development. To a considerable extent, the following discussion concentrates upon its history and ultimate capitulation to the main primary tone of the movement, g².

Example 259 presents a greatly distilled version of the development, showing its essential voice leading without the complicated prolongations at middleground and foreground levels. What this very abstract sketch shows is a prolongation of scale degree $\hat{2}$ over V moving to $\hat{1}$ over I, at which point the reprise begins with a restatement of theme 1 and the primary tone $\hat{5}$. Scale degree $\hat{2}$ is itself prolonged by a descending third-progression, a motion which we will see replicated several times at other levels within the development. Indeed, this motion is thematic, for it is the first part of the linear progression set out in theme 1 in the exposition, the descending progression from g^2 to e^2 (Example 253, p. 303).

EXAMPLE 259. Haydn, *Sonata in C major*, I: Schematic of Development

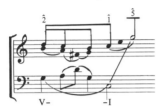

A schematic such as that provided by Example 259 is relatively meaningless from the analytical standpoint apart from the musical material that expands it. This will now be considered in connection with Example 260.[6]

It will be recalled that the development takes up each theme in order, beginning with a complete statement of theme 1 in the mediant, a closed form which prolongs d^2 through a linear progression of a fifth. At m. 63 the transition begins, but not exactly as it did in the exposition, since m. 63 corresponds to m. 10. That is, the transition here does not begin by repeating the opening of theme 1 as it did in the exposition.

The foreground of the transition is more intricate than it is in the exposition, and this is not reflected in the analytic sketch, which emphasizes middleground structures. The foreground might, in fact, occasionally be confusing here were it not for the prior statement of the model passage in the exposition. For example, in m. 64 the stepwise motion from g^2 to d^2 might be interpreted incorrectly as part of a larger descending motion g^2–f^2–e^2 (m. 65). This would obscure the correct middleground motion in m. 65, which is the neighbor-note formation d^2–e^2–d^2, corresponding to m. 12 of the exposition.

The transition leads to theme 2 in the "key of A minor" at m. 71. The foreground at this point is not that of theme 2, part 1, in the exposition, but of theme 2, part 2 (m. 27), which is developed here *both at foreground and*

---

6. In Schenker's analytic sketches, such as those in *Das Meisterwerk in der Musik* and FGMA, he customarily included information of the type shown in Example 259 at the higher structural levels, aligned with representations of foreground and middleground events at the

Example 260. Haydn, *Sonata in C major*, I: Development

middleground levels, in the way shown on the analytic sketch. In m. 69 the transition introduces c² in the upper voice, the main melodic note within the large section of the development governed by A minor (correctly designated II of V on the sketch). This is the passing note shown in Example 259.

After c² is introduced in m. 69, it is prolonged in the following way. First there is the short descending linear progression of a third. Then e² appears in the upper voice in m. 73, preceded by the thematic arpeggiation. Ultimately (m. 78) this descends through d² to c², a linear progression of the prefix type, the goal of which is the tail note of the progression, here c². The head note of this linear progression, e², is itself prolonged by an elaborate and very dramatic foreground: a stepwise ascending motion from inner to outer voice that culminates on f² in m. 75, an incomplete neighbor note. The bass of this motion is, if anything, more elaborate, featuring consonant skips and incomplete neighbor-note diminutions that prolong the motion from c¹ (I⁶) to d¹ (IV).

---

lower levels. This practice, although admirable, requires a large format and, moreover, is not appropriate to a pedagogical method that concentrates upon the presentation of shorter segments of music.

In mm. 78–80, the previous upper-voice motion is recapitulated in miniature: e^2–d^2–c^2. Beginning at m. 80 is a passage that has no counterpart in the exposition, although it comes in where a version of the *minore* section of mm. 36ff. might have occurred. What happens in this section is clear from the sketch: c^2 is further prolonged as the head note of a descending linear progression of a third which is completed in m. 83. The two measures that follow have as their goal the Neapolitan (N^6) on the downbeat of m. 85, with bb^1 in the descant. This melodic note is a large-scale passing note which belongs to the descending beamed linear progression of a third c^1 (m. 78)–bb^1 (m. 85)–a (m. 88). At this point in our consideration of Schenkerian analysis, it is probably not necessary to remind the reader that a^1 over d♯ at the end of m. 86 does not resolve the unusual chromatic note bb^1, but is a passing note at the foreground level that connects bb^1 down to g♯, as indicated by the slur in the sketch.

The closing theme, which begins in m. 88, repeats the descending third below the main note of the "A minor" section, here placed in the upper octave as c^3.

At m. 92 a 7–10 linear intervallic pattern begins. Remarkably, this too carries the upper-voice third motion c^2–b^1–a^1. But perhaps the most important aspect of the closing theme in this location in the music is the reorientation of harmony, directing the large-scale structure back to the main tonic at the beginning of the reprise. In the closing theme the A-minor triad, which is understood locally to be II of V, becomes VI of I (C major). This reinterpretation is effected by the linear intervallic pattern, which ends with an F-major triad. The F-major triad can only be understood as IV of C major (since it has no position within the diatonic structure of V—the dominant triad). Thus, in the analytic sketch a slur is drawn from bass note a up to bass f^1, corresponding to the roman numeral annotations below the lower staff.

With the resolution of d^2 to c^2 at the end of the development (the long-awaited capitulation of d^2), the underlying harmonic and melodic structure is in place for the reprise in the tonic, which is immediately forthcoming. The fact that d^2 is not literally present in m. 95 should not present any difficulty to the reader at this point in our discussion, since, as illustrated by Example 259, d^2 is the main melodic note of the entire development and is represented throughout at various structural levels by prolongational elements that refer to it directly.

Two general and interrelated aspects of the development require brief attention before we proceed to the reprise. First, the descending melodic third is everywhere. Second, descending melodic thirds are often "nested" within larger descending thirds, as in mm. 78–88. These are clearly visible as beamed structures on the analytic sketch.

Haydn, Piano Sonata in C major, *Hob. XVI/21, I: Reprise*

Since theme 1 and the transition are the same in the reprise as in the exposition, there is no need to provide redundant analytic sketches. The reader may refer to Examples 253 and 254 (pp. 303–4). As far as the transition is concerned, however, it is well to recall that this did not include a modulation to V, but only cadenced on V (a "half cadence"). Thus, in the reprise theme 2 begins on the tonic following this cadence on V in m. 113, a natural progression which requires no recomposing of the transition.

The foreground of theme 2, part 1, in the reprise is almost identical to that of the exposition. Because of the transposition, however, the middleground now has quite a different meaning. Example 261 provides an overview, omitting the measure-by-measure phase of the analysis given with the previous examples.

EXAMPLE 261. Haydn, *Sonata in C major,* I: Reprise, Theme 2

As can be read from the sketch, Example 261, the middleground descant of the first part of theme 2 consists of a linear progression of a fourth from g^1 to d^1, with corresponding bass progression I–V, producing an interruption form. The head note of the linear progression, g^1, of course refers to the primary tone of the movement, but not in the obligatory register. There is, however, a strong reference to that register in m. 118, at the beginning of the second phrase of the theme, indicated by the flagged g^2.

Part 2 of theme 2 varies considerably from its counterpart in the exposition. There (Example 256, p. 306, m. 28) the arpeggiation g^1–b^1–d^2 was a secondary feature in the foreground. Here in m. 123, the arpeggiation clearly repeats the motivic arpeggiation of theme 1. Moreover, Haydn avoids g^2 in m. 124 (which corresponds to m. 29 of the exposition), delaying reference to the obligatory register until two measures later. The most important modification in this part, however, is the introduction of E♭ in m. 125, which is clearly associated with the *minore* section in the third part of theme 2 (Example 257, p. 306). Now the motivic arpeggiation appears in its minor form, a traditional way of intensifying a motive and drawing special attention to it. This is further heightened in m. 126, when g^2 enters and becomes the head note of a descending minor arpeggiation (somewhat concealed by the foreground detail). It is important to recognize that this minor part does not duplicate the foreground of the *minore* part of the exposition. However, it clearly replaces it in the formal design, as is evident at the end of the minor part on the downbeat of m. 132, for this measure corresponds exactly to m. 41 of the exposition, the end of the *minore* part.

Theme 2 merges with the closing theme as it did in the exposition: As the linear progression of a third ends on e in m. 139 the descant brings in g^1 via the motivic arpeggiation, which, of course, is the arpeggiation that has been so strikingly presented at the end of the previous section (m. 123 ff.). This and the remainder of the end of the movement are shown in Example 262.

EXAMPLE 262. Haydn, *Sonata in C major*, I: Reprise, Closing Theme

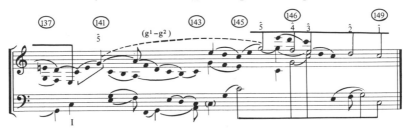

Although the closing theme in the reprise is almost identical to the closing theme in the exposition, it is read in a different way because of its position in the formal design with respect to the fundamental structure. Here the primary tone G is emphasized and, in particular, the very significant coupling g^1-g^2 which restores the obligatory register in m. 145. It is precisely at this point that Haydn changes from the exact transposition of the closing theme of the exposition. Instead of dropping down to g^1 at the end of m. 145 in accord with the model m. 53 of the exposition, the melody retains g^2 in the obligatory register. Superimposed above it is the subsidiary line $e^3-d^3-c^3$, which accompanies the descent of the fundamental line segment $\hat{5}-\hat{4}-\hat{3}$. Scale degree $\hat{2}$ then enters in m. 148, preceded by a foreground diminution attached to $\hat{3}$, and the close of the fundamental structure on $\hat{1}$ over I follows.

In this analysis, compared with the analysis of Beethoven's *Piano Sonata*, Op. 10, No. 1, III (Examples 222–42, pp. 281–93) we have not placed as much emphasis upon motivic structures of foreground and middleground. Instead, we have highlighted the relations between sections of the form as they are transformed over the three main parts of the sonata design. The analysis is also intended to give a lucid picture of the middleground structures that provide continuity within and between the various parts, unifying them over the span of the entire movement.

Example 263 outlines the form of this sonata movement so that the reader can review conveniently and so that this particular form may be easily compared with the general shape given in Example 219 (p. 277).

EXAMPLE 263. Haydn, *Sonata in C major*, I: Summary of Form

Exposition: I–V

Theme 1: I	Transition: I–V	Theme 2: V			Closing Theme: V
		Part 1	Part 2	Part 3	
1–6	7–18	19–27	27–36	36–44	45–57

Development: V–
58–95

Reprise: I

Theme 1: I	Theme 2: I	Closing Theme: I
96–113	113–37	137–49

Sonatina Form

The sonatina form is generally regarded as a variant of the sonata form.[7] It is a sonata without development section. Exposition and reprise follow the harmonic pattern of the sonata form, with theme 2, closing theme, and coda based (normally) upon the dominant harmony in major and the mediant harmony in minor. There may be a short transition between exposition and reprise, and this may have developmental characteristics, but it is not a full-fledged development in its own right. Development-like passages may occur in both exposition and reprise. An example of the latter is provided by Exercise 21/4, from Mozart's "Dissonant" Quartet.

Although the term *sonatina* may suggest a miniature form or a work of trivial nature, this is far from being true in general. The following works are among many examples of sonatina form in tonal music: Brahms's *Fourth Symphony*, II; Beethoven's *Eighth Symphony*, II; Schubert's *Unfinished Symphony*, II; and the Overture to *The Marriage of Figaro* by Mozart.

Sonatina forms are often found in second (slower) movements of multimovement instrumental works. Three famous examples are cited above. The work which will be analyzed in this section as an instance of sonatina form is also a second movement, the expressive Adagio movement of Mozart's *Piano Sonata in F major*, K. 332. The analytic sketches (Examples 264–67)

7. For some reason Schenker does not include sonatina form per se in the section on form in FC, but cites examples of it under the rubric "Four-part form" in §317, p. 141 (for example, Beethoven's *Piano Sonata in C minor*, Op. 10, No. 1, II). Perhaps he was concerned that the sonatina form might be confused with the many pieces called sonatinas, which are often trivial tonal compositions.

retain the barlines for easy reference to the full score and omit surface diminutions.[8]

The melodic structure of theme 1, as shown in Example 264, is rather complicated. At the foreground level the upper voice of m. 2 parallels that of m. 1: both outline a major triad, then drop back to an inner voice. The middleground structure of the sketch places these repeated foreground patterns in perspective, showing that they are internal to the large motion from bb^1 up to f^2, the primary tone, $\hat{5}$. At the foreground level the most important motion is d^2–c^2 in m. 1 and its match in m. 2, g^2–f^2. The latter pair, of course, introduces the primary tone, and is notated as a neighbor note (by the slur). The arpeggiation in each measure comes about as the result of a consonant skip. Thus, the second of these, in m. 2, lies above the primary tone, pointing to a still higher register, one that is touched briefly in m. 7 and which becomes prominent in the closing theme as well as in theme 2 in the reprise (Example 266).

EXAMPLE 264. Mozart, *Sonata in F major*, II: Exposition, Theme 1 and Transition

Still at the foreground level, the accented ascending chromatic passing tone is clearly a basic motive. This chromatic motive returns in various guises throughout the movement and is always flagged for special attention.

The middleground upper-voice motion of the second phrase of theme 1 (mm. 2–4) is straightforward: a linear progression of a descending fourth that terminates on c^2 to form an interruption. In the foreground the upper neighbor g^2 in m. 3 is carried forward from m. 2, where it was also attached to the primary tone f^2. There are two occurrences of the special chromatic

---

8. In the *Sonatas and Fantasies for the Piano*, edited by Nathan Broder (Theodore Presser, 1956), two versions of the reprise are given. The first is taken from Mozart's holograph, the second from the first edition published by Artaria in Vienna and by Schott in Mainz. The latter contains additional and voluminuous foreground diminutions.

motive: e², in the upper voice of m. 3 and b in the voice above the bass in the same measure. Also, as shown in the sketch, the voice exchange, which was a secondary feature of m. 2 is twice repeated in m. 3.

The transition begins in m. 5 with a statement of the opening phrase of theme 1 in B♭ minor. One effect of this change of mode is to bring into play the note D♭. This first occurs in the bass at the end of m. 6 as d♭, then immediately afterward as the climactic note in the foreground of the upper voice, d♭³, an appoggiatura that relates to the special chromatics of mm. 1–2, hence flagged. This d♭³ couples down to d♭², which resolves to c² on the downbeat of m. 8. The tie from c² in m. 8 to c² in m. 9 indicates that the former prepares the latter, which is the primary tone of theme 2. Thus, the structural role of the emphatic d♭³ in m. 7 is to introduce the main melodic note of the second theme.

Theme 2 begins with the accompanimental figure at the end of m. 8, which highlights the motion a–b♭, bracketed in Example 265. This prepares the entrance of the first note of theme 2, b♭¹, on the downbeat of m. 9, a dissonance that arpeggiates down to the inner voice e¹ before resolving to a¹ on the third beat of the measure over bass f. The resolution of the dissonant b♭¹ is covered by c² in the upper voice, a kind of overlapping. The dissonant seventh above the bass, b♭¹, does not move up to c²—thereby constituting the long-awaited case of the upward resolving seventh—but down to a¹. The latter progression is given directly in the tenor and is represented in the small motion c²–a¹–c² in the foreground of the upper voice on the third beat of the measure.

EXAMPLE 265. Mozart, *Sonata in F major*, II: Exposition, Theme 2 and Closing Theme

The second occurrence of the motto figure of the second theme is followed in mm. 10–11 by a descending configuration that begins with a superimposed

note, a². As shown in the sketch, Example 265, this couples down to a¹ on the third beat of m. 11, a note that progresses immediately to bb¹ to form the "accompanimental" motive of theme 2, bracketed in mm. 8–9 and here as well. Thus, the passage in parallel thirds that begins at the end of m. 10 effects an expansion of a characteristic motive of theme 2, a–bb, and in this specific sense is developmental. The motive is also repeated in the detail of the configuration as e²–f², c♯²–d², and finally as the goal motive a¹–bb¹.

At the middleground level, the analytic sketch (Example 265) shows that the goal bb¹ at the end of m. 11 is a passing note in the descending linear progression of a third, the head note of which is the primary tone of theme 2, c². However, before bb¹ connects to a¹ at the end of the progression it is prolonged by a rather elaborate unfolding at the foreground level. A few words about this are in order, since this is typical of many passages that may offer difficulty to the beginning student at first.

First, it should be apparent that the unfolding tritone bb¹–e¹ here is an expansion of the upper-voice tritone that began theme 2 in m. 9. In the expanded form it is articulated by the harmonic progression II–V, as shown. The first part of the unfolding is based upon the exchange between Bb and G, shown by the crossed arrows in the usual way. (It will be recalled that the exchange is a feature of theme 1.) The upper component of the exchange, bb¹–g¹, is part of a diminution which includes notes that cover it, specifically, d² and c² on the sketch. That these are decorative at the very surface of the melody becomes clear when f¹ enters on the second beat of m. 12 and the covering decorative voice is abandoned. This is an accented passing note, part of the ⁶₄, and resolves to e¹, completing the upper-voice unfolding. Above bass f on the third beat of m. 12 a¹ is brought in to complete the middleground linear progression. The analytic sketch, Example 265, shows all the relations within the unfolding using slur notation. Notice that the unfolding motion consists of two adjoined thirds, bb¹–g¹ and g¹–e¹. The whole is a particularly beautiful example of a foreground unfolding which carries its own diversionary ornaments, an unfolding in the service of a middleground element, namely, the passing tone bb¹ in the descending linear progression. The end of the unfolding, on e¹, is of course an elegant expression of the special chromatic motive of theme 1.

The closing theme begins in the middle of m. 16 following the repetition of the unfolding just discussed, which is shown in truncated form in Example 265. This thematic component is especially interesting because of the sudden change of register, the coupling a¹–a². This initiates a progression in parallel tenths that culminates on d³ at the end of m. 17, a clear reference to db³ of m. 6, the chromatic that introduced the primary tone of theme 2, as discussed above. In the extreme foreground, beginning on the third beat of m. 17, the ascent to d³ is emphasized in the most expressive way by the stepwise diminution that connects d² to d³.

On the third beat of m. 18 the middleground $\hat{2}$ enters, and this is followed by $\hat{1}$ on the downbeat of m. 19, to complete the linear progression of a fifth that began with the primary tone of theme 2, c^2, in m. 9. The tail note of the progression, f^1, of course, represents $\hat{5}$ of the fundamental structure and is notated accordingly as an open note. It is not, however, in obligatory register; the definitive restatement of $\hat{5}$ occurs only with the return of theme 1 in the reprise in m. 21.

Both here at the end of the exposition and at the end of the reprise we have omitted the codetta. In both places this short section contains multiple motivic references, including, in the reprise, the tritone eb^2-a^1, an allusion to that motive as it occurs in theme 2 of the reprise.

The reprise begins with a repetition of theme 1 and the transition, unchanged at the middleground level. (See note 8, p. 314.) Thus, the analytic sketch in Example 266 begins with the entrance of theme 2 in m. 29. Here, with the transposition to the tonic in effect, the dissonant seventh eb^2 resolves to d^2 and is covered by the primary tone $\hat{5}$ (f^2). What was middleground structure in theme 2 in its appearance in the exposition now becomes background (fundamental) structure in the reprise. As shown by the beamed open notes, $\hat{5}$ descends through $\hat{4}$ to $\hat{3}$ in m. 32. In the closing theme, mm. 36–39, the fundamental structure is closed, with the descant descending from $\hat{3}$ to $\hat{1}$ over the I–V–I succession.

EXAMPLE 266. Mozart, *Sonata in F major,* II: Reprise, Theme 2 and Closing Theme

At the foreground level in theme 1, mm. 30–31, we again find the downward coupling, this time from d^3 to d^2. Once again, d^3, in the highest register of the movement, refers to the apex note db^3 of m. 7. Here the downward coupling to d^2 prolongs the connection from f^2 to eb^2 ($\hat{3}$).

The unfolding in mm. 31–32 is an exact transposition of that in mm. 11–12. Because the analytic sketch in Example 266 shows the diagonal relation between descant e♭² and bass f, the voice exchange (with its diagonal lines) is omitted.

The closing theme in the reprise differs markedly at the foreground level from its counterpart in the exposition, as can be seen in the analytic sketch. In mm. 36–37 the succession of parallel tenths carries the upper voice to f² (at N.B.). This motion, of course, relates directly to theme 1 in the exposition, specifically to the arrival on f² ($\hat{5}$) at the end of m. 2. It is just at this point that the composer changes the foreground so that it is not simply a transposition of the closing theme in the exposition. The consonant skip up to b♭² is clearly a reference to that same note as it is associated with f² in m. 2 of theme 1. The allusion to theme 1 does not end there, however, for the descant continues upward to g², and this note has a descending arpeggiation attached to it, an exact replica of the neighbor note g² and its arpeggiation at the beginning of m. 3 in Example 264. Only the surface diminutions differ. In the upper voice of m. 38 there is a final reference to theme 1: the foreground ascent from f² to b♭² just before the entrance of $\hat{2}$ (c²). There is no corresponding motion in the closing theme of the exposition.

The foregoing analysis of the slow movement of Mozart's *Piano Sonata in F major*, K. 332, an instance of sonatina form, has emphasized the interaction of musical components at middleground and foreground levels and the significance of changes in the foreground of the reprise with respect to the exposition. In constructing an analysis it is always essential to understand, insofar as possible, every level of the composition as it contributes to the progression of the whole. It is not sufficient only to display the fundamental structure. For this reason we have devoted considerable space to a discussion of certain intricacies of structure, such as the large-scale unfolding in theme 2.

In selecting a sonatina form to present as the final example of this large chapter, we intend to make an important general point: that although the sonatina lacks a development section per se, it has many developmental features. A good demonstration of this is the closing theme in the reprise, which begins as an exact transposition of the closing theme in the exposition, but is then developed in such a way as to bring out its resemblance to theme 1, thus adding another facet to the overall unity of the composition.

Example 267 summarizes the form.

EXAMPLE 267. Mozart, *Sonata in F major*, II: Summary of Form

Exposition: I–V
Theme 1 and Transition: I–V   Theme 2: V   Closing Theme: V
1–8   9–15   16–19

Reprise

Theme 1 and Transition: I	Theme 2: I	Closing Theme: I
21–28	29–36	36–39

Exercises

Following the pattern of the examples in this chapter, the exercises are to be completed as vertically aligned analytic sketches: The upper graph retains barlines and shows foreground detail, with some indications of middleground structures, while the lower graph is a clear representation of middleground and background structures. Brief written comments on the analysis are suggested, especially concerning motivic structures.

1. Mozart, *Piano Sonata in B♭ major*, K. 333, II

> This is one of Mozart's many beautiful slow movements. The exposition is straightforward (the beginning was given as Exercise 20E/3, p. 275), although special attention needs to be given to theme 2 (m. 14ff.). In particular, the seventh e♭² in the upper voice resolves downward to d². Mozart often covers the resolution of the seventh in this artistic way, as he did in the theme 2 of the movement from the *F-major Sonata*, K. 332 (Examples 264–67). And beginning with m. 18 a careful reading of the detail should sort out the foreground components from those of the middleground. Although the middleground voice leading of the development is clear and the fundamental melodic-contrapuntal motion is uncomplicated, the foreground introduces a number of digressions which require careful study and, above all, careful listening.

2. Mozart, *Piano Sonata in F major*, K. 280, II

> This movement was perhaps modeled on Haydn's *Piano Sonata in F major*, Hob. XVI/23, II. It contains many unusual features, such as the $^6_4$ at the beginning of theme 2 (m. 9), and a false reprise in m. 33. The development is challenging, and may not be immediately clear to the analyst. Consider how it connects exposition and reprise.

3. Haydn. *Symphony in F♯ minor*, Hob. I/45, II

> A carefully done sketch of the foreground of this movement will prove rewarding alone, for it contains many motivic associations and elegant arpeggiations, overlappings, and unfoldings.

4. Mozart, *Quartet in C major*, K. 465, II

> This movement, in sonatina form, is from the last of the six quartets dedicated to Haydn, sometimes called the "Dissonant" Quartet, because of the unusual opening of the adagio introduction to the first movement. The composition is rich in detail, with many special moments, such as the distinctive music that first occurs in m. 32. The reprise begins in m. 45. Beginning in m. 57 is a long section that may be described as transition qua development, leading to the return of theme 2 in m. 75. A "new" melodic element enters in the closing section of the reprise, at m. 102.

22

Variation Form and Structural Levels

The "theme" of a theme and variations is in most cases not a single theme, but a self-contained musical form. This is, of course, a fact that we have already acknowledged; Part Two, recall, depended heavily on variation themes as a source of small but complete formal units. At the same time, the variation theme is obviously part of a larger musical form—theme plus variations plus coda (the latter optional)—and it is in this role that we approach it here.

As a type of composition, the theme and variations has been common throughout every period in which music (particularly instrumental music) has been written. Variation technique lies at the heart of the study and practice of improvisation, no matter what the idiom. If we accept the basic notion that the theme, by definition, is the structural model for each of the ensuing variations, we can see that the variation process is essentially the reverse of the reductive process with which most of this book has been concerned.[1] Therefore, in sets of variations where the key of the theme is preserved throughout—as was the standard practice in the Baroque and Classic periods—it is generally valid to let a background sketch of the theme stand for the entire piece or movement, and to presume that those factors that change from variation to variation will be at the middleground and foreground levels.

The foreground level, through the process of diminution, is where the preponderance of variation activity takes place. This brings us full circle to the beginning of this book, specifically to Examples 3–6 (pp. 9–15). An additional illustration, by way of review, is given in Example 268, whose source is the familiar Mozart theme first cited in Example 137 (p. 133). Though the surface details exhibited at *a*, *b*, and *c* are all different, each is reducible to the melodic outline graphed in Example 137.

---

1. An obvious exception would be those instances where a variation may be a simplification of the theme.

EXAMPLE 268. Mozart, *Piano Sonata in A major*, K. 331, I

The operatons shown in Example 268 are typical of variation procedure prior to the nineteenth century, where such elements as meter, phrase length, and key (save for brief excursions into the parallel minor mode) tended to remain constant. Such was no longer necessarily the case in the Romantic period, where we can observe a gradual and general loosening of these constraints. Obviously, the freer the relationship between theme and variation, the greater the chance for the deeper structural levels to be affected. The ways in which this can occur may be summarized as follows:

1. Variations will tend to expand upon motives introduced in the theme.
2. A correct background reading of the theme will be reinforced by the variations, while an incorrect reading will be refuted.
3. Variatons in keys other than the tonic will tend to constitute middleground prolongations within the background structure of the set of variations as a whole.

A dramatic illustration of observation 1 occurs in a set of variations by Brahms, on another of the themes initially cited in Example 137, the *Chorale St. Antoni*, attributed to Haydn. The two motives of importance in the theme—the neighbor note and the descending third-progression (both highlighted in Example 138, p. 135)—received varied and pervasive treatment in Brahms's variations. This fact is evident from the very beginning, as we see in Variation 1, mm. 1–10 (Example 269; compare Example 138).

Regarding Example 269, look first at the neighbor-note motive in its pitch-specific form, D–E♭–D. This motive occurs at least once in each of the three contrapuntal strands, and as a consequence makes at least one appearance as part of the descant, inner voice, and bass. Its occurrence in the bass (mm. 35–36) is new to this variation, a fact which is underscored by the coupling of bass D–E♭ with d–e♭ (mm. 35–37, in imitation of the descant d^2–e♭^{2}–d^3–e♭^{3} in mm. 30–32), and the close proximity of the upper octave of this coupling to the inner-voice e♭–d in m. 37 (marked N.B.).

In short, Variation 1 emphasizes the neighbor note in its foreground

EXAMPLE 269. Brahms, *Variations on a Theme by Haydn*, Op. 56b, Variation 1

aspect. Interestingly, the situation is just the opposite with the other important motive, the descending third-progression D–C–B♭. This motive, though traceable at the middleground level over the length of the passage, is conspicuously absent as a foreground detail. As an indication of this fact, notice that the foreground representation in mm. 2–3 of the theme (that is, the descent from D to B♭ harmonized by I–V–VI) is omitted from the present variation (again, compare Example 269 with 138).

Observation 2, which was in essence stated earlier (beginning of Chapter 12), is crucial to our approach to themes and variations. To begin with an already familiar example, we cite the Mozart *A-major Sonata* (K. 331, I): specifically, how the reading of E (5̂) as primary tone of the theme is confirmed subsequently in the movement. As pointed out previously (recall p. 320, note 1), an obvious instance is found in the eight-measure coda appended

EXAMPLE 270. Mozart, *Piano Sonata in A major*, K.331, I
    a. Coda to Variation 6

---

2. A secondary feature of this last variation and the coda which follows is the use of 4/4 time instead of 6/8.

b. Variation 5, mm. 13–16

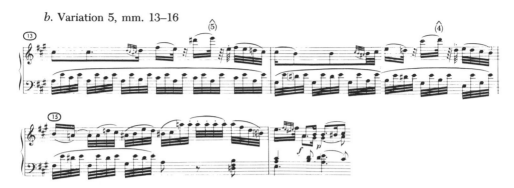

to the sixth and last variation,[2] in which the descent from scale degree $\hat{5}$ is recapitulated and then stated once more for emphasis (Example 270*a*). No less striking is Variation 5, where in the reprise of the A section (recall the graph of the corresponding portion of the theme in Example 152, p. 162) scale degrees $\hat{5}$ and $\hat{4}$ are echoed in the highest register used in the piece, specifically e^3 and d^3 respectively (Example 270*b*).

Our last introductory example concerns observation 3—that is, how best to address the situation where a variation is in a key other than that of the theme. The source of this example is anything but "introductory": it is the massive double set of variations by Brahms, for piano, on Paganini's twenty-fourth caprice for solo violin. Nonetheless, the theme of the work has the advantage of being well known; moreover, there is one variation, number 12, in Book 2, which illustrates observation 3 in an exemplary fashion.

The relevant excerpts from the Brahms Paganini Variations are shown in Example 271. At *a* is the theme, as adapted by Brahms. Although we have not graphed the theme itself,[3] it should be clear upon even a cursory examination that the theme establishes E (scale degree $\hat{5}$ in the key of A minor) as the

EXAMPLE 271. Brahms, *Variations on a Theme of Paganini*, Op. 35, Book 2
  a. Theme

---

3. The reader is referred to Schenker's graph in FC, Fig. 40/9.

b. Variations 12, 13 (beginning)

Un poco più Andante

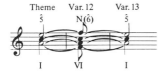

c. Schematic overview

d. Variation 12 (foreground and middleground)

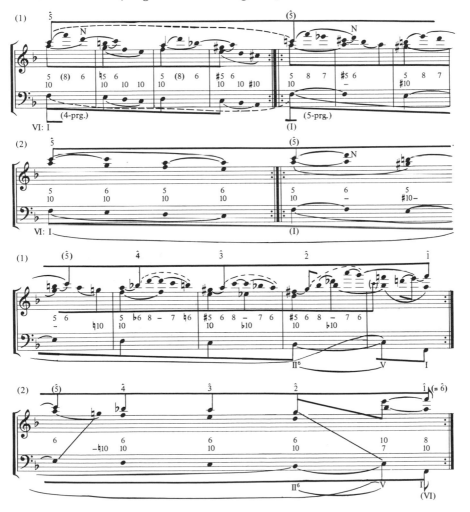

primary melodic tone. Variation 12, shown at b along with the beginning of Variation 13, is in F major. On a large scale, we can read Variation 12 as a prolongation of scale degree $\hat{6}$ (F) over VI (F major), resolving to $\hat{5}$ over I at the start of the following variation. This larger picture is graphed in the schematic at c; a more detailed view of Variation 12 is given at d. To summarize, Variation 12 can be viewed as prolonging an element which, though it lies outside the background structure per se, occupies a significant position within the middleground—specifically, as the harmonized upper neighbor to the primary tone.

This last point warrants further explanation. If, for the moment, we treat Variation 12 as a separate piece in the key of F major (as we have done in Example 271d), we see quickly that the primary melodic tone within Variation 12 is not F, but C. This is true despite the prominence given the consonant skip c^3–f^3 (mm. 1, 5), which would seem at first to suggest F as being more important. The reason is that in this consonant skip and all those that follow (for example, a^2–d^3 in m. 3, b^2–e^3 in m. 7, etc.), the upper tone is invariably an octave duplication of the bass. Were we to read these consonant skips according to their respective upper tones, we would end up with a reading of the entire variation as a succession of parallel octaves in the upper voices. The correct reading, therefore, is the one shown in the graphs here. The primary tone, within the key of F (VI of A minor) is scale degree $\hat{5}$, whose validity is confirmed by the neighbor-note motions at the beginning of each section of the variation (most notably the double neighbor over mm. 5–8). The descent from scale degree $\hat{5}$, which takes place over mm. 8–12, is complicated by one very important factor: a registral shift which thrusts the concluding tone of the descent back into the same octave as the f^3 of the initial consonant skip. It could thus be argued that, perceptually, the variation ends, not on scale degree $\hat{1}$, but scale degree $\hat{8}$ of F major—which in turn is equal to scale degree $\hat{6}$ (upper neighbor to $\hat{5}$) of A minor. Lastly, by way of review, the graphs in Example 271d provide an excellent study in the recognition and notation of linear intervallic patterns (recall Chapter 4).

In a manner parallel to the preceding chapter, we now proceed to treat in detail a complete set of variations on a single theme. The tremendous number of possibilities inherent in variation form makes it an unwieldy subject for any kind of exhaustive categorization; for that reason it must be made clear that the ensuing discussion is, in the general sense, intended only to show the kinds of things one looks for in studying a theme and variations. The extent to which these things may or may not be present is, of course, an index of the quality of the composition.

Beethoven, Piano Sonata in E major, *Op. 109, III: Theme*

From among the last group of Beethoven piano sonatas, the one most accessible to the listener is likely to be Op. 109. It is also one of two late sonatas to conclude with a theme and variations (the other is Op. 111). As with any late work of Beethoven, Op. 109 is a highly personal statement fraught with complexities and subleties that stretch the imagination to its fullest. As testimony to these special qualities, we cite Schenker's *Erläuterungsausgabe* (Critical Edition) of Op. 109,[4] which concentrates on the foreground and performance aspects of the music, and in this way serves as companion to his celebrated performing edition of the sonatas.[5]

The score of the theme is reproduced in Example 272, along with two analytic graphs. The first, shown at *b*, reflects the kind of detailed examination which is indispensible to a proper understanding of the theme and, in turn, of the variations which follow.

EXAMPLE 272. Beethoven, *Sonata in E major*, III: Theme

---

4. Beethoven, *Die letzten Sonaten: Sonate E dur Op. 109. Erläuterungsausgabe* [critical edition] *von Heinrich Schenker*. New edition, ed. Oswald Jonas (Vienna: Universal Edition, 1971); originally published 1913. Similar volumes were completed for Op. 110, 111, and 101, with original publication dates of 1914, 1915, and 1920 respectively.

5. Beethoven, *Complete Piano Sontas*, edited by Heinrich Schenker, with a new introduction by Carl Schachter (New York: Dover Publications, 1975). This edition was originally published by Universal, first c. 1923, then in a revision by Erwin Ratz in 1947.

Virtually every note of the theme is retained in the graph at *c*, and judgment is deliberately withheld concerning the deeper structural levels. The relatively simple texture of the theme has permitted us to leave in more surface detail than might otherwise have been practicable (compare, for instance, the graph at (1) in Example 271*d*). Moreover, a well-composed theme and variations will tend to endow such detail with greater significance as the piece progresses.

In this particular piece the interval of a third is paramount, in two ways: first, it is used with remarkable consistency; second, it receives special emphasis in two pitch-specific forms, namely G♯–E and G♯–B. The former is announced at the very beginning and, in the measure immediately following, imitated (by D♯–B) through overlapping. The statements in mm. 1 and 2 are both supported by a voice exchange with the bass. In the graph at *b*, under N.B., we have highlighted G♯–E as follows: at its initial appearance (m. 1), its transformation into a sixth (mm. 7, 11), and (most surprisingly of all) its alteration into a minor third (m. 8).[6] As we have shown in the graph, this last

---

6. The exclamation mark in parentheses, which calls attention to the unusual nature of this particular event in the graph, was one of Schenker's favorite notational devices.

event can be read within the context of a coupling from e¹ downward to e (note the retention of the upward direction of the stem on the lower note); moreover, the motion g♮–e in the right hand is supported by an exchange with E–G♮ in the left. Although this exchange takes place ostensibly between two inner voices, the parallelism between it and the voice exchange that begins the piece is unmistakable. In addition, as we have already pointed out, the upper voice of the exchange in m. 8 can be interpreted, through the process of coupling, as a register transfer of the descant. (This last matter will be more clearly addressed in the second graph.)

Interacting with the third G♯–E is its triadic complement G♯–B; however, the latter receives distinctly different treatment in the theme. Rather than occurring as a skip supported by voice exchange, the interval from G♯ to B is consistently expressed as a stepwise succession, with either A or A♯ as the intervening note. The various representations of the filled-in third from G♯ to B (or vice versa) are indicated by either brackets or beams in the graph at *b*. Those which are beamed extend over longer durational spans and have full harmonic support, while the bracketed segments occur simply as notes in direct succession.

The interplay between the beamed and bracketed segments—in effect, between the foreground and middleground levels—is an ongoing feature of the entire theme. The first beamed progression, g♯¹–a♯¹–b¹ (mm. 3–4), is foreshadowed in the left hand by bass G♯–A♮–B (mm. 1–2) and accompanied in part by a small replica of itself (bracketed g♯–a♯–b in the left hand). A similar phenomenon can be observed when we relate the beamed progression b–a–g♯–a♯–b (mm. 5–8) to the bracketed segments spanning the motion from B to G♯ and back to B in the bass (mm. 4–5).

The second half of the theme contains one correspondence that is even more remarkable: the middleground progression b¹–a¹–g♯¹ (mm. 9–11), and the way in which it is followed immediately (in m. 12) by b–a♯–g♯ at the foreground level in an inner voice. The remaining bracketed and beamed progressions (mm. 15–16) are joined together in a single gesture: the motion from g♯¹ to b¹ and back to g♯¹ (almost a mirror image of what happens at the end of the first half of the theme). There is, meanwhile, a more fundamental progression which the motion to and from g♯¹ masks, namely the descent to e (transferred to the same inner voice that contains the descent to g♯ in m. 12).

---

7. This principle explains the stem on d♯ in the bass line of m. 10. Despite the fact that the measure reiterates the same linear intervallic pattern as m. 9 in three of the four voices, the fact that the one remaining voice (tenor) remains stationary on b counteracts whatever surface parallelism that might be suggested by the former. The consequence, taking all four voices into account, is that, in m. 10, d♯ is the proper bass counterpoint for the descant a¹, making the resultant harmony V$_5^6$. The recurrence of the same pair of outer voices—and the same resultant harmony—in m. 14 is a contributing factor in enabling us to establish the larger pattern shown in the second graph over mm. 9–14.

There are two areas we have not yet discussed in connection with this particular example: harmony and large-scale melodic organization. With regard to the first of these, notice now, in the first graph, the stemmed melody notes all have their counterparts in the bass, so that it is possible to extract these notes from the surrounding material to form a succession of outer voices that will be both intelligible and appropriate to the piece.[7] This is the point of departure for the second graph, shown at *c*, in which these elements are notated anew and brought into sharper focus.

Included in this new graph at *c* is a reading of the background structure of the theme, a subject which is very much open to discussion. Indeed, a real question exists— and persists—as to whether G♯ (scale degree $\hat{3}$) or B (scale degree $\hat{5}$) is the primary melodic tone. On the one hand, a case for B can be made on the following grounds: 1) it is the highest active triadic degree in the piece (with the single exception of the foreground e^2 in m. 11, omitted from the second graph); 2) it is the goal note of the ascent in mm. 3–4, and is prominently featured throughout the theme from m. 4 onward; 3) there is a clear linear descent leading from that note, beginning in m. 9. Meanwhile, on the other hand, the role of G♯ as a melodic focal point is clearly established at the very beginning of the piece. It is, after all, the common tone between the two motivically important intervals, G♯–E and G♯–B; moreover, the pull of the linear progression b^1–a^1–g♯^{1}, in every one of its three iterations in the second half of the theme, can be perceived more aptly as toward the G♯ rather than away from the B. (The internal harmonic prolongation of III supporting an extension of g♯^{1} in m. 12 lends credence to this perception, as does the reappearance of g♯^{1} as the ostensible melodic goal in the final cadence.)

If in fact the primary tone is G♯, then B becomes a cover tone (recall Chapter 18, especially Example 190, p. 224). The graph at *c* reflects this interpretation, and should be studied carefully.

Beethoven, Piano Sonata in E major, Op. 109, III: Variation 1

The sophistication and subtlety of this work, already amply demonstrated in the theme, is carried still further in the variations. In Variation 1 (Example 273) we find several noteworthy changes: the note B, which we read as a cover tone in the theme (Example 272), is thrust into relief in the variation's first five measures, only to return in the same octave (b^2) in m. 9. Within the first five measures, however, the moving voice is the one below the voice bearing b^2 (that is, e^2 ascending to g♯^{2}); and this fact continues to suggest that B is a cover tone and not the primary melodic tone. Another clue as to the identity of the primary tone comes in mm. 13–15, where we find the note a^3 resolving to g♯^{3}. Although it is possible to read a^3 as a registrally displaced passing note—in analogy to the large third-progression b^1–a^1–g♯^{1} in the latter half of the theme (see Example 272c, mm. 9–14)—it is significant that a^3 represents a register invoked for the very first time. It is also the highest note in the movement thus far. The sforzato marking on a^3 reinforces the view that this note was intended by the composer to be set apart from the earlier b^2 of m. 9, hence the neighbor-note interpretation given in the graph following the score in Example 273.

EXAMPLE 273. Beethoven, *Sonata in E major*, III: Variation 1

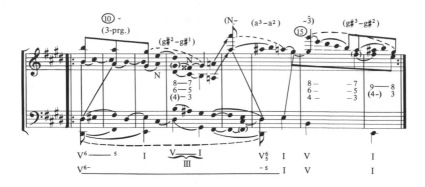

In terms of analytic procedure, this graph represents a level midway between the two stages shown in the analysis of the theme given in Example 272. In the amount of detail that is retained (barlines, specific registers, foreground diminutions), the graph of Variation 1 in Example 273b resembles Example 272b; however, this new graph includes some of the interpretive overlay previously reserved for Example 272c. Instances of this are the labeling of such middleground events as linear progressions and couplings, and the labeling of harmonies at the middleground level. Although the background notes are not explicitly notated as such, they remain the same as in the theme, albeit expanded registrally.

Before proceeding further, mention must be made of several subsidiary harmonic changes that occur in Variation 1. In mm. 1–4, although the measure-by-measure succession I–V–I–V is preserved, the bass line now moves by step, with only one note per measure. The filled-in skips E–B–e–b (downbeats of mm. 1–4 in the theme) are thereby replaced by the stepwise progression E–F♯–G♯–A. The G♯ on the downbeat of the following measure is the first place since the beginning where the bass lines of the theme and Variation 1 coincide; however, while the theme has the bass moving upward by step from G♯ to e in mm. 5–7, the first variation shows it retracing its path back to E—in other words, a descending third rather than an ascending sixth. The overall harmonic prolongation is still the tonic triad, as it is in the theme, until m. 8, where a definitive motion toward the dominant takes place. The preparation of the dominant is different, however: V of V in Variation I as opposed to the augmented-sixth chord in the theme. (Notice at the same time that melodic G♮ is retained despite this harmonic change.) Finally, there is the greater attention given to the leading tone in the bass in the second half of this variation: first, the substitution of D♯ for B on the downbeat of m. 9 (thus establishing a connection with the recurrence of this note in the same register on the downbeat of m. 14); second, the fact that this leading tone and its resolution (bass D♯ and E) are the lowest notes in mm. 9–16.

Beethoven, Piano Sonata in E major, *Op. 109, III: Variation 2*

Beginning with Variation 2, and excluding only Variation 4 among those following, Beethoven abandons the literal repeats of mm. 1–8 and 9–15 in favor of a through-composed treatment. Consequently, if the form of the theme is ‖:A:‖:B:‖, then the form of Variation 2 can be expressed as AA'BB'. Although the same can be said for the other through-composed variations, Variation 2 has the unique attribute of being a true double variation. The surface features of the A and A' sections are distinctly different from one another, likewise the B and B' sections; at the same time, those of A and B—and of A' and B'—show a distinct resemblance. The sectional form of Variation 2, analyzed in Example 274, can thus be summarized as follows:

A (1–8)   A' [1–8]   B (9–16)   B' [9–16]

Within this overall form, the A and B sections are relatively easy to describe verbally. There we find essentially the same notes as in the corresponding portions of the theme, initially in the same register, but thereafter moving upward in stages (first beat of m. 3, second beat of m. 5, and first beat of m. 8, to be precise). Although the pattern of registers in the B section of Variation 2 is not nearly so uniform in direction, it is still possible to discern a general reversal over mm. 9–16 (though more so in the bass than in the descant). Of course, the most immediately apparent surface feature, the fragmentation of the theme's quarter-note verticals into individual sixteenth notes, is consistent throughout the A and B sections.

In short, the A and B sections of Variation 2 adhere closely to the harmonic and melodic structure established by the theme. The A' and B' sections are quite different in this respect. The beginning of the A' section prolongs the goal harmony of the A section by means of a dominant pedal point instead of returning to the root-position tonic. Over this pedal point the upper voices, taking as their point of departure the theme's opening dyad g#[1]–e[1], initiate a pattern of overlapped thirds, which begins again an octave higher in m. [5].[8] This overlapping is intriguing in that not only are the successive thirds overlapped, but also the notes within these successive thirds—a fact which we have tried to communicate through the judicious use of stems and slurs in Example 274. (The same overlapping is to return later in the movement, on a grander scale, as the motivic mainstay of Variation 5.) Yet

8. The use of bracketed measure numbers for the repeat sections follows the method used by Schenker in the *Erläuterungsausgabe*.

it is important to remember that this seemingly new material is firmly rooted
in the theme's single, most elementary motive: the descending third G♯–E.
And despite the underpinning by the dominant pedal, we can point to the
recurrence of the coupling g♯¹–g♯², the descending fourth-progression from
the higher of these two notes, and the augmented-sixth chord at the
cadence—all as evidence that the A′ section is not altogether unlike the eight
measures that make up the A section of this variation.

EXAMPLE 274. Beethoven, *Sonata in E major*, III: Variation 2

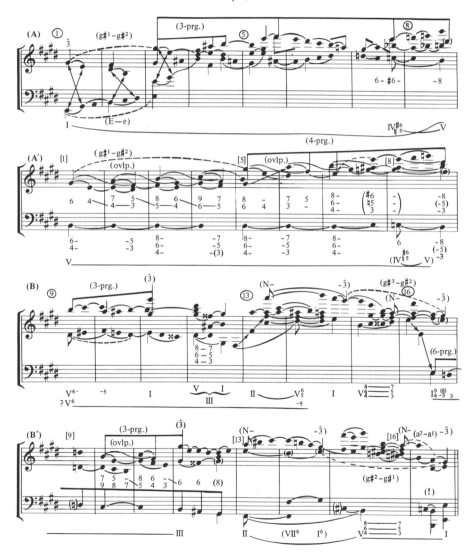

Like the overlapping in the A′ section, the unison D that opens the B′ section is an element whose significance extends beyond the confines of the present variation: in fact, it appears at the same place in every variation thereafter, with the exception of Variation 3. Contrapuntally, we can explain the D♮ of m. [9] as a passing note between the E of m. 16 and the C♯ of mm. [10–11]; the larger context, as shown in the graph, is a linear progression in the bass that spans the descending sixth from e (m. 16) to G♯ (m. [12]). This sixth-progression connects I with III and strengthens the position of the latter; what disappears, meanwhile, is the prolongation of V that comes at the beginning of the B section of the theme. The connection between the end of the B section and the beginning of the B′ section is made clear by the fact that D♮ (to be registrally specific, d♮) actually makes its appearance before the B section is completely finished— as an upbeat to the following measure.

As with the graph of Variation 1, the graph of Variation 2 in Example 274 concerns itself with the foreground and middleground levels. Once again, the background is $\hat{3}$ over I, more clearly so in this variation than in the one preceding.

Beethoven, Piano Sonata in E major, Op. 109, *III: Variation 3*

Variation 3 contrasts with the previous two variations in several respects. It is the first to use duple instead of triple meter; also, it is the first variation to bear a new tempo designation (allegro vivace). At the same time, it must be noted that the score of Variation 2 ends without a double bar, implying that Variation 3, contrasting though it may be, is to follow without pause. Above all, Variation 3 is a study in double counterpoint using elements distilled directly from the theme, with no new or derived motives added. The right hand of mm. 1–4 duplicates the bass line of the corresponding measures of the theme almost exactly, while the left hand presents, with diminutions, a registrally expanded version of the theme's opening upper-voice material. The result, graphed in Example 275 (compare mm. 1–3 of the theme), is a succession of voice exchanges in contrary motion, resolving to the vertical B_1–b^2 in m. 4. This two-voice counterpoint is repeated in mm. 5–8 with the parts exchanged; as a result, the contrary motion of the voices is in the reverse direction—inward instead of outward. The linear intervallic pattern of each voice exchange is also reversed in the process: specifically, the pattern 6–10 now becomes 10–6.

The written-out repeat of the A section (which we again call A′) restates the content of mm. 1–8, with the addition of eighth-note diminutions in the right hand and with a slight alteration in the pattern of sixteenth-note diminutions in the left. As in the A section, the parts change hands beginning in m. 5. The graph in Example 275 shows the A′ section in the same stage of reduction as the A section: that is, without the diminutions. (For the sake of

EXAMPLE 275. Beethoven, *Sonata in E major*, III: Variation 3

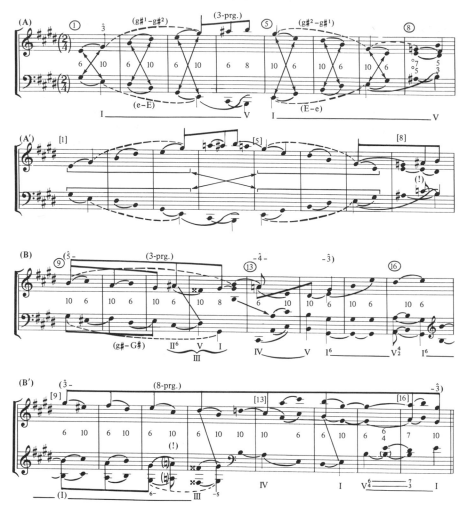

readability, the small voice exchanges are highlighted only in the graph of the A section, the larger exchange of parts only in the graph of the A′ section.) The cadences in mm. [4] and [8] are shown in greater detail because the changes here could be more significant: for example, in mm. [7–8] we see a reiteration of the linear progression G♯–A♯–B accompanied by the reintroduction (marked with an exclamation point) of the flatted upper neighbor to B in the bass (compare the theme, m. 8, and Variation 2, mm. 8, [8], and [16]).

The second half of Variation 3 is predictably more complex than the first half, owing to the more complex structure on which it is based. Instead of a symmetrical treatment such as we find within the respective A and A′ sections, we now find, in the B and B′ sections, a symmetry between them:

that is, an exchange of parts between mm. 9–16 and [9–16]. (Notice that symmetry within each section is no longer possible, since the foreground succession of harmonies in mm. 13–16 does not duplicate that which occurs in mm. 9–12). Once again, the exchange of parts causes the linear intervallic patterns to reverse themselves (compare corresponding measures in the B and B' sections). There are occasional inconsistencies in this regard, for two reasons: either the notes themselves are altered (compare m. 12 with m. [12]), or the part merits a different interpretation according to whether it is in the treble or the bass (compare mm. 15–16 with mm. [15–16]).

The latter consideration is also responsible for differences between linear progressions elicited in the B section and those in the B' section. A case in point is the octave-progression in the treble of mm. [9–16]. Although it is possible to find the same notes in the bass of the previous eight measures, the harmonic pull toward G♯ (III) in m. 12 precludes the reading of a stepwise descent from D♯ to C♯ in the left-hand part of mm. 12–13. In comparing the treble of mm. 9–12 with the bass of mm. [9–12], meanwhile, we find one small but significant change: from A♯ (m. 11) to A♮ (m. [11]), to which we have drawn attention in the graph by means of an exclamation point and a flag. As a result of this change, the note in question is more likely to be perceived as a neighbor to G♯ (the latter the primary melodic tone, here prolonged harmonically) than as a passing note from B.

Beethoven, Piano Sonata in E major, *Op. 109, III: Variation 4*

Variation 4, occurring at roughly the midpoint of the movement, is marked by changes in both tempo ("somewhat slower, like the theme") and meter (9/8). The compound nature of the latter—three within three—is symbolic of the role played by this variation. Motivically, Variation 4 is a synthesis of all that has come before it; moreover, much of this variation's motivic richness occurs at the submetrical level. An additional characteristic of Variation 4 is that each section begins on an upbeat. This includes the opening section, whose upbeat occurs at the end of the last measure of the preceding variation, and in general accounts for the odd placement of repeat signs in the score (i.e. after the first full measure of each section rather than at the beginning). The detailed nature of the graph in Examples 276 has made it necessary to retain this arrangement therein; however, we have added double bars to clarify the sectional divisions. (One exception is the double bar at the end of the variation, which occurs in the score as well—in contrast to the absence of double bars at the end of Variations 2 and 3.)

To appreciate the motivic complexity of Variation 4, we need only look at the first two measures. Already, within the right hand's first six notes, we can find the three thirds essential to the theme: the lower and upper thirds of the

EXAMPLE 276. Beethoven, *Sonata in E major*, III: Variation 4

tonic triad (the latter filled in by step), and the lower third of the dominant. The order in which these intervals appear—even the notes themselves—is also significant. The first six notes of the right hand virtually replicate the melody of mm. 2–4 of Variation 3, while the latter's opening third E–G♯ (m. 1) is stated by the left hand at the upbeat. When we consider that the melody that begins Variation 3 is in turn derived from the bass line of the corresponding measure of the theme, then we can begin to comprehend just how intimately the details of Variation 4 relate to the basic material of the piece.

The succession of thirds described above is clarified in Example 276 by means of brackets. In addition to those, notice the descending third g♯¹–e¹ that occurs between the left and right hands in m. 1 (the same interval that begins the theme, in the identical register), also the thirds g♯–e and a–f♯ in mm. 1–2 (the same pattern introduced through overlapping in Variation 2 and, as we shall see momentarily, reintroduced in Variation 5). There is, finally, a larger motive highlighted in Example 276 by the designation N.B. plus a bracket (right hand, mm. 1–2; left hand, mm. 5–6), which appears to be a direct descendant of the opening melody in Variation 1.

As we mentioned earlier, the graph in Example 276 is fairly lavish in its attention to foreground detail. The foregoing discussion should make it clear why this is so. At the same time, we have tried to be more concise in cases where a particular figure has been introduced previously; there, as established practice dictates, we have substituted the prolonged note or interval for the kind of detailed analysis shown in the first few measures. Notwithstanding this fact, the graph in Example 276, when compared with the score, should be readily comprehensible with a minimum of commentary. The linear progressions at the close of the A section and at the beginning of the B section are cause for speculation, however. The fourth-progression from g♯^{2} in mm. 7–8 is in conformity with similar progressions in the theme and in the first two variations, except for the chromatic alterations that occur midway through it. The tail note of this progression, d♯^{2}, is subsequently interpreted as the head note of a descending fifth-progression to g♯^{1}. The two taken together form a descending octave progression, g♯^{2}–g♯^{1}, over mm. 7–12. This is not the case when the B section is repeated, since the tonic—rather than the dominant—is the goal in the measure immediately preceding (i.e. m. 16). We have therefore read the linear progression to g♯^{1} as commencing on e^2 (see first ending, m. 16). Both versions of the progression contain d♮^{2} as an important passing note (compare Variation 2, m. [9]).

Beethoven, Piano Sonata in E major, *Op. 109, III: Variations 5 and 6*

The fact that Variations 5 and 6 were not explicitly labeled as such in the autograph score (although they were in the first printed edition) may simply represent an oversight on the composer's part, or it may be a signal that these final two variations are to be understood as a continuum set apart from the others. Both are through-composed (as are Variations 2 and 3); however, each one contains additional measures beyond the established thirty-two. In Variation 5 the B′ section is stated twice (first forte, then piano); in Variation 6 the B′ section is lengthened by three measures prior to a virtually literal restatement of the theme without repeats. (As a result, Variations 5 and 6 total forty and forty-nine measures respectively.) There are several other clues pointing to a break between Variation 5 and the preceding variations. The rest and double bar at the end of Variation 4 is one; the metrical change from triple to duple is another. There is also a change in tempo (Allegro ma non troppo)—and, for the first and only time since the beginning of the movement, the tempo direction begins with a capital letter. In contrast, Variation 6 is clearly meant to follow without break, leading as it does directly from the latter half of the concluding measure of Variation 5. There is no double bar, and the tempo direction (tempo primo del tema) is not capitalized.

Variation 5 begins with a stretto treatment of the motive marked N.B. in Example 277, which is almost identical with the opening melody in the first two measures of the theme. Resulting from this stretto, in which the top two voices participate (until mm. 4–5, where the motive marked N.B. appears in the bass), is an ascending series of overlapped thirds, an idea first introduced in the B′ section of Variation 2 (compare Example 274, mm. [1–4]). What is different here is that the overlapped thirds are counterpointed by 10–6 voice exchanges with the bass (an extension, of course, of the idea presented in the first measure of the theme). Owing to the resulting series of parallel tenths on the downbeats of mm. 1–4—and the absence of a dominant pedal point, as in Variation 2—we can now read the descant at face value: that is, as forming an ascending line from g♯ to c♯^{1} (again, compare Example 274, mm. [1–4]). Because the last note of this line falls back to b in m. 5, we have, in the graph, flagged c♯^{1} separately as a neighboring tone rather than showing it as the goal note of the opening linear progression. To summarize the reading of the descant in mm. 1–6, we have a stepwise ascent from g♯ to b (third-progression), the upper neighbor c♯^{1}, followed by a descending third-progression back to g♯. Over the same span of time, in the bass, we can read an ascending fifth-progression from bass E to B, an octave transfer (m. 5) from B down to B$_1$, and a return of the tonic E in m. 6. The prolonged harmony is therefore the tonic rather than the dominant.

EXAMPLE 277. Beethoven, *Sonata in E major*, III: Variation 5

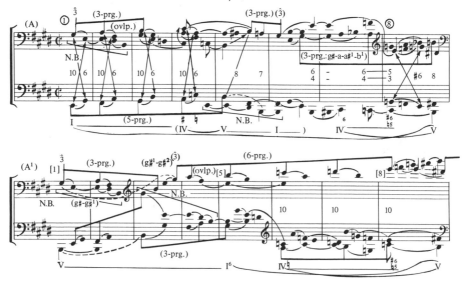

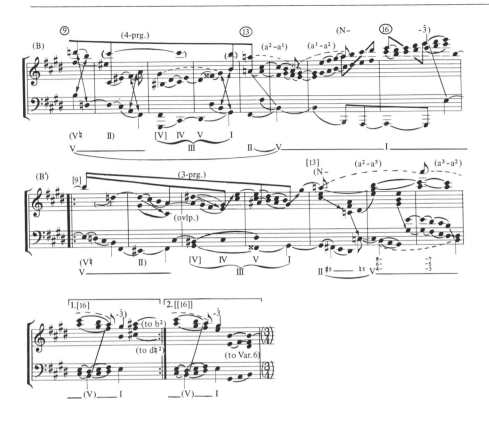

The latter is not the case with the opening measures of the A′ section. There, through m. [4], the goal harmony of the A section, V, is prolonged. Meanwhile, in mm. [3–5], it is possible to discern a motion directed briefly toward the tonic in the bass third-progression B–a–g♯ (an interesting reversal of the descant's g♯–a–b[1] in mm. [1–3]). Following this, again in the bass, we find a prolongation of IV (culminating in the augmented-sixth chord with bass c♮[1]) leading to V. Melodically, there is a significant change: the opening third-progression is repeated in a higher register and then extended, forming a sixth-progression from g♯[1] to e[2] (end of m. [3] through the downbeat of m. [8]). The interval spanned by this sixth-progression remains fundamental, however; compare, for example, the leap g♯–e[1] in m. 6 of the present variation—to say nothing of the identical leap of the seventh measure of the theme.

The dominant chord in m. [8] is spaced as in m. 8, only it is two octaves higher. Its bass note, b, begins m. 9 as well; its third, d♯[3], is replaced in m. 9 by d♮[3]. As in the analyses of earlier variations in which a similar change occurs, it is our position here that d♮[3] is best explained as part of a linear progression. In the present instance, however, the linear progression is complicated by two transfers of register: from d♮[3] to c♯[1] in mm. 9–10, and from c♯[1] to b[1] in mm. 11–12. The appearance of a[2] on the downbeat of m. 13

in effect restores the progression to its proper register, the interval of progression being the descending tritone d♯³–a². This interval, a structural component of the dominant seventh, links the prolonged dominant (continued through mm. 9–10 from m. [8]) with its return via II in m. 14. As a consequence of this interpretation, the prolongation of III in m. 12 is subordinated to a larger prolongation of V—an event not without precedent, as witness the theme, Variation 1, and the B (but not the B') section of Variation 2 (recall Examples 272–74). Though the linear progression itself may not be thoroughly convincing, its position is strengthened by the return of both a² and d♯³, joined together as an unfolding in m. 15. (The latter resolves, through register transfer, to the unfolded interval e³–g♯³ in m. 16.)

As mentioned earlier, the score of Variation 5 contains two written-out repeats of mm. 9–16. However, since the only difference between the first and second of these repeats (whose measures are respectively numbered [9–16] and [[9–16]] in the *Erläuterungsausgabe*) is one of dynamic, we have been able to use repeat signs in the graph. In other words, the sectional form analyzed in Example 277 can be summarized as A A' B||:B':||. The B' section does not have the analytic problem discussed above, due to the fact that B and not D♮ is the emphasized melodic tone in m. [9]. To be specific registrally, we can trace a linear progression b²–a¹–g♯¹ in mm. [9–11] contained within a larger linear progression spanning the same interval: that is, b²–a♯¹–g♯¹ in mm. [9–12] (compare Variation 3, mm. 9–12). The voice leading from d♮², in the meantime, is shown in the graph with the aid of arrows (denoting register transfer, as is customary): that is, to c♯¹ in m. [10], then d♯²–e¹–e² in m. [11]. The last of these notes resolves, in m. [12], to d♯², which in turn heads a foreground descent to b¹.

If Variation 5 is the finale to Op. 109, then Variation 6 is most certainly the postscript. This attribute is due not only to the reprise of the theme that comes at the end, but to the retrospective nature of Variation 6 as a whole. Not only do the tempo and meter return to those of the theme, but so do most of the details of the opening melody. The latter, which migrates from the alto voice to the descant in the course of the first eight measures, is essentially the same in both its initial statement and written-out repeat. The resemblance of these measures to the corresponding measures of the theme (compare Example 278 with Example 272b) is closer than anything we have seen thus far. However, there are two noteworthy differences. The expression of the foreground harmonic succession in the form of linear bass progressions is one: notice the contrary motion between melody and bass in mm. 1–4 and the parallel tenths in mm. 5–7. Again, the written-out repeat is much the same, though there is one subtle change worthy of mention: the embellishment of the bass note E by its upper neighbor in mm. 1–2 versus its lower neighbor in mm. [1–2]. The other significant difference between the opening of Variation 6 and that of the theme is the explicit presence of the cover tone b¹.

EXAMPLE 278. Beethoven, *Sonata in E major*, III: Variation 6

The role of the note B in general has been a continual topic in the discussion of this movement. Our position, as shown in the background sketch of the theme (Example 272c) is that, while B (scale degree $\hat{5}$) maintains a consistent position as the upper boundary of melodic activity, G♯ ($\hat{3}$) remains the focal point of this activity. Scale degree $\hat{3}$ persists in this capacity throughout the movement; indeed, the very fact that each variation ends on G♯ (specifically, either g♯^{1} or g♯^{2}) is itself an indication of this note's importance. At the same time, the third above this note is equally persistent in its own way—and nowhere is it more so than in Variation 6. In the A and A' sections (mm. 1–8 and [1–8] respectively), the note b^1 (doubled two octaves lower in the left hand) is sustained as a cover tone until the end of the fourth measure, at which point the octave transfer of the melodic line leaves b^1 as an inner voice. (Remember that the cover tone was initially defined, in Chapter 18, as a registrally transposed inner voice; in the present instance it reverts to being an inner voice through the register transfer of the main melody.) This doubled inner voice leaves b^1 in the seventh measure, presumably because the outer voices are about to proceed to the vertical B$_1$–b^2 in the eighth. Again, the A and A' sections are the same in this regard.

The manner in which the cover tone is "sustained," as we initially put it above, is an element of detail which merits attention. What actually happens in the score is that repeated notes (mm. 1–5) lead into a measured trill (mm. 6–8, [1–4]), which finally becomes an unmeasured trill on the upbeat to m. [5]. The bass picks up the trill on B$_1$ in m. [8] and continues on that note until the third beat of m. 16. Beginning with m. [9] and continuing until the reprise of the theme ten measures thereafter, the right hand maintains the trill as an inner voice: on b^2 (mm. [9–17]), then on b^1 (mm. [18–19]). In all, the trill is confined to some form of the note B (i.e. in whatever register) for all but two measures, and thus crucially links detail (the trill) with structure (the dominant). This fifth degree of the tonic scale, which acts as a cover tone at the opening of the A and A' sections and acquires harmonic significance at the close of those sections, continues in the latter regard in the B and B' sections: first as a pedal point, then as a sustained inner voice. The pedal point on B$_1$ in mm. 9–11 gives a dominant underpinning to the sequence of broken chords in the right hand, and corroborates our reading of the melodic note D♮ here and at the same place in earlier variations: that is, as a passing tone within the context of a dominant prolongation.

Another harmonic prolongation which we have come to expect in the second half of every variation occurs in the form of a shift toward III, with the goal being reached—each time—in the twelfth measure. In some variations the pull toward III has been quite strong (as in the B' section of Variation 2, both the B and B' sections of Variation 3, the B section of Variation 4, and the B' section of Variation 5). Elsewhere, as we have shown in the graphs, the arrival on III is overshadowed by the larger prolongation of the dominant that we have judged to be in force. But only in Variation 6 is III actually deserted. In m. 12, the two voices directly below the descant, c$\sharp^2$ and a($\natural$)^1, resolve to b^1 and g$\sharp^1$ respectively at the end of the measure, forming the intervals $\frac{9-8}{7-6}$ above the bass B$_1$. However, the descant remains on e^2; its resolution to d$\sharp^2$ does not come until m. 13. By that time the harmony is clearly V^7, and as a result any feeling of III that might have occurred in m. 12 (i.e. by the stepwise resolution of all three voices) is bypassed. As shown in Example 278 by the two sets of figures above and below the lower staff, the linear intervallic succession over mm. 11–13 reduces to the familiar pattern $\frac{8-7}{6-5}_{4-3}$. At the corresponding place in the B′ section, m. [13], we also find a vertical that does not resolve as expected: this time $^6_4$ over d$\sharp$ resolving, not to $^5_3$ on the next beat (as in the theme and elsewhere), but to $^6_5$ in the following measure—once again, a form of the dominant seventh. If III is to be found at all in m. [12], it is in the form of a $^6_4$ chord and therefore questionable indeed.

The B′ section of Variation 6, with the extreme register of the right hand and the intricacy of the left, poses obvious textural problems. The left-hand sequence in mm. [9–11] must be simplified substantially, even in a foreground sketch such as we have in Example 278. The first step, which Example 278 bypasses but should be easy enough to reconstruct, is to eliminate the neighbor-note diminutions that occur on almost every half beat; the next is to eliminate the passing notes. The result, as shown in the graph, virtually duplicates the contents of the right hand of the corresponding measures in the B section (compare mm. 9–11). Since the sustained trill on B$_1$ in the left hand is now replaced by a trill on b^2 in the right, we can see that the technique of double counterpoint exploited in Variation 3 is subtly reintroduced. Added to this is the syncopated descant line which recapitulates, two octaves higher, the melody of the second half of the theme. Two octaves lower—that is, in the same register as the theme—we find this melody reproduced within the left-hand part, through m. 11, shown graphically by the upward stems. (Additionally, the line can be traced, an octave lower still, through m. 13.) We have interpreted the descant as in the theme: as a small third-progression contained within a larger one spanning the same interval.

We now come to what would normally be the last two measures of the variation. The tonic chord at the beginning of m. [15] is admittedly questionable, as it may simply be part of the $^6_4$ chord arpeggiated within the second beat. As in the theme and in Variation 1, the upper voices of the dominant seventh are carried over from the third beat to form a suspension on the downbeat of the next measure. However, in Variation 6 the suspension is sustained for all of m. [16] plus three additional measures, during which time the descant (which bears the suspended fourth) undertakes a downward register transfer spanning two octaves. The resolution of a^1 to g$\sharp^1$ coincides with the reprise of the theme on the downbeat following m. [19], and the resolution of the other note in the suspension (i.e. 9 and 7, both to 8) is implied at that time as well. In short, the extra measures leading to the reprise of the theme constitute an elaborate written-out fermata.

As we mentioned earlier, the reprise of the theme (shown only at the background level in Example 278) is complete and literal, save for the absence of repeat signs. There is, however, one subtle but significant change (for which the reader is referred to the score): a single passage in the bass which is doubled at the lower octave in the reprise of the theme and not in its initial statement. The added low notes, beginning with the eighth note before m. 5, comprise the descending semitone A_1–$G\sharp_1$ followed by the stepwise ascent of a sixth from $G\sharp_1$ to E. The occurrence of a–$g\sharp$–e^1 in the descant in mm. 6–7, at just the point when the left hand finishes the ascent to E, is a coincidence that should not be lost to the reader or listener—nor, for that matter, should we overlook the whole network of associations brought into play by these particular notes.

Summary

It is always helpful to summarize a detailed study such as the foregoing, especially when the subject is sectional in nature. Toward this end, Example 279 presents a table showing how the specific variations relate to the theme and to each other. Most of its contents have already been discussed in connection with the theme and the individual variations. Shown side by side in capsule form, they reflect a complex of connections that binds the parts into a coherent whole. It is appropriate, for example, that Variation 6, notwithstanding its direct resemblance to (and subsequent recapitulation of) the theme, would also share, in places (see under Remarks in Example 279), several characteristics found in earlier variations.

Notice that some variations generally relate to the theme more directly than do others.These include Variation 6, of course—but also part of Variation 2, all of Variation 3, and to a lesser extent, Variation 4. Variation 4 also recalls the opening of Variation 1, while the overlapped thirds introduced in Variation 2 return in Variation 5. In Example 279, these generalized relationships are shown at the top by lines with arrowheads: solid lines for direct links with the theme; dotted lines for connections based on derived material.

The remainder of Example 279 is self-explanatory, although every item there is potential cause for comment. Even the headings given to the theme and the respective variations are of more than routine significance. To summarize, tempos different from that of the theme are indicated only three times: the two allegro variations in duple time (Variations 3 and 5), and the one variation slower than the theme (Variation 4), in compound triple time. What we have not mentioned yet is Beethoven's use of German directions.

EXAMPLE 279. Beethoven, *Sonata in E major*, III: Summary

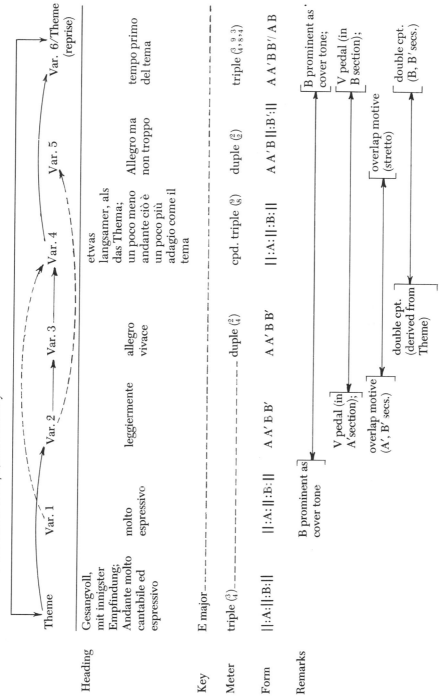

	Theme	Var. 1	Var. 2	Var. 3	Var. 4	Var. 5	Var. 6/Theme (reprise)
Heading	Gesangvoll, mit innigster Empfindung; Andante molto cantabile ed espressivo	molto espressivo	leggiermente	allegro vivace	etwas langsamer, als das Thema; un poco meno andante ciò è un poco più adagio come il tema	Allegro ma non troppo	tempo primo del tema
Key	E major						
Meter	triple $(\frac{3}{4})$			duple $(\frac{2}{4})$	cpd. triple $(\frac{9}{8})$	duple $(\frac{2}{2})$	triple $(\frac{3}{4},\frac{9}{8},\frac{3}{4})$
Form	‖:A:‖:B:‖	‖:A:‖:B:‖	A A' B B'	A A' B B'	‖:A:‖:B:‖	A A' B‖:B':‖	A A'B B'/A B
Remarks		B prominent as cover tone	V pedal (in A'section); overlap motive (A', B' secs.)	double cpt. (derived from Theme)	overlap motive (stretto)	B prominent as cover tone; V pedal (in B section); double cpt. (B, B' secs.)	

Though these appear from time to time in the late sonatas, it is interesting to note that the present movement is the only one within Op. 109 to bear them. Even so, directions in German are given in addition to the Italian only for the theme and for Variation 4. Although this is not so with the theme, the German heading given Variation 4 does not add anything to what is simultaneously given in Italian, and thus its value must be judged as purely symbolic. A review of the discussion of Variation 4, above, will show that this variation is a fitting choice for such a symbol.

The fact that all of the variations remain in E major makes it unnecessary to construct a schematic such as was given earlier (Example 271c, p. 325) for a portion of the Brahms Paganini variations. Instead, as stated at the beginning of this entire section, we can let the background structure of the theme stand for the background structure of the movement. (By background structure, we mean only the open notes in Example 272c.) As we have shown, the successive variations continue to reinforce the background notes $\hat{3}$ over I, albeit through numerous shifts in register. (It is appropriate, for example, that the most extreme juxtaposition of registers should take place, as it does, in Variation 6.) An additional task, left here to the student, would be to show, in a single graph, a synopsis of the various expansions and contractions of register that occur throughout the movement. Such a synopsis would of course be gleaned from the graphs we have already presented.

In conclusion, we must stress that the third movement of Beethoven's Op. 109, though exemplary as a theme and variations, can hardly be called "typical," and that it would be premature to select a work of comparable difficulty as a first exercise. Two works that invite comparison are the second movement of Op. 111 and the *Diabelli Variations* of Op. 120, either of which could be attempted as a more advanced project. A far more approachable set of variations on a theme is the air and variations from the E-major keyboard suite of Handel. The air (popularly called *The Harmonious Blacksmith*, and the subject of Exercise 16/1) bears a marked resemblance to the theme of Op. 109.

Exercises

Following the pattern of Examples 272–79, analyze the theme carefully and provide two graphs, one emphasizing the foreground, another emphasizing the middleground and background (as in Examples 272*b* and *c*). Next, proceed through the variations, making a combined foreground-middleground graph of each one. Finally, make a tabular and, if needed, a graphic summary of the entire piece or movement. Some verbal commentary, like the discussion accompanying Examples 272–79, is also advised.

1. Handel, *Keyboard Suite in E major*, Air and Variations

    The air (see Exercise 16/1) resembles the theme of Beethoven's Op. 109, III in several important respects: key, form, and the question of whether G♯ ($\hat{3}$) or B ($\hat{5}$) is the primary tone. (On the last point, the answer may not be the same as in the Beethoven work.)

2. Mozart, *Piano Sonata in D major*, K. 284, III

3. Mozart, *Clarinet Quintet*, K. 581, IV

    This theme and variations are basically the same as the *Six Variations on an Allegretto*, K. Anh. 137 (see Exercise 12B/3); however, the quintet version is preferable for this exercise.

4. Beethoven, *Thirty two Variations on a Waltz by Diabelli*, Op. 120

    Though a larger work and chronologically later than the variation movement of Op. 111 (Exercise 5), the Diabelli variations pose one less problem in that each variation is reasonably self-contained. The theme itself, trivial though it may be, provides a good example of initial ascent.

5. Beethoven, *Piano Sonata in C minor*, Op. 111, II

    Coming from the same stylistic period as Op. 109, this movement is at least the equal, technically and artistically, of the variation movement of the earlier work. As mentioned at the close of this chapter, this exercise should be undertaken only as an advanced project. As with the last two variations in Op. 109, the variations in this movement are not headed by number, and follow one another without break. The change of key toward the end of Variation 4 is one technical feature of this set of variations that is not found in the other.

6. Mendelssohn, *Variations sérieuses*, Op. 54

    Above all, the theme of these variations needs careful analysis at the foreground as well as the deeper levels. As in Beethoven's Op. 109, the stepwise motion spanning a third is of paramount importance at all structural levels.

23

Structural Levels in Compound and Rondo Forms

Chapter 21 dealt with the sonata, a major form for tonal compositions and the design that many of the finest musical works of the so-called common-practice period exemplify. The set of variations on a theme (Chapter 22) is also a basic form type for instrumental movements, with many wondrous instances in the tonal repertory. Two additional designs complete what may be regarded as a roster of basic forms in tonal music: the compound (ternary) form and the rondo form, of which there are essentially three varieties.[1]

Here, as in previous chapters, we shall be concerned not only with the skeletal outline of the form type but also with the way in which the music is shaped within the formal divisions at various structural levels. Once again, it is worthwhile to remind the reader that the components of the structural levels vary greatly from work to work, as does the manner of their interaction. Accordingly, we again focus on the analysis of individual exemplars of these forms, drawn from the works of Schubert, Mozart, Chopin, Mendelssohn, and Haydn, and do not attempt to generalize about the content of structural levels for other representatives of these forms.

Compound Ternary Forms

Chapter 17 introduced and illustrated the *simple* ternary form ABA. The *compound* ternary form, which is the subject of this section, is an expansion of the simple ternary form.[2] In this large compound form the main parts are still

---

1. The rondo form is especially difficult to categorize because there are so many variants of it. For example, the Mozart piano concertos contain a number of rondo movements which do not fit neatly into the schemata normally considered to be rondos.

2. The compound binary form, although important, is omitted from this presentation. It consists of two large parts, each of which is a complete binary or ternary form in itself. There are many examples in the operatic literature—for instance, No. 7 in Mozart's *Don Giovanni*, the duettino "Là ci darem la mano" (Don Giovanni and Zerlina).

labeled ABA, but each of these contains a simple binary or ternary form that is complete in itself. A model compound ternary form might be represented in the following way:

Main Parts: A   B   A
Sections: a_1 b a_2 a_1 b a_2 a_1 b a_2

To designate any of the sections of the compound form we first give the letter-name of the main part, which is always upper case. The lower-case letter-name of the section, with its subscript, is attached, preceded by a hyphen. Thus, A-b designates the middle section of the large A division, while B-a_2 represents the return of the small a section within the main B section.

The compound ternary form is a staple of tonal music. Sometimes called song form with trio, it is amply represented in instrumental movements such as the minuet and trio, the scherzo and trio, and the march and trio. In all these cases, the trio is part B of our schema above. Normally only A and B are notated in score; there is no repetition in notation of the second A. By tradition, parts A and B are performed with all repetitions of the sections, then the final A is performed again with no repetitions of the subparts. The same procedure holds for the da capo (from the beginning) aria, where the performance instruction "da capo" tells the singer to repeat the A section, concluding the aria. The compound ternary form is, however, not restricted to minuets and trios, da capo arias, and similar genres, but is exemplified by a diversity of compositions. For example, Schubert's Op. 94, No. 4 (*Moments musicaux*), in A♭, is a compound ternary, as is Chopin's *Prelude in D♭ major*, Op. 28, No. 15. In the latter, the B part consists of a binary form. Brahms's *Intermezzo in E♭ major*, Op. 117, No. 1, is a compound ternary and so is his *Intermezzo in E minor*, Op. 119, No. 2. These are only a few of the many instances of the form in the repertory of tonal music.[3]

Schubert, String Quartet in G minor, *Op. posth. (D. 173), Menuetto: Part A*

As our first example of a compound ternary form, let us consider a movement by Schubert, from the *String Quartet in G minor*. Example 280 shows section A-a_1 in its entirety, reducing out eighth-note diminutions. The descant of the first four measures presents an arpeggiation which serves as prefix to the primary tone d^3. At the end of this phrase (m. 4), d^3 couples down to d^2, the melodic note which initiated the music. The second four-measure phrase begins on the tonic triad, but modulates to III.

---

3. An expansion of the compound ternary is represented by the ternary with different B sections: ABACA, effectively creating a five-part form. A famous example of this is the scherzo of Schumann's *First Symphony*, which has two (different) trios.

Coextensive with the modulatory progression is the upper-voice ascending linear progression bb^2–c^3–d^3. Thus, the arrival on III in m. 7 coincides with the restatement of d^3 ($\hat{5}$) in the upper voice. As can be seen in the sketch, the bass motion to B♭ (III) is the first step in a long-range arpeggiation of I which spans and unifies the entire section A-a₁: G–B♭–D.

EXAMPLE 280. Schubert, *Quartet in G minor*, III: Section A-a₁

In mm. 7–8 the upper voice descends through c^3 to bb^2 over the cadential progression, leaving d^3 still implicitly active as the controlling note of the fundamental structure (since the progression from d^3 to bb^2 does not take place over tonic harmony).

Over the first four measures (mm. 9–12) of the second part of the section the bass has the neighbor-note formation d–e♭–d, which was foreshadowed in m. 3. Above this the descant unfolds from d^2, which represents the continuation of the primary tone. This is a single unfolded interval; the resolution of $f\sharp^1$ to some G is implicit with the resumption of the tonic triad in m. 13 at the beginning of the last four-measure phrase.

In the final portion of this section, mm. 13–16, the upper voice descends from d^2 to an implied a^1. Although this could have been notated as a linear progression, we have chosen not to do so—mainly because of the absent a^1 and attendant parallel fifths with the bass—but have used stemmed filled notes to indicate the configuration. Most striking in this final section is the middle-ground coupling d^2–d^3, a return to the obligatory register. Just at the cadence the bass brings back the neighbor-note motive e♭–d, and against this the upper voice echoes the arpeggiation of mm. 1–2.

Thus, this first section of part A has a great deal of diversity at the middleground level, including arpeggiations (both in upper voice and, of longer range, in the bass), a linear progression, a large-scale unfolding, a neighbor-note figure, and a middleground coupling. The interaction of all these features is intensified, of course, in the repetition.

Section b of part A (A-b) is set out in Example 281. This begins on the mediant triad, without any preparation (modulation).[4] At the foreground level, the arpeggiation of A-a₁ is reintroduced in imitative fashion, forging a motivic link between the two sections. A more complex middleground structure develops over the first ten measures (in contrast to the regular four-measure groups of the preceding section). This proves to be a descending linear progression of a sixth, with head note f² (m. 18) and tail note a² (m. 26). How is it that the tail note is in the same register as the head note? Because in m. 21, just as the bass moves to the motivic neighbor note, E♭, the descant couples upward from b♭¹ to b♭² and the latter is prolonged until the resolution to a² in m. 26. Meanwhile, the bass E♭, which was assumed to be a neighbor note back in m. 21, becomes a passing note and ascends through E♮ in m. 25 to F. Notice that this chromatic passing note, E♮, sets the upper-voice b♭², which then descends to a² to complete the linear progression.

EXAMPLE 281. Schubert, *Quartet in G minor*, III: Section A-b

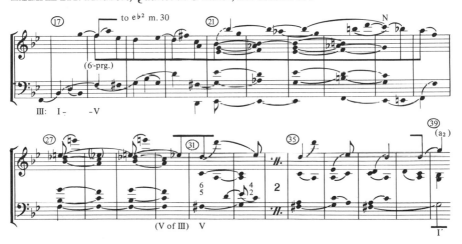

The remainder of section A–b can be viewed most succinctly in Example 282. This shows the descending linear progression of a sixth, without change of register, arriving at tail note a¹ in m. 26. This progression prolongs the head note f², which is therefore still effective at m. 26. At m. 30 e♭² is brought in in the descant, and this represents the continuation of f², as shown by the beam.

---

4. Note that in the Schenkerian sense this is not to be construed as a progression from a D-major triad at the end of A-a₁ to a B♭ triad at the beginning of A-b. Since the D-major triad (V) is a result of the bass prolongation by arpeggiation of the tonic triad, I is still effective at the join of the two sections. Thus, the progression is from the governing harmony of A-a₁, I, to the governing harmony of A-b, III.

This and similar events should cause no problems to the burgeoning analyst, provided that very basic concepts are borne in mind. Here the critical factor is the interpretation of the descending linear progression over the consonant sixth. This progression leaves the note f^2 still effective. It has not moved to a^1, but has connected down to it, since a^1 belongs to an inner voice. Thus, the entrance of eb^2 in m. 30 does not represent some kind of discontinuity but is a logical voice-leading event that originates from f^2. Example 281 shows how the chromatic passing note $e\natural^2$ highlights the entrance of eb^2.

EXAMPLE 282. Schubert, *Quartet in G minor*, III: Section A-b, Summary

To complete the analysis of section A–b, let us remain with Example 282. The critical descant note eb^2, which enters in m. 30, resolves downward by step, as must all dissonant real sevenths; however, the bass changes simultaneously, redirecting the harmony away from III and back to I. Thus, the definitive setting for d^2 in m. 31 is the tonic triad which is brought in at the beginning of the next section, A–a_2.

The middleground upper-voice structure of section A–b therefore consists first of a descending linear progression of a third f^2–eb^2–d^2, a progression which prolongs the tail note ($\hat{5}$). Within this linear progression is still another, the descending sixth from f^2 to a^2, which prolongs the head note of the outer progression. The bass prolongs f, introducing the characteristic neighbor-note figure d–eb in mm. 20–21, which proves to have another meaning (direction) over the span of the whole section, as described above.

Section A-a_2 is shown in Example 283. It begins just as did section A-a_1, with the arpeggiation restoring the primary tone d^3 in its obligatory register and then coupling back down to d^2 in m. 42. The second four-measure phrase of this section, however, departs radically from its counterpart in Section A-a_1. Now, the descant arpeggiates upward to the climactic note eb^3, the neighbor-note motive, then drops down abruptly to bb^2 in m. 45, scale degree $\hat{3}$ of the fundamental line. The subsequent closure of the fundamental line is shown in Example 283. What is remarkable here is the substitution in m. 44 of the motivic eb^3 for the expected c^3—expected on the basis of the arpeggiation $f\sharp^2$–a^2–c^3 which would have paralleled the thematic arpeggiation of mm. 39–40 exactly. Here is an interesting case of a middleground component replacing a component of the background.

EXAMPLE 283. Schubert, *Quartet in G minor*, III: Section A-a₂ and Coda

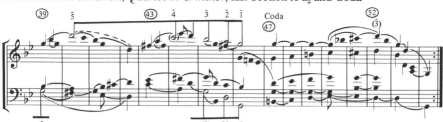

The coda of eight measures, also shown in Example 283, contains direct references to the A₁ sections. In the bass, the initial figure B–C (mm. 47–48) is imitated in the next two measures to become the motivic d–e♭. In parallel sixths to this bass motion the inner voice ascends from g¹ to d² (m. 52), the latter a reference to the initial note of the movement. And in the upper voice g² is sustained until the bass reaches the motivic e♭, then arpeggiates upward to d³ to create an expanded form of the thematic arpeggiation from the opening music.

Schubert, String Quartet in G minor, *Op. posth. (D. 173), III: Part B*

Part B lies entirely within III, and, like many trios, is relatively inactive from the standpoint of harmonic progression.[5] As shown in Example 284, the primary tone $\hat{5}$ is stated in m. 56 in its obligatory register and prolonged through an unfolding from e♭³ in to a². The head note of the unfolding, e♭³, is the familiar upper-neighbor-note motive, undisguised. Beginning in m. 59 the descant descends from d³ to c³, completing an interruption form in m. 62.

EXAMPLE 284. Schubert, *Quartet in G minor*, III: Sections B-a₁ and B-b

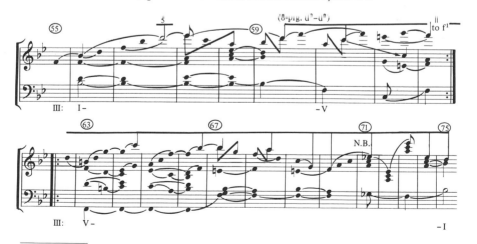

5. This is an important historical and stylistic consideration, but one which lies outside the domain of this textbook, as does the matter of the traditional continuous eighth-note descant diminutions of the trio.

Notice that f³ covers the structural voice at the cadence, in preparation for the upbeat f¹ of the repetition.

The most important motion in the section is the linear progression of an octave that spans measures 59 to 75. This has its origin in the coupling of d² and d³ in the A section. As soon as it is completed, in m. 75, the primary tone is regained in obligatory register through the coupling d²–d³.

Some readers will realize that a long segment of this descending octave progression is accompanied by a bass pedal, thereby violating the usual conditions regarding harmonic and/or contrapuntal support for a linear progression. Here we have taken a liberty with respect to normative analytic procedures, since the upper voice moves slowly in the way a linear progression does and since the inner-voice motion that accompanies it so effectively substitutes for the kind of harmonic or contrapuntal change one normally expects in the presence of a linear progression.

The structure of section B–a₂ can be read from the sketch in Example 285. Most striking here is the bass motion in mm. 79–80 from a♭ to g which supports the neighbor-note motive d³–e♭³ in the descant, just before the close to b♭² in m. 82.

EXAMPLE 285. Schubert, *Quartet in G minor*, III: Section B-a₂

Part B is followed by the repetition of part A, the structure of which is shown in the sketches of Examples 280, 281, and 283. Thus, the primary tone of the B part, d³ is the same as the primary tone of part A, and there is a perfect common-tone voice-leading connection between the two contrasting parts of the ternary form.

The Schubert minuet just discussed presents a clear example of compound ternary form. Each part and section has an individual foreground identity, but they coalesce at middleground and background to form a completely unified work. Example 286 reviews the large outline of the movement.

EXAMPLE 286. Schubert, *Quartet in G minor*, III: Summary of Form

A: I   B: III   [A]

a₁: I–III–V   b: III   a₂: I   a₁: III   b: V of III   a₂: III
1–16   17–38   39–54   55–62   63–74   75–82

Chopin, Mazurka in A minor, *Op, 17, No. 4*

At every structural level this composition is quite different from the Schubert quartet movement just discussed, although it too exemplifies compound ternary form.[6] The work begins with an enigmatic introduction of four measures, shown in Example 287. Framed by bass a and upper voice f^1, the inner voice unfolds the third $b–d^1$. At the end of the introduction this resolves to c^1 over a, as summarized in Example 287*b*, still leaving the tonality indeterminate, since there has been no clear statement of tonic and dominant.

EXAMPLE 287. Chopin, *Mazurka in A minor*, Introduction

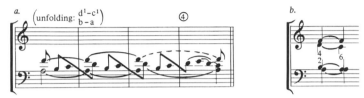

With the beginning of section A–a_1 proper (Example 288) a linear progression begins its ascent, arriving at the primary tone $\hat{5}$ (e^2) on the downbeat of m. 8. However, the bass has already moved away from the (assumed) tonic note a in m. 5 and has embarked on a stepwise descent to the dominant e in m. 11. Thus, the primary tone and its structural support are widely separated, an extreme instance of a familiar phenomenon caused by linear development in one or more voices—here the bass.

EXAMPLE 288. Chopin, *Mazurka in A minor*, Section A-a_1

---

6. Again (as explained in note 5), there are historical and stylistic matters here which lie beyond the purview of this textbook. They do not, however, affect our reading of the structure of the composition.

The motive featured in mm. 5–7 of Example 288 is the ascending third filled by a passing note. This is labeled α on the sketch. In the "consequent" phrase that begins in m. 9 the inversion of motive alpha occurs twice, without connective passing tone, and is then stretched out over some three measures as d^2–c^2–b^1, a motion which prolongs the seventh above bass e.

In m. 13 the tonic note A is restated in a new register of the bass and the unfolding from b^1 out to d^2 resolves as before. This brings in c^2 on the downbeat of m. 14 to conclude the linear progressions of a descending third, the head note of which is the primary tone e^2 in m. 8. Characteristic of Chopin's music, the inner voice carries the same linear progression, a simpler doubling, indicated by the figures between the staffs—the 7–6 linear intervallic pattern.

At m. 14 the upper voice again ascends by step to the primary tone. As soon as this is reached (m. 16), the descent begins, this time, however, completing the fifth from e^2 to a^1 in m. 20. In the final A part of the mazurka this motion will constitute the close of the fundamental line (Example 294).

The analytical problems posed by section A–a_1 of this unusual composition are three. First, there is the determination of the primary tone and its harmonic setting. As shown in Example 288, the primary tone is taken to be e^2 at the end of the first phrase, related diagonally to bass a of m. 5. The inner voices here show a simpler aspect of the voice leading that supports this reading, namely the suspended f^1 in the left-hand part, which finally resolves to e^1 on the downbeat of m. 8, doubling the primary tone an octave lower. It is only this f^1, a neighbor note, that keeps the harmony in m. 6 from being a tonic A-minor triad. (As will be seen, this feature plays a special role at the very end of the composition.) Second, the upper voice in mm. 9–12 must be correctly understood in terms of structural levels. The $f\sharp^2$ in m. 9 and the $f\natural^2$ in the next measure belong to the foreground as diminutions (the consonant skip of Chapter 1) which have motivic significance, as explained above. The middleground motion is of longer range, spanning the entire phrase. This consists of the descent from e^2 in m. 8 to d^2 in m. 10. The latter then becomes the seventh above the dominant in the bass.

The third problem then appears: the motion from d^2 down to an implied b^1 in m. 12, an inversion of the original alpha motive. This is not a continuation of the linear progression from e^2, but an accessory foreground motion that prolongs d^2. This is supported by the inner voice d^1 and indicated in the sketch by the figure 7. That is, c^1 in m. 12 is a passing note; it does not resolve the seventh d^2. That resolution occurs only in m. 14, the second measure in the repetition of the opening music.

Section A–b, graphed in Example 289, is by no means as complicated as section A–a_1. It features a repeated descending motion in the descant, e^2–d^2–c^2, which recalls the linear progression in the previous section. On the sketch, the third of these is beamed as a linear progression and continued downward to b¹ in mm. 43–44 to complete a linear progression of a fourth which determines an interruption form. The bass remains stationary on the dominant, E. Again, because of the voice-leading activity of the inner voices, we have taken the liberty of showing the upper voice as a beamed structure, contravening the usual rule of special harmonic-contrapuntal support for the components of a linear progression.

EXAMPLE 289. Chopin, *Mazurka in A minor*, Section A–b

The melodic foreground of section A–b is so rich in detail that only a few aspects can be shown on the analytic sketch. These include the several occurrences of the alpha motive, among which is now the major third descending from e², the emphatic d♯¹ at the end of m. 40 that refers to the inner-voice d♯ of m. 9 and elsewhere, and the sixth c³ over e² flagged in m. 42. The latter is clearly an allusion to c³ which occurs (uniquely) just at the end of section A–a₁. The reader will discover many other foreground features from section A–a₁ in this section as well, some transformed in ways characteristic of Chopin's sophisticated compositional language, such as the motion b♭¹–a¹–g♯¹ in mm. 43–44, which is a variant on b¹–g♯¹ in mm. 11–12, also at the end of a section.

Example 290 first presents the end of section A–a₂ (the end of Part A), then section B–a₁. The juxtaposition of the end of A–a₂ with the beginning of B–a₁ in the example is intended to emphasize the correspondence of c³–b²–a¹ with c♯²–b¹–a¹, the major version of the same scale segment. The descant has two basic components here: the alpha motive c♯²–b¹–a¹ answered by d¹–c♯¹–b (m. 62) and the neighbor-note figure f♯¹–e¹ (m. 62). The latter is clearly the

EXAMPLE 290. Chopin, *Mazurka in A minor*, Section B–a₁

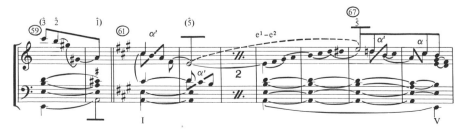

EXAMPLE 291. Chopin, *Mazurka in A minor*, Comparison of Motives of Sections A-a
and B-a

major-mode version of the neighbor-note figure f^1–e^1 of the opening music in
Section A-a_1. But the other component is also related in a very specific way to
the melodic configurations of section A–a_1, as partially indicated above.
Example 291 shows the correspondence. At *a* we see the melodic theme of
section A–a_1 placed above that of section B–a_1. The way in which their
elements match is shown in Example 291*b*; there we see that the elements of
the theme of B-a_1 are the retrograde of those of A-a_1, as indicated by the small
letters on the example at *b*.

To return to Example 290, the primary tone first occurs as e^1 in m. 62,
preceded by its upper neighbor. This is followed by the upward coupling to
e^2, which comprises the stepwise progression shown. When the primary tone
$\hat{5}$ is reestablished in its obligatory register, a descending linear progression of
a fourth ensues which incorporates small foreground unfoldings of the alpha
motive, a subtle reference to the opening of the section.

The coupling e^1–e^2 in mm. 62–67 is not arbitrary, for these are the registers
which are linked at the beginning of section A–a_1. (See Example 288, m. 8.)

Section B–b begins as did section B–a_1, but it ends in quite a different way,
as shown in Example 292. Instead of the coupling e^1–e^2 we now have a
motion from e^1 up to $c\sharp^2$ (mm. 73–74). This may be regarded convincingly as
a development by inversion of the thematic material of the opening, in mm.
69–70. Chopin then continues to develop this idea, bringing in e^2–$c\sharp^2$ in m. 75
to answer the ascending sixth, and, finally, expanding the third e^2–$c\sharp^2$ through
the passing tone d^2 in mm. 76–77, the alpha motive once again.

EXAMPLE 292. Chopin, *Mazurka in A minor*, Section B-b

Section B–a_2 spans measures 77–84. Because it is identical to section B–a_1,
it is not sketched again. Instead, we go directly to the transition from section
B back to section A, Example 293. This begins as did sections B–a_1 and B–b,

but does not end in the same way as either one. (Indeed, what distinguishes these sections from one another is not their beginnings, but their endings.) In m. 89 the stepwise coupling from e^1 to e^2 is initiated; however, in a dramatic gesture e^2 is bypassed and the melodic goal proves to be f^2 in m. 91, the upper neighbor to e^2 which first occurred in m. 7 (Example 288). Below this, doubling at the octave, is f^1. Here unlike the first occurrence, the note is sustained through measures 92–95, not repeated in even quarter notes as before. But, just as in the opening music, it resolves to e^1 in m. 96, when e^2 is restated as $\hat{5}$ in the descant.

EXAMPLE 293. Chopin, *Mazurka in A minor*, Transition

The final statement of part A is represented by section A–a_1 only, a truncation not uncommon in ternary forms, and the close of the fundamental line thus occurs in mm. 104–8, as represented in Example 294.[7]

EXAMPLE 294. Chopin, *Mazurka A minor*, Close of Fundamental Line

There follows a coda that comprises two distinct sections, indicated as C-a and c-b on Example 295. In section C-a the descant descends from e^2 to a^1 over a pedal bass A, while the inner voices follow in parallel motion. Example 295*b* presents a slightly reduced version of this Chopinesque motion, in which the verticals are entirely incidental to the linear motion created by the component lines.

Section C-b of the coda refers twice to the alpha motive of the opening music—the second an inversion of the first—lending credence to our statements concerning inverted motives in section B-a_1 and elsewhere.

---

7. Following the voice leading of the inner voice, the descending line might also be read $\hat{5}$–$\hat{4}$–$\hat{3}$—i.e., not a complete close to $\hat{1}$.

EXAMPLE 295. Chopin, *Mazurka in A minor*, Coda, Sections C-a and C-b

Finally, the introduction returns in mm. 129–32, leaving the piece in the enigmatic state in which it began, with the special note f¹ still sounding at the very end.

Example 296, Summary of Form, is hardly an adequate representation of the work in all its detail. Still, it provides an overview of the parts and helps to give a picture of the large-scale organization of the work.

EXAMPLE 296. Chopin, *Mazurka in A minor*: Summary of Form

Introduction	A: I			B: I♯		
	a₁: I	b: V	a₂: I	a₁	b	a₂
1–4	5–36	37–44	45–60	61–68	69–76	77–84

Transition	A: I	Coda: I	
	a₁	a	b
85–92	93–108	109–124	125–32

Mozart, String Quartet in D minor, K. 421, III: Section A

The Menuetto from Mozart's late D-minor quartet (the second of the six quartets dedicated to Haydn) is a perfect example of compound ternary form. Each large part is composed of a small ternary form. Since section A–a₂ is identical to section A–a₁ and section B–a₂ is identical to section B–a₁, only four analytic sketches are required for this work.

At the opening of section A–a₁ the primary tone $\hat{5}$ is reached by arpeggiation, as graphed in Example 297. In fact, there are two arpeggiations, the large middleground arpeggiation, beamed, and its embedded foreground replica, which begins at the end of m. 2. The opening thematic gesture contains two other patterns of interest, the consonant skip from d^2 to a^1 in m. 1 and the descending third f^2–d^2, which prolongs f^2 at the foreground level. The descending skip of a fourth is featured in the foreground of the remainder of the descant of this section, becoming a descending fifth in m. 9. And the descending third returns in m. 8, again prolonging f^2.

EXAMPLE 297. Mozart, *Quartet in D minor*, III: Section A-a₁

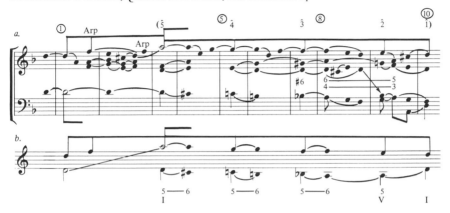

From m. 3 to m. 8 the bass descends over the fourth d^1–a, with chromatic passing notes interpolated. This motion supports a linear progression of a fifth from a^2 to d^2. Although this is shown as a middleground progression in Example 297 it becomes the descending fundamental line in the final statement of A. As explained at the beginning of the present section, the second A is not notated in full (by tradition, when it is identical to the first A) but is represented only by the d.c. (da capo) at the end of Part B.

In Example 297b the essential counterpoint formed by the descending fifth progression and its bass is given. This consists of the linear intervallic pattern 5–6, where the vertical sixths ameliorate the succession of parallel fifths. To understand this in terms of the paradigm given in Example 88 (p. 89) it is only necessary to exchange the upper voice with the lower in that example. Only the verticals on d^1 in m. 3 and on a in m. 9 have harmonic value.

The prolongation of f^2 in m. 8 is worthy of comment, since this kind of situation may still cause difficulty to the analyst. In the worst case, this would be read as a descent from $\hat{3}$ to $\hat{1}$—an arrival on $\hat{1}$ two measures too soon—in which case e^2 in m. 9 would be (mis)understood as some kind of neighbor note. In fact, what we have here is an idiomatic foreground prolongation of $^6_4$. The bass of the $^6_4$ is a on the downbeat of m. 8; the resolution of the $^6_4$ occurs on the second quarter note of m. 9 over bass a, with a dissonant passing note, f¹, in second violin. Prior to its resolution, the $^6_4$ is prolonged first by the descending motion in parallel sixths between descant and bass that occupies all of m. 8 and then by the flagged lower neighbor note g on the downbeat of m. 9 which delays the return of the bass a and the resolution of the $^6_4$ to $^5_3$.

Each component of the descending linear progression that begins in m. 3 takes up two measures, except for the last two, which have one measure each; thus, the entire motion occupies eight measures. Had the upper-voice prolongation in m. 8 followed the pattern of the preceding measures, it would have consisted of a skip from f² to c², then back to e². This would have caused the progression to take quite a different harmonic direction, one out of the direct control of the main tonality, D minor. Such changes in foreground pattern are always interesting and worthy of the analyst's attention.

Section A-b, shown in Example 298, establishes a new key, A minor, immediately, and this, of course, is a tonicization of the minor dominant of the main tonality, D minor. Let us first consider the harmonic components of the section.

EXAMPLE 298. Mozart, *Quartet in D minor*, III: Section A-b

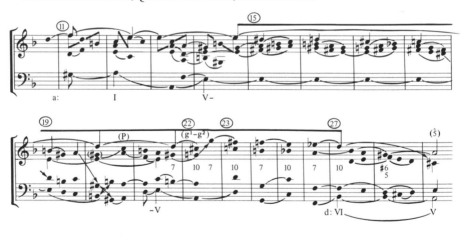

The temporary tonic in m. 12 leads to its dominant in m. 14, which is then extended all the way to m. 21. At m. 22, the bass moves from e to A. The latter note would represent a resolution back to the temporary tonic, A minor, were it not for the upper voices. What happens here is clearly indicated in the sketch, Example 298: a linear intervallic pattern takes over the foreground, terminating in m. 27 on the B♭ triad. As indicated, this proves to be the dominant preparation VI in the main tonality; the dominant then follows in m. 29, preparatory to the return of section A–a₁ in m. 30 (not shown).

Section A-b lasts for nineteen measures reflecting the unusual, "irregular" prolongations in the upper parts, which will now be discussed.

The section begins with two pairs of foreground unfoldings that span mm. 11–14, a regular four-measure phrase. The net effect of these is to introduce e^2 in the descant, prefixed by its upper neighbor, f^2, as shown.[8]

Once e^2 is established in m. 14 as the main note in the descant a descending stepwise progression commences, which is motivically associated with the descending chromatic bass of section A–a_1 (Example 297). When this reaches b^1 in m. 19 the bass suddenly begins to move, descending from e to B in mm. 19–20. Just at that point the descending upper-voice motion ceases, and the descant takes up a new note, d^2. As shown in the sketch, this is the continuation of the initial e^2 in m. 15. This e^2 has been prolonged by the stepwise descent which ends on $g\sharp^1$ (implied) in m. 20. Measures 20–21 are critical to the understanding of the middleground of the section and are subject to a variety of misreadings. The first analytic pitfall occurs with the entrance of c^2 over bass A on the last quarter-note of m. 20. This does not resolve d^2 in the upper voice, but is a passing tone in the longer motion to $g\sharp^1$, which is grouped beneath a slur in the sketch. That is, c^2 here is a consonant passing tone at the foreground level, not an element of the middleground. The definitive setting of d^2 occurs only on the last quarter note of m. 21 in second violin over bass e. It is at this point that the dominant harmony of m. 14 is resumed, and it seems that the temporary tonic A-minor triad should ensue.

However, although the bass descends to A on the downbeat of m. 22, the upper voices form a seventh chord, not a consonant triad, above it, and it immediately becomes clear that this is the second member of a 7–10 linear intervallic pattern which will terminate in m. 27 on VI, as described above. The paths followed by the upper voices over this linear intervallic pattern can be read from the sketch. In m. 22, g^1 is thrown up an octave (by first violin) to g^2 and from there descends chromatically to d^2 in m. 27. The lower of the two upper voices continues its downward path from $c\sharp^2$ in m. 22 to a^1 in m. 26, the note which represents the primary tone when it is properly defined with the support of the dominant in m. 29 at the end of the section. From m. 30 to m. 39 section A–a_2 repeats exactly the music of section A–a_1.

Mozart, String Quartet in D minor, *K. 421,III: Part B*

Example 299 is a sketch of section B–a_1, the first section of the trio of this movement. In style and structure it differs markedly from the minuet. Unlike the minuet, the trio falls into phrases of regular four-measure length. The first of these presents a pair of unfolded intervals: a sixth from f^1 out to d^3 followed

---

8. If f^2 in m. 11 is given middleground status, then the main descant motion over the entire section incorporates the third f^2–e^2–d^2 and is an enlarged replica of the foreground motive of mm. 2–3. Tempting as this reading is, we have rejected it.

by an augmented fourth from c♯³ in to g². (The resolution of c♯³ is implied through the harmonic change in m. 44.) At the foreground level these unfoldings are prolonged by arpeggiations, creating an idiomatic instrumental configuration.

EXAMPLE 299. Mozart, *Quartet in D minor*, III: Section B-a₁

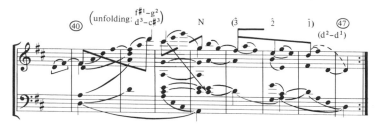

Passages such as the first four measures of this trio sometimes cause difficulties to the beginning analyst, difficulties which pertain directly to structural levels. Here it is obvious that the foreground consists of arpeggiations. The question that needs to be asked is: How do these fit into the middleground? (We assume, of course, that there is more to the structure than foreground arpeggios.) Perhaps the best general strategy for answering this question is to work from the bass up. The bass divides the four-measure group into two measures each: the first two governed by the tonic, the second two by the dominant. We then ask: what takes place over the tonic bass? Answer: the ascent from f♯♯¹ to d³. And over the dominant bass? Answer: the arpeggiation from c♯³ out to g³ and the drop back to g² on the downbeat of m. 43. Because of the continuation we take g² to be the note that defines the interval here, hence an augmented fourth is outlined. Putting this together with the motion from f♯♯¹ to d³ then permits us to synthesize the passage in terms of its component unfolded intervals.

The primary tone of the trio, f♯♯², introduced by its upper neighbor at the beginning of the second four-measure phrase of part B–a₁, is the head note of a linear progression of a third, as shown in Example 299. In section B-a₂, which is an exact repetition of section B-a₁ (and thus not explicitly shown here), this becomes the closure of the fundamental line of the trio, a complete small piece in itself.

Section B–b, shown in Example 300, continues the unfoldings of the previous section, with the head note, g², of the first interval a large-scale neighbor note to the primary tone of the trio, f♯♯², in m. 50. Notice that in reading the upper voice of mm. 50–51 we regard f♯♯³ as subsidiary to f♯♯², since the linear continuity of the section occurs in the register of the latter. This linear continuity, more precisely described, is represented by the stepwise ascent f♯♯²–g♯♯²–a², an ascending linear progression that prolongs the head note f♯♯². It would be incorrect to regard this as a definitive ascent to a², since with the return of section B–a_2 in m. 56 all motion centers around the primary tone of the trio, f#^{2}. The motion to a^2, however, is clearly a reference to the primary tone of the entire movement, $\hat{5}$, as indicated in m. 54 of the sketch.

EXAMPLE 300. Mozart, *Quartet in D minor*, III: Section B-b

This minuet and trio transcend the simple dancelike form typical of the period. The minuet is especially unusual, with its Mozartean chromaticism and elaborate prolongations. But the trio, too, is most interesting in the way it combines idiomatic instrumental arpeggiation with the unfolding type of prolongation to create middleground structures. Example 301 summarizes the form of this movement.

EXAMPLE 301. Mozart, *Quartet in D minor*, III: Summary of Form

A: I			B: I#			[A]
a_1: I	b: V	a_2: I	a_1: I#	b: V	a_2: I#	
1–10	11–29	30–39	40–47	48–55	56–63	

The minuet and trio are unified through key, since the trio represents only a change to major mode. They are also unified with respect to register, since the main middleground components are in a single location. Finally, the trio may be considered as a melodic development of the third of the triad, the note f^2 which is singled out in the theme of the minuet by the foreground prolongation f^2–e^2–d^2 in mm. 1–2. This motion, expanded, becomes the linear progression f#^{2}–e^2–d^2 of section B–a_1

Rondo Forms

The rondo form is characterized by the periodic recurrence of its initial formal component, a part known as the *refrain*. The refrain in the highly developed rondo of the late eighteenth and nineteenth centuries is a complete piece in itself, a ternary or binary form. Occurrences of the refrain alternate with contrasting parts, called *episodes*, which are also complete pieces in themselves. In the case of one recurrence of the refrain, then, we might represent the succession of parts ABA, where B designates the single episode.

How, then, does this differ from the compound ternary form? The answer resides in an additional feature of the rondo form: the often elaborate transitions between its component parts. A transition need not occur between every pair of parts, however, nor is it necessary that the transition be lengthy. The content of the transition is determined by the particular melodic and harmonic circumstances of the individual composition.

By its very nature, the rondo form is exemplified by many of the longest works in the tonal repertory. Assignment of a rondo to one of the three basic types—called first, second, and third rondo—depends upon *the number of recurrences of the refrain*.[9] In some instances, there may be a question as to whether a given form is first rondo or compound ternary, and a good case might be made for either. However, there is never any question about the other types of rondos.

Examples of extended rondos are numerous. Some famous instances are the final movements of Brahm's *Second* and *Third Symphonies*. The finale of Beethoven's *Second Symphony* is a complicated rondo of large scale, one that contains very interesting transitions, especially between the episodes and the refrain. It has the pattern AB_1ACAB_2A Coda. The finale of Haydn's *Symphony in D major, No. 101* ("The Clock") is a second rondo which includes a fugato based upon the thematic motive of the refrain. The rondo may also incorporate features of other forms. For example, the marcia funebre of Beethoven's *Third Symphony* ("Eroica") is a second rondo with a fugal development.[10] In this connection it should be pointed out that the transition sections of rondos are often highly developmental; they are not merely filler.

Our coverage of the rondo form includes only the first and second rondos, since the third rondo is such a long form. However, we include an example of third rondo in the exercises for this chapter.

Mendelssohn, Nocturne *from* Music to A Midsummer Night's Dream : *Refrain*

As an example of first rondo form let us study Mendelssohn's Nocturne from his *Music to A Midsummer Night's Dream*. Obviously an analytic sketch cannot represent all the wonderful surface features of this famous work. In particular, it makes no attempt to indicate the exquisite orchestration, which only the full score can reveal. However, the analytic sketches that begin with

---

9. In some texts rondo forms are classified on the basis of *the number of different episodes*. This is incorrect, since the third rondo form has only two different episodes, displaying the pattern AB_1ACAB_2A: three occurrences of the refrain but only two different episodes (B and C). Part B_2 differs from B_1 usually in that it is transposed to the tonic key, however.

10. A complete analysis of the *Eroica Symphony* was published by Schenker in the third volume of *Das Meisterwerk in der Music* (1930), entitled "Beethovens Dritte Sinfonie zum erstenmal in ihrem wahren Inhalt dargestellt" (Beethoven's Third Symphony, represented for the first time with its true content).

Example 302, if played at the piano, are complete enough to give a convincing rendition of the voice leading and harmony. For this work the sketches preserve barlines, so that the reader may easily follow the details of the analytic interpretations.

The melodic theme of the refrain is quite elaborate. It begins with the characteristic foreground motto, the fanfarelike ascending fourth b–e¹, bracketed in Example 302 and labeled motive *a*. This is followed by the stepwise ascent to the primary tone, $\hat{3}$, in m. 2 (motive *b*), and a descent from b¹ through the interval of fourth (motive *c*). As the final gesture of the first phrase, motive *c* joins with the ascending fourth f♯¹–b¹ in mm. 3–4, a replica of the opening motive *a*.

EXAMPLE 302. Mendelssohn, *Nocturne*: Refrain, Section A

Motive *c* contains, as its first three notes, a motive marked *d*, which proves to be important both at the foreground and middleground levels.

Although it might be possible to regard b¹ on the first beat of m. 4 as the primary tone, $\hat{5}$, there is no fundamental line that descends from it, whereas there is a clear descent from $\hat{3}$. Therefore, we regard the latter as defining the main melodic interval of the work. As the work progresses it becomes increasingly clear that b¹ is the upper-voice representative of b, the first note of the piece. This reading is reinforced, as suggested above, when b¹ is associated with f♯¹ to form the motto fourth (motive *a*) in mm. 3–4. In the coda this and other aspects of melodic structure are succinctly recalled. (See mm. 101–2, for example.)

The second part of the melody, from m. 4 to m. 8, prolongs the superimposed b¹ by a linear progression at the middleground level, as shown in the sketch. This progression descends from b¹ in m. 4 to a¹ in m. 7 and is then completed in the inner voice by the resolution of a to g♯ at the beginning of the second phrase in m. 9. The entire motion, B–A–G♯, is, of course, an enlargement of motive d, a remarkable example of an enlarged repetition that unifies foreground and middleground.

Associated with the linear progression from b¹ are the two unfoldings shown on the sketch, Example 302. First, b¹ unfolds in to e¹. This is followed by the stepwise ascent from e¹ to a¹ containing, in the notes e¹–f♯¹–g♯¹, an explicit reference to motive b (shown bracketed in mm. 5–6). The bass, meanwhile, from m. 4, consists of descending skips of thirds that culminate on F♯ in m. 7. This note, which provides special support for the upper voice a¹, is flagged because it returns in a crucial role in the transition, to be discussed below.

Only the close of the second part of the section (mm. 15–16) differs from the first. Again a¹ in m. 15 is taken over by the inner-voice a, while the descant presents $\hat{2}$ and $\hat{1}$ to close the fundamental structure. When the refrain is stated for the second and last time this will be the final close in the work, and is so represented here.

The melodic note a¹ in m. 7 presents an analytic problem, the solution to which involves a correct assignment to structural level. If it is regarded as a foreground element, then it is a consonant skip above f♯¹ in m. 6 and effectively disappears after it is stated. (Or it might be regarded as an incomplete neighbor to g♯¹ in m. 4; but that seems implausible.) The bass provides the clue to the correct interpretation. The F♯-minor triad, II, is dependent upon the dominant that follows it. Thus, the melodic note which it carries, a¹, bears a diagonal relation to the bass of the dominant in m. 8 and is still effective there. It is not resolved by g♯¹ in m. 7; that note is only part of the foreground prolongation of a¹, the unfolding down to d♯. Indeed, as explained above, a¹ never resolves to g♯¹, but is taken over by the inner voice, which resolves a to g♯ over the barline between m. 8 and m. 9. Once it has been determined that the problematic a¹ belongs to the middleground, it is not difficult to see that it is, in fact, the continuation of the b¹ that was abandoned in m. 4 when the upper voice connected down to the inner-voice e¹ in m. 5. The complete reading—a linear progression of a descending third—places all components properly in middleground or supporting foreground.

Example 303 shows section B of the refrain in its entirety. Here the main upper-voice note is b¹, introduced by the octave skip from b at the very outset, which clearly shows the association of those equivalent pitches. The middleground motion of largest scale over the span of the first four-measure phrase of the section is the coupling b¹–b. Within this are two motivic fourths, bracketed on the sketch: b¹–f♯¹ followed by e¹–b¹, a remarkable development of the opening motion of section A.

Section B takes places entirely over a dominant pedal, with an expanded $^{6-5}_{4-3}$ voice leading, and is therefore a good example of a one-part (unary) form.

EXAMPLE 303. Mendelssohn, *Nocturne*: Refrain, Section B

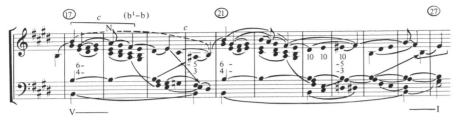

With this exception, the entire refrain is a compound ternary:

A   B   A

binary unary binary

Mendelssohn, Nocturne: *Episode*

The episode preserves rhythmic and some diminutional features of the refrain. The first section of its binary form is shown in Example 304. Let us consider first its harmonic organization. This is a prolongation of VI, as shown by the roman numerals in the sketch. Each of the component eight-measure phrases moves from I to V within VI, which leaves the large-scale progression "open" at the end of the section, since there is no definitive return to VI as tonic.

EXAMPLE 304. Mendelssohn, *Nocturne*: Episode, Section A

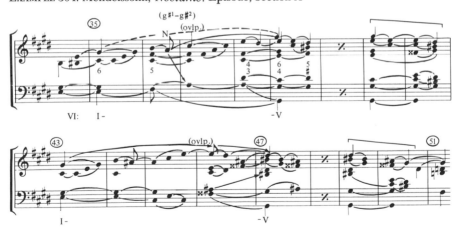

The most prominent middleground features of this part of the episode are the coupling from g♯¹ to g♯² and the repeated motivic fourth, g♯²–d♯², which becomes the fifth g♯¹–d♯² in the second eight-measure phrase. In these respects this part of the episode resembles the second part of the refrain, and, indeed, may be regarded as a development of it.

The primary tone of the refrain, G♯, remains the primary tone of the episode as well, occurring in two registers, as g♯^{1} (obligatory register) and as g♯^{2}, the prolongational register.

In the second and final section of the episode (Example 305) the prolonged harmony is II (F♯ minor). Thus, with respect to the main tonality, both sections of the episode are based upon preparations for the dominant of the main tonality, the dominant which arrives in m. 71 at the end of the transition to the refrain.

EXAMPLE 305. Mendelssohn, *Nocturne*: Episode, Section B

Section B of the episode is quite different in content from section A. At the foreground level, beginning in m. 51, it presents expanded variants on the ascending third (motive *b*) at the opening of the refrain, and these prove to be in the service of an ascending arpeggiation of II^7 (of II). At the still deeper middleground level the descant prolongs the primary tone by a descending linear progression of a third, one that suggests an expansion of foreground motive *d* of the refrain, b^1–a^1–g♯^{1}, in mm. 2–3. This linear progression in the descant is accompanied by an unfolding in the bass, as shown in the sketch, from f♯ down to d, resolving to g♯ over c♯ in m. 54.

In the second phrase of section B, mm. 55–58, the linear progression from the primary tone G♯ is repeated, but this time there is a further motion through an overlapping to g♯^{2}, completing the coupling from g♯^{1} in m. 54, as indicated in the sketch. This in turn leads to the climactic note of the episode, c♯^{3} on the first beat of m. 59, which moves to g♯^{2} to create the fourth motive that was so prominent in the first part of the episode. Simultaneously, this is the definitive arrival on the tonic for this section, I of II.

Mendelssohn, Nocturne: *Transition to the Refrain*

The transition to the refrain begins almost imperceptibly in m. 61, marked, however, by a change in orchestration. Now the climactic c♯^{3} turns out to be the head note of a descending linear progression, as shown in Example 306. This is beautifully composed with the fourth motive in the foreground, here represented by its inversion, the fifth. First we have c♯^{3}–f♯^{2} (mm. 61–62), then b^2–e^2 (mm. 63–64), then the tail note of the linear progression, a^2, to which is attached the skip of a fourth down to e² (m. 65), echoed immediately by e¹ up to a¹ (bracketed in mm. 65–66), a replica of the thematic motive itself, from which all the preceding fifths and fourths were derived. Thus, the foreground is literally saturated with fourths and fifths, in preparation for the forthcoming return of the theme of the refrain.

EXAMPLE 306. Mendelssohn, *Nocturne*: Transition from Episode to Refrain

The tail note of the linear progression, a², is the main element in the middleground; the head note, c♯³, is subordinate to it. This is because, as shown in the analytic sketch, Example 306, a² of m. 65 becomes the seventh over the dominant harmony in m. 72 and thus serves as upper neighbor to the primary tone 3̂, when it returns in the upper register at m. 73. The head note of the linear progression, c♯³, has no further continuity in the middleground.

From m. 66 to the return of the refrain in m. 73, the harmonic progression consists of the dominant preparation II, which moves to the dominant in m. 71, then to the tonic in m. 73. Above this are two occurrences of the motivic motion a¹–b¹–c², followed by a²–c♯³ in mm. 70–72, a reference to the linear progression from c♯³ that began in m. 61. Both motions, of course, prolong the key middleground pitch A, which resolves to the primary tone with the return of the refrain in m. 73.

Mendelssohn, Nocturne: *Coda*

The refrain returns in m. 73 and is represented by section A only, an abbreviation common in rondos. The final phrase of the refrain does not cadence, but merges with a long coda that contains four distinct sections. This is based entirely within the tonic harmony and is clearly developmental with respect to the thematic motives of the refrain and a figure characteristic of the episode, the foreground appoggiatura. In the coda this is attached to the important triadic note b¹ at special points. In the sketches that follow, it is always flagged for special attention.

The middleground descant of the first section of the coda, shown in Example 307, consists of a linear progression that ascends from e¹ in m. 85 to an implied g♯¹ in m. 91 via a prolonged neighbor note, a¹. This, of course, is a middleground expansion of motive *b*, the initial ascent to the primary tone in the refrain. Since this takes place within the frame of a $\frac{5-6}{3-4}$ voice leading, the arrival in m. 91 is not as strong as it would be otherwise. And, indeed, this section proves to be preparatory to section B, which follows. There; the linear progression extends upward all the way to b¹, with both a¹ and b¹ supplied with motive *d* and the characteristic appoggiatura figure of the episode. Motive *d* occurs also in the foreground of the bass, in alternation with the upper-voice form, while the middleground bass motion traverses the third from e to g♯, within the 10–7 linear intervallic pattern. As soon as it reaches g♯ it drops back to e, which is sustained while the upper voice introduces a motive characteristic of the coda: f♯¹–b¹–g♯¹. This is, of course, a reference to motives *d* and *c* of the refrain. Section B of the coda then ends with a descent from $\hat{3}$ to $\hat{1}$, an allusion to the end of the refrain.

EXAMPLE 307. Mendelssohn, *Nocturne*: Coda, Sections A and B

Section C of the coda (Example 308) again presents an ascending linear progression to $\hat{3}$, this time incorporating the special version of motive *c* introduced at the end of the previous section: b¹–g♯¹–f♯¹. In an ingenious fashion this motive joins with motive *c'* (i.e., the notes of motive *c* in reverse order) at the end of m. 102, which, in turn, interlocks with motive *a* in m. 103, to introduce the highest note thus far in the movement, e³. The downward coupling to e², which ensues, adjoins two forms of motive *d*, as indicated in the sketch. After the arrival on e² in m. 106 the descant brings in the appoggiatura, c♯², which resolves to b¹ in m. 108 to conclude the section. This final upper-voice motion creates the pattern e²–c♯²–b¹, a form of motive *a*, (identified as *a'* in the sketch). This, of course, is a transposition of the *c* motive in mm. 101–2.

EXAMPLE 308. Mendelssohn, *Nocturne*: Coda, Section C

The final section of the coda, section D (Example 309), begins with the motion of closure associated with the end of the refrain, here identified as motive *b'*, and the opening motive of the refrain, motive *a*. In m. 113 the high e^3 is introduced once again, in the context of motive *a*. The only moving voice-leading component at the middleground level is a^2, which is effective from m. 113 until its resolution to $g\sharp^2$ in m. 119. This motion may be regarded as a reference to the transition from the episode to the refrain, mm. 61–72 (Example 306).

EXAMPLE 309. Mendelssohn, *Nocturne*: Coda, Section D

In the final portion of section D of the coda the tonic triad is arpeggiated, with emphasis upon E and B. In m. 123 violins play the highest note of the movement, e^4, a final, ethereal reminder of the opening of the refrain. While this is sustained, a melodic lower voice descends from e^1 to b, pausing on c^1 in the next-to-last measure. This enigmatic final gesture in m. 125 is a reference to the sonority of mm. 66–70 of the transition (Example 306).

Finally, the cadential chord of the movement, in m. 126, is orchestrated in such a way that $g\sharp^1$, the primary tone, emerges as the predominant pitch, a final allusion to the focal melodic element of the music.

The essentials of this first-rondo form are reviewed in Example 310, the Summary of Form. Notice the characteristic rondo features (in addition to refrain and episode)—the transition (mm. 61–72) and the extensive four-part coda.

EXAMPLE 310. Mendelssohn, *Nocturne*: Summary of Form

Refrain: I
Section A: I   Section B: V   Section A: I
1–16   17–26   27–34

Episode: VI–II
Section A: VI   Section B: II   Transition: II–V
35–50   51–60   61–72

Refrain: I
Section A: I
73–84

Coda: I
Sections A and B: I   Section C: I   Section D: I
85–99   100–8   109–26

Haydn, Piano Sonata in D major, *Hob. XVI/37, III: Refrain*

The last movement of a familiar piano sonata by Haydn will serve well as an instance of second rondo form. Instead of measure-by-measure sketches, we present regular Schenkerian graphs of this work.

In comparison with the Mendelssohn Nocturne, this composition is relatively uncomplicated. Moreover, it is an excellent example of the rondo form of the Classic period. Each part is a complete small piece in itself, a small ternary form. There is only one transition, from Episode 2 back to the final statement of the refrain.

Example 311 is a sketch of the entire refrain. The primary tone $\hat{5}$ is given at the very outset, but not in the obligatory register. Its definitive statement occurs only in m. 8 over the dominant harmony, and is the completion of an upward coupling from a[1] at the beginning.

EXAMPLE 311. Haydn, *Sonata in D major*, III: Refrain

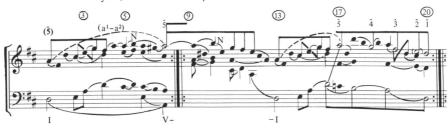

At the middleground level, a¹ is prolonged by a descending third, beamed in the sketch.[11] This involves a registral displacement and incorporates an unfolding diminished fifth c♯²–g², which resolves to f♯² over d², as indicated. At the completion of this motion, a² is superimposed and prolonged by upper and lower neighbors, prior to its definitive statement at the end of the phrase.

The B part of this small ternary form is only four measures long (mm. 9–12) and takes place over the dominant harmony, extended from the cadence in m. 8. The descant middleground is straightforward: a descending linear progression of a fourth, prolonging the primary tone, a², with an additional foreground prolongation, the upper neighbor b² in m. 10.

In m. 13 the final section of the refrain begins as did the first. As a² is reached by coupling, the bass begins to descend, providing contrapuntal support for the descending fundamental line as shown on the sketch (Example 311). This descending fundamental line is somewhat concealed by the foreground. Specifically, scale degree $\hat{3}$ is embedded in the arpeggiation a²–f♯²–d² of m. 19. In addition, scale degree $\hat{2}$ is represented by c♯¹, a substitution. The voice leading supports the reading given, however, since g² in m. 18 is supported by bass b, forming a sixth. When the bass continues stepwise to a, the upper voice continues to follow, forming another sixth with f♯².

Haydn, Piano Sonata in D major, *Hob, XVI/37, III: Episode 1*

Episode 1, shown in Example 312, is in the parallel minor mode—not an infrequent occurrence in the rondo form. Its primary tone, f¹, $\hat{3}$, is first

EXAMPLE 312. Haydn, *Sonata in D major*, III: Episode 1

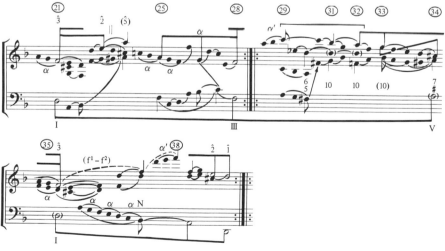

---

11. It would not be entirely remiss to show g² as a neighbor note to f♯² rather than as a passing tone between a¹ and f♯².

prolonged by the progression to $\hat{2}$, as shown, and at the end of the phrase there is a brief reference to the primary tone of the refrain, a^2.

The second four-measure phrase begins abruptly on the mediant in m. 25, with the foreground melodic motion a^1–g^1–f^1, in imitation of the opening motive (marked alpha) in mm. 21–22. This proves to be an embedded miniature version of the middleground linear progression that prolongs the tail note f^1, which is attained at the end of the section in m. 28.

The middle part of this ternary form (mm. 29–34) is somewhat more difficult to read than the first part. In the upper voice c^3 is introduced via the inversion of the alpha motive, and this is answered by an enlarged form of the same motive in bass and inner voice. In m. 31 this c^3 resolves to $b\flat^2$ over bass g^1, which has the harmonic value IV and is the crucial element in directing the motion back to the main tonic, D minor. As shown in Example 312, a linear progression of a third follows, with head note a^2, another enlargement of motive alpha and one that links part B of the form to part A (m. 35 ff.). Passing note g^2 in the linear progression (m. 33) is prolonged by a foreground unfolding in to $c\sharp^1$, which arrives at the cadence on V. At this point—the conclusion of part B—the bass has completed an arpeggiation of the tonic triad, beamed in the sketch to emphasize its unifying function with respect to part A and part B.

In this reading of the upper voice both c^3 and $b\flat^2$ are prefixes to a^2 in m. 32, the head note of the linear progression. To include them as stepwise elements of some linear progression would contradict the harmonic goal of the progression—a situation that has been amply discussed in previous sections. One problem remains, however, in this interpretation of the upper voice: the position of the head note of the linear progression, a^2, within the second element of a 10–10 linear intervallic pattern. Because of this location it is not as clearly articulated as the head note of a progression usually is.

The section ends with two foreground flourishes, typical of Haydn's style: the bass motion of a seventh from a to $B\flat$ and the successive coupling of the primary tone to f^2, then f^3 (m. 38). The latter has the shape of motive alpha inverted. Closure of the fundamental line for episode 1 is uncomplicated, and the first recurrence of the refrain follows in its entirety.

Haydn, Piano Sonata in D major, *Hob XVI/37, III: Episode 2*

Episode 2, a complete ternary form, lies entirely within the subdominant harmony ("G major") and is the simplest of all the sections of this rondo. Part A prolongs the primary tone of this episode, b^2 ($\hat{3}$), with an uncomplicated close to $\hat{1}$ in m. 68 (Example 313). Part B is an interruption form, moving from tonic to dominant, and part A returns to complete the structure.

EXAMPLE 313. Haydn, *Sonata in D major*, III: Episode 2

Episode 2 is stated without any intervening transition from the refrain. How does this section, in the subdominant harmony, fit into the overall organization of the rondo? That question is answered in the transition that follows the episode, the return to the last statement of the refrain.

Haydn, Piano Sonata in D major, *Hob. XVI/37, III: Transition*

Beginning in m. 81 is a passage thirteen measures long, the transition from episode 2 to the refrain. Although the foreground changes markedly in rhythmic and melodic configuration at the beginning of this passage, the primary tone b^2 remains, as shown in Example 314, moving to a^2 at the end of the first four-measure phrase, as the bass changes to the dominant. In m. 85 the descant brings in d^3, a superimposed inner voice, and this couples down to d^2 in m. 86, involving $g\sharp^2$ in the process. While $g\sharp^2$ resolves to a^1, d^2 resolves to $c\sharp^2$, to complete the unfolding shown in the analytic sketch.

EXAMPLE 314. Haydn, *Sonata in D major*, III: Transition from Episode 2 to Refrain

The concluding note of the transition, a^1, although locally related to $g\sharp^2$, has a more important relation of longer range: It is the continuation of b^2 at the beginning of the transition over the subdominant harmony. Specifically, b^2 is the upper neighbor of a^1 (with octave displacement, of course). Thus, in the transition, the subdominant loses its quasi-independent status and resumes its position within the orbit of the main tonic, D minor. (See Example 109, p. 105.)

The second and final recurrence of the refrain spans some forty measures and includes internal repetitions of all the parts of the refrain, each with additional figurations involving bass and tenor. Otherwise, the structural motions it presents are identical to those shown in Example 311.

The overall plan of this second rondo form, with its characteristic two episodes, is shown in Example 315. In this work there is only one transition, it will be recalled. Harmonically, this effects a change from IV to V, as indicated.

EXAMPLE 315. Haydn, *Sonata in D major*, III: Summary of Form

Refrain: I	Episode 2: IV	Transition: IV–V
1–20	61–80	81–93

Episode 1: I♮	Refrain: I
21–40	94–122

Refrain: I
41–60

Mozart, Serenade in G major (Eine kleine Nachtmusik), K. 525, II

As in the case of the Haydn rondo above, we use analytic graphs without barlines to represent the structure of the third and last example of rondo form, the familiar Romance from Mozart's *Eine kleine Nachtmusik*. It is considerably more elaborate than the Haydn work, both within the individual parts and in overall form. An overview of the form is given in Example 316.

EXAMPLE 316. Mozart, *Serenade in G major*, II: Summary of Form

Refrain: I   Simple Ternary
1–16

Episode 1   Binary (open)
Section A: I   Section B: I–V of VI (III♯)
16–20   21–28
Transition: V of VI–I   Phrase
28–30

Refrain: I   Truncated (first part only)
31–38

Episode 2: I♭–III–V   Binary
38–45
Transition: V–I   Extended Phrase
45–50

Refrain: I   Simple Ternary
51–66

Coda: I   Extended Phrase
67–73

Within this second rondo design episode 1 plays an interesting role, one reminiscent of a development section in a sonata form. Also especially interesting are the two transitional passages between the episodes and the recurring refrains. These and episode 1 will be discussed at an appropriate point below.

Mozart, Serenade in G major, *K. 525, II: Refrain*

Example 317 is a sketch of the refrain in its entirety. The primary tone, $\hat{3}$, is stated directly, without complications. Attached to it are two motions: the ascending third with upper neighbor note and the descending sixth from c^3 to e^2. In the second phrase these foreground motions change to descending arpeggiations that prolong $\hat{3}$ and $\hat{2}$.

EXAMPLE 317. Mozart, *Serenade in G major*, II: Refrain

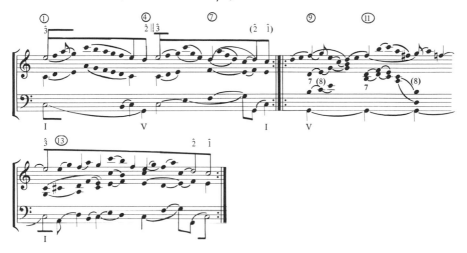

Section B of the refrain (m. 9) features a prolonged neighbor note, f^2, in the descant, and this note itself is twice embellished by an upper neighbor note, forming the 7–(8) motion indicated on the sketch, before it returns to the primary tone at the beginning of the last section of the refrain.

In the concluding section the ascending third from e^2 to g^2 is elevated to the status of a middleground progression by virtue of the bass and harmonic support it receives there. With this exception, the middleground of the final section is essentially that of the second phrase of the first section: a prolongation of $\hat{3}$ in the upper voice over tonic harmony and a close of the fundamental line at the end.

Mozart, Serenade in G major, *K. 525, II: Episode 1*

Episode 1 (Example 318) preserves the primary tone in the descant and prolongs it, first through an interruption form that encloses a descending third, then through an ascending linear progression e^2–$f\sharp^2$–g^2 (m. 19), which may be regarded as a middleground development of the initial foreground motion of the refrain. From m. 19 to the end of section A in m. 20, g² couples down to g¹, dividing the octave at d², as indicated by the slurs in the sketch. At the cadence in m. 20 it is clear that the dominant has been tonicized. However, the possibility for extending that harmony as a temporary tonic is not realized, for with the repetition of the section the main tonic resumes its governing role.

EXAMPLE 318. Mozart, *Serenade in G major*, II: Episode 1, Sections A and B

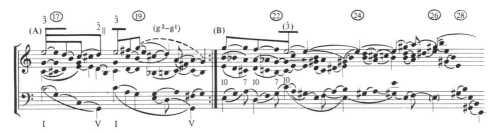

At the beginning of section B of episode 1, g² reappears in the descant against e in the bass and a 10–7 linear intervallic pattern ensues. With respect to harmony, this effectively negates the preceding tonicization of the dominant. With respect to the upper voice, g² becomes the head note of a descending linear progression that returns to the primary tone in m. 22.

As remarked earlier, episode 1 has a very interesting feature, which we can now specify as the passage from m. 22 to m. 28. As soon as the primary tone is restored in the descant in m. 22 there is an abrupt shift away from the tonic triad to the E-major triad in m. 24, shown by the bass slur in Example 318. This is reached in such a way that it sounds like the dominant harmony in A minor (VI). However, it never fulfills its dominant function.[12] Instead, it supports the primary tone e² in the descant until m. 26, when g♯² is

EXAMPLE 319. Mozart, *Serenade in G major*, II: Transition to Refrain from Episode 1

---

12. An analogous situation arises in the development sections of the first movements of the two piano sonatas in F major, K. 280 (m. 78) and K. 332 (m. 123). The goal of motion in both cases is an A-major triad (III♯) just before the transition to the reprise. Beethoven may well have modeled the close of the development of the first movement of the *"Spring"* Sonata for violin and piano after these unusual Mozartean passages.

superimposed. In the transition that follows, shown in Example 323, g♯♯²
connects downward chromatically to f² above the dominant harmony, and
this leads to the return of the primary tone over tonic in m. 31 at the
beginning of the refrain.

Example 320 shows, schematically, how the E-major triad fits into the
structure. With respect to the bass it is part of an arpeggiation of the tonic
triad, shown at *a* in the example, a third-divider in Schenkerian terms. With
the return to V⁷ the upper voice moves to its upper neighbor, G♯, then falls
back to G, while the common tone B remains fixed. The elaboration of this is
shown at *b* in the example. There g♯¹ is coupled upward to g♯², which
returns by chromatic step to f² as a motion in the linear intervallic pattern.
This motion prevents the direct connection e²–f² from taking place. Moreover, the bass arpeggiation shown at (a) does not occur in the actual piece;
the dominant seventh is in the $^6_5$ position, with B in the bass. Thus, in the
music the emphatic bass motion is C–e. The motivic significance of this, as
well as the motivic significance of g♯² in the descant at the end of episode 1,
are questions which cannot be discussed here without digressing from the
topic at hand, namely, the structural design of this second rondo form.

EXAMPLE 320. Mozart, *Serenade in G major*, II: Episode 1 and Transition to Refrain
— Schematic

Mozart, Serenade in G major, *K. 525, II: Episode 2*

This part of the rondo is a binary form in the parallel minor mode. Perhaps
the most important large-scale unifying factor is the bass arpeggiation
C–e♭–g, shown in Example 321c. Thus, like episode 1, this part is "open," in
the sense that it does not end in C minor.

Example 321c presents the basic middleground structure of the music
here: g² is prolonged in the descant against the bass arpeggiation. Example
321b fills out the graph at *c*, showing more foreground detail. Notice in
particular the second part of this binary form, from m. 43 (including the
upbeat in m. 42) to m. 45. Enclosed in brackets there are the skips from b♭²
to e♭² and from c³ to f². These are bracketed because they are doublings of
voice-leading components that lie below them. The upper voice does not
ascend b♭²–c³–d³ against the bass e♭–f–g, creating a succession of three

EXAMPLE 321. Mozart, *Serenade in G major*, II: Episode 2

parallel perfect fifths, nor does the upper voice move e♭²–f²–g² against the bass e♭–f–g, creating parallel octaves! These upper voices enrich the voice leading by doubling voices below them, but they do not represent the real progression, which is the 5–10 linear intervallic pattern shown in the analytic sketch, Example 321*b*. At the foreground level, shown in Example 321*a*, the imitation of first violin by cello is shown by the broken diagonal arrows. It is this imitative pattern that causes the pseudo-voice-leading descant. In analyzing an instrumental composition such as this it is always important to take into account the way in which the instruments interact. Here, in this work for four instruments, not all the lines are real voice-leading components.

The sketch in Example 321*a* incorporates the essential foreground motions of episode 2. Of these the most prominent are the accompanimental inner voices (second violin and viola) and the descending skip of a sixth in first violin, imitated by cello. Both patterns are derived from the refrain. The repeated ascent $e\flat^1$–f^1–g^1 in the accompaniment is the minor version of the first foreground motive of the refrain, e^2–f^2–g^2. And the second foreground motive of the refrain, the sixth which descends from c^3 to e^2 (mm. 2–3), is the model for the descending skips of sixths that recur throughout this episode.

This descending skip, which characterizes episode 2 as melodic motive, is carried forward in expanded form at the beginning of the transition, shown in Example 322. This is the large-scale unfolding from g^2 in m. 45 in to b in m. 47, completely filled in by step, which is perhaps more clearly shown in Example 322*b*. The unfolding, as well as other foreground features of the

EXAMPLE 322. Mozart, *Serenade in G major*, II: Transition to Refrain from Episode 2

transition, occurs over a dominant harmony. As shown in Example 322*b*, the middleground descant is a prolonged 8–7 above that harmony. When this arrives at $\hat{3}$ at the beginning of the refrain in m. 51, a linear progression of a third is completed, spanning the third between scale degrees $\hat{3}$ and $\hat{5}$ which was established at the outset of the refrain as a basic prolongational interval in the composition.

A comparison of the aligned graphs in Example 322 will help to sort out the structural levels and place the components in proper perspective. For instance, c^3 in the upper voice of m. 47 resolves in the voice-leading texture to b, as indicated by the diagonal arrow. And the bass motion from g down to C via the unfolding (m. 47 ff.) is not to be understood as a motion from dominant to tonic. Rather, C is a consonant skip below the controlling bass note g, although, to be sure, the motion does prepare the definitive descent to the tonic in m. 51 when the refrain recommences.

Mozart, Serenade in G major, *K. 525, II: Coda*

The coda begins in a remarkable way (Example 323), with an encapsulated version of the 5–10 linear intervallic pattern from the second part of episode 2 (mm. 43–45). However, the pattern breaks just at the end, on the downbeat of m. 68, where c^2 replaces the expected b^1 in the upper voice. Just at this point, viola enters with the descending sixth motive of episode 2 and first violin brings in the descending third e^2–d^2–c^2, recalling the refrain and the opening of episode 1. In m. 69 the melodic theme of the refrain returns, but instead of ascending to g^2, skips away to c^3, so that f^2 in m. 70 serves as upper neighbor to e^2. Finally, the last two measures carry a complete allusion to the opening melodic motion of the refrain, e^2–f^2–g^2, and to the last note is attached the descending sixth of episode 2. Clearly the coda here, as in many compositions, is a kind of summary of the movement.

EXAMPLE 323. Mozart, *Serenade in G major*, II: Coda

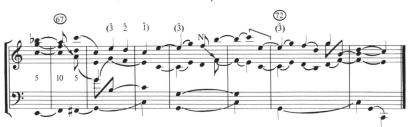

Conclusion

In this section we have presented analyses of large ternary and rondo forms, illustrating procedures and interpretations as well as sketching techniques. We have also touched upon certain analytical problems and suggested solutions to them.

At this stage the reader is able to follow more complex analyses and to read analytic sketches. Here and throughout the text, however, we stress the essentiality of the exercises. Only by working these out carefully can the student achieve a high level of competency and prepare himself for advanced study of musical structures. It is with this in mind that we retained much of the foreground detail in the analytic sketches. Experience has shown that neglect of the foreground in a misguided effort to penetrate the middleground and background structures without adequate interpretation of foreground leads only to poor analytical work. Indeed, here at the end of the last chapter of this introduction to Schenkerian method it is appropriate to remind the reader that a good complete analysis will show clearly the components of each level and, beyond that, will indicate precisely the way in which all the levels interact to create the complete musical work. It is this high degree of precision which distinguishes the well-constructed Schenkerian analysis from other analyses and which enables the person who wishes to study the analysis to obtain an unambiguous reading, one that can be thoughtfully and critically evaluated.

Exercises

A. Construct a measure-by-measure analytic sketch of each of the following compound ternary works and write a brief commentary on your analyses, emphasizing the interaction of foreground and middleground elements.

1. Beethoven, *Piano Sonata in F minor*, Op. 2/1, III (Menuetto)

> Small unfoldings are featured in the foreground of the minuet. Be sure to read beyond these to understand the middleground motions. It is probably wise to postpone a decision about the primary tone until the analysis is well underway.

2. Schubert, *Moments musicaux*, Op. 94, No. 6

> This work contains a great deal of melodic detail that is worth special attention. Note in particular the role of F and its chromatic counterpart F♭. The first part can be done as a separate piece. If the trio is analyzed, explain the structural relation between its governing harmony and that of the first part.

3. Beethoven, *Piano Sonata in D major*, Op. 28, Scherzo

This piece, although short, contains some passages that require special consideration. In m. 8 and corresponding places it is important to include the implied note in your analysis in order to understand the continuity of middleground. How does the trio relate to the scherzo? Do they share any features? Since no transitional passage links scherzo with trio or trio with scherzo, how are they connected?

Note: This composition has a primary tone but no fundamental line, and thus constitutes an exception to the axioms of fundamental structure. Similar exceptions occur elsewhere in the literature, mainly in short pieces. For example, Brahms's *Intermezzo in B♭ major*, Op. 76, No. 4 (whose middle section is cited in Exercise 20D/2, p. 274) exhibits the fundamental line $\hat{4}$(N)–$\hat{3}$, with no descent beyond $\hat{3}$. Another example is Chopin's *Prelude in E major*, Op. 28, No. 9, which has as its primary melodic tone $\hat{5}$, but no fundamental line.

B. The refrain and episode(s) of the following rondo forms may be analyzed as though they were separate small pieces. If this is done, give special attention to the transition(s) and to the way in which the separate pieces are linked to form a complete work. The analytic sketches need not contain barlines, but should indicate measure numbers clearly. As always, a brief written commentary is useful, to present and clarify your ideas about the structure of the movement.

1. Beethoven, *Piano Sonata in E♭ major*, Op. 7, II

The opening of this movement was given as Exercise 2A/1 (p. 139), and it is suggested that the reader refer to that exercise before commencing this one. The work has many extraordinary features which will reveal themselves as the analysis proceeds. Only in the coda does the fundamental line close.

2. Haydn, *Piano Sonata in C major*, Hob. XVI/48, II

This is the finale of a two-movement sonata. As in the Haydn rondo presented in the text, the various parts are clearly set out in this work.

3. Beethoven, *Piano Sonata in C minor*, Op. 13, III

This work, although well known, still offers the analyst interesting problems to solve. Begin by outlining the form, then study the music part by part, first making a measure-by-measure sketch, then deriving a more reduced graph from that. The movement shares certain features with the sonata form, although it is basically a rondo, and was so titled by Beethoven.

Index of Examples
and Exercises

After Bach
  Chorales (*see also under* Bach, Johann Sebastian)
    Allein Gott in der Höh' sei Ehr, (No. 32), 42 (p. 51)
    Christus, der ist mein Leben (No. 316), 56 (p. 59)
    Jesu meine Freude (No. 356), 53 (p. 57)
    Wo soll ich fliehen hin (No. 331), 51 (p. 56)
  Bach, Anna Magdelena, Notebook for, 16/4 (p. 213)
Bach, Johann Sebastian
  Aria variata, 5 (p. 13)
  Art of Fugue, The
    Contrapunctus I, 93 (p. 92)
    Contrapunctus IV, 80 (p. 84), 103 (p. 97)
  Cantata No. 61, *Nun komm der Heiden Heiland*, 19/7 (p. 248)
  Cello Suites
    in C major, Courante, 20A/1 (p. 271)
    in C minor, Gavotte II, 11 (p. 21)
    in D minor, Courante, 182 (p. 211); Sarabande, 181 (p. 210)
    in C major, Menuet II, 63 (p. 70), 16/6 (p. 213)
  Chorales (*see also under* After Bach)
    Ach Gott, wie manches Herzeleid (No. 217), 13/1 (p. 185)
    Ach wie nichtig, ach wie flüchtig (No. 48), 13/5 (p. 185)
    Als der gütige Gott (No. 159), 161*b* (p. 179), 162*b* (p. 180), 13/2 (p. 185)
    Befiehl du deine Wege (No. 367), 110 (p. 106)
    Christus, der ist mein Leben (No. 6), 166 (p. 184)
    Du Friedensfürst, Herr Jesu Christ (No. 42), 156 (p. 175)
    Ein' feste Burg ist unser Gott (No. 20), 137*c* (p. 134), 163*a* (p. 181)
    Herr, ich habe misgehandelt (No. 287), 43 (p. 51)
    Herr, wie du willst, so schick's mit mir (No. 317), 11/4 (p. 165)
    In dich hab' ich gehoffet, Herr (No. 118), 160*c* (p. 178), 13/4 (p. 185)
    Jesu, meine Freude (No. 356), 141*a* (p. 143), 160*b* (p. 177), 13/8 (p. 186)
    Mach's mit mir, Gott, nach deiner Güt' (No. 44), 13/7 (p. 186)
    Nicht so traurig (No. 149), 14 (p. 22)
    Nun lob' mein' Seel' den Herren (No. 296), 106 (p. 99), 113 (p. 108)
    Nun ruhen alle Wälder (No. 117), 157 (p. 176)
    O Ewigkeit, du Donnerwort (No. 274), 45 (p. 53)
    O Mensch bewein' dein' Sünde gross (No. 306), 55 (p. 59)
    Schmücke dich, O liebe Seele (No. 22), 160*b* (p. 178), 13/6 (p. 186)
    Schwing' dich auf zu deinem Gott (No. 142), 158 (p. 176)
    Seelen-Bräutigam (No. 141), 159*b* (p. 177), 161*a* (p. 179), 162*a* (p. 180)
    Sei gegrüsset, Jesu gütig (No. 172), 11/2 (p. 164)
    Valet will ich dir geben (No. 24), 13/9 (p. 186)
    Vater unser im Himmelreich (No. 47), 13/10 (p. 186)
    Vom Himmel hoch, da komm' ich her (No. 46), 163*b* (p. 181)
    Warum betrübst du dich, mein Herz (No. 300), 47 (p. 54)
    Was frag ich nach der Welt (No. 291), 15 (p. 23)
    Was mein Gott will, das g'scheh (No. 41), 159*a* (p. 177), 13/3 (p. 185)
    Weg, mein Herz, mit den Gedanken (No. 298), 111 (p. 107)
    Werde munter, mein Gemüte (No. 233), 11/3 (p. 164)
    Wir Christenleut' (No. 55), 11/1 (p. 163)
  English Suites
    in A minor, Sarabande, 1/7 (p. 40)
    in D minor, Sarabande, 2/2 (p. 64)
    in F major, Menuet II, 127 (p. 120), 20B/2 (p. 272)
    in G minor, Allemande, 85 (p. 87); Gavotte I, 12A/2 (p. 170); Prelude, 4/2 (p. 101)
  French Suites
    in B minor, Menuet, 189 (p. 223)
    in C minor, Sarabande, 16 (p. 23)
    in D minor, Sarabande, 180 (p. 209)
  Inventions
    in C major, No. 1, 19/6 (p. 248)
    in D minor, No. 4, 213 (p. 264)
    in E♭ major, No. 5, 99 (p. 95)
    in E major, No. 7, 3/1 (p. 80)
    in F major, No. 8, 15/2 (p. 205)
    in A minor, No. 13, 70 (p. 74)

Italian Concerto, I, 123 (p. 117)
Partitas
  I in B♭ major, Allemande, 28 (p. 34)
  V in G major, Sarabande, 25 (p. 31)
  for Solo Violin in B minor, Bourrée, 77 (p. 79); Sarabande, 78 (p. 79), 211 (p. 262)
  for Solo Violin in D minor, Gigue, 3/7 (p. 82)
Passacaglia for Organ in C minor, 58 (p. 60)
Preludes
  in C major (*Twelve Short Preludes*, No. 1), 14/4 (p. 199)
  in A minor (*Twelve Short Preludes*, No. 12), 15/1 (p. 204)
  in C minor (*Six Preludes for Beginners*, No. 2), 129 (p. 121)
Sinfonia 15 in B minor, 30 (p. 35), 31 (p. 36), 205 (p. 255), 208 (p. 258)
Suite in D major for Orchestra, No. 2, Air, 16/2 (p. 213)
Trio Sonatas
  in C major (BWV 1037), III, 60 (p. 63)
  in G major (BWV 1038), II, 59 (p. 62)
Variations on O Gott, du frommer Gott, 61 (p. 68)
Well-Tempered Clavier, Book I, *Preludes*
  in C major, No. 1, 167 (p. 188), 169a (p. 190), 176 (p. 202)
  in C minor, No. 2, 14/5 (p. 199)
  in E♭ major, No. 7, 18/2 (p. 229)
Well-Tempered Clavier, Book II
  Fugue in B major, No. 23, 64 (p. 71)
Beethoven, Ludwig van
  Bagatelle in D major, Op. 33, No. 6, 20E/1 (p. 275)
  Piano Concertos
    Fourth in G major, Op. 58, II, 10/3 (p. 157)
    Fifth in E♭ major, Op. 73, II, 2/1 (p. 64), 12A/5 (p. 171)
  Piano Sonatas
    in F minor, Op. 2, No. 1, I, 9/2 (p. 152), 195a (p. 238); II, 22 (p. 29); III, 20E/2 (p. 275), 23A/1 (p. 387)
    in E♭ major, Op. 7, II, 7/1 (p. 139), 20C/1 (p. 273), 23B/1 (p. 388); III, 20C/3 (p. 273)
    in C minor, Op. 10, No. 1, I, 9/3 (p. 152); II, 9/4 (p. 152); III, 222–42 (pp. 281–93)
    in F major, Op. 10, No. 2, I, 12A/4 (p. 170)
    in E major, Op. 14, No. 1, 220 (p. 279)
    in G major, Op. 14, No. 2, I, 1/1 (p. 38)
    in B♭ major, Op. 22, I, 1/6 (p. 40)
    in D major, Op. 28, III, 197 (p. 241), 23A/3 (p. 388)
    in F minor, Op. 57, II, 147 (p. 155), 179b (p. 209)
    in E♭ major, Op. 81a, I ("Les Adieux"), 188d (p. 223), 194 (p. 236), 200 (p. 245)
    in E major, Op. 109, I, 190 (p. 224); III, 272–79 (pp. 327–47)
    in C minor, Op. 111, II, 22/5 (p. 349)
  Sonata for Piano and Cello
    in F major, Op. 5, No. 1, I, 4/3 (p. 101), 6/1 (p. 126); III, 82 (p. 86)

String Quartets
  in D major, Op. 18, No. 3, I, 46 (p. 53)
  in C major, Op. 59, No. 3, I, 54 (p. 57)
Symphonies
  Second, I, 114 (p. 111); II, 19/4 (p. 247)
  Fifth, I, 188a (p. 222)
  Sixth, I, 8/5 (p. 147)
  Seventh, Introduction, 20B/3 (p. 272); I, 8/6 (p. 148); II, 44 (p. 52); III, 26 (p. 32)
  Eighth, I, 121 (p. 116), 122 (p. 117)
  Ninth, III, 6 (p. 15)
Variations
  C minor, 6/2 (p. 126)
  Diabelli, Op. 120, 22/4 (p. 349)
  on an Original Theme, 12B/5 (p. 173)
  on Quanto e bello l'amor Contadino (Paisello), 12B/1 (p. 171)
  WoO 78, 1/3 (p. 39)
Berlioz, Hector
  Symphonie fantastique, II, 1/5 (p. 39)
Bovicelli, Giovanni Battista
  Regole Passagi di Musica, 1 (p. 8)
Brahms, Johannes
  Capriccio in D minor, Op. 116, No. 7, 66 (p. 72)
  Es hing der Reif, Op. 106, No. 3, 199 (p. 244)
  Intermezzi
    in B♭ major, Op. 76, No. 4, 20D/2 (p. 274)
    in E major, Op. 116, No. 6, 124 (p. 118)
    in E♭ minor, Op. 118, No. 6, 17 (p. 24)
    in B minor, Op. 119, No. 1, 183 (p. 215), 193 (p. 227), 18/1 (p. 229)
  Requiem, Op. 45, III (chorus only), 125 (p. 118)
  Rhapsody in E♭ major, Op. 119, No. 4, 21 (p. 28)
  Sonata for Violin and Piano in A major, Op. 100, I, 73 (p. 76)
  Second Symphony, I, 7 (p. 18)
  Variations
    on a Theme of Handel, Op. 24, 4 (p. 12)
    on a Theme of Paganini, Op. 35, 271 (p. 323)
    on a Theme by Haydn, Op. 56b, 269 (p. 322)
Chopin, Frederic
  Etudes
    in C major, Op. 10, No. 1, 168 (p. 189), 169b (p. 190), 177 (p. 203)
    in C minor, Op. 10, No. 12, 196 (p. 239)
    in A♭ major, Op. 25, No. 1, 14/2 (p. 197)
    in C minor, Op. 25, No. 12, 14/3 (p. 198)
    in A♭ major (*Trois nouvelles Etudes*, No. 2), 14/6 (p. 199)
  Mazurkas
    in A minor, Op. 17, No. 4, 287–96 (pp. 357–62)
    in G♯ minor, Op. 33, No. 1, 67 (p. 72), 10/4 (p. 157)
    in A minor, Op. 59, No. 1, 217 (p. 269)
    in C♯ minor, Op. 63, No. 3, 10/5 (p. 158)
    in G minor, Op. 67, No. 2, 69 (p. 73), 17/8 (p. 219)
  Nocturnes
    in D♭ major, Op. 27, No. 2, 20 (p. 27)
    in C minor, Op. 48, No. 1, 131 (p. 122), 206 (p. 256)

in F♯ minor, Op. 48, No. 2, 1/9 (p. 40)
Preludes
  in C major, Op. 28, No. 1, 170–74 (p. 191),
    175 (p. 202)
  in G major, Op. 28, No. 3, 178 (p. 203)
  in E minor, Op. 28, No. 4, 15/3 (p. 207)
  in A major, Op. 28, No. 7, 9 (p. 19)
  in F♯ major, Op. 28, No. 13, 192*b* (p. 226),
    17/3 (p. 219)
  in E♭ minor, Op. 28, No. 14, 89 (p. 89)
  in C minor, Op. 28, No. 20, 141*c* (p. 143), 191
    (p. 225)
Waltzes
  in A♭ major, Op. 42, 14/1 (p. 195)
  in B minor, Op. 69, No. 2, 1/2 (p. 38)
  in C♯ minor, Op. 69, No. 3, 212 (p. 263)
  in E minor (posth.), 27 (p. 33)
Corelli, Arcangelo
  Sonata da camera a tre, Op. 4, No. 5, 16/7 (p.
    213)
Fundamental Structure, Forms of, 136 (p. 133)
Handel, George Frideric
  Joy to the World, 164 (p. 182), 165 (p. 183)
  Keyboard Suites
    in D minor, Air, 128 (p. 120); Menuetto, 3/3
      (p. 81)
    in E major, Air, 16/1 (p. 212), 22/1 (p. 349)
    in F major, III, 2/6 (p. 66)
    in F minor, Courante, 209 (p. 259)
    in G major, Air, 18/5 (p. 230)
    in G minor, Sarabande, 74 (p. 77)
  Leçon in B♭, Air, 3 (p. 9), 143 (p. 150), 144 (p.
    151), 179*a* (p. 208)
  Sonatas for Flute and Continuo
    in A minor, I, 68 (p. 73)
    in D major, IV, 3/6 (p. 82)
    in E minor, No. 1*a*, II, 117 (p. 113), 4/5 (p.
      102), IV, 3/4 (p. 81)
    in E minor, No. 1*b*, II, 23 (p. 29)
  Sonata for Oboe and Continuo in C minor, 24
    (p. 30)
  Trio Sonata in B♭ major, Gavotte, 17/2 (p. 218)
Haydn, Franz Joseph
  Divertimento in B♭ major, Hob. 11/46 II (*Cho-
    rale St. Antoni*), 10 (p. 20), 137*a* (p. 133),
    138 (p. 135), 140*a* (p. 000), 142 (p. 000),
    148 (p. 160), 151 (p. 162), 154*a* (p. 167)
  Piano Sonatas
    in C major, Hob. XVI/21, I, 8/4 (p. 147),
      252–63 (pp. 302–13); III, 119 (p. 115)
    in E major, Hob. XVI/22, II, 115 (p. 112),
      243–51 (pp. 294–302)
    in G major, Hob. XVI/27, I, 10/1 (p. 156)
    in E♭ major, Hob. XVI/28, I, 12A/1 (p. 169)
    in A major, Hob. XVI/30, 12B/2 (p. 172)
    in C major, Hob. XVI/35, I, 8/3 (p. 147)
    in D major, Hob. XVI/39, III, 311–15 (pp.
      376–80)
    in C major, Hob. XVI/48, II, 23B/2 (p. 388)
  String Quartets
    in F major, Op. 74, No. 2, II, 57 (p. 60); IV,
      83 (p. 87)

    in G minor, Op. 74, No. 3, I, 96 (p. 93); II, 52
      (p. 57)
    in G major, Op. 76, No. 1, III, 135 (p. 125)
    in B♭ major, Op. 76, No. 4, II, 50 (p. 56); III,
      91 (p. 91)
    in D major, Op. 76, No. 5, II, 218 (p. 269)
    in E♭ major, Op. 76, No. 6, II, 49 (p. 55)
  Symphonies
    in F♯ minor, No. 45, II, 21/3 (p. 319)
    in G major, No. 92 ("Oxford"), I, 92 (p. 91),
      4/4 (p. 102); III, 132 (p. 123)
    in G major, No. 100 ("Military"), III, 133 (p.
      124)
    in D major, No. 101, III, 18/3 (p. 229)
    in D major, No. 104 ("London"), II, 130 (p.
      122); III, 8 (p. 18)
Kirnberger, Johann Philipp
  Dance Pieces, Bourrée, 16/5 (p. 213)
Linear Intervallic Patterns, Paradigms of
  5–6, 88 (p. 89)
  5–10, 93 (p. 192)
  6–5 (two paradigms), 90 (p. 90)
  6–6, 81 (p. 86)
  7–6, 102 (p. 96)
  7–10, 100 (p. 95)
  8–5, 86 (p. 88)
  8–10, 104 (p. 98)
  10–5, 95 (p. 93)
  10–6, 84 (p. 87)
  10–7, 97 (p. 93)
  10–10, 79 (p. 84)
Mattheson, Johann
  Pièces de Clavecin, Sarabande, 16/5 (p. 213)
Mendelssohn, Felix
  Music to A Midsummer Night's Dream, Op. 61,
    Nocturne, 302–10 (pp. 369–76)
  Praeludium IV, Op. 35, 62 (p. 69)
  String Quartet in D major, Op. 44, No. 1, 19/1
    (p. 246)
  Variations sérieuses, Op. 54, 22/6 (p. 349)
Mozart, Wolfgang Amadeus
  Clarinet Quintet, K. 581, IV, 22/3 (p. 349)
  Dies Bildnis ist bezaubernd schön (*Die Zauber-
    flöte*), 203 (p. 252)
  Minuet in D major, K. 94, 17/4 (p. 219)
  Piano Concertos
    in D minor, K. 466, II, 12A/3 (p. 170)
    in A major, K. 488, II, 75 (p. 77)
  Piano Sonatas
    in F major, K. 280, I, 20B/1 (p. 272); II, 21/2
      (p. 319)
    in G major, K. 283, I, 1/4 (p. 39); II, 3/2 (p. 81)
    in D major, K. 284, III, 22/3 (p. 349)
    in C major, K. 309, I, 145 (p. 154)
    in D major, K. 311, I, 10/2 (p. 156); II, 120
      (p. 115)
    in C major, K. 330, II, 3/5 (p. 82), 207 (p.
      257)
    in A major, K. 331, I, 137*b* (p. 134), 139 (p.
      137), 140*bc* (p. 138), 150 (p. 161), 152 (p.
      162), 154*b* (p. 167), 268 (p. 321), 270 (p.
      322); III, 155 (p. 168)

in F major, K. 332, II, 264–67 (pp. 314–19)
in B♭ major, K. 333, I, 141*b* (p. 143), 8/1 (p. 145); II, 195 (p. 238), 20E/3 (p. 275), 21/1 (p. 319); III, 7/3 (p. 140)
in C minor, K. 457, I, 29 (p. 35), 76 (p. 78), 146 (p. 154)
in F major, K. 494, I, 101 (p. 96)
in C major, K. 545, I, 65 (p. 71), 221 (p. 279); III, 7/4 (p. 141)
in D major, K. 576, II, 116 (p. 113)
Serenade in G major (Eine kleine Nachtmusik), K. 525, II, 316–23 (pp. 380–86)
String Quartets
in A major, K. 169, II, 4/1 (p. 100)
in G major, K. 387, I, 20A/2 (p. 271)
in D minor, K. 421, III, 297–301 (pp. 363–67)
in C major, K. 465, II, 21/4 (p. 319)
String Quintet in C minor, K. 406, III, 105 (p.98)
Symphonies
in D major, K. 385, II, 19/2 (p. 246)
in C major, K. 425 ("Linz"), II, 215 (p. 267); IV, 19 (p. 26), 71 (p. 75)
in E♭ major, K. 543, I, 126 (p. 119); III, 6/4 (p. 126)
in G minor, K. 550, I, 198 (p. 242); IV, 6/5 (p. 127)
in C major, K. 551 ("Jupiter"), I, 98 (p. 94), 19/5 (p. 248); II, 6/3 (p. 126)
Variations
on an Allegretto, K. Anh. 137, 12B/3 (p. 172); K. 500, 12B/6 (p. 174)
on "Come un agnello," K. 460, 12B/4 (p. 173)
Overlapping, 186–87 (p. 221)
Purcell, Henry
Dido and Aeneas, Dido's Lament, 2/4 (p. 65)
Register Designations, 201–2 (pp. 250–51)
Register Displacement, 185 (p. 220)
Schubert, Franz
Das Wandern (Die schöne Müllerin), 188*c* (p. 222)
Deutsche Tänze, Op. 33, No. 5, 20D/1 (p. 275); No. 10, 216 (p. 268)
Deutsche Tänze, Op. 171, No. 3, 210 (p. 261)
Du bist die Ruh', 214 (p. 266)
Erste Walzer, Op. 9, No. 6, 87 (p. 89)
Ihr Bild (Schwanengesang), 17/1 (p. 218)
Impromptus
in G♭ major, Op. 90, No. 3, 7/5 (p. 141)
in A♭ major, Op. 142, No. 2, 1/8 (p. 40), 9/1 (p. 151)
in B♭ major, Op. 142, No. 3, 7/2 (p. 140)
Moments musicaux, Op. 94, No. 6, 134 (p. 124), 23A/2 (p. 387)

Ständchen (Schwanengesang), 12 (p. 21), 13 (p. 22)
String Quartets
in A minor, Op. 29, II, 48 (p. 55)
in B♭ major, Op. 168, III, 118 (p. 114)
in G minor, Op. posth. (D. 173), III, 280–86 (pp. 352–56)
Symphonies
in B minor, I, 18 (p. 25); II, 188*b* (p. 222)
Thränenregen (Die schöne Müllerin), 72 (p. 75)
Valses sentimentales, Op. 50, No. 2, 20C/2 (p. 273); No. 19, 18/4 (p. 230)
Schumann, Robert
Album for the Young
°°°, 2/5 (p. 65)   Mu: replace asterisks
Nachklänge aus dem Theater, 17/5 (p. 219)
Rundgesang, 2/3 (p. 65)
Aus meinen Thränen spriessen (Dichterliebe), 8/2 (p. 146)
Du Ring an meinem Finger (Frauenliebe und Leben), 184 (p. 216)
Ich grolle nicht (Dichterliebe), 17/7 (p. 219)
Ich kann's nicht fassen (Frauenliebe und Leben), 17/6 (p. 219)
Schenker, Heinrich
"Mozart: Sinfonie G-Moll," *Das Meisterwerk in der Musik,* Vol. II, 107 (p. 104)
Simpson, Christopher
The Division-Viol, 2 (p. 9)
Six-four, The, 112 (p. 108)
Sonata Form, Summary of, 219 (p. 277)
Species-Counterpoint Exercises
Bellermann, Heinrich
Second-species exercise, 36 (p. 45)
Fourth-species exercise, 40 (p. 48)
Fux, Johann Joseph
First-species exercise in four voices, 34 (p. 44)
First-species exercise, 32 (p. 42)
Third-species exercise, 37 (p. 46)
Fourth-species exercise, 39 (p. 47)
Mozart, Wolfgang Amadeus
First-species exercise (c.f. by Fux), 33 (p. 43)
Third-species exercise, 38 (p. 47)
Roth, Hermann
Second-species exercise, 35 (p. 44)
Schenker, Heinrich
Combined-species exercise, 41 (p. 49)
Subdominant in Relation to I and V, 109 (p. 105)
Tchaikovsky
Romeo and Juliet, Overture Fantasy, 19/3 (p. 247)
Unfoldings (characteristic), 204 (p. 253)

General Index

Analytic notation. *See* Notation, analytic
Anstieg. *See* Initial ascent
Anticipation, 22
Applied dominant, 88 n
Appoggiatura, 15
Arpeggiation
  of the bass, 131
  of consonant harmony, 32
  and consonant skip, 32
  as diminution, 7
  first-order, 153
  as motive, 32–37
Ausfaltung. *See* Unfolding
Auskomponierung. *See* Composing-out

Background, 130
  and analytic notation, 132
  coupling of elements of, 260
Bar form. *See* Form, bar
Bass arpeggiation. *See* Arpeggiation, of the bass
Bassbrechung. *See* Arpeggiation, of the bass
Binary form. *See* Form, binary

Cambiata. *See Nota cambiata*
Cantus firmus, 41
Composing-out, 241

Compound melody, 67–80
  compared to arpeggiation, 67
  compared to single voice, 74
  conclusive motion in, 77
  connective motion in, 77
  partially compound type, 72
  rhythmic displacement resulting from, 70
  variable span and continuity in, 77
  and voice leading, 70
Compound ternary form. *See* Form, compound ternary
Consonant $^6_4$, 52
Consonant skip, 9
  as diminution, 7
Counterpoint. *See* Species counterpoint
Coupling, 167–69, 220, 260–65. *See also* Register transfer; Obligatory register
Covering progression, 224
Cover tone, 221, 223–26

Deckton. *See* Cover tone
Descant, 68 n
Development. *See* Form, sonata
Diagonal line. *See* Notation
Diminution(s). *See also* Passing note; Neighbor note Consonant skip; Arpeggiation
  derivation of term, 7

as displacement, 14
in durationally expanded form, 11
function of, 11
as prefix, 10
representing embellished note, 9
and rhythmic structures, 18
as suffix, 10
in suspensions before resolution, 59
in theme-and-variations genre, 9, 320
and voice exchanges, 112
Dissonance
stepwise resolution of, 44
Divider
fifth, 203
third, 105
Divisions (on a ground), 8
Dominant preparations, 105
Dominant substitutes, 105

Échappée, 15 n
Embellishing notes. *See* Diminutions
Episode, 367
Exchange. *See* Voice exchange
Exposition. *See* Form, sonata
Extended binary form. *See* Form, rounded binary

Fifth
diminished and perfect, in combination, 54
Figured bass, 49–63
figures
♭ referrng to third, 51
♯ referring to third, 51
4, 58
$\frac{4}{2}$, 56
$\frac{4}{3}$, 55
$\frac{5}{3}$, 50
$\frac{5}{4}$, 58
$\frac{5}{4}\frac{}{2}$, 61
5–6, 51
♯6, 57
$\frac{6}{4}$, 52
$\frac{6}{5}$, 54
6–5, 50
$\frac{7}{4}\frac{}{2}$, 61
8–7, 53
solidus (/), 51 n12

realization of, 50
and roman numerals, 54
Foreground, 130
and rhythmic notation, 132
and rhythmic reduction, 136
Form
bar, 175
binary, 159, 208–11
compound binary, 350 n
compound ternary, 350–67
designation of parts of, 351
expansion of, 351 n
and first rondo, 368
model of, 351
one-part, 201
rondo
episode, 367
first and compound ternary, 368
refrain, 367
transition, 368
type dependent upon recurrences of refrain, 368
rounded binary, 159, 208, 214–17
simple ternary, 214–17
and rounded binary, 217
sonata, 276–319
design of, 276–78
summary of, 277
sonatina, 313–19
variation, 320–48
and deeper structural levels, 321
Fundamental line, 131
notation for, 131–32
Fundamental structure, 130–33
in complete units, 166–69
models of, 130–32
in thematic statements, 132–33

Graphic notation. *See* Notation, analytic

Harmonic function(s)
correct determination of, 105
of diatonic triads, 105
Harmonic progressions, 106
Harmonic relations, 103–04. *See also* Harmony
key and modulation, 104
and tonicization, 104
Harmony. *See also* Harmonic relations
and diminutions, 108–9

in the large, 103
and species counterpoint, 44
and voice leading, 106–8
Head note. *See* Primary tone: Linear
    progression, head note of

Illusory linear progression. *See* Linear
    progression, false
Implied notes, 119–23
Initial descent, 182
Interruption, 158, 201
Intervals
    diminished and perfect, in combina-
        tion, 54
    fourth, in species counterpoint, 43
    second, in species counterpoint, 43
    unfolding of, 159–63
Inversion, 107
    and rule of substitutability, 107

Kopfton. See Primary tone
Koppelung. See Coupling

Leerlauf. See Initial descent
Levels. *See* Structural levels; Fore-
    ground; Background; Middle-
    ground
Line. *See* Linear progression
Linear intervallic patterns, 83–100
    5 6, 88 89
    5–10, 91–92
    6–5, 89
    6–6, 85–87
    7–6, 96–97
    7–10, 95–96
    8–5, 87–88
    8–10, 97–99
    10–5, 92–93
    10–6, 87–88
    10–7, 93–95
    10–10, 83–85
    constituents of, 83
    defined, 83
    as determinants of voice leading, 84
    and figured bass, 84–85
    and harmony, 86, 100
    and larger organization, 86
    as primary structural constit-
    and stepwise motion, 99
    with voice exchange, 114
Linear progression, 133
    in the bass, 238–40

dissonant, 240–43
false, 243–45
head note of, 238
of a seventh, 244–45
tail note of, 238
and unfolding, 259
in upper voices, 237–38

Metrical value, 11
Middleground, 130
    and analytical notation, 132
    coupling of elements of, 260
Modulating dominant, 107
Modulation, 104
Motive. *See* Motivic structures
Motivic structures, 267–70
    concealed forms of thematic motive
        in, 268
    expansions of motives in, 268

Neighbor note
    as adjacency, 19
    chromatic lower, 16
    complete form of, 11
    diatonic lower, 16
    as diminution, 7
    incomplete, 12
    incomplete lower suffix type, 13, 22
    indirect, 16
    as motive, 17–24
Non-chord tones. *See* Diminutions
Nonharmonic tone, 12 n. *See also* Dim-
    inutions
Nota cambiata, 46
Notation
    analytic
        arrowheads, 167
        diagonal line, 138
        double vertical line, 203
        doubly curved slur, 166
        flag, 17
        and middleground, background,
            132
        open notes in, 131–32
        stem and slur, 10
        of unfoldings, 252
        versus rhythmic, 133–38
    figured bass. *See* Figured bass, fig-
        ures
    rhythmic. *See* Rhythmic notation

Obligatory register, 169, 262
Octave progression, 180–84
Overlapping, 221–23, 265–67

Passing note, 9, 9 n
   accented, in the bass, 61
   as connective, 19
   consonant, 28–29, 29 n
   as diminution, 7
   within the fourth, 17
   indirect, 25–27
   as motive, 24–32
Passing tone. See Passing note
Pedal point, 86–87
Primary melodic tone. See Primary tone
Primary tone, 131
   designation of, in chorale, 178–80
   prolongation of, 149–50, 153–56
Prolongation, 142–45
   and diminution, 143
   harmonic, 142
   main types of melodic, 143–44
   melodic, 142–43
   of primary tone, 149–50, 153–56
Prolongational line. See Linear progression

Reaching over. See Overlapping
Recapitulation. See Form, sonata
Reduction, 130. See also Rhythmic reduction
   techniques for, 178–80
Refrain, 367
Register
   designations, 250–51
   displacement, 220
   obligatory, 169, 202 nl, 262
   transfer, 123–25, 220–28, 260–67. See also Coupling; Overlapping
Reprise. See Form, sonata
Resolution, transfer of. See Transfer of resolution.
Rhythmic notation
   and analytic, 133–38
   and foreground, 132
Rhythmic reduction, 10
   and foreground, 136
Roman numerals
   and figured bass, 54
   and analysis, 33

Rondo form. See Form, rondo
Rounded binary form. See Form, rounded binary

Secondary dominant, 88 n, 106–7
Sequence, 85. See also Linear intervallic patterns
Simple ternary form. See Form, simple ternary
Slur, 10
Sonata form. See Form, sonata
Sonatina form. See Form, sonatina
Song form. See Form, compound ternary, simple ternary
Species counterpoint, 41–49
   combined species, 48–49
   fifth species, 48
   first species, 42–44
   fourth species, 47–48
   and harmony, 44
   second species, 44
   third species, 45–47
Stimmtausch. See Voice exchange
Structural levels, 130, 235–37. See also Foreground; Middleground; Background
Substitution, 120
Suspension. See also Species counterpoint, fourth species
   ascending resolution of, 58
   in the bass, 61
   consonant, 48
   diminutions attached to, 59
   formation, 47
   preparation of, in dissonant context, 59
   species, 47

Teiler. See Divider
Ternary form. See Form, simple ternary; Form, compound ternary
Third divider, 105
Tonicization, 104
Tonic substitutes, 105
Transfer
   of register. See Register, transfer of
   of resolution, 61–62
Tritone, 55
   as augmented fourth, 55 n
Two-part form. See Form, binary

Übergreifung. See Overlapping
Unfolding, 159–63
  characteristic types of, 253–55
  distinguished from linear progression, 259
  false, 255
  of larger scale, 257–60
  notation of, 252
  in pairs, triples, quadruples, 252
  series of, of small scale, 257
  of small scale, 251–57
Unterbrechung. See Interruption
Urlinie. See Fundamental line
Urlinie-Tafel, 132
Ursatz. See Fundamental structure

Variation form. *See* Form, variation
Verticalization, 70
  pitfalls of, 74

Voice exchange, 23, 36, 110–19
  and diminutions, 112
  within dissonant interval, 116
  with linear intervallic pattern, 114
  and prolongation, 111
  as replacement, 111
  10–8–6, 111
  10–10–6–6, 113–14
Voice leading
  and compound melody, 70
  figured bass model of, 49–63
  and implied notes, 119–23
  and linear intervallic patterns, 99
  species counterpoint model of, 41–49
  verticalization of. *See* Verticalization

Zug. See Linear progression.